Red Smith On Baseball

TH… TER
ON… EARS

CHICAGO
Ivan R. Dee

 For information, address: Ivan R. Dee, Publisher, 1332 North Halsted Street, Chicago 60622. Manufactured in the United States of America and printed on acid-free paper.

Photo credits: AP/Wide World, pages 28, 287; Brace Photos, pages 21, 58, 60, 69, 112, 193, 241, 309, 334; Brown Brothers, page 14; Culver Pictures, page 97; University of Notre Dame, page iii.

Library of Congress Cataloging-in-Publication Data:
Smith, Red, 1905–1982.
Red Smith on baseball : the game's greatest writer on the game's greatest years / with a foreword by Ira Berkow.
p. cm.
Includes index.
ISBN 1-56663-415-6
1. Baseball—United States—History. I. Berkow, Ira. II. Title.
GV863.A1 S675 2000
796.357'0973—dc21 99-053675

Contents

Foreword
by Ira Berkow

AT THE END of this millennium, the magazine *Editor & Publisher*, the respected "bible" of print journalism, commissioned a blue-ribbon panel to choose for its special centennial issue the twenty-five most influential newspaper people of the twentieth century. On the final list were publishers like Joseph Pulitzer and Adolph Ochs and Katharine Graham, to be sure, and writers like H. L. Mencken and Walter Lippmann and Ernie Pyle. And one sportswriter: Red Smith.

It was a designation I could not quarrel with. I was an admirer of Red Smith's writing from the time I began reading him in the 1950s as a teenager in Chicago, where I grew up. He appeared in the *Chicago Sun-Times*, one of some 250 newspapers that carried his sports column nationwide, a column that then emanated from his flagship paper, the *New York Herald Tribune*.

Smith could make me laugh out loud from his stories and metaphors (an outfielder leaped for a ball against the outfield wall "and stayed aloft so long he looked like an empty uniform hanging in its locker"), and he could make me contemplative when he composed a kind of legal brief in entertaining prose on a serious subject (when outfielder Curt Flood in 1970 shocked the baseball hierarchy by refusing to accept a trade from the St. Louis Cardinals to the Philadelphia Phillies without being able to seek a team of his choice, even though he was making the then huge salary of $90,000 a year, Smith wrote: "You mean," baseball demands incredulously, "that at these prices they want human rights, too?").

In time I would learn that he was also called "The Shakespeare of the Press Box," and that his fans included people from Bing Crosby to Bernard Baruch, the brilliant financier and counsel to presidents, from professors who taught him as "literature" in their English classes to truck drivers to housewives to Ernest Hemingway, who, in his novel *Across the River and into the Trees,* wrote of how one of his characters "was reading Red Smith, and he liked him very much."

And in 1976, at age seventy and now a columnist for the *New York Times,* Smith was awarded the Pulitzer Prize for Commentary, an honor that was widely viewed as long overdue. "In an area heavy with tradition and routine," the Pulitzer citation read, "Mr. Smith is unique in the erudition, the literary quality, the vitality and freshness of viewpoint he brings to his work and in the sustained quality of his columns."

When I went away to college—Miami University in Oxford, Ohio—I had my sights set on becoming a lawyer, for want of something better to do. A quirk of fate sent me in a different direction. It happened this way: a guy living across the dormitory hall from me in my junior year, a fellow named Dave Burgin, the sports editor of the school newspaper, was also a huge fan of Red Smith.

Now, a lot of college boys had *Playboy* centerfolds taped on their walls. Not Burgin. On his wall was a recent cover of *Newsweek* magazine (this was 1959) which featured the face of Red Smith—receding hair line, glasses, small-boned features, and generous, wise, perhaps somewhat skeptical eyes.

The cover headline read: "Red Smith: Star of the Press Box." Burgin and I clearly shared an enthusiasm for Smith. Burgin suggested I take a stab at writing for him on *The Student.* Warily—I had never considered anything like this before—I did. I fell in love with it. And one day I wrote to Red Smith, sent him two of my columns, and, with aplomb, asked for advice. He gave it to me straight, though gently:

"When I was a cub in Milwaukee," he wrote, "I had a city editor who'd stroll over and read across a guy's shoulder when he was writing a lead. Sometimes he'd approve, sometimes he'd say, 'Try again,' and walk away.

"My best advice is, try again. And then again. If you're for this racket, and not many really are, then you've got an eternity of sweat and tears ahead. I don't mean just you: I mean anybody."

I took Smith's best advice and tried again. And again. I sent him a few more of my attempts over the next few years, and, I am pleased to report, he found me improving. So did Dave Burgin, apparently, who elevated me to a columnist on the school paper. When I became a professional, Red Smith and I crossed paths numerous times and developed a friendship. We overlapped at the *New York Times* for nine months, from the time I joined the staff in March 1981 until his death, at age seventy-six, in 1982.

Dave Burgin went on to become one of the distinguished editors in American journalism in the last decades of the century. He was sports editor of the *Washington Daily News,* a city editor of the *Washington Star,* and editor-in-chief of the *Orlando Sentinel*, the *Dallas Times-Herald*, the *Houston Post*, the *San Francisco Examiner*, and the *Oakland Tribune*. He is now editor and publisher of Woodford Press, a book publishing firm in San Francisco, near his home. We have been in touch over the years, and he once told me a story about Red Smith that I still treasure.

"I got a job at the *New York Herald Tribune* just a couple of years after we were in college," Burgin said. "One of my first assignments was with the *Herald Tribune* news service, which was in the middle of the newsroom. The columnists for the paper would send in their pieces by Western Union. I would take them, paste them up in a book, edit them, and then give them to the teletype operator who would punch in the columns, sending them out to the newspapers, like the *Chicago Sun-Times* where you first read Red, and the *Dayton Journal* and the *Cincinnati Enquirer*, where we both read him when we were in school.

"On this day—it was in the summer of 1963—Red was in Philadelphia. He had written a baseball column. He sent it in. It was all very routine. My instructions from the editor, a no-nonsense guy with a quick temper named Tom, were to edit some of the other columnists but leave Red Smith and Art Buchwald alone. I was told, 'They don't need your help.'

"So all I had to do with Red's column was paste it up, put in the dateline, and designate the paragraphs with those copy-editing hook-marks. That's it.

"The column comes in four takes. I accidentally transpose the first take with the third take, so that the third paragraph becomes the lead.

"The column is sent out just this way. Red is still in Philadelphia. He gets up the next morning, where the column appears in the *Philadelphia Inquirer*, and, as he routinely does, reads it. Any other columnist would have gotten an uzi and gone looking for me.

"Red just gently waits until he gets back to New York, a couple of days later. He comes into the newsroom, as he does maybe once a week to get his box of mail, to say hello and leave. I see him and I'm standing there with my mouth hanging open. I have no idea what's going to happen to me. Red walks right by me and says hello to Tom, the editor in charge of the news service. Red says, 'Tom, I'm just curious, what was wrong with my column the other day, the one you changed?'

"Tom says, 'What! We didn't change anything, Red.' Then Tom looks right at me. 'What did you do, kid, goddam it? This is Red Smith here.'

"Red says, 'Well, what we have here is transposed paragraphs.' He's low-key, amiable.

"Tom says to me, 'You're on probation! If you ever do anything like this again, you're fired! You're not to edit Red Smith again under any circumstances!'

"And Red says, 'Well, Tom, all I wanted to say was that I thought you made the column better.'

"Then Red turns around and walks out. He doesn't look at me, though he surely knows that I'm standing in fear and about ready to burst into tears. Tom never said another word to me about being fired.

"Red figured out very quickly that I had made a mistake, was sorry about it, and got me off the hook in the most gracious of ways."

I recall this story at some length because it says so much about Red Smith the man and Red Smith the writer. It displays his sensitivity and his ingenious, even poetic way of handling a subject, delicate or otherwise, and getting to the core of a problem rather than flying off the handle. And while he gave Tom a kind of comeuppance, it was not devastating to him ("You made the column better," he said to Tom). Both Tom and young Burgin were left with their dignity—and Dave with his job. It also served Red's self-interest—no small item for a writer—since more care would surely be taken with his column in the future.

While Smith the columnist wrote on subjects from the Olympics to harness racing, from Super Bowls to hoops, from world heavyweight title fights to fishing, it may well be that he loved to write baseball best of all. He became a baseball writer in 1929 for the *St. Louis Star-Times*, covering the St. Louis Browns and later the Cardinals. When he took a job in Philadelphia in 1936, he was the beat writer for the Phillies and the A's. He did this for ten years—while also writing columns—until he joined the *Herald Tribune* in September 1945. There he was a sports feature writer for three months before being given the column, and a columnist exclusively he remained for almost thirty-seven years.

He once wrote that the distance of ninety feet between bases, as devised in 1845 by Alexander Cartwright, is "the nearest to perfection that man has yet achieved. It accurately measures the cunning, speed and finesse of the base stealer against the velocity of the thrown ball."

And he would think of baseball, as he wrote, "as an evocation of childhood," and recall his playing it in his hometown of Green Bay, Wisconsin: "It was a game played in a pasture lot on hot summer afternoons, leisurely afternoons, and it was great fun, even for nonathletes like me." And "as a boy I never willingly missed seeing a game in the Wisconsin-Illinois League."

He maintained a lifelong enthusiasm for the game. "Baseball is dull only to dull minds," he once wrote. "Today's game is always different from yesterday's game, and tomorrow refreshingly different from today."

Included in the pages that follow are stories relating to baseball that Red Smith wrote from the 1940s to the 1980s. In them are descriptions of some games that are part of a dusty history and whose result only the most profound of sports archaeologists might conceivably be interested in. But Red Smith's view of the people who played them, his insights into the human condition, or the human comedy, as it were, the stories he weaves and the art of his prose, transcend to a remarkably high degree the timeliness of many of these stories, and they continue to delight. As do the pieces on baseball people away from the ballpark.

Such as when he covered the funeral in Washington, D.C., of the great and gentlemanly fastball pitcher from Kansas, Walter Johnson:

". . . Another said, 'Remember the time Ruel and Milan were hurrying to a show with him and some fan spoke to him and held 'em up half an hour? They kept signaling him to break away and when he finally did they gave him hell. He said he was sorry, but the fan was a fellow who grew up in Kansas and knew his sister well and he didn't want to be rude.'

"Milan said, 'I didn't know you had a sister.'

"'I haven't,' Walter said. 'But he was such a nice feller!'"

Or about Jackie Robinson, making a sensational play in an extra inning of a critical, end-of-season game: "the unconquerable doing the impossible."

Or when Reggie Jackson hit three home runs in three consecutive at-bats, and on three straight first pitches, in a World Series game in 1977 against Los Angeles. Red captured the moment with this quote: "I must admit," said Steve Garvey, the Dodgers' first baseman, "when Reggie Jackson hit his third home run and I was sure nobody was listening, I applauded into my glove."

And then there is his widely quoted lead on what is almost universally considered to be the most extraordinary game in baseball history, when on October 3, 1951, Bobby Thomson hit a home run in the last inning of the final playoff game to give the Giants the game, 5–4, and the National League pennant over the archrival crosstown Dodgers:

"Now it is done. Now the story ends. And there is no way to tell it. The art of fiction is dead. Reality has strangled invention. Only the utterly implausible, the inexpressibly fantastic, can ever be plausible again."

Having read Walter Wellesley (Red) Smith rather closely over the years, I remember some baseball columns I particularly enjoyed that are not in this anthology. And yet I'm not sure which columns I'd have taken out to put in some of my favorites. I would suggest to the editors of *Red Smith on Baseball* a solution: *Red Smith on Baseball II.*

By the way, of the two columns from 1963 that are represented in this volume, neither is datelined Philadelphia. Which may be just as well. No need to cause a onetime young editor of the *New York Herald Tribune* news service any further chagrin.

Red Smith
On Baseball

1940s

Winning by Striking Out

IT COULD HAPPEN only in Brooklyn. Nowhere else in this broad, untidy universe, not in Bedlam nor in Babel nor in the remotest psychopathic ward nor the sleaziest padded cell could The Thing be.

Only in the ancestral home of the Dodgers which knew the goofy glories of Babe Herman could a man win a World Series game by striking out.

Only on the banks of the chuckling Gowanus, where the dizzy-days of Uncle Wilbert Robinson still are fresh and dear in memory, could a team fling away its chance for the championship of the world by making four outs in the last inning.

It shouldn't happen to a MacPhail!

As Robert W. Service certainly did not say it:

Oh, them Brooklyn Wights have seen strange sights.
But the strangest they ever did see,
Today was revealed in Ebbets Field
When Owen fumbled strike three!

Among all the Yankee fans in the gathering of 33,813 who watched the fourth game of the World Series, only one was smiling when Tommy Henrich faced Hugh Casey in the ninth inning with two out, nobody on base, the Dodgers in front by one run, and a count of three balls and two strikes on the hitter.

That one gay New Yorker was Jim Farley, whose pink bald head gleamed in a box behind the Dodger dugout. He sat there just laughing and laughing—because he hadn't bought the Yankees, after all.

Then The Thing happened.

Henrich swung at a waist-high pitch over the inside corner. He missed. So did catcher Mickey Owen. Henrich ran to first. Owen ran after the ball but stopped at the grandstand screen.

That was Mickey's biggest mistake. He should have kept right on running all the way back home to Springfield, Missouri.

That way he wouldn't have been around to see and suffer when Joe DiMaggio singled, Charley Keller doubled, Bill Dickey walked, Joe Gordon doubled, and the Dodgers went down in horrendous defeat, 7 to 4.

Out of the rooftop press box in that awful instant came one long, agonized groan. It was the death cry of hundreds of thousands of unwritten words, the expiring moan of countless stories which were to have been composed in tribute to Casey.

For just as Owen has taken his place among the Merkles and Snodgrasses and Zimmermans and all the other famous goats of baseball, so now Casey belongs with the immortal suckers of all time.

The all-American fall guy of this series—round, earnest Casey—was only one pitch short of complete redemption for his sins of yesterday.

Remember that it was he whom the Yankees battered for the winning hits in the third game of the series. It was he whom Larry MacPhail castigated for failing, in MacPhail's judgment, to warm up properly before relieving Fred Fitzsimmons yesterday.

Now he was making all his critics eat their words. He was making a holy show of the experts who snorted last night that he was a chump and a fathead to dream that he could throw his fast stuff past the Yankees.

He was throwing it past them, one pitch after another, making a hollow mockery of the vaunted Yankee power as each superb inning telescoped into the one before.

No one ever stepped more cheerfully onto a hotter spot than did Casey when he walked in to relieve Johnny Allen in the fifth inning.

The Yankees were leading, 3 to 2, had the bases filled with two out, and the hitting star of the series, Joe Gordon, was at bat.

Casey made Gordon fly to Jim Wasdell for the final putout, and from there on he fought down the Yankees at every turn.

He made Red Rolfe pop up after Johnny Sturm singled with two out in the sixth. He breezed through the seventh despite a disheartening break when DiMaggio got a single on a puny ground ball that the Dodgers swore was foul.

Leo Durocher said enough short, indelicate words to Umpire Larry Goetz on that decision to unnerve completely anyone within earshot. But

Casey, determined to hear no evil and pitch no evil, shut his ears and shut out the Yanks.

In the clutch, the great Keller popped up. The ever-dangerous Dickey could get nothing better than a puerile tap to the mound.

So it went, and as Casey drew ever closer to victory the curious creatures that are indigenous to Flatbush came crawling out of the woodwork. They did weird little dances in the aisles and shouted and stamped and rattled cowbells aloft and quacked derisively on little reedy horns.

Their mouths were open, their breath was indrawn for the last, exultant yell—and then The Thing happened.

Far into this night of horror, historians pored over the records, coming up at last with a World Series precedent for "The Thing."

It happened in the first game of the 1907 series between the Cubs and Detroit, when the Tigers went into the ninth inning leading, 3 to 1. With two out and two strikes against pinch-hitter Del Howard, Detroit's Wild Bill Donovan called catcher Charley Schmidt to the mound for a conference.

"Hold your glove over the corner," Donovan said, "and I'll curve a strike into it."

He did, but Schmidt dropped the strike, Howard reached base, and the Cubs went on to tie the score. The game ended in darkness, still tied after twelve innings, and the Cubs took the next four contests in a row.

That's about all, except that it should be said that experts certainly knew their onions when they raved about the Yankee power. It was the most powerful strikeout of all time.

—October 1941

Oh, Those Wondrous Rookies

By now it must be clear to all readers of the sports pages that Florida and California are places where ball players of the Cobb-Wagner-Ruth kidney hang from every tree like bunches of bananas. Never within living memory has there been another spring when so many total strangers played such incomparably wondrous baseball in print.

Managers count that day lost when they fail to think up a dozen new superlatives to describe some lop-eared newcomer who not only hits like Ted Williams, throws like Dom DiMaggio, runs like George Stirnweiss and fields like Terry Moore, but also can cook, sew, sing, play the piccolo and talk Sanskrit like a native.

Thus Mel Ott takes a gander at young Bill Rigney in the hotel lobby and forthwith announces that here is the greatest shortstop he's ever seen, not excluding Travis Jackson, Glenn Wright or Slats Marion. Joe Hatten takes his first turn at throwing for the Dodger scrubs and the telegraph wires erupt quotes: "Best rookie I ever saw . . . speed, curves, control, change of pace . . . can't miss."

Dick Sisler hits like Charley Keller and Bill Wight is another Lefty Grove and Bill McKechnie says his man, Ed Shokes, is "a Marion or a Joe Gordon" around first base and fellow travelers with the Red Sox call Sam Mele "our other .400 hitter." Leo Durocher's bright and roving eye even found a "new Paul Waner" on the Montreal squad.

It is noted, however, that the Phillies were willing to fork over more than $7,500 for Rollie Hemsley, who is in his thirty-ninth year and has played seventeen uncommonly full seasons behind the plate. And that Pinky Higgins and Ken Keltner and Dick Bartell are expected to play third base again this year, and Spud Chandler and Red Ruffing will be out there pitching and the top man on Cincinnati's mound staff is Bucky Walters, thirty-six.

The South is crummy with young phenoms and boy wonders this spring, but when the championship season opens the managers will depend, for the most part, upon players whose major-league quality has been proved in the major leagues.

This doesn't necessarily mean all the managers will be eating all their pretty words all summer. Some rookies will live to justify at least some of their praises and possibly the year's crop of first-rate operatives will be uncommonly large.

Probably one reason for the exuberance of the managerial statements is the happy contrast between this spring's camp and those of the last three years. Even those who ordinarily like to reserve judgment on rookies go all starry-eyed and mush at the sight of able-bodied citizens on the field once more.

It may be, too, that more finished ball players are reporting as recruits this year than in pre-war camps. A kid who was almost ready for a major-league trial before the war has had three or four years to mature and develop.

If he had come up in 1942 the critics might have said, "He's got promise but he's a couple of years away." Now he has been away that couple of years, and even if he didn't play much baseball in the service, he was subjected to physical training which kept him fit.

Professional baseball men are leery of accepting service league records as proof of a youngster's class, since those games weren't played under championship conditions. But the chances are most Army and Navy players competed with better talent than the big leagues had. Some must have developed.

The Dodgers' Hatten, for instance, is twenty-eight, a comparatively advanced age for a rookie. He showed promise when the Dodgers first saw him four years ago. If he is endowed with one-tenth the native ability his cheering section claims for him, he simply had to improve in the interim.

If the rookie crop is bigger than usual this year, so is the harvest of injuries. Hardly a day goes by without additions to the hospital lists—Joe Gordon with a severed tendon in his left hand, Hoot Evers with a broken leg, Rigney with a sprained ankle. Some went to what seemed extreme lengths to meet misfortune, like Rigney, who stepped on a loose baseball.

However, an authority on the subject reports that Fred Fitzsimmons still holds the unlikely injury title, although Dizzy Dean once made a strong bid for this distinction when he was attacked by a telephone in his hotel room. Sitting in a rocking chair one spring, Fat Freddy bent to snatch a newspaper from the floor and rocked on his pitching hand.

—March 27, 1946

Plagiarists from the Polo Grounds

THE DODGERS SHOULD sue. What happened in Ebbets Field yesterday had the Brooklyn copyright stamped all over it. It was redolent of Flatbush. It fairly smoked with the rich, aromatic, pungent, pervading bouquet of the Gowanus. But the perpetrators were Giants, low, skulking plagiarists from the Polo Grounds.

One customer and one center fielder caught batted balls with their profiles; the Dodgers stole five bases, including home plate, four of them in one inning; a Brooklyn base runner was ruled out on an interference play without a murmur of protest from stands, field or dugout; a Giant runner went gamboling dreamily around the bases on an infield pop and got himself doubled off the bag by 180 feet; Ernie (Wingfoot) Lombardi laid down a bunt and had it beaten easily when it rolled foul, then he outsped an infield single. Through it all, a lone trumpeter played a brassy paean of joy, and toward the end a male quartet made with the tonsils under the stands.

Neighbors, summer is back in Brooklyn.

It was opening day in Ebbets Field, but not just an ordinary opening day, assuming any ball game in Brooklyn can be ordinary. This was a Dodgers-Giants opener, which is like crepe suzette for breakfast, or, a circus opening with the tigers uncaged.

As you came up out of the subway, and later when you turned into McKeever Place, cops grabbed you and demanded, "Got a ticket, bud?" Later it developed that the crowd of 31,825 was somewhat less than capacity, suggesting that the law was there not to turn away loiterers but to mooch an extra ticket for Mayor William O'Dwyer.

That pillar of horse-race society, New York's first gentleman of the turf, occupied a box seat beside the Dodgers' dugout. This couldn't have happened in the day of Commissioner Landis, who tolerated no union between baseball and the horsey set.

Bill-O stood up with his hat on and brandished a baseball aloft in his right fist while flash bulbs blazed. Then he stood up with his hat off, revealing an almost unnecessarily wide part of his coiffure and brandished the ball some more. Then he threw the ball, a weak little blooper that plopped almost unnoticed on the turf.

By this time the band was parading to the flagpole, flanked by enough military to occupy Formosa. The players didn't march, having had enough of that these last four years.

On the first play of the game, the Giants' Bill Rigney stretched a single, sliding into second just as the ball arrived. "Safe," said George Magerkurth, a large umpire. From the stands came the poignant, haunting, melodious mating call of the Greenpoint jungle.

"You," Billy Herman advised Mr. Magerkurth, with simple dignity, "are a short word of Anglo-Saxon origin."

"And," said Pee Wee Reese, more in sorrow than in anger, "a blind, bug-eyed one into the bargain."

"Now," Mr. Magerkurth mused, "I know I'm in Brooklyn." Some of Mr. Magerkurth's fondest memories concern Brooklyn. It was there a customer leaped from the stands a few years ago, a small customer in a large rage, who clambered aboard Mr. Magerkurth's wishbone and struck him with repeated blows.

No such indelicacies marred this lawn party, however. The utmost in punctilio was observed as each side was retired scoreless for two innings. The Giants' Harry Feldman was a no-hit pitcher for this space, and his success was seized upon as evidence by those who contend Mel Ott (benched with a gimpy leg) is a better manager in the dugout than in the field.

"See," they argued, "how much more effectively Mel thinks sitting down."

At that point the Dodgers scored five runs on five hits, including a triple by Billy Herman, who first bounced a foul off a patron's nose. It was time for a statement by Ott regarding Feldman.

"Ugh!" Ott said, putting it in a nutshell. In came Mike Budnick, to be succeeded soon by Jack Brewer. Brewer was the pitcher when a ground ball hit by Reese caromed off Babe Young's features in center for a triple and Brooklyn's sixth run.

Jack was still pitching in the fifth. That was the inning when Pete

Reiser walked, stole second, ran to third as Lombardi's throw bounced into the outfield, then stole home; when Gene Hermanski walked and stole second; when Carl Furillo singled Hermanski home, and stole second. The thefts were committed against Brewer, not Lombardi.

With one out and two on base in the sixth, Buddy Kerr bunted and was thrown out. Walker Cooper then batted for Brewer.

"What kind of strategy is that?" a witness demanded. "Bunting when they're eight runs behind!"

"I think," a man said, "Ott feared a double play. Wanted to be sure to get a pinch hitter up there, so he wouldn't have to look at Brewer again before June."

—April 19, 1946

Social and Slightly Revolting

BASEBALL'S SOCIAL REVOLUTION turned out to be one of the politer social affairs of the season with results which were moderately revolting to those who fancied the ball players were going to get a new Bill of Rights.

Meeting by invitation of their bosses to formulate demands for a more abundant life, the player delegates sat and listened while they were told what to demand, then obediently did as directed. Except that they demanded nothing at all; they merely made recommendations. The National League meeting here was run by Ford Frick, president of the league, and when it was over he dictated the handout telling the press what happened. The players didn't open their mouths.

All of which makes it fairly evident how this bloodless "revolution" has been engineered from the top. The owners, clearly disturbed over the double-barreled threat of the Mexican League and the baseball labor movement, sought to forestall trouble by tossing the help a bone. They decided in advance how little they could offer and get by with it. Then they called in the hired men and made a pretense of asking them what they wanted.

There has been much talk about formation of a company union to hold the field against any independent labor organization. But it seems unlikely now that the players will bother to organize at all. Chances are they'll accept the benefits handed to them—which do not, in fact, amount to much more than the increases that inevitably would be demanded after this obscenely profitable season—and settle back into the old rut.

Certainly the committees chosen to represent the players in further conversations aren't the sort calculated to agitate for bigger and better gains. All three of the National League delegates are in the $15,000 to

$20,000 salary class with nothing to gain by way of minimum-wage agreements and such.

Of the six representatives named from the two leagues, only the Cardinals' Slats Marion is young enough so that he could hope to get anything out of a pension system. The Dodgers' Dixie Walker and Boston's Billy Herman and Joe Kuhel, Mel Harder and Johnny Murphy, of the American League, are close to the end of the string. They don't want to make any trouble in the little time they have left.

What ball players refused to realize is that they could form their own organization and call their own tune. The owners know they couldn't buck organized labor on the field, and their hasty efforts to placate the players show they know it. In Pittsburgh, where organizational work was farthest advanced, the club is pleading that unionization would be "completely destructive of the game of baseball." There never has been a child labor law proposed whose opponents didn't bleat that it would destroy their business.

Big league ball players in the main are unschooled, self-centered and reactionary. Their anti-labor attitude is perhaps natural since they reached the top because of individual talents and individual effort. They are all capitalists or would-be capitalists. So they snoot unions, refusing to see beyond their batting averages.

Probably the owners would have made some changes in the player contract this year even if the Baseball Guild hadn't come along to betray signs of unrest in the ranks. Lawsuits with the Mexican League have brought the validity of the standard contract under fire and impelled the owners to strengthen their legal position, just as the National Football League altered its contract form when war with the All-America Conference developed. The invitation to the players to participate in proposing changes is pap for noisy brats.

Not that the "demands" as dictated don't represent gains for the players. A $5,500 minimum wage would involve many substantial increases. There are more $2,500 rookies in the majors than the fans imagine. A $5-per-day allowance for spring training expenses (when no salaries are paid) is no more than fair. However, both these points would be taken care of in many instances through the salary increases which would have to be given next year.

There is no reason why a sound pension plan can't be worked out. But not by ball players or baseball writers. Actuaries would have to figure out a scale of payments for the majors and minors, for players whose career is short and those who give long service. Substituting sixty days' severance pay for the ten-day release clause doesn't afford job security, of course. It only greases the slide, easing the departing player's exit.

Probably the biggest reform proposed is a rule providing that when a club asks waivers on any player the waiver request cannot be withdrawn if another club puts in a claim. Fans are not advised to give odds that this rule will pass. It would put unwelcome obstacles in the path of owners who dote on evading the waiver rule to smuggle fellows like Hank Borowy out of the league.

—July 31, 1946

They Can't Lose for Winning

AMONG THE PEOPLE who are supposed to be competent judges—meaning baseball managers and players and umpires and writers and fans and the neighbor who is getting rich running hot toilet tissue and Rinso—the consensus is that the Dodgers are not good enough to win a pennant.

This practically guarantees the National League championship to the Cardinals or Cubs except for one purely technical detail: i.e., the fact that the Dodgers are, and have been, and give every appearance of intending to remain in first place.

What keeps them up there is one of those questions like how long is a piece of string. On the surface, they appear to have four ball players. There is a Mr. Pete Reiser who is, gimpy shoulder and all, about as fine a ball player as a human being can be. There is a Mr. Dixie Walker, having pretty close to the best season of a blameless life. There is a Mr. Pee Wee Reese, a peerless shortstop and incomparably discerning literary critic. There is a Mr. Ed Stanky, a compact little bundle of distilled malice.

Along with this quartet, there is an assortment of characters who wander into the lineup and out again, and a slew of pitchers who win one day and are strictly dog-meat the next. It is a virtual certainty there won't be a twenty-game winner in the lot, and it could very well be nobody will win more than fifteen. The leader of this band is a little lefthanded cutie of the sort scouts make a career of ignoring.

What the Dodgers have is a strong weakness for winning. Call it chutzpuh or opportunism or elan or moxie or, to go first class like Funk and Wagnall, the guts of burglars. Whatever the word is, they've got it. And they win the big ones.

That was the point Tuesday night when the Cardinals came to Ebbets Field. St. Louis was second by two and a half games. A sweep of the three-game series would mean first place for the Cards. They tossed in Howie Pollet, whom the Dodgers hadn't beaten, against Rube Melton, who hadn't beaten anybody. And the Dodgers won the big one, 2 to 1. This was the key game. It made the series a "lock" for Brooklyn. It robbed yesterday's St.

Louis victory of its meaning. It left the Cards with no place to go but away, still in second place.

Brooklyn was lucky to win, which is no rap. In a game as tightly contested as this, it usually is the luckier team which wins. Pollet had beautiful control and walked only one batsman, yet it was his wild pitch that put the winning run in position to score.

He'd given a sample of his control just before. Reese had opened the home seventh with a triple and Pollet, pitching with painful caution to Reiser, missed the plate with his first three throws. Nevertheless, he had enough to work the count to three-and-two and then make Reiser pop up. After Walker singled Reese home for a tie, Pollet threw one into the dirt and Dixie took second, whence he scored when Furillo's drive bounced into the left field seats. Save for the wild pitch, Walker would have been stalled at third on Furillo's ground-rule double.

Everybody wrote that Stanky saved the game in the ninth. He did. With Stan Musial on second, Whitey Kurowski on first and one out, Harry Walker slashed one over the mound, which Stanky chased into short center, overtook, and flung backwards as he raced toward the fence. His under-arm throw forced Kurowski.

Sometimes you see an infielder run down a ball like that, but not once in a hundred times can he complete a play on it. True, the ball ticked Hank Behrman's glove, which slowed it down just enough to give Stanky a chance. But the point was, the little guy never quit on the ball, hopeless though the effort seemed.

There was an earlier play that stirred less comment but was equally important. After Slats Marion opened the sixth with a walk, Pollet grounded to Reese. The ball hopped high as it reached Pee Wee—and for a second or so he couldn't pluck it out of his glove. Still groping for the handle, he ran to cover second himself, stepped on the bag, then got the ball free and threw for a double play. Red Schoendienst then doubled, but instead of setting off a big inning the hit only got him exercise.

This pedestrian took a ride yesterday in the glittering maroon Cadillac of another of baseball's proved pros, one Leroy Satchelfoot Paige, who pitches for the Kansas City Monarchs against the New York Black Yankees in Yankee Stadium tonight.

The Satchel, who's been wheeling the high hard one through there for nineteen years, says he's only thirty-nine and good for six, seven more years of almost nightly work averaging four innings per hitch eight months a year. He's a blithe and cocky sliver of midnight without a touch of gray in mustache or poll.

"It's runnin' a club makes you gray-headed," he says. "Could you age whisky like you age a manager, you have 2,000 proof inside of a week."

Kansas City pays Satchel $1,000 a month plus ten per cent of gates in all big parks, bringing his possible earnings to $20,000 and up. He'd still like a big league chance but not at a rookie's salary.

"Ain't no doubt I could win pitchin' relief every day. Name off one of you guys can hit three deliveries like I throw, overhand, sidearm and underhand."

His first manager, Bill Blakewell, taught him control, making him warm up with a baseball as his target instead of a plate. "If I'd be five inches off center, why, that'd still be a strike but he'd give me hell. Today I can lay a cigaret paper down and pitch across it seven times out of eight. Never been sore but once down in Mexico in 1937. Like Joe Louis, only one arm like this comes along in fifty years."

—*August 1, 1946*

Model Ball Player

By special arrangement with the Hudson Tubes, an expedition to this model political community was made today to get a look at Jackie Robinson, the model Negro infielder of the Dodgers' model Montreal farm. It was a brief look because Robinson, having jimmied an ankle sliding into third base, didn't play against the Itsy-Bitsy Giants. It is possible to report, however, that he looked good retrieving balls for the batting practice pitcher, being blessed with the sort of contours that make baseball rompers seem stylish.

Although he had been injured several times this season, Robinson is the second batter in the International League with an average of .352, the second base stealer with thirty-one thefts and, playing second base instead of shortstop for the first time in his life, constitutes one-half of the league's deftest double-play combination.

He is a major attraction at home and on the road and a major cog in a machine that had a thirteen-game lead this morning. He just got through winning three of Montreal's four games in Newark. The Royals have drawn 365,000 paid admissions on the road this year and expect home crowds to pass 500,000. At this time last season they led the league by fifteen games and had played for 124,000 witnesses on tour.

Clay Hopper, the Royals' manager, was warming up for a hitch on the mound while Robinson piddled around the infield, limping noticeably.

"Yes," Hopper said, "I think he's a major leaguer. He goes hard all the time and he has great hands for an infielder. He seems a little frail, though. Gets hurt. Maybe because he goes so hard."

Jackie Robinson signing his contract with Branch Rickey to play for the Brooklyn Dodgers

Robinson, who weighs 190 pounds and was a rugged halfback at U.C.L.A., chuckled at the word "frail" when he came off the field. After his chores behind the rubber he strolled into the outfield to shag a few flies, flung a ball to a crowd of clamoring kids in the bleachers, and paused on the way in to autograph score cards for two Negro fans.

"I'm not brittle," he said. "Football never hurt me. Anybody hitting a bag the way I did the other night would have hurt his ankle. Anyhow, that ankle always has been bad. It's been broken but I played six years of football with the ankle taped and it never bothered me."

Last winter he told Al Laney that racial discrimination wouldn't disturb him; his only doubt then concerned his ability to play well enough.

"I know now I can play International League ball," he said.

He hasn't heard what plans Brooklyn may have for him for next year, although now and then Hopper has told him scouts for the parent club were watching him. For that matter, Branch Rickey brings his brain bund to most of Montreal's night games in Jersey City and Newark.

As for his color:

"There's been no trouble at all. I haven't heard anything worse than you hear in college football. In any game they'll call you names if they think they can rile you. That's just competition. Same as they get on Ed Stanky, of the Dodgers. Syracuse was a little rough early in the season but when I didn't pay any attention they dropped it.

"Then one day in Syracuse I hit a home run and that seemed to get 'em started again. I was talking back until I realized I was just encouraging 'em. One of the umpires got kind of sore and shouted something to the Syracuse bench and I told him to forget it. That was all."

He shares the club's accommodations everywhere save Baltimore, where he occupies a different hotel. This, he concedes, might create a problem on a club with a number of Negro players.

"Depends on the type of fellow. I don't drink or stay out late and I don't think Hopper knows where I stay in Baltimore. But if a manager had a lot of players living out like that, he might have trouble controlling some of them."

"Some people," he was told, "think the battle against Jim Crow is won. Now that you've made the grade, they believe there'll be no further argument about it."

"I think it's won, for now," he said. "But it could easily start all over if something should happen."

"Do you see any material difference between this baseball and the Negro National League?"

"Only in the organization of teams, accommodations, parks and such. The baseball here is better than down the line. That is, there are more good players. Negro kids used to give up in school or on the sandlots, figuring there was no future for them. Now I think they'll produce more good players."

"Did it bother you when Montreal's exhibition games in the South were canceled because of you?"

He laughed. "Not me. It wasn't my problem. They have their laws down there. I don't happen to think much of 'em, but as long as they have 'em you have to observe 'em."

Since the season opened, Robinson has not hit less than .330. He is not a powerful hitter, "legs out" a good many hits on sheer speed, excels at beating out bunts. He has made 106 hits and scored seventy-eight runs in 301 chances, with three triples, three home runs and fifteen doubles. Batting second, he has knocked in forty-four runs. He was shifted from shortstop to second base because his arm isn't particularly strong.

Club followers believe pitchers throw at him occasionally, but probably no oftener than at other dangerous batters. One day when he was pinked on the wrist and the umpire called it a foul ball, the first out of the dugout to protest the decision was a Texan.

In the recent Newark series he doubled in the ninth to win one game, saved another with a diving catch of a low line drive near first base when the bases were filled, doubled in the tenth to win a third game. He enjoys playing before big crowds, such as he saw in college, seems to rise to these occasions. Trapped in a run-down on the baseline one day, his sparkling footwork kept him jockeying safely until almost the entire Baltimore team got into the play. When he finally was retired, a full house in Montreal cheered as though for a home run.

—August 4, 1946

A Man Who Knew the Crowds

WHEN THE ICEMAN cometh, it doesn't make a great deal of difference which route he takes, for the ultimate result is the same in any case. Nevertheless, there was something especially tragic in the way death came to Tony Lazzeri, finding him and leaving him all alone in a dark and silent house—a house which must, in that last moment, have seemed frighteningly silent to a man whose ears remembered the roar of the crowd as Tony's did.

A man who knew the roar of the crowd? Shucks, Tony Lazzeri was the man who made the crowds and who made them roar. Frank Graham, in his absorbing history of the Yankees, tells about the coming of Lazzeri and about the crowds that trooped into the stadium to see him, the noisily jubilant Italian-American crowds with their rallying cry of "Poosh 'em up, Tony!"

"And now," Frank wrote in effect, "a new type of fan was coming to the stadium. A fan who didn't know where first base was. He came, and what he saw brought him back again and again until he not only knew where first base was, but second base as well."

It was a shock to read in the reports of Lazzeri's death that he was not yet forty-two years old. There are at least a few right around that age still playing in the major leagues. One would have guessed Lazzeri's age a good deal higher because his name and fame are inextricably associated with an era which already has become a legend—the era that is always referred to as the time of "the old Yankees."

You can't think of Tony without thinking also of Babe Ruth and Bob Meusel and Herb Pennock and Waite Hoyt and Lou Gehrig and Mark Koenig and Benny Bengough and Wiley Moore, all of whom have been gone from the playing fields for what seems a long time.

And you think of Grover Cleveland Alexander, too, for it was Lazzeri's misfortune that although he was as great a ball player as ever lived the most vivid memory he left in most minds concerned the day he failed.

That was, of course, in the seventh game of the 1926 World Series when the Yankees filled the bases against the leading Cardinals, drove Jesse Haines from the hill and sent Rogers Hornsby from his position at second base out toward the Cardinals' bullpen where Alexander drowsed in the dusk.

Everyone knows that story, how the St. Louis manager walked out to take a look at Alexander's eyes, how he found them as clear as could be expected and sent Old Pete in there to save the world championship by striking out Lazzeri. Come to think of it, Alex wasn't a lot younger then than Tony was when he died.

It was after that game that someone asked Alexander how he felt when Lazzeri struck out.

"How did I feel?" he snorted. "Go ask Lazzeri how he felt."

Tony never told how he felt. Not that it was necessary, anyway, but he wasn't one to be telling much, ever. He was a rookie when a baseball writer first used a line that has been worn to tatters since. "Interviewing that guy," the reporter grumbled, "is like mining coal with a nail file."

Silent and unsmiling though he was, Lazzeri wasn't entirely devoid of a taste for dugout humor. Babe Ruth, dressing in haste after one tardy arrival in the stadium, tried to pull a shoe out of his locker and found it wouldn't move. He didn't have to be told who had nailed it to the floor.

When other players found cigarette butts in their footgear or discovered their shirts tied in water-soaked knots or were unable to locate their shoelaces, they blamed only one man.

Lefty Gomez used to tell of the day, long after Lazzeri's experience in the 1926 World Series, when he lost control and filled the bases. Lazzeri trotted in from second base to talk to him. Lazzeri always was the man who took charge when trouble threatened the Yankees. Even in his first season when he was a rookie who'd never seen a big league game until he played in one, he was the steadying influence, the balance wheel. So after this incident Gomez was asked what words Lazzeri had used to reassure him in the clutch.

"He said," replied Lefty, who didn't necessarily expect to be believed, "'You put those runners on there. Now get out of the jam yourself, you slob.'"

They chose Lazzeri "Player of the Year" after one of his closing seasons. They could just as well have made it "Player of the Years," for in all his time with the Yankees there was no one whose hitting and fielding and hustle and fire and brilliantly swift thinking meant more to any team.

Other clubs tried to profit by those qualities of his when he was through. He went to the Cubs and the Dodgers and the Giants. None of these experiments was particularly happy; none endured for long. He managed Toronto for a while and then just before the war he went back home to San Francisco. That was the last stop.

—August 9, 1946

Mr. Horwitz Meets Mr. Williams

BOSTON—BACK IN 1938 when Ted Williams wasn't a national institution like Yellowstone Park or even a New England gentleman of letters like Henry Wadsworth Longfellow, a wandering baseball writer named Al Horwitz encountered the young man en route to his first major league training camp in the custody of Bobby Doerr.

The three rode through the South talking, naturally, of the gentle art of massaging curves, and the rookie Williams, naturally, held up his corner of the discussion. Held it up so ably, in fact, that Mr. Horwitz regarded him slantwise and remarked that there were some pretty fair country hitters on the Red Sox.

"Wait," he said, "until you see Jimmy Foxx hit."

Mr. Williams leaned back and turned a tranquil gaze out the window.

"Hmmmm," he said, "wait until Foxx sees me hit."

Today Mr. Foxx, currently a golden voice on a Boston radio station, saw Williams hit. It wasn't the first time nor is it likely to be the last. It was just a typical Williams stroke in a typical Williams spot, with Johnny Pesky on base and the Yankees threatening to make a contest of their match in Fenway Park. Ted took three called balls from Tiny Bonham and urged the three-and-oh pitch on a level, evil line into the distant bleachers high over the bullpen.

This made the score read 4 to 1 for Boston and simplified Dave Ferriss's task of preparing the ground for Larry MacPhail's 1947 reconstruction project. After this 7-to-4 dismantling, the razing of the Yankees was deemed complete.

Newspaper advertisements of games in Fenway Park stress the point that the Sox have nothing to sell except baseball—"no fireworks, no nylons, no bathing beauties."

Never willing to be outdone, the Yankees responded with no pitching, no hitting, no throwing and no fielding.

There has been a curious reluctance in baseball's tall forehead department to put the imprimatur of greatness on chubby Joe Cronin's team.

The Sox have been compared, to their disadvantage, with the champion Yankees and Athletics of the last fifteen years, and even today an expert insisted they weren't fourteen games better than the rest of the league. They just happen to be fourteen games ahead in the standings, except in a Boston paper that has invented a mathematical system that puts them twenty-eight games ahead.

Watching them these last two days in comparison with their closest pursuers, one wonders what they're expected to do besides win. From this corner of the Fenway rooftop, the Sox not only look like several of Tom Yawkey's millions, they also give signs of being ready to boss the clambake for some years to come, for their farms are developing some estimable products named Mele, Albright and such.

Before the war, the Sox had been built up to a level not hopelessly far below that of the Yankees. Whereas fellows like Joe Gordon and Joe DiMaggio seem to have lost something in the armed forces, players like Williams and Johnny Pesky, being a few years younger, appear to have brought back everything they took away.

The Yankees stood pat and waited for their veterans to return. The Red Sox caulked the pre-war seams, adding Ferriss to the pitching staff, Rudy York at first base, Hal Wagner behind the plate and Wally Moses in right field.

To say that all have been helpful is like saying a million dollars is cute. This also goes for another post-war pick-up, Rip Russell, an experienced hand at first base, third and the outfield. When Cronin asked him which position he played best, Rip smiled pleasantly and said, "none of 'em."

As for the threadbare argument about Cronin's proper ranking among managers, here's the record for 1946: There have been four key games which the Six simply had to win. They won 'em all.

The Yanks won their first game here, 12 to 5. This looked like the business the old Yanks always gave their most menacing rivals. Well, this Boston team came back and won the next day, 12 to 5.

Later the Sox won fifteen in a row but were stopped by Bonham, 2 to 0. Now, the experts said, the honeymoon was over. Next day Spud Chandler pitched a three-hitter, but so did Boston's Mickey Harris. In most such struggles, the proof of a champion is in the defense. This time it was the Yankees who cracked, and lost, 3 to 1.

Inevitably, the Sox had to hit a slump. On a Western tour, they lost six out of seven games, went into Cleveland to face Bob Feller. Cronin had the gambler's nerve to lead trump. He pitched Tex Hughson, who beat Feller, 1 to 0.

Finally there came a visit to Detroit after the Sox lost two series out of three in Chicago, Cleveland and St. Louis. It was August, the month when Ferriss is supposed to faint at the first sniff of pollen. Dave followed his sensitive nose out to the hill and slammed the door on the Tigers.

Cronin remarked today that Ferriss, big, quiet, friendly but intensely combative, has the ideal baseball temperament. Doerr is much the same sort. As for Pesky, his implausibly apt name recalls a personal memory. A small boy in Green Bay, Wis., was helping a gentleman named Leo Van Der Plas feed a pen of pigs. The boy and man stood watching the snorting melee around the trough.

"They sure named them right," Leo mused, "when they called 'em pigs. Ain't they the most hoggish things you ever saw?"

—August 18, 1946

It Doesn't Sound Like Greenberg

THE REPORT IS that Hank Greenberg will retire after this season, and if this is so then baseball is about to lose one of the greatest players of our time, one of the most unselfish team men, one of the finest gentlemen. Since he joined the Detroit Tigers in 1933, nothing has gone into the record of this big, quiet, courteous man which wasn't a credit to him, unless it is the published reason for his decision to quit.

Hank has been having an indifferent season. He has heard more jeers than cheers from the Detroit public that used to worship him. The story is that he is fed up, that he has said it's a great game when you're hitting .350 but a miserable life for the fellow batting .250.

That's true, of course. And yet it doesn't seem like Greenberg to quit just because the sledding is a little tough. It doesn't sound like the fellow Al Simmons was talking about when it was announced that Hank, discharged by the Army, was coming back to the Tigers.

"This is the test," Al said, "for all ball players past thirty who have been away for more than a year. Hank has more equipment than the rest of 'em, more natural ability. He'll come back in good shape, because he's always kept himself in shape. And he'll be out there working at 8 o'clock every morning if necessary to get back on his stride.

"If he doesn't make it, the rest of 'em might as well not try. They better just take what pay they're entitled to and go home to the farm."

Simmons's words were recalled the day Greenberg returned to the Tigers' line-up. It was a day that won't be forgotten soon by anyone who was

Hank Greenberg

present. There was a double-header with the Athletics and Hank's appearance had been advertised, bringing out a crowd that filled big Briggs Stadium.

Tempestuous applause saluted announcement of his name in the batting order and even more tumultuous cheers welcomed him home on his first trip to the plate. He hit two or three baleful line drives on his first trip to the plate. Then he got hold of a pitch by a left-hander named Charley Gassaway and drove it into the left field seats on a line as flat as old beer.

What one remembers is not so much the look of him as he loped around the bases nor the unrestrained joy of the crowd. Rather, it was the undisguised pleasure that the other players showed, not only the other Tigers but the Athletics as well. Detroit had won the game before Hank connected, so the hit didn't affect the outcome. Members of both teams crowed about it for hours, and even Gassaway went around with his chest out as though being on the receiving end of that comeback blow were the biggest thing that ever happened to him.

This day saw a sample of the respect in which Greenberg has been held by the men of his sport, a respect he earned fairly, just as he always earned his big salary. He worked hard to become the best first baseman in the game and then, when he had established his right to that ranking beyond dispute, he gave it up and worked even harder to become an outfielder because his team needed him there.

He earned the honors that came to him when he was twice selected for the league's "most valuable" player award, and no other player ever was heard to begrudge him his position as the most highly paid operative since Babe Ruth. On the contrary, there was unanimous sympathy for him when he was called up for pre-war military training a few weeks after starting work on a $55,000 contract. The war came along before he could get back to baseball and he re-entered the Army and stuck until the job was done.

If he regretted the sacrifice he had to make at the peak of his career, he gave no sign. He has a sense of dignity that always has become him. At World Series, for example, he has been pestered to pose for photographs with Hollywood hams or others trying to gain personal publicity.

On more than one such occasion he refused quietly, explaining that since he didn't go up onto the stage to crowd into the ham's act, why should the ham be allowed on the field to louse up his game?

No one questioned his right to return to the Tigers at his pre-war scale of $55,000. He batted .311 as the Tigers struggled for the 1945 pennant and it was his home run with the bases filled which won the championship on the last day. Except for his three-run homer which won the second game of the World Series, Detroit wouldn't have had a chance for the world title. The Cubs probably would have won the first three games and finished the job in the sixth.

So Hank received a contract for this year that is supposed to pay him $60,000. Baseball has done pretty well for him and he has done very well for baseball. He is in his thirty-sixth year, which is up there close to the retirement age. Some of his old physical hurts must come back to plague him now and then. Financially he is in a position to quit. And yet, wouldn't you hate to see a guy who has been that sort of guy just take the $60,000 and walk out without trying to give his club one more good year?

—August 27, 1946

It's All Genuine, Although Synthetic

TO THE AVERAGE Dodger fan who can't get out to Ebbets Field to see a ball game, the next best thing is to tune in on Red Barber. That's what the Dodger fan thinks and he's wrong. Next to seeing a ball game, the best thing is to sit in the studio with Mr. Barber and watch and listen as he takes the skeletonized report of a game coming over the telegraph wire and wraps up the bare bones with flubdub and pads it out and feeds it to the customers so it sounds as though he, and they, were seeing the plays.

"This is just a business," Mr. Barber explained before the wire opened for the third game of Brooklyn's series in St. Louis. "We don't try to fake it. We have the telegraph sounder right in here near the microphone where it can be heard because we don't try to kid the listeners that this is anything but a telegraphed report.

"From spring training on, Connie Desmond and I are studying the mannerisms of the players in the National League and memorizing them so that when we do a game like this we can visualize them on the field. For instance, I remember how Ed Stanky stands at the plate, how he crouches lower and lower when he's trying for a base on balls. So when I describe it over the air I'm not faking. I know he's doing that."

For a "reconstructed" game a telegraph operator in the studio copies the wire report on a typewriter. Barber stands beside him talking into a microphone which is hung over one of those thingummies that orators use to support their notes and elbows. Because this is radio, the thingummy is painted robin's egg blue. Although Barber sits down in his booth at Ebbets Field, he prefers to stand in the airless studio because sitting makes him loggy.

At his elbow, propped up on a sort of music rack, are the line-ups of the two teams with the current batting average of each player. John Paddock, a left-handed statistician who is a cousin of the great sprinter Charley Paddock, keeps the averages up to the minute, writing in a new figure after each new time at bat. He doesn't do the arithmetic himself but uses a "Ready Reckoner," one of those little books that show at a glance what a man is hitting when he has 104 hits for 396 times at bat. A passionate Dodger fan, Paddock daren't talk during a broadcast but roots for his guys with ardent gestures.

Here's the way Barber builds up a play:

The telegraph types: "Reiser up—bats left."

"And here's Pete Reiser," says Red. "Hitting .283, 106 base hits. He's having a tough year, fighting that bad shoulder. Dickson will pitch very carefully to him. Reiser up, square stance, he's one of those square-built guys, not very tall. Strength is not necessarily dependent upon height. The Cards are playing this fellow a step in because of his speed." . . .

All this time there's been nothing over the wire except the bare fact that Reiser is up. The rest all comes out of Barber's memory and knowledge, filling the gap until the typewriter adds: "B 1 OS (Ball one, outside)." . . . "Dickson comes down," Barber says, "and misses the plate. Ball one, outside." . . . Or "S 1 C (Strike one, called)." . . . "Dickson comes in with one," Barber says, "and Reiser is caught lookin'. Strike one, called."

The telegrapher writes: "H. Walker up—bunt, foul—hit—Walker singled to right."

Barber says, "Harry Walker, who's always nervous and pickin' at that cap of his, has to have it sittin' just right. He cuts at the first pitch and tries to bunt it, fouls it off. One strike. Melton working very deliberately. That's his custom, you know. Walker, with that two-toned bat of his—swings on it, bloops a single to right, turns first and stops as his brother Dixie fields the ball."

The Cardinals get Harry Walker and Stan Musial on the bases, and Barber reminds his listeners that they're there: "Walker and Musial takin' a lead off first and second. They both of 'em can run like scalded cats, you know."

It infuriates the announcer when a friend remarks after a broadcast, "What were you doing reporting all those pick-off throws to first base. Trying to fill in?"

It infuriates him, because he doesn't add a pitch or play that doesn't happen. He merely embroiders each play with words. He can't read Morse code and doesn't want to learn because he doesn't want to know too soon how the next play is coming out. "If you know in advance what's happening, you're no longer a broadcaster," he says. "You're a dramatic artist." Ordinarily, he waits until the telegrapher finishes a sentence before he announces the play.

Once, however, he got himself trapped. The Dodgers had Stanky on first with the tying run, and the operator wrote: "Stanky was picked off first, Dickson to Musial." . . .

At that point Barber said, putting a lift of excitement into his voice, because after all, he's a Brooklyn fan: "Dickson wheels, throws, and Stanky is picked off."

"But," the operator wrote, and went on to report how Stanky, trapped off the bag, fled toward second, jockeyed, retreated, and finally regained first base safely. Barber had a hell of a time talking fast enough to fill in until he could get the play straight on the air.

There were a couple of excusable errors when Barber or Desmond, reading over the telegrapher's shoulder, mistook a swing for a called strike, or vice versa. Generally, though, the broadcast was painstakingly accurate, including only the telegraphed facts and the "color" provided by the announcer.

—August 28, 1946

Slaughter—Series Hustler

ST. LOUIS—Enos Slaughter is a thickly built, low-slung man with thin, pale hair, a fairish amount of nose and a greater store of all-around ability than any other member of the travel-stained company whose baseball show is threatening the longevity record of "Life With Father."

No matter what he does tomorrow when he and his gimpy elbow go out to right field in the seventh and possibly last World Series game, Slaughter already has proved himself The Complete Ball Player of this competition.

Unlike Ted Williams and Lauren Bacall, his classic features decorate no magazine covers. Unlike Stan Musial, he is neither a batting champion nor a candidate for the league's "most valuable player" award. Unlike Slats Marion, he has never been acclaimed the greatest living practitioner in his field. He makes less money than Williams and inspires fewer feature stories than Johnny Pesky.

But when you add up the factors that make a ball player great, when you consider hitting, fielding, running, throwing, hustle and the combative spirit that pays off biggest when the pressure is heaviest, Slaughter scores more points than any other.

The only man on either team whose all-around play has challenged that of Slaughter is Dom DiMaggio, without whom the Red Sox wouldn't have a chance. And although DiMaggio has made six hits, his contribution to the Boston cause has been chiefly a defensive one.

Slaughter finished the season with a bigger total of runs-batted-in than any other player in either league. He wound up in characteristic style with a two-run triple in the final game of the pennant play-off with Brooklyn, smashing the key hit and scoring the winning run after Joe Hatten purposely walked Whitey Kurowski and pitched to Slaughter.

"I don't want to second-guess Durocher," Eddie Dyer said that night. "He was playing the percentage, having his left-hander pitch to a left-handed batter. But Enos swung against all kinds of pitching when he led both leagues in R.B.I.s, and it made me very happy when they passed Kurowski to get to him."

Slaughter is one of three men—the others are Bobby Doerr and Kurowski—who have made seven hits in the World Series. With three bases on balls, he has been on base ten times, more than anyone else except Williams, who has walked five times. One of his hits was a double, one a triple and one a home run.

He has thrown out one Boston runner and made assorted plays of top class in the outfield. In yesterday's tense wrangle Leon Culberson sliced a fly to right which looked like an impossible chance. Mickey Harris, starting from first base, and Culberson were tearing around the bases at top speed, the wind was pushing the ball toward the foul line, and Slaughter, playing over toward center for a righthanded batter, seemed to be running in an utterly forlorn cause.

But he kept running, and made the catch look easy.

His right elbow was damaged so sorely by one of Joe Dobson's fast balls on Friday that Slaughter was a doubtful starter yesterday until he talked with Dr. Robert F. Hyland, the baseball surgeon, just before the game. Yet the first time he came up with men on bases, he teed off with a run-scoring single which detached Harris from the box score.

After hitting once he walked twice, being the only player in the game to get on base three times. He insisted the pain in his elbow was only annoying and not punishing, but he aggravated the injury sliding back to first base, and this sent him to a hospital today for a second set of X-ray pictures.

The examination disclosed no fracture. "Hoematoma" is Dr. Hyland's $4 word for a severe bruise. Slaughter just says he'll be in there again tomorrow. He hasn't had to throw hard since he was hurt.

"But," he said, "if I have to I'll cut loose—and the hell with the arm."

Which may help explain why his playmates, who call him "Country," also call him the greatest hustler alive.

Something has to give tomorrow, and Dr. Hyland hopes it won't be Slaughter's arm. The Cardinals never have lost a seven-game World Series; the Red Sox never have lost one of any length. They can't both hold the pace.

Today's papers carried a story about a genuine ghost occupying Borley Rectory in England. As published here, the yarn had a wistful note, this being the only ghost not writing under the by-line of some St. Louis or Boston player.

—October 15, 1946

Silvertooth Mike Is Right Again

ST. LOUIS—Old Silvertooth Mike Gonzalez, the Cuban with the smile like Cartier's window, replied to the Amalgamated Brotherhood of Grandstand Coachers today and his answer was worth $1,200 to every Cardinal. Which is better than they could do on a quiz program.

Because Mike was right when he had to be, the Cardinals are baseball champions of the world for the sixth time. Because Old Silvertooth had the wit to see a chance and the gambler's gall to take it, Harry Brecheen rode out of Sportsman's Park on his playmates' shoulders, the first pitcher in twenty-six years to win three games in a World Series. Because of Mike's $40,000 decision, Joe Cronin walked alone through the crowd that poured out from the stands staring at his shoes as though trying to memorize them.

Old Silvertooth is the Cardinals' third-base coach, and the grandstand brotherhood has been second-guessing him ever since this series began away back there in the good old days. He should have sent Country Slaughter home when he tripled in the first game. He should have held up Whitey Kurowski and Joe Garagiola in the fourth game. And so on.

Mike paid no attention. He just flashed his metallic grin and stuck to his knitting out there on the white line, watching the play and shouting his orders: "You go. He stay. Come on, Slats, you can do." And then today the big question was asked, and Mike had the answer.

It was in the eighth inning with the score tied, two out, Slaughter on first base and Harry Walker at the plate. Walker hit a long drive that slanted out to the left of Leon Culberson in center field, and Slaughter took off.

If the ball had got by Culberson, as seemed likely, there'd have been nothing to it. But it bounced high on the hard, knobby earth and leaped into Culberson's glove before Slaughter was far past second. Johnny Pesky, in shallow center field to take the relay, caught Culberson's throw just about the instant Slaughter came charging into third.

You'd have called it a fantastic notion that even the fleet Slaughter could score. Walker was so far short of second base a quick play there would have retired him for the third out. But Gonzalez never hesitated. He was waving Slaughter on from the moment Enos turned for third. Slaughter wheeled sharply at the corner and fled for home.

Pesky, still out behind second, stood morosely studying Ford Frick's signature on the ball. His interest was natural, for the ball he's accustomed to play with is signed by Will Harridge. At length he turned dreamily, gave a small start of astonishment when he saw Slaughter halfway home, and threw in sudden panic.

The throw was weak. Roy Partee, the catcher, had to take a step or so from the plate and as he caught the ball Slaughter slid in behind him.

Chances are the run that got the bully's share of the swag for St. Louis might never have scored if Dom DiMaggio hadn't doubled home two runs to tie the score for Boston in the top half of the eighth. DiMaggio was injured running out the hit and had to leave the game. It is unlikely Gonzales would have dared challenge Dom's squirrel rifle arm if he'd been playing center instead of Culberson.

Anyhow, that was the payoff in one of the most exciting World Series games ever played. Ten minutes later, witnesses were comparing it with the

Enos Slaughter scoring what proved to be the winning run in the seventh game of the 1946 World Series

seventh game of the 1926 series, which Grover Alexander saved for the Cardinals when he relieved Jesse Haines and struck out Tony Lazzeri with the bases filled.

There was some similarity, too, for this one was saved by the relief pitching of bandy-legged little Brecheen, called to the aid of his friend, Murry Dickson.

Possibly because they're little squirts in a game populated mostly by big, sweaty, muscular lumps of gristle, Brecheen and Dickson have been pals as long as they've played for the Cardinals. They room together, eat together, sit up nights talking baseball together, and after the season they team up on hunting and fishing junkets.

So when Rip Russell singled and George Metkovich doubled at the start of the eighth for the fourth and fifth Boston hits off Dickson, Murry dumped a large load of grief on his friend. Dickson walked alone to the dugout, his head down, and the crowd made with a Comanche yell when Brecheen started in from the bullpen.

Brecheen, a nine-inning pitcher on Sunday, rarely is at his best with less than four days rest but don't waste your winter trying to sell the Red

Sox that idea. He was almost good enough to put out the fire right away, for he struck out Wally Moses and got Pesky on a fly so short that Russell didn't dare run even against Slaughter's gimpy arm. But then DiMaggio doubled on a three-and-one pitch, putting the question up to Slaughter, Walker and Old Silvertooth.

At the end the Cardinals hoisted Brecheen to their shoulders but other players, clamoring to get near him, reached up and hauled him down like a goal post. As they disappeared from the field, Cronin came out of the first-base dugout and pushed slowly through the crowd. Now and then a man hurrying past reached out to tap his big shoulders. Joe didn't lift his head.

—October 16, 1946

The Big Train and His Buddies

WASHINGTON, D.C.—Walter Johnson, one of the most beloved of baseball players and perhaps the greatest of all pitchers, was buried today beside the grave of his wife in a little country cemetery. A funeral procession three blocks long wound through the thickets of Maryland to Rockville Cemetery after services in the National (Episcopal) Cathedral, which contains the crypt of an ardent Johnson fan, Woodrow Wilson.

"Big Barney's" casket was carried by eight of the men who were his comrades when he whipped the Giants in the deciding game of the 1924 World Series—Oscar Bluege, present manager of the club; Nick Altrock, now a coach; Muddy Ruel, new manager of the Browns; Joe Judge and Roger Peckinpaugh, who served with Bucky Harris and Bluege in Washington's finest infield; Sam Rice, outfielder; Tom Zachary, pitcher; and Mike Martin, who was the club trainer throughout Walter's twenty years with the Senators. All are graying or balding or both.

Bucky Harris, present manager of the Yankees, who was the "boy wonder" leader of the 1924 Senators, was an honorary pallbearer. So were Clark Griffith, president of the club; Edward Eynon, secretary; Clyde Milan, who roomed with Johnson for fourteen seasons; Jack Bentley, the Giant pitcher who lost that final World Series game; E. Lawrence Phillips, the Griffith Stadium announcer in megaphone days; Bill McGowan, dean of American League umpires; Spencer Abbott, scout and manager of Washington farm teams; Jim Shaw, a colleague of Johnson's on the pitching staff; and Lu Blue, former first baseman for Detroit and St. Louis. George Weiss, Yankee farm administrator, came down from New York, and Dick Nallin, a former American League umpire, from his farm near Frederick, Maryland.

"How he could pitch!" a man said. "How many bases on balls would you say he allowed in 1913 when he won thirty-six and lost seven games? Well, he had forty-three decisions that year and he walked thirty-eight men. In Hal Newhouser's best year, when he won twenty-nine, he walked one hundred and two."

"The best pitching I ever saw," Altrock said, "was in Detroit. The Tigers filled the bases on two boots and a walk with none out. Three left-hand hitters, Cobb, Veach, and Crawford, came up. Walter struck 'em out on nine pitches."

"That wasn't his best pitching," Griff said. "Neither was his game in the '24 Series or the time he beat New York three times in four days. The best of all was in 1912 against the Athletics with Eddie Collins, Home Run Baker, and the rest of that one-hundred-thousand-dollar infield. We'd been feuding with the A's all season and while we were fighting, the Red Sox slipped in and won the pennant.

"We had a three-game series in Philadelphia to close the season and the team that won that odd game would take second place. Jim Shaw over there started the series, the first game of a doubleheader, and led, three to nothing, until the seventh. Then the A's tied the score and Johnson came in. He shut 'em out until the nineteenth, when his catcher got hurt. We put in Rippey Williams, who always wanted to catch Johnson, and the first pitch got by him and clipped Billy Evans, the umpire, on the ear. Billy clapped a hand to his ear and it came away blood.

"'You're not gonna get me killed,' he told Williams. And he called the game on account of darkness, although it was only about four-thirty. Next day another doubleheader was scheduled and the same thing happened. Walter had to come in again with the score three to three after seven innings. This time it went to the twenty-first before we won, four to three. So he worked twenty-six innings against the greatest team of its time without allowing a run."

Johnson's eighty-year-old mother; his sons, Walter, Jr., and Edward and William, and his daughter, Barbara, were among the mourners. The simple services were conducted before a congregation of several hundred, mostly of middle age or older who packed one nave in the vast cathedral. Earlier in the day there had been a stream of visitors to the funeral home in suburban Bethesda, a few blocks from the house Johnson occupied until he moved to a Montgomery County farm.

These former neighbors stood in knots outside the funeral home, dropping in singly or in pairs, then lingering to talk of the plain, gentle man who is dead. A Montgomery County trooper came in alone and knelt before the casket. Walter was a member of the county commission, the only Republican. At each election, the voters would name four Democrats and Johnson.

"That woman," Griffith said, nodding, "was his nurse. She took care of him like a baby, and when she knew he couldn't get well she resigned. She couldn't bear to stay."

"See that man?" Griff said. "As long as Walter could eat anything, he took a quart of ice cream all the way out to the farm every day."

"Did you ever see such a guy for eating ice cream?" Bucky Harris said. "He hardly ever smoked or drank, except once in a while he'd take a few puffs out of a cigar, looking as awkward about it as a girl.

"What a sweet guy! My first year as manager I was young and I didn't know how some of the older players might take to me. We took the pitchers to Hot Springs for early training and Walter was the bellwether, setting an example that made 'em all work.

"You know, he pitched fifty-six consecutive scoreless innings for me. The last six innings of the streak he had St. Louis shut out, but then we scored six runs and I said to myself, 'Good night, here it goes.' I knew he'd coast on that lead, and I'd advertised him in Detroit, where we were going next, and Cobb had been promising to score on him and I knew we'd get a crowd up there.

"Sure enough, he threw a nothing ball to Ken Williams, who hit a triple. Joe Gedeon tripped Williams at second, fell on him, hollered for the ball and tagged him. But Billy Evans sent Williams on to third for interference, and he scored on a fly."

"Cobb," somebody said, "once confessed that if he hadn't been so sure of Walter's control and didn't know how careful Walter was not to hit anybody Ty couldn't have batted .100 against him. As it was Ty knew he could take a toehold."

Another said, "Henry Edwards once told me he asked Walter if he'd ever used a spitter. Walter said just once. It almost got away from him and he never tried it again for fear he'd kill somebody."

"When we had squad games in training camp with Walter pitching," Bluege said, "practically everybody that was supposed to hit against him would suddenly get sick or hurt."

Another said, "Remember the time Ruel and Milan were hurrying to a show with him and some fan spoke to him and held 'em up half an hour? They kept signaling him to break away and when he finally did they gave him hell. He said he was sorry, but the fan was a fellow who grew up in Kansas and knew his sister well and he didn't want to be rude.

"Milan said, 'I didn't know you had a sister.'

" 'I haven't,' Walter said. 'But he was a nice feller!' "

—December 1946

The Pot, the Kettle and the Czar

IT NOW APPEARS that Happy Chandler's decision in the celebrated case of Larry (The Pot) MacPhail versus Branch (The Kettle) Rickey will be, "Let's make like nothing ever happened." Dispatches from Florida suggest that when baseball's Solomon has heard all the testimony regarding who's been calling whom a bad name he will call the belligerents together and suggest that they shut their traps for the good of the game.

If Happy settles upon this solution, it will be his first completely smart move since his running broad jump from the Senate to the major leagues' payroll. It will also be altogether out of character, a form reversal demanding investigation by the stewards.

Any time Happy counsels anybody else to button his lip and act like an adult, the other guy has legitimate grounds to retort, "Look who's talking." And yet, what can you do with such incorrigibles as Rickey, MacPhail and Leo Durocher except to make them go wash out their mouths with soap?

Under the rules, Happy has the theoretical authority to bar from baseball anyone whose words and actions seem to him sufficiently offensive to justify the penalty. From now until a decision is announced, this office will be open twenty-four hours a day to accommodate bettors who believe that baseball's czar has the courage to banish MacPhail and/or Rickey.

It becomes wearisome to keep on making a comparison that must be odious to the gentleman from Kentucky. But does anyone seriously believe these middle-aged brats would have dared to put on their mud-slinging act during the administration of Kenesaw M. Landis?

Away back last winter when MacPhail made his first pass at Charley Dressen, an employee of the Dodgers, the judge would have snatched Larry baldheaded for violation of the rule against tampering. Rickey would have opened his face just long enough for the judge to stuff a gag into it.

It is unnecessary to labor the point that the judge is dead and times and manners have changed. If the change has been for the better, the point remains to be proved.

Meanwhile, it is noted that the Yankees, who celebrated the marriage of baseball and booze last year by transforming the Stadium into a genteel ginmill, are making an even greater cultural advance this year.

Beginning Monday, April 14, and continuing throughout the baseball season, the club will sponsor a radio program of symphonic music over WQXR every afternoon.

A lot of people are going to wonder what possible need Larry MacPhail has for a horn, not to mention a whole orchestra. This is a mystery which remains unexplained by the publicity release announcing the program.

However, the release does list the compositions which will be offered during the first week of the broadcasts. By some oversight, the "Nutcracker Suite," by Tchaikovsky, is not included.

Instead, the first number listed is "The Flying Dutchman Overture," by Wagner. Here is a selection that fairly drips with nostalgia for those who remember a time when the Yankees, representing the ultimate in dignity and class, were under the direction of Ed Barrow, the man who discovered Wagner, the Flying Dutchman.

The first week's program runs the gamut of Bach, Beethoven, Strauss, Verdi, Grieg, Haydn and Liszt. In view of the bathing beauty parades, kooch dances and similar circus acts which go on in the Stadium these days, Glazunov's "Carnival Overture" is appropriately included. So is "Symphonie Espagnole," which commemorates the Yankees' adventures in Puerto Rico, Caracas and way stations.

It is not clear whether the sponsors had any particular person in mind when they chose Liszt's "Mephisto Waltz" for one of the shows, but it is reasonably certain that the decision to offer the immortal love story, "Tristan und Isolde," was not intended as a tribute to their modern counterparts, Leo and Laraine.

Studying the program with which Mr. MacPhail hopes to sooth the savage bleacher fans, one is struck by an inexplicable omission. Nowhere on the list does there appear that most appropriate of selections from I Pagliacci—"Laugh, Clown."

—March 26, 1947

Open a Window, Albert

LARRY MACPHAIL, FOR reasons best known to that magnanimous gentleman, has asked that Happy Chandler reopen the Durocher case. Previously, in a speech before a St. Louis church congregation, Chandler had said the case was closed. Mr. Chandler was mistaken. The case is not closed. It will not be closed until the public is satisfied that something approaching justice has been done.

As baseball commissioner charged with administration of the national game, Chandler works for the people, the millions of baseball fans in the land. He does not, whatever his decisions may suggest and whatever his own opinion in the matter may be, work for Larry MacPhail. The fans are asking for a look at the record of the hearings which preceded the one-year suspension of Leo Durocher.

They have a right to study the evidence which convinced Chandler that Durocher was guilty and MacPhail innocent of conduct detrimental to baseball. The Brooklyn club, as defendant in the case, has a right to have that evidence made public. And this, by the way, is written by one who holds no brief for Durocher as an individual nor for the Brooklyn club as an organization.

It is, however, a fact that the Brooklyn club never has made, before or during or after the hearing, any public statement of any kind with reference to MacPhail's charges of defamation. MacPhail made numerous statements, and in view of the publicity attending his statements, the Brooklyn club demanded the right to defend itself in an open hearing. This demand was refused by Chandler.

In this respect, Chandler has spoken the truth. The case has been closed. It has been altogether too snugly closed from the outset. It is time someone opened a window and let in some fresh air. Let's consider the circumstances.

On Nov. 22 last, Durocher was in Hollywood rehearsing a radio show with Jack Benny when a telephone call interrupted him. He returned to the studio so upset he was scarcely able to go on with the rehearsal. There is no secret about this; the story was all over Hollywood within twenty-four hours.

The telephone call was from Happy Chandler summoning Durocher to Oakland for a conference. There is no secret about that, either. Durocher has told how Chandler questioned him about his acquaintance with assorted Hollywood characters and Eastern gamblers and warned him to keep away from people of that sort.

This following publication of Westbrook Pegler's columns concerning George Raft's crap game in Durocher's apartment. The question is, did Chandler act on his own initiative for the good name of baseball when he called Durocher on the carpet? Or did the commissioner have to be pushed?

Well, Durocher went to the Dodgers' training camp in Havana and there can be no doubt he went out of his way to avoid contact with gamblers there. Then at two Yankee-Dodger games he saw MacPhail sitting in close proximity to two racetrack characters.

Leo blew up and popped off. He said, in effect, that if he were to appear publicly with these men it would mean his finish in baseball. Branch Rickey echoed him. MacPhail's response was a charge that Durocher and Rickey had maligned him as an associate of gamblers.

MacPhail said a number of other things. Charley Dressen, who had quit as Durocher's coach to take a job as coach of the Yankees, said a number of things. The Brooklyn club said nothing.

Rickey did not point out that he had been MacPhail's sponsor in baseball since Larry's earliest days in the game. He did not mention that after

MacPhail's financing of the Medical Science Building in Columbus, Rickey helped him get a baseball job in Cincinnati and, following his departure from Cincinnati, recommended him as general manager of the Dodgers. Rickey did not suggest that now MacPhail was deliberately pumping up a "feud" with his former sponsor simply to get publicity for a Yankee ball club whose players seemed unable to get it for themselves.

Instead, the Dodgers went into Chandler's star chamber hearing as defendants. They did not go in to charge Dressen with jumping a contract; yet the commissioner found that Dressen had jumped a contract and Charley was suspended for thirty days. The Dodgers did not go in to charge MacPhail with tampering, yet the commissioner found MacPhail did hire Dressen when Charley was under oral contract to Brooklyn. Why did Chandler act against Dressen and not against MacPhail? What does the record say?

"The evidence," Chandler says, "shows that the alleged gamblers were not guests of MacPhail and did not sit in his box."

Was Mike Suarez, manager of the Havana Stadium, asked what disposition was made of the twenty-eight seats in Boxes 117A, 117B, 118A and 118B? Was the Brooklyn club asked who received tickets for these seats? Was the Yankee club asked what happened to these tickets? Did anyone explain how Memphis Engelberg and Connie Immerman happened to wind up in two of these seats, and MacPhail in another? What does the record say on this, Mr. Chandler?

Public statements had been made that Durocher tried to get the job as Yankee manager and also the job as manager of the Pittsburgh Pirates. If true, this might reflect dissatisfaction on Durocher's part, and any employer has a right to know it if his manager is dissatisfied. If untrue, stories like these could be the unjustifiable cause of turmoil within a club.

Was Durocher asked whether he sought either job? Was MacPhail asked whether he sought Durocher? Was the same question put to the Pittsburgh club? What were the answers? What is on the record?

Was Durocher suspended on the basis of evidence adduced at the hearing? If so, what was the evidence and where did he come off worse than MacPhail? Or did Chandler go beyond the evidence of the hearing and belatedly punish Durocher for past sins? If so, why bother conducting a hearing? And if Durocher's past has been "an accumulation of unpleasant incidents," what is the official opinion of MacPhail's past?

In his St. Louis church speech, Chandler said, "There was a case in which one fellow wanted a man suspended for a month. Another wanted him suspended for ninety-nine years."

Hey, Mr. Commissioner, was the decision based on the evidence or on what somebody else wanted? There is only one way to answer these questions to the public's satisfaction, and if justice has been done this is the way to prove it. Let's look at the record. Who is afraid?

—April 18, 1947

Losing Pitcher: Mulcahy

THE NEWS ITEM tucked deep down near the bottom of the page told the story in seventeen words: "Roy Hamey, general manager of the Pittsburgh Pirates, today announced the unconditional release of Hugh Mulcahy, pitcher."

So, Losing Pitcher Mulcahy has lost another decision. Quite possibly it was his last one, as far as major league baseball is concerned, for he has now been included out by the Phillies and Pirates successively, which is double zero on any wheel. When you've reached a point where a team like the Phillies, whose leading pitchers are as nearly prehistoric as Dutch Leonard and Schoolboy Rowe, can gaze without love into your soft gray eyes, then it's a cinch that your future lies somewhere beyond Joplin, Mo.

Common sense doesn't allow for a separate period of mourning for every good ball player and good guy who finishes his hitch in the majors and has to move along. Not even for all guys as good as Hugh Mulcahy. It happens to them all, and they all know before they come up that there'll come a day when they'll have to go down. But the case of Hugh Noyes Mulcahy is a special case.

Chances are there has not been in modern times another ball player with ability comparable with Mulcahy's who put so much into baseball and took so little out, that is, no one who wasn't at least partly at fault, no one at once so deserving and so unlucky.

In a strictly professional sense, Mulcahy is the major war casualty among big-league players. He didn't get shot, like John Grodzicki or young Bob Savage. He wasn't knocked out of the skies and imprisoned, like Phil Marchildon. But those fellows were young enough to come back and start over. Mulcahy only lost a career that seemed just about to come to full flower when he had to give it up.

He was the first major league player called into the Army in the prewar draft. He was in longer than any of the others. And when he came out his success was behind him. It wasn't anybody's fault that he never began to get the rewards he deserved. He had come to the Phils in 1935 as a kid of twenty-one and the Phillies had farmed him out to Hazleton, Pa., where he won twenty-five games in 1936. Then they brought him back and put him to work.

Really to work. In his first season he pitched in fifty-six games, which was a National League record then. In 1938, when he lost twenty games, and in 1940, when he was licked twenty-two times, he suffered more defeats than any other pitcher in the league.

That's when he got his nickname. The Phillies of those days lost with regularity and surpassing ease no matter who was pitching. Because Mul was big and strong and quite earnest and ready to work at the drop of a fly ball, it seemed he was in there nearly every day, and as he strode out to the hill the fellow keeping the box score would sigh and write, "Losing pitcher: Mulcahy." It got to be a litany in the press box.

But his won-and-lost figures deceived no one in baseball. He'd always had strength and stuff and an incomparable disposition, and he was developing poise the hard way. Jimmy Wilson, who was his first manager in Philadelphia and didn't make mistakes about pitchers, used to mumble at the press a little, saying, "Call him Losing Pitcher Mulcahy if you like, he's the very hell of a pitcher."

So after 1940, when he and Kirby Higbe had won twenty-seven of the team's fifty victories between them, there wasn't a club in the league that wouldn't have jumped at the chance to buy either of them. It was taken for granted Mul would be sold and would start making real money.

That was the stamp of success for a member of the Phillies of those days. Gerry Nugent, saving string and old tinfoil in the front office, couldn't afford to pay stars salaries. For his players the road to financial success was a highway leading to Brooklyn or New York or Chicago.

But they never had a chance to sell Mulcahy. In March, 1941, eight months before Pearl Harbor, he was drafted. Chances are he lived on his Army pay and nothing else in the years that followed, for the rather foggy recollection here is that before he went away he had spent what small savings he had providing a home for his parents and setting his father up in business.

The recollection also is that he didn't play ball in the service. When the war ended he was crowding his thirty-second birthday. Not too old for a comeback, you'd say, but last season when he was rising thirty-three he was able to win only twice for the Phillies. They let him go and the new Pittsburgh ownership, reaching out indiscriminately for loose talent, picked him up. So now he's through with the Pirates.

At a baseball writers' show during the war, Arthur Mann had a song that went: "Bless 'em all, bless 'em all, let their names echo out in the hall; start with Mulcahy, the first to go in, shout 'Captain Greenberg' and set up a din." . . .

By coincidence the item about Mul's release appeared directly below a longer story about the difficulty Hank Greenberg is having with a gimpy elbow. There's a fellow whose name is associated mentally with Mulcahy's because he, too, was nailed by the pre-war draft at the peak of his earning power. He was pulled out of a $55,000 job when he went into the Army three months behind Mulcahy.

But Hank had been a star making big money when Mul was a rookie in Woonsocket. And Greenberg, having come back to a $55,000 salary, is getting even more now. Two guys equally deserving but not equally fortunate.

"Well, more power to Hank," Mulcahy would say, being that sort of a guy.

—May 14, 1947

Profile of a Sports Reporter

THE CHILDREN WERE restless on a recent evening and wanted a bedtime story. It was but the work of a moment to switch on the radio in search of something soothing like a triple ax murder in a haunted madhouse. Halfway around the dial, however, the quest was interrupted by a voice of singular urgency.

"Profile of a medal," it screamed. A story followed.

Six years ago (the tale went) a great man died. Name of Lou Gehrig. Well, this was the story of Lou Gehrig and a trip to Japan. Some years ago he toured the Orient with an all-star baseball team. In Tokyo there was a huge celebration in his honor, and all the fuss embarrassed him, but he was still more embarrassed at a banquet in the Japanese Imperial Palace, when a high official of the government arose to speak.

Here the narrator paused, and here came the tinny squeak which is the voice of all Japanese on the radio. The voice presented a gold medal to Lou Gehrig. Back now to the narrator.

After Gehrig's death, with the United States and Japan at war, a package arrived in the War Department in Washington. It contained the Lou Gehrig medal and a note requesting that it be returned to Tokyo with the first consignment of American bombs. And so it happened that when Jimmy Doolittle's flyers raided Tokyo the Lou Gehrig medal fell with the explosives.

That, the intense voice conceded, could be the end of the story, but it wasn't. Long afterward a Japanese submarine in the Pacific attacked an American Liberty ship. Attacked without warning, surfacing and preparing to blow the defenseless ship out of the water.

But that Liberty ship was not so defenseless as the Japs thought. It rammed and sank the submarine, and several survivors were captured. One of those survivors was found—the Lou Gehrig medal!

Well, that was all of the story except for one more item. That Liberty ship which rammed the Japanese sub and captured the survivors and recovered the Lou Gehrig medal was a new Liberty ship bearing the name—S.S. Lou Gehrig!

Profile—of a medal!

Coincidence is a noun meaning the condition, fact or instance of coinciding; occupying the same place in space or the same period of time. Coincidence also is a horse that runs occasionally in the Greentree colors. Since Coincidence is a gelding, it will, unfortunately, never get a colt to be named Bill Stern.

People who think that a truly dramatic coincidence is a rarity are commended to this program, any station, any night. Recently someone was telling of his good luck in happening to tune in on this one:

Before the war there was a great racehorse in France. Toast of the Riviera, winner of zillions of francs, darling of millions, all that sort of thing. But the horse came upon unhappy times, slid miserably down the equine social scale until at last he was pulling a milk wagon in Paris.

Now, it came about that the man who owned the horse in his golden years also fell upon evil days. After the war he was tried as a collaborationist, convicted and sentenced to death. He was executed and his body tossed into a cart—drawn by the very same horse that had carried this man's racing colors to glory and to wealth!

And that man, sports fans, that man whose lifeless body was hauled to a traitor's grave by the once-great horse that had won so gloriously in his name, that man's name was—Pierre Laval!

There is here nothing but profound admiration and respect and, perhaps, just a smidgeon of envy for a reporter so diligent and indefatigable and so richly blessed with news sources that he can obtain the registration papers of the horses which pull charnel carts in Paris.

It is unlikely that a reporter of such stature has any need for volunteer assistants. Nevertheless, here is a story recently obtained from unimpeachable sources in the heart of the Blue Grass country and now offered, free of encumbrances or obligations, for such use as it may be suited.

About eighty years ago an American cavalry officer visited the horse farms near Lexington, Ky. There he had an opportunity to buy a colt of superb breeding and brilliant speed, a colt so fast, its owner said, that no Indian pony alive could ever catch its rider.

The price was $50, and the officer said no, he wouldn't pay that much. So he passed up the opportunity.

And that man, that military leader who declined to spend $50 for a horse that could outrun the fastest Indian pony that ever lived, that man was—General George Armstrong Custer!

Take it away, Bill.

—June 10, 1947

No Surprise to the Writer

A HIGH POINT in the commencement exercises at St. Raymond's was reached when a graduate's relative, who must be psychic or else had copped a sneak out to some radio set during the baccalaureate address, came over and said, "Did you know Ewell Blackwell just missed another no-hitter? One out in the ninth, and that Stanky hit one back at him."

Except for the time and place and manner of its arrival, the news was not particularly surprising. There is a theory, long subscribed to here, that you can figure the form on good pitchers just about the way you can figure it on good horses. Years of observation with this point in mind have inclined to support the theory, although admittedly there are no figures at hand which can be quoted to prove it.

Race players know that when a horse of class attains a sharp edge he is likely to remain sharp over a considerable period of competition, provided the race conditions don't change materially and he has a trainer who knows how to take care of him. First thing a player wants to know from the form sheet is how the horse has been going lately, and after that he considers weights, jockeys, track conditions, distance, probable odds, purse values and what the butcher's wife said about the trainer's cousin.

In pretty much the same degree, a pitcher of class who reaches peak form can be expected to hold his edge through several games, at least, provided he also takes reasonably good care of himself. One exceptionally well-pitched game suggests that the next will be well pitched, too. And probably the one after that.

Thus at the start of the 1944 season, Jim Tobin kept his flutterball behaving in a series of three or four low-hit games immediately preceding his no-hitter against the Dodgers and, unless memory is playing tricks, he got pretty well along toward another no-hitter in his next start before the roof fell in. And, of course, Johnny Vander Meer's no-hitter against the Braves in 1938 was followed by another in Brooklyn four days later.

It is not intended to suggest that when a man goes through nine innings today without allowing a hit you can get rich betting he'll duplicate the performance next weekend. He should, if form holds up, come back with a good game but the no-hitter is largely accidental.

All conditions must be right. The pitcher must have all his stuff and all his control, he must catch up with the opposition at a time when it isn't hitting, and he generally needs better-than-average fielding behind him. Probably there've been hundreds of occasions when pitchers were just as good as Vander Meer in two straight turns, but in the whole history of baseball Vander Meer was the only one who had that subtle blend of skill and luck twice in succession. Which illustrates how rare a blend it is.

Chewing over the matter yesterday, our Mr. Rud Rennie remarked that he has found no-hit ball games to be dreary spectacles. The entertainment value of baseball, he feels, is in its action—hitting, base running, great catches and close plays. Says it's no fun just watching some guy throw a ball.

It was, Mr. Rennie recalled, great fun watching Joe DiMaggio through his hitting streak of fifty-six consecutive games in 1941. Each game was a new drama, loaded with suspense. One day Joe would get only two official chances at bat, and he'd come through. Another time he'd have to wait until his fifth and last trip to the plate before he connected. And every day the crowds would come clamoring out just to watch one man, and even if they were enemy crowds the same tight, strained silence would fall on all of them when Joe walked up.

As a matter of fact, it's almost always the crowd that makes the excitement at a ball game. For example, on the last day of the 1946 season Bobby Feller and Hal Newhouser met in Detroit with Feller gunning for a strikeout record for a season.

Now, you can't see a strikeout record except in a book. The game meant nothing to either team in the pennant race. Yet something like 50,000 customers came out on a cold, wet day and made it a carnival of excitement. Every time Feller got two strikes across the mob would start to roar. Time after time, the batter would hit the next pitch and the noise would subside until the next chance came. It seemed hours before Feller got Newhouser for the strikeout he needed. It didn't mean a blessed thing except one line in a record book. But it made a show you wouldn't want to miss.

—June 24, 1947

A Day for Hank Greenberg

THE FIRST GAME ended amid alarums and excursions with the Pirates on top, 11 to 10, and the Giants scrambling vainly to get the tying run home from third base and Kirby Higbe out on the mound nervously probing for a weak spot in the New York batting order. He squirmed out from under at last and all the players jogged for the clubhouse in center field. All, that is, except Clyde Kluttz, the Pittsburgh catcher, who chased Higbe out to second base, tapped Kirby's shoulder and shook hands, then returned to the dugout to unbuckle his armor.

A couple of guys fiddled with a microphone on home plate. In a little while, Hank Greenberg came in from the clubhouse alone, his eyes on the ground as he walked swiftly with his loose, shuffling gait. Waves of applause followed him in, growing in volume as he neared the packed boxes behind the Pittsburgh bench.

An American Legion color guard marched to the plate. They had to break stride to step around groundskeepers who were painting in the batter's box and didn't lift their heads. Then came fifteen members of the James Monroe High School team with whom Greenberg played ball in 1927, and the uniformed players of the 1947 team. The older squad, mostly hatless and wearing shorts, looked so trimly athletic you'd swear it couldn't be a day more than twenty years since they last played ball.

Greenberg came out then and went weaving through the crowd of former playmates. Tallest of them all, he stooped a little to shake hands. He wore the slightly hesitant smile of a man who hoped he'd remember all the names.

James J. Lyons, Borough President of the Bronx, read a speech and made presentations. Hank got a $500 check for the New York University Rehabilitation Institute, a plaque, a portable radio and a wrist watch sent on by Bing Crosby, part owner of the Pirates. Bing helps pay Hank's salary, which Pittsburgh newspaper men believe to be $90,000.

"This makes it $90,000 and a watch," somebody observed.

When Hank stepped to the microphone the crowd sat up in an effort to hear the words, which is strictly unorthodox at baseball ceremonies. Hank said it used to be customary to have a "day" for some rookie ball player, give him a traveling bag and then turn him loose so he could use it; now it was customary to have a "day" for a veteran and then give him his release. So he guessed this day represented the handwriting on the wall.

"I've never wanted a 'day' in a ball park," he said. "The only kind of day I ever desired was one with a chance to hit in the winning runs, and fortunately I've had a few of those in my time."

The gifts, he explained, weren't supposed to be on the program. He told how he had at first opposed the plan for a Hank Greenberg Day but consented on condition that all contributions go to his favorite charity, the Rehabilitation Institute. He talked briefly of the work the institute does with the physically handicapped.

Giants and Pirates sat watching from the clubhouse windows. To right and left of the knot at the plate, Preacher Roe and Andy Hansen warmed up for the second game, paying no apparent attention.

Hank turned to his high school classmates, some of whom, he said, he hadn't seen in fifteen years. "Looking at the bald heads," he added, "it seems longer. But they'd probably do a better job of hitting today than I."

When he was through, a man in the press box said, "You can safely say that's the longest speech ever made by a ball player at home plate."

"And the most intelligent," another said.

Hank walked to the clubhouse along the left field wall, followed by more waves of handclapping. Elbie Fletcher was to take his place at first base in the second game. Hank hadn't got a hit in the first game and had struck out with the bases filled.

The memory of other days kept coming back. Days when Hank had won World Series games all by himself. A poignantly thrilling day in Detroit when Hank, returning from war, stepped into the line-up and smashed a home run off a left-handed pitcher named Charley Gassaway.

Up in the press box guys were telling little stories about him—how even today when there's a night game in Pittsburgh, he shows up at the park by early afternoon to work on his hitting and to instruct kids who show up with him; how he has helped young Ralph Kiner this year, rooming with him, advising him, polishing the kid's style.

"He told me something interesting this summer," said Chile Doyle, of the "Pittsburgh Sun-Telegraph." "A lot of people think he's ready to quit but he told me, 'Next year I'm really going to have a big season for this club.' "

—August 24, 1947

A Man of Honor

IN 1942 THE president of the Dodgers, whose name is lost in antiquity, hired Louis Norman Newsom as pennant security. Mr. Newsom, one of the most distinguished of latter-day poets, responded with a telegram:

> *"Have no fear,*
> *Bobo is here."*

Brooklyn didn't win in 1942, but Bobo Newsom is a man of honor, to whom a promise is a gilt-edged bond. Yesterday he put the Dodgers into a World Series. He did it belatedly and not altogether voluntarily, but when he had pitched an inning and two-thirds for the Yankees in their third and most sordid encounter with Brooklyn, the Dodgers were on their way to victory, 9 to 8.

It wasn't Bobo's fault that the way turned out to be the longest ever traveled by a team in a nine-inning game. The blame there belongs to the Brooklyn pitching, which squandered the whole of the six-run lead constructed on the foundation which Bobo laid. If, during the gruesome hours between Newsom's departure and the arrival of Joe Page, the Yankees had dredged up a single pitcher who could get somebody out, New York could end the series today.

About halfway through the third hour, Yogi Berra came up with a World Series batting average of .000 to hit for Sherman Lollar, .667. He drove the ball over the scoreboard for the eighth Yankee run. This was, incidentally, the seventy-second World Series homer ever made by a Yankee, which is two more than all National League players put together have made in the competition.

"Does it look to you," a man asked his neighbor, "as though the Yanks are toying with 'em?"

"It looks to me," the other man said, "like a bad grinding job by a dentist. A 50-cent dentist with trouble at home."

No description could be more accurate, yet all the same this eerie pursuit race did have the quality of excitement which had been utterly lacking in the two affairs in Yankee Stadium.

There hadn't been a sound from the customers when the line-ups were announced. Some thought this indicated that the real Dodger fans weren't in Ebbets Field, but subsequent developments proved they were on hand and studiously giving their demigods the silent treatment.

As soon as the attack on Bobo started, the species of fauna fondly described as typical of Brooklyn began coming out of the woodwork. With half the capacity of Yankee Stadium, the joint shuddered with twice the noise. Colored balloons floated from the stands. A blimp rode overhead, almost obscuring Bobo in its shadow.

The slightly musical organization known as the Dodger Sym-Phony materialized in the lower stands and serenaded Mr. and Mrs. L. Durocher with "For He's a Jolly Good Fellow." Mr. Durocher arose and shook the leader's hand. Mrs. Durocher, a music lover, blushed.

At the first blast from the trombone, Happy Chandler leaped to his feet and spun around to face the music. With the agility born of long practice at Dodging issues, he spun right back, sat down and stared stonily at the diamond.

Yes, the joint was jumping, and it never did go entirely flat again. Nevertheless, the Dodgers in victory showed the same mortal illness that has beset them in defeat, the apparently incurable weakness which, one is forced to believe, must be their downfall eventually.

They didn't have the pitching. They scraped and scrambled and couldn't find enough pitching to protect a six-run lead. They couldn't, that is, until Hugh Casey came in and protected a one-run lead.

This strapping son of Buckhead, Ga., the only relief pitcher in the big leagues who lives upstairs over a saloon, was making his fifth World Series appearance for Brooklyn, and was destined to win his first decision. Last time he faced the Yankees in Ebbets Field was six years ago next Sunday when he mislaid a victory with Mickey Owen as his accomplice. Until yesterday, that was the slowest of World Series games.

Well, he came in there with the Yankees threatening and swiftly closed out the seventh inning. He opened the eighth by walking Tom Henrich, whereupon Johnny Lindell singled.

Two on, none out, the tying and winning runs aboard, and Joe DiMaggio up there at the plate looking bored and contemptuous of the things his eyes had seen. The yard was so still you could hear a pretzel drop away off in Casey's saloon.

DiMaggio grounded into a double play. There was no further nonsense of any kind. Not with Casey around. But Casey can't pitch 'em all.

—October 3, 1947

A Shrine in Brooklyn

THE GAME HAS been over for half an hour now, and still a knot of worshippers stands clustered, as around a shrine, out in right field adoring the spot on the wall which Cookie Lavagetto's line drive smote.

It was enough to get a new contract for Happy Chandler. Things were never like this when Judge Landis was in.

Happy has just left his box. For twenty minutes, crowds clamored around him, pushing, elbowing, shouting hoarsely for the autograph they snooted after the first three World Series games. Unable to get to Lavagetto, they were unwilling to depart altogether empty-handed. Being second choice to Cookie, Happy now occupies the loftiest position he has yet enjoyed in baseball. In Brooklyn, next to Lavagetto is next to godliness.

At the risk of shattering this gazette's reputation for probity, readers are asked to believe these things happened in Ebbets Field:

After 136 pitches, Floyd Bevens, of the Yankees, had the only no-hit ball game ever played in a World Series. But he threw 137 and lost, 3 to 2.

With two out in the ninth inning, a preposterously untidy box score showed one run for the Dodgers, no hits, ten bases on balls, seven men left on base and there were two more aboard waiting to be left. There still are two out in the ninth.

Hugh Casey, who lost two World Series games on successive days in 1941, now is the only pitcher in the world who has won two on successive days. One pitch beat him in 1941, a third strike on Tommy Henrich which Mickey Owen didn't catch. This time he threw only one pitch, a strike to Tommy Henrich, and this time he caught the ball himself for a double play.

Harry Taylor, who has had a sore arm half the summer, threw eleven pitches in the first inning, allowed two hits and a run, and fled with the bases filled and none out. Hal Gregg, who has had nothing at all this summer—not even so much as a sore arm—came in to throw five pitches and retired the side. Thereafter Gregg was a four-hit pitcher until nudged aside for a pinch hitter in the seventh.

In the first inning George Stirnweiss rushed behind second base and sole a hit from Pee Wee Reese. In the third Johnny Lindell caught Jackie Robinson's foul fly like Doc Blanchard hitting the Notre Dame line, and came to his feet unbruised. In the fourth Joe DiMaggio caught Gene Hermanski's monstrous drive like a well-fed banquet guest picking his teeth, and broke down as he did so. Seems he merely twisted an ankle, though, and wasn't damaged.

Immediately after that play—and this must be the least credible of the day's wonders—the Dodger Sym-Phony band serenaded Happy Chandler. The man who threw out the first manager for Brooklyn this year did not applaud.

In the seventh inning two simp-phony bandsmen dressed in motley did a tap dance on the roof of the Yankees' dugout. This amused the commissioner, who has never openly opposed clowning.

In the eighth Hermanski smashed a drive to the scoreboard. Henrich backed against the board and leaped either four or fourteen feet into the air. He stayed aloft so long he looked like an empty uniform hanging in its locker. When he came down he had the ball.

In the ninth Lindell pressed his stern against the left-field fence and caught a smash by Bruce Edwards. Jake Pitler, coaching for the Dodgers at first base, flung his hands aloft and his cap on the ground.

And finally Bucky Harris, who has managed major-league teams in Washington, Detroit, Boston, Philadelphia and New York, violated all ten commandments of the dugout by ordering Bevens to walk Peter Reiser and put the winning run on base.

Lavagetto, who is slightly less experienced than Harris, then demonstrated why this maneuver is forbidden in the managers' guild.

Cookie hit the fence. A character named Al Gionfriddo ran home. Running, he turned and beckoned frantically to a character named Eddie Miksis. Eddie Miksis ran home.

Dodgers pummeled Lavagetto, Gionfriddo and Miksis pummeled each other. Cops pummeled Lavagetto. Ushers pummeled Lavagetto. Ushers pummeled one another. Three soda butchers in white ran onto the field and threw forward passes with their white caps. In the tangle, Bevens could not be seen.

The unhappiest man in Brooklyn is sitting up here now in the far end of the press box. The "V" on his typewriter is broken. He can't write either Lavagetto or Bevens.

—October 4, 1947

Mine Host Dons a Fireman's Hat

OUT OF THE murky twilight in left field, the burly figure of Hugh Casey came striding, his glove swinging like a dinner pail as he walked. For the fourth time in four consecutive days he hiked in on feet that were neither eager nor reluctant, a prosperous saloon keeper on his way to work, or, if you prefer, fireman Casey answering a night alarm. You half expected him to pull on a white jacket and apron, rub his hands hospitably and inquire: "Well, gents, what'll it be?"

If he had, there'd have been only one answer possible for the Yankees: "The usual."

Arriving at work, he paused and took stock. He saw eight runs on the scoreboard for the Dodgers, five for the Yankees and no Yankee outs in the ninth. He saw two Yankees on the bases and the tying run waiting at the plate, where Phil Rizzuto stood waggling a bat.

Briskly, mine host Casey opened for business. He served fifteen pitches and the Dodgers were home free in what had threatened to be the only night game in World Series history.

A stranger reading the box score today could be excused for assuming the ball clubs had opened spring training uncommonly early. The Yankee batting order included all those characters who normally expect to be used, three innings apiece, in March against Dazzy Vance's semi-amateurs in Homosassa Springs, Fla.

Not that the Dodgers' line-up was a great deal tidier. Burt Shotton, resident genius on the Brooklyn bench, obviously was unwilling to let Bucky Harris, licensed brain of the Yankee dugout, out-think him for either distance or accuracy. The result was appalling carnage among the official scorers, who finished up barefoot, using their rubber heels for erasers.

The sixth World Series game was the longest and most intemperate orgy of ratiocination ever flung by a couple of managers. Before the game, Harris made like a statue by Rodin and put a rookie, Jack Phillips, at first base, and another rookie, Sherman Lollar, behind the plate so he'd have right-handers batting against the left-handed Vic Lombardi.

As soon as Lombardi was knocked out, Bucky celebrated some more and substituted George McQuinn for Phillips, Aaron Robinson for Lollar and Yogi Berra for the damaged Johnny Lindell.

Next time Bucky lifted his throbbing head, another southpaw was pitching for Brooklyn, Joe Hatten having replaced Ralph Branca, Lombardi's successor. Now Harris was stuck with the left-handed batters whom he hadn't wanted to start. But it can't fairly be said these rapid changes hurt his cause, for he was careful to keep the club pro, J. DiMaggio, insulated against strategy.

Concerned not at all with left or right handers, with logic, metaphysics or percentages, Joseph just hauled off in the sixth inning and poked one that would have been the ball game ninety-nine times in a hundred. With two runners on base and the Yankees three runs behind, he aimed a home run at the Dodger bullpen 415 feet away.

It failed by a few feet to get there because Shotton, thinking like a dervish, had waved his wand a few minutes earlier and caused Al Gionfriddo to appear in left field, like a genie.

There were 74,065 customers in the yard, including the sixty-five who had heard Gionfriddo's name before the series started. Now he has two legs on a pedestal at Cooperstown. Running in frenzied, hopeless pursuit of DiMaggio's drive, Al twisted to look back so often that he got himself wound up like a yo-yo. Somehow, a step or so short of the bullpen gate, he unwound himself and stole three runs from the Yankees.

It goes without saying that having Gionfriddo in there at just that moment makes Shotton the most astute tactician of all time. His other moves worked well, too, as pinch hitters like Cookie Lavagetto and Bobby Bragan came through for him and even his horizontal pinch runner, Dan Bankhead, got home safely after rolling himself out like a plush carpet between third base and the plate.

Meanwhile Harris was having similar success with his medulla oblongata. He got pinch hits out of such infants as Bobby Brown and Ralph Houk. But his unshakable faith in Joe Page's relief pitching—a faith that is richly supported by Page's record for the season—turned out to be the chink in the armor.

When the Dodgers started teeing off in the sixth, Bucky couldn't call for Page. Page was already in there. Those were his brains being scrambled.

Except in the four-run third inning, every pitcher Shotton picked did exactly what he was asked to do in the situation for which he was chosen. Shotton says, "You take the judgment and I'll take the luck," but he has made superlative use of comparatively skimpy mound material in this series.

At the outset, the Yankees were favored because "they've got the pitching." Now they've got Bill Bevens left, a guy who loses no-hitters.

—*October 6, 1947*

Pitching Takes Brains

"MY ALL-STAR all-screwball team," Al Schacht said, "starts with Art Shires on first base—no, that's wrong. It starts with Moe Berg behind the plate. Berg is a kind of nut, you know. He's an educated mental case. An educated catcher, which is the worst kind. Then there's Smead Jolley in the outfield. Did I ever tell you about Smeadie in Boston? Don't answer.

"Smeadie was playing left field when there was a hill in Fenway Park. A sort of incline up to the left field wall—Duffy's Hill they called it, for Duffy Lewis. Every time Smeadie started up after a fly he'd trip and fall on his face and finally they got him out mornings and had him practice running up the hill after fungoes.

"Well, Washington comes to town and somebody says: 'Smeadie, how you going to manage Duffy's Hill today?' Smeadie says: 'Don't worry about me, I got it mastered.' Well, the first ball hit out there is one by Joe Cronin that looks like it might be caught if Smeadie can make the hill.

"Jolley turns and dashes up the hill and wheels with his back pressed against the fence. Then he sees he has overrun the ball, so he starts down. One step and, oops, here he goes flat on his kisser, the ball hits him on the head, Cronin slides into third base, and Smeadie is out of the ball game.

"Well he's sitting there on the bench rubbing the knot on his head and cussing. 'A lot of smart guineas on the nine,' he says. 'Ten days you spend teaching me how to go up the hill and there ain't a guinea in the crowd with the brains to teach me how to come down.'

"The next day they decided to make a catcher out of him. He's a great big guy, you know, that can hit. That's all he can do. So he's behind the plate and the first batter up is Joe Judge. Smeadie ain't caught a pitch yet in a major-league game, but Joe turns to him and says: 'Smeadie, how do you like this catching racket?'

"'Well, Joe,' Smeadie says, 'I'll tell you. Out there in the outfield you're all alone by yourself, but here you got conversation.' With that, there's a pitch and Judge hits a high foul straight up in the air.

"Now, Smeadie was getting a little bald and his wife was always telling him to wear a tight cap. 'When your cap flies off, Smeadie,' she'd tell him, 'you look like an old man.' He used to wear a cap so tight he'd have to wrench it off like this in the clubhouse.

"When this foul went up, Smeadie yanked off his mask, and of course the cap came off, too. Smeadie thought of his bald spot. He claps his mitt over the top of his head and turns to the stand, 'I got it, Mary!' he yells. Then he turns to the third baseman and hollers: 'Okay, guinea, it's all yours!'

"The next day he was in the minors."

"My all-screwball team," said a man at the luncheon table, "would start with the pitcher."

"What do you mean?" Mr. Schacht demanded. "Pitching takes brains. Strategy. Lemme tell you about when I was in the International League. We're playing a double-header in Baltimore and between games I play a screwy golf game with a fungo stick and one of those ten-cent baseballs we called Rockets. It's just like a regular baseball only it's sawdust. When I finish the act I stick the Rocket in my hip pocket.

"Sixth inning of the second game our pitcher is getting belted and Chief Bender sends me into the game. Three men on bases. Seems like there's always three on when I'm pitching.

"In those days you could discolor the ball with licorice or tobacco juice. As I walk in, I'm reaching back in my pocket for my licorice and I feel the Rocket. 'Oh-oh,' I say, 'oh-oh,' I stick the Rocket in my glove and, when I'm on the mound, I turn my back to the crowd and slip the real ball into my shirt.

"Joe Boley's the first hitter. I lay one in for him and he tees off with everything he's got. Ffzzz, it goes in a little pop fly to the shortstop. One out. Len Stiles is next, and he tees off. Phzzz, another pop fly. Two out. The third guy is big Rube Parnham, which I can always beat him because I talk to him and get his goat. This time, though, I'm busy massaging that Rocket back into shape, because it's pretty lopsided. Finally I lay one in and he swings and it goes spiraling up over my head. It's just the shape of this hard roll here. I wave everybody away and make the catch myself. Three out.

"But now I can't leave the Rocket on the mound and I can't get the real ball, which has worked around here to the back of my shirt. So I carried the Rocket into the dugout, but before I could get the real ball out, Bill McGowan, the umpire, starts hollering and I got to roll the Rocket out to him. It goes skipping and hopping out across the grass.

"Of course, there's a terrific howl, and after a lot of argument I say: 'Well, all right. I confess I tricked the Rube, but I got Boley and Stiles legitimate.' I figure I'm going to get fined anyway, and I might as well get away with something.

"So McGowan rules it an illegal pitch to Parnham, and I take the real ball out of my shirt and go out to pitch to the Rube again. I get two strikes on him, and then I start working on him. I reach into my shirt, and the crowd starts yelling: 'Watch him!' and McGowan comes storming out to me. 'You just live your life, and leave me live mine.' I tell him. 'See, here's the ball, and it's okay.' So he goes back, and I throw one more to the Rube right up here under his chin, and he strikes out.

"Well, he's so mad he comes howling out to the mound, and I say: 'Here's the ball, look at it.' And I toss it to him. He grabs the ball and whirls and throws it clean out of the park, and McGowan fines him twenty-five dollars.

"See what I mean," Mr. Schacht asked, "about pitching strategy?"

—December 17, 1947

Prexy Swings to the Left

WASHINGTON—The first pitch of 1948 in America's national capital was a fast ball that whistled straight toward Snuffy Stirnweiss's left ear. Stirnweiss removed the ear with celerity and 31,728 witnesses wondered about the political significance of the duster. It seemed unlikely it had been ordered by Harry Truman on the theory that Snuffy, an old University of North Carolina halfback, must be a Southern Democrat.

Nor can the Thomas committee read anything subversive into the fact that the president posed for photographers as a right-hander and then swung to the left when he threw out the first ball. By that time, Happy Chandler had worn out his right pumping it.

An hour or so before the annual Presidential preview of the slum-clearance project called Griffith Stadium, there was a rumor that Mr. Chandler had the flu and wouldn't be able to show up. Shortly afterward, however, Happy arrived and the day was saved. Not only that, but the sun also beamed upon this almost unbearably fortunate community.

The Yankees, as stolidly indifferent as if this were only another World Series game with the Dodgers, lounged in their dugout, but long before the President appeared, the Senators were out on the field ogling the Presidential box, jostling the Secret Service operatives on funeral chairs before it, and sniffing the tangy scent of mothballs in the bunting. The Senators are mostly genteel young men from Chattanooga, eager to see all the sights of a town they may not be around for long.

Mimeographed sheets were distributed bearing the repertoire of the United States Army band, but the musicians rang in some added starters, including "Dixie," "Suwanee River" and "Maryland, My Maryland," but emphatically not the "Missouri Waltz." At length Prexy showed up and Commissioner Chandler, crouching with every muscle tensed, sprang from ambush, his right hand extended. The band made with "Hail to the Chief" and the players straggled out for the hike to the flagpole.

They were led in their meandering, unmeasured march by Representative Joseph Martin, Speaker of the House; Clark Griffith, proprietor of the Senators, and baseball's jocund czar. The only Yankee owner in evidence was Del Webb, who visited the Presidential box and held Mr. Truman in such earnest discussion it was apparent he was selling him a year's subscription to the magazine "Arizona Highways."

Coming back from center field, Happy Chandler waved joyously to customers in the stands. Before leaving the field he turned and waved his hat to the bandsmen. He did not sing. Griffith just marched along looking thoughtful, like a man trying to multiply the admission price by 31,728 in his head.

The world's most famous ambidextrous pianist and porch-builder then faced the cameras, waggled a new white ball aloft in his fist, switched, aimed his high hard one at the file of Senators lined up along the first-base line. He threw fiercely, as though all Senators were named Taft. Senator Sid Hudson (Democrat), of Tennessee, caught the ball.

It was the last time all afternoon that a resident of Washington's threw a pitch with impunity. Every time Early Wynn tried it, the Yankees brought blood. There'd been, when he walked to the mound and glowered down at Stirnweiss, the same old delightful tingle of anticipation which comes with the opening of any season. But before the first inning ended, the season was over in Washington.

Both Wynn and his opponent, Allie Reynolds, are noble Redmen and this was the grisliest Indian massacre since Little Big Horn. Starting with seven runs in the first round, the Yankees beat Wynn with sticks until they had accumulated sixteen hits and twelve runs. And not until then, with one out in the ninth inning, did Joe Kuhel instruct Early to impersonate the Vanishing American.

Joe was dead set on not getting panicky on his first day as a big league manager and yanking his pitcher hastily.

The Yanks have been trying to get Wynn from the Senators, and today they seemed to think they already owned him. Tommy Henrich, favoring a weak wrist, sliced his first hit instead of pulling it, and drove it no more than five rows in the remote left-field seats. Aged Joe DiMaggio singled and doubled, scored two runs, raced from first to third on a short single to center, twice slid magnificently into third, and tired out his new arm with an extravagantly terrific throw to the plate. Infirm Charley Keller slashed a double to left center and pulled a screaming single into right.

In the latter half of the seventh inning, Mr. Truman stood for the Senators. The rest of Washington must stand for 'em all summer. And yet hundreds of men come right out and ask the voters to send 'em here.

—April 20, 1948

News Aboard Ship

ABOARD M. V. BRITANNIC—The story made page one of "The Ocean Times" immediately below the bulletin about the Kremlin conversations. The headline read "Death of Baseball Idol," and the dispatch announced: "Babe Ruth, baseball's beloved home-run king, died in his sleep last night. The fifty-three-year-old famed Sultan of Swat died after a week-end rally that had raised the fading hopes of his legions of admirers. The end came swiftly."

Even in mid-ocean, news like that arrives punctually. It was news, too, in Japan and Pakistan and Johannesburg and Canberra. There are a great many places on this earth where baseball is not played, but very few indeed where the name of Babe Ruth was unknown. Which could be, if you liked, a way of saying how much bigger the man was than the game.

The end came swiftly, the dispatch said. Not swiftly enough. Not without years of unceasing, remorseless pain. Not so suddenly as to take anyone by surprise. Not anyone at all. "I haven't much farther to go," the Babe told his friend, Frank Stevens, in the hospital last winter, "but I'm not going to die in here. I'm going to get out and have some fun first."

The betting was against him on that, but he did get out as he said he would. How much fun he had only he could have said. It didn't look like fun being convoyed around Florida, where he'd had, in his time, some fun that really was fun. You'd encounter him in Miami and Tampa and St. Petersburg and Clearwater at the spring training games or maybe at a dinner, always with a squad of cops fending off the autograph hounds and a horde of junior executives chuffing and scurrying like tugboats around a liner.

There always seemed to be junior executives around him in those last few months. In Florida he had some sort of business tie-up with a motor company and later, back home, there was a great fuss about the launching of his autobiography into the market, and after that came the screening of the book in Hollywood. Seemed as though everyone had an idea how to make some more money, but there wasn't much time and it had to be hurry, hurry, hurry.

Always there was the pain that never went away. He was so dreadfully sick even to the layman's eye. There was a sadness even in the jauntiness of his tan cap and camel-hair polo coat. Still, probably it was better than the hospital, and maybe he did have some fun of a sort.

There was a day at a ball game in St. Pete's Al Lang Stadium, the shiny new playground on the site of old Waterfront Park where Babe and the other Yankees used to tee off in the spring. Somebody asked him about the old days in St. Pete. He pointed to the weathered façade of the Gulf Coast Inn which, when the old park was up, had stood an everlasting distance beyond the outfield wall. He remembered, he said in the husk of voice which he had left, how he'd really got his adjectival shoulders into a swing and had knocked the indelicacy ball against the Anglo-Saxon Hotel out there.

His eyes gleamed with something like pleasure. Some of the old joie de vivre remained, all right. But the end didn't come swiftly, really. The Yankees of Ruth's day who have gone, they didn't get many breaks at the end. There was the Babe with his intractable pain these last several years. There was Lou Gehrig dying by inches and knowing it and facing it. There was Tony Lazzeri alone in the dark when the finish came. Little Miller Huggins was luckier. He went tragically, but suddenly.

Now that Babe is gone, what's to be said that hasn't been said? Nothing, when you come down to it. Just that he was Babe Ruth. Which tells it all, for there never was another and never will be. Probably he was the greatest ball player who ever lived, Ty Cobb and Honus Wagner and the rest notwithstanding.

It's a typically shabby trick on history's part that, as time goes by, he will be remembered merely for his home runs. He was also, remember, a genuinely great pitcher, a genuinely great outfielder, a genuinely great competitor, a truly great personality.

Merely by being part of the game, he wrought lasting changes in its strategy, its financial standards, its social position and the public conception of it. Somebody else will come along to hit sixty home runs, probably very soon. That won't make somebody else a second Babe Ruth. There won't ever be a second Babe Ruth. Never another like him.

—August 19, 1948

Heat Wave in New England

BOSTON—It was a good while before noon and the thermometer was whistling up into the nineties, but already the narrow little intersecting streets around Fenway Park were jammed. It was suggested to the cab driver that this town seemed to be slightly steamed up, with both of its teams in first place. He said yeah he guessed so, and swore at a driver cutting in on his left.

Outside Fenway, a public-address system was warning the thronged streets that nothing save bleacher seats was available. It turned out that the crowd that finally got in for the second game of the Cleveland-Boston series was under capacity, a mere 30,745 being counted. It had been different last night. There'd been maybe 25,000 locked out of the joint and many of them were still milling in the streets when one of the radio stations gave off its stock announcement: "For the information of those who live close to the park, there are still plenty of seats available."

Matter of fact, with the Red Sox and Indians scrambling for first place in the American League, Boston's saloons have been doing a booming business. For the first time since the second Louis-Walcott fight, they've been able to charge for seats in front of the television set, besides charging for drinks.

For all of that, things were quiet on the Boston bench. Joe McCarthy was sitting there, his flat face as expressionless as ever. A photographer was being extraordinarily apologetic, explaining that he hated to bother him but he'd had a special request for a photograph of McCarthy and Lou Boudreau shaking hands. Joe said no, he'd refused a similar request by another camera man, and much as he liked the Cleveland manager he didn't think he ought to pose with him in the circumstances.

A guy said, "Joe, I've been away a long time. When I left, your club was beginning to win by scores like 11 to 9, but you still had no pitching. Now you're in first place. What has happened to your club?"

"Nothing," McCarthy said.

"Didn't some pitchers come through for you?"

"Yes," Joe said, "Kramer came along." Then he frowned, and kind of shook all over.

"I don't want to talk about 'em," he said. "Dammit, every time I say something nice about a guy, something happens. I remember one time in Chicago I was telling a guy about DiMaggio. I said, 'I've never seen him make a bad play.' I said, 'He's never thrown to the wrong base. He knows exactly when he can catch a guy trying to stretch a hit and when he can't.' I said. 'And when he's behind second, he always knows when he can stretch a hit. He's never thrown out.'"

Joe said, "That's what I told the guy. And that afternoon Joe was on first and a ball was hit to left center. Joe rounded second, started for third and came back. The ball was thrown to second base, and he was tagged out coming back. They threw the ball behind him, and tagged him out!"

"I said to him afterward, 'What happened, Joe?' He told me, 'I thought I saw the ball coming into third ahead of me, so I ran back.' Well, that's why I don't like to talk about guys."

It didn't really make any difference, though. McCarthy could have talked all day and he'd never have changed today's ball game.

The simple fact is, the guys McCarthy had in there pitching just couldn't do today. Denny Galehouse started, and by the time he was finished the Clevelands had four runs and seven hits. Already, ears were aching from the rum-tum-tum of line drives against the left-field wall.

Dave Ferriss came in, and by the time three innings had ended, the score was 6 to 0 and the Indians had twelve hits. There'd been a moment when the temper of the crowd seemed to swell almost to the point of explosion. In the third inning, Joe Gordon singled and Larry Doby wrapped a triple around the flagpole in center.

This colored outfielder, Doby, he needs a few lines to himself. He is a black and slender gentleman who bats left-handed and uses the stick like a whip. When he tees off, he is all eyes and wrists and shoulders. He had got himself a single the first time up and now, snapping his wrists, he golfed a drive into center field which tucked itself in between the flagpole and the wall and rattled around like a pair of dice while Dom DiMaggio scrambled for it.

A low growl grew in the bleachers. There had been cheers for Ted Williams the first time he came up, mixed with a few boos emitted by people who knew he'd made only one hit in twelve times at bat. He lashed a single into right field, and the boos dropped away to silence among the cheers.

But that had produced no runs, and now the growl grew louder, with a menacing note, because McCarthy let Ferriss stay in there after Doby hit. It grew louder still as Eddie Robinson banged a single to right, and it was downright mean when Jim Hegan, the Cleveland catcher, followed with the Indians' twelfth hit.

After that it didn't matter much. Now and then the Indians banged another run home. None of the Red Sox got a good bite out of Bob Lemon's malevolent side-arm speed. The Red Sox just kept toying with that slot machine, and all they saw was Lemons.

—August 26, 1948

Heat Waves and Brain Waves

BOSTON—Mr. Lou Boudreau, resident genius of the Cleveland Indians and one of the greatest switch thinkers of our day, put in a tortured afternoon of thinking in the hot sun today, thinking on his feet, thinking on the back of his lap, thinking on the run and thinking from a crouch. Beads of perspiration as big as pingpong balls stood out on his dark sconce as he struggled to fight off Boston's challenging Red Sox by sheer brain power.

But in a disheartening triumph of muscle over intellect, Bobby Doerr knocked a baseball out of Fenway Park and Mr. Boudreau's Indians out of first place with a single coarse stroke. Bobby's home run in the eighth inning with two playmates on base and the score tied at 3-all enabled Boston to win the rubber game of this impassioned series, 8 to 4, send the Indians to New York a half-game behind the Sox, and shake Mr. Boudreau's faith in the force of pure logic.

It was a disenchanting business for Mr. Boudreau, for only a few minutes earlier he had risked heat prostration by thinking the Indians into a tie. His had been an awesome performance that impressed even the 20,322 Bostonians who, along with a number of mad dogs, had come out in the noon-day sun for the garish conclusion of the series. The noon-day sun, by the way, hiked the thermometer to 99 and apparently unhinged the corporate mind of the Red Sox management, for in the second inning the directorate invited all customers who were broiling in the cheap bleacher seats to move into the shade of the grandstands.

Sitting there wallowing in unwonted creature comforts, the clientele had watched an absorbing struggle between Mel Parnell, the slender southpaw pitcher of the Red Sox, and big, left-handed Gene Bearden, of Cleveland. Both were wonderful, and Parnell was also lucky because the Indians handed him a gratuitous two-run bulge in the third inning.

With one out in that inning, Birdie Tebbetts walked and fled all the way to third when Ken Keltner booted a wobbly grounder by Parnell. (Tebbetts broke his own track record of 47.6 for the 180-foot course on that dash.) Then Keltner pawed at a ground ball off Dom DiMaggio's bat, recovered it in time for a force play at second, but missed a double play and enabled Tebbetts to score. John Peskey bounced a hopper near first base. The Cleveland first baseman, Eddie Robinson, glowered at the ball, addressed it as though he could see bubonic-plague germs parading down the seams in a column of fours, and it skipped on past him for a hit that scored DiMaggio, who had trotted to second while Bearden took a dreamy windup.

Well, that put the Sox ahead and kept them there. In spite of Bearden, who allowed only three hits in seven innings. The Indians chipped a couple of runs off Parnell, but they weren't getting far. Nobody gets very far against

Lou Boudreau

the Sox in Boston, where they have won forty-two of their sixty-one games. The wonder was that Bearden, in spite of the heat, looked as though he might last nine innings. Until Bob Lemon did it yesterday, not one in the last thirty starting pitchers had worked a complete game against Boston at home.

Now Mr. Boudreau started thinking. With the Indians one run behind, Keltner doubled opening the eighth. Joe Gordon popped up. Here came Larry Doby, a willowy Negro gentleman who looks like he's becoming one of the genuinely great players of all time. He fouled a ball, took a called strike, fouled another and missed an outside curve. Two out.

Eddie Robinson started for the plate, but Mr. Boudreau waved him back. Bob Kennedy batted instead, and lined a double to left that tied the score. That was managerial thinking that couldn't be improved upon.

The Indians went out. DiMaggio went out starting the Boston eighth, and then Pesky beat out a bunt. Ted Williams got his only hit, a characteristic drive to right, low and baleful. Up came Junior Stephens, the very big guy in Boston's batting attack recently. He lifted a pop fly toward third base.

Mr. Boudreau thought like a three-ply Solomon as this ball curved downward. It was an important out, a vital out, not to be entrusted to underlings. Mr. Boudreau nudged Mr. Keltner aside and made the catch himself. Mr. Boudreau is not a man to delegate jobs like that to hirelings.

Now, with two out, Doerr stepped up. Mr. Boudreau, thinking on the walk, strolled in and conversed quietly with his pitcher. He must have considered the advisability of walking Doerr, a great clutch hitter, and taking a chance on Stan Spence, who is batting .218 in his saddest season. But the idea was discarded.

Mr. Boudreau returned to his post at shortstop. Thinking from a crouch, he turned and waved Doby, his center fielder, a half-dozen steps toward left field. Then Bearden threw one pitch. It rocketed into the big wire catch-all atop the left-field wall, and the ball game was in for the Red Sox.

That's about all there is to the story, except that one ought to give Mr. Doerr a respectful paragraph. He has been one of the real pros in this game for a long, long time. He is batting .288, has driven in ninety-four runs and is shooting for the American League record of seventy-one games without an error. This year he played thirty games without a boot, made one error and then ran through sixty-five perfect games.

He's still on the streak. He makes no fuss about it. He's hardly ever spectacular on a play. He's just one of the guys who have hauled the Red Sox up from the second division to the top of the American League.

—August 27, 1948

When Stan Has His Health

ON A RAINY March day in St. Petersburg, Fla., Stan Musial sat with a guy in the Cardinals' hotel chewing over the club's pennant prospects, as guys always do in all baseball health camps in the spring. "For one thing," the guy said, "you don't figure to have another lousy year like last season. That makes the club stronger."

Musial kind of took back at that, stiffening a trifle. But he didn't protest and the discussion went on. Four or five times while they talked, something was said about Musial's miserable year in 1947, and each time Stan stiffened a bit but said nothing.

That evening the guy was going through the records and discovered that in 1947 Musial batted .312 and knocked in ninety-five runs. So the next day he said to Musial: "Either I owe you an apology or you should

Stan Musial

thank me for the compliment, calling it a lousy year when a fellow hits .312. Why didn't you call the record on me yesterday when I was knocking you?"

"For me," Musial said mildly, "it was a lousy year."

There was no vanity in that statement. He was merely reporting on a fact. Stan Musial is the sort of ball player to whom a batting average of .312 and a runs-batted-in figure of ninety-five represents failure. Last summer he played with appendicitis. This year he has demonstrated what he's like when he has his health.

Last Thursday the Giants moved into St. Louis with a six-game winning streak. They lost the first game of a double-header, 7 to 2, without any special help from Musial, who merely made one hit and knocked in one run. In the second game Stan made only one hit, too. It was his thirty-second home run, good for two ninth-inning runs which broke a tie, won the game, 7 to 5, and moved the Cardinals into second place in the National League.

Next day the idle Cardinals slid to third place, but on Saturday they played another double-header with the Giants. Musial hit a home run, a double and a single and for the second consecutive time his home run won the game, 5 to 4, in the twelfth inning. In the second game he contributed a single to the Cardinals' fourth straight torture of New York.

When the Dodgers whipped the Cards twice on Sunday, Musial made a home run, a double and a single in the first game, driving home two runs, and a double and triple in the second. His three-base hit came with two out in the ninth, sent two runs across the plate and tied the score at 4-all. Stan stood there with the winning run on third base while Dom Lank struck out.

These were not isolated instances when Musial happened to excel himself. Matter of fact, he isn't having an especially hot streak at the moment. Since Aug. 15, he has made six home runs, five doubles and two triples in seventeen games, batted in fourteen runs and hit for an average of .365. That's fair, but not wonderful for him, because his average for the season was .381 yesterday morning.

He is, of course, the leading batter in his league. He has scored far more runs than anyone else. In total hits, he is more than thirty ahead of his closest pursuer. His total of thirty-four home runs is exceeded only by Ralph Kiner's thirty-five. He leads the league in runs batted in. And although current figures are not immediately available here, the belief is that he has hit more triples, doubles and singles than anyone else.

He is the best left fielder the Cardinals have, the best center fielder they have, the best first baseman they have. He is, in short, the best ball club in St. Louis and one of the best in the world.

Yet there was a time last spring when the Cardinal directorate was mumbling bravely about facing the summer without him. That was during contract discussions. Musial had received $31,000 in 1947, which placed him second to Hank Greenberg among the highest-salaried first basemen of National League history. Probably because of his appendix, whose uncooperative disposition wasn't suspected at the time, he had a dreadful struggle getting started. While he was scrambling to raise his batting average to .200, the Cardinals dropped so far behind they never were able to overhaul the Dodgers, even with Musial hitting .400 in the closing months.

Bob Hannegan, having taken over the team from Sam Breadon, reasoned that Musial's early slump had deprived him of any claim to a salary increase. Musial disagreed. Or, at least, he reasoned that it would be nice to get more money, which is not a unique attitude. So he returned his contract unsigned, and Hannegan was offended.

Bob, innocent of experience in dealing with holdouts, was all for sitting tight and letting Musial come to him. When a friend urged him to make peace with Musial, he replied stubbornly that he didn't see why he should have to court the ball player.

"Look," the guy said, "do you want to fight him until you break him down and he comes in begging your favor and resenting it? Or do you want to have the guy on your side, satisfied and ready to hustle as he always has hustled? Get on the phone and talk sense to him; he's ready to listen."

Hannegan reluctantly consented. He phoned Musial, had a straight talk with him, and the league's most valuable player came in cheerfully enough for $31,000. In today's market, when high-school wonders get $75,000 bonuses and can't play, that's like shaking a Ty Cobb out of a tree.

—August 31, 1948

The Mortgage Is Lifted

BOSTON—In the twenty-eighth inning of their New England ordeal, the Yankees called upon the club pro today and he lifted the mortgage. That is, he lifted a corner of it, personally trouncing the Red Sox and salvaging the fragment that was left of this preposterous series.

Because the Yankees have a man named Joe DiMaggio, an outfielder, they are still second in the American League tonight, two and a half games behind Boston, instead of languishing in a tie with Cleveland four and a half games out.

The Boston baseball authors have a song they sing, more or less to the tune of "Maryland, My Maryland," whenever their own dandy little center fielder gets a hit or makes a handsome catch. It goes:

"He's better than his brother Joe—Dominic DiMaggio!"

As home-grown music goes it isn't a bad song and it's all good fun and it keeps the vocalists happy. But let's have no mistake about this; there simply isn't anybody else in the world like Dominic's brother Joe. And nobody knows how long we must wait to see his like again.

Look, here were 27,329 Bostonese having themselves a large time rooting for a third straight Red Sox conquest of the runners-up. They had seen some fairly frightful baseball and some very good baseball and some weirdly implausible theatrics.

They had seen a game which the Yankees would have won breezing if it hadn't been for a couple of Joe McCarthy's less celebrated operatives whose activities helped demonstrate the talent this manager has for making use of the material at his command.

Billy Hitchcock and Wally Moses are a couple of slightly used part-time workers whom McCarthy is employing currently at second base and in right field. Between them, they kept the Red Sox alive today when they should have been dead.

Leading, 2 to 0, in the second inning, the Yankees put runners on second and third base with none out. Gus Niarhos hit a twisting foul behind first base which Hitchcock chased down and caught with his back to the plate for the first out. Bobby Brown, on third base, started for the plate, but Hitchcock wheeled, his throwing arm cocked, and drove him back.

With the infield in close, Vic Raschi grounded to Hitchcock, who made a tough stop and flung the ball home, retiring Brown at the plate. Then he went to his left for a great stop on George Stirnweiss's sinking liner and threw him out, retiring the side.

This was a clear case of plucking the baby out of the burning building. So was the double play which Hitchcock started with two aboard and one out in the third inning. So was the job Moses had done earlier in that inning when he reached into the right-field seats and made a putout on a ball that lacked no more than an inch of being Tommy Henrich's second home run.

So, what with one thing and another, the customers had been having themselves a show, including a glorious rhubarb which developed when a photographer in the tunnel beside the Red Sox dugout got into a play in the home half of the third. And what with one thing and another, the score eventually got itself tied. Naturally, the talent anticipated that, for the script for this series has required Boston to come from behind in each game and the management neglected to change writers for today's show.

Well, it went along through the ninth inning with the score tied, and in the tenth the Yankees filled the bases with two out and up came Joe DiMaggio. Earl Caldwell was pitching. For twenty-seven innings the Yankees had been getting their lumps in Boston. But now they had the bases filled and DiMaggio at bat.

A guy in the press box said, "I would rather be anybody in the world than Earl Caldwell right now. I'd rather be Wallace. I'd even rather be Happy Chandler."

What is it they call it? Hobson's choice? If Caldwell walked DiMaggio, he'd force in a run and lose the ball game. If he threw the ball within Joe's reach, why, he'd lose the ball game. No question about it.

No room for doubt. That guy down there at the plate, legs spraddled wide, but sticking up high like an anti-aircraft gun, he's the club pro, the champ.

Caldwell threw the first one within reach. Joe hit it, but not well. The ball went skittering up the screen toward the press box, a foul nobody could reach.

Caldwell threw another within reach. Joe hit. The crowd made a noise like a fat man punched in the stomach, some 27,000-odd fat men. But the screaming liner went a few feet foul before it rocketed into the wire catch-all surmounting the left-field wall.

Caldwell threw the next one wide for a ball. He threw the fourth one wide for ball two. Somebody muttered, "Better not waste another, chum. Do you want the count to be three—and—two?"

So Caldwell threw another within reach. Joe's brother Dom in center field whirled and started running. Then he stopped. There's a niche in the center-field wall where the flagpole stands, and a sign there says it is 379 feet from the plate. That's just to the left of the bleachers, whose lowest row is very high.

The ball went a bit to the right of the flagpole, six, eight, maybe ten rows up in the bleachers.

There had been five pitches. Three were within reach. All three went out of the ball park. One was a fair ball.

That is the end of the story.

—September 11, 1948

They Played It by Radio

BOSTON—It was a day when malice lay over everything, thick as mustard on a frankfurter, and you could reach out and feel it like something tangible. The Yankees, killed off by the Red Sox yesterday, were out here in Fenway Park to gouge back an eye for the one they had lost, and the Red Sox, inspired by the loftiest sort of cupidity, wanted that World Series money so badly they could taste it.

The 31,354 specimens penned in the park had a sort of shine on their faces, the sweatily eager look that a bullfight crowd wears when the bull is five runs ahead of the matador in the ninth inning.

It was the third inning and the Red Sox, who had been two runs behind, had scored three times and had two runners on the bases, with one out and Bill Goodman at bat. Chuck Dressen, the Yankees' opulent coach, was out in the middle of the diamond talking to Bob Porterfield, the rookie pitcher, and the crowd started to scream.

At first, the notion was that the customers were only trying to work on Porterfield, hoping to shake the kid's unnatural poise. But there was a different sort of note in the crowd's voice. People behind the Boston dugout were standing and cupping hands to mouths and shouting things to the players, and after a little while it was apparent what was happening.

There were portable radios in the stands and the customers had just heard about that third inning in Cleveland. The word had reached the press box. The Tigers had a run home and the bases filled with one out. Then another flash came "Wakefield doubled."

You should have seen that crowd. Everybody was on his feet, and everybody was screaming, but the ball players acted as though they hadn't heard anything. Goodman singled, driving in Boston's fourth run.

The crowd made a fair fuss about that, but that was nothing. The small, unseen man who lives in the scoreboard swung a panel open and took down the number of the Cleveland pitcher and put up another. He took down 19 and put up 26, which meant that Bob Feller had been replaced by Sam Zoldak.

You should have heard that crowd. They weren't watching the Red Sox, who were scoring another run just then on a force-out by Birdie Tebbetts. They were watching the scoreboard, where the figure 5 went up for Detroit. That was a mistake, and a moment later the sign was changed and the number 4 was posted, the real Detroit score for the third inning.

Now the third inning was over up here. The Red Sox were in front, 5 to 2, and out in Cleveland the Tigers were leading, 4 to 0. Everybody knew Hal Newhouser was pitching for Detroit. Everybody knew that if Boston could stay ahead, there would be a tie for the American League pennant. Nobody thought for a moment that Newhouser would blow a four-run lead.

Of course he didn't. And of course the Red Sox won, setting up the first play-off the American League has had. But it wasn't easy. The Yankees have a guy named Joe DiMaggio. Sometimes a fellow gets a little tired of writing about DiMaggio; a fellow thinks, "there must be some other ball player in the world worth mentioning." But there isn't really, not worth mentioning in the same breath with Joe DiMaggio.

That guy, DiMaggio, had hit a double in the first inning and driven in New York's first run. He had grounded out in the third, but in the fifth Phil Rizzuto singled. Bobby Brown doubled Rizzuto to third, and then Joe came up. There were two runs on the bases and DiMaggio was the tying run at the plate.

First base was open. Up in the press box, people said, "I don't care how wrong it is to put the tying run on base. They have got to put this guy on."

But Joe McCarthy didn't. Heaven knows, the Red Sox manager is aware of what DiMaggio can do. The champ did it often enough for McCarthy when they were together on the Yankees. But McCarthy let Joe Dobson pitch to the guy. So, naturally, the guy hit another double, slamming the ball to the left-field fence and dragging his dead left leg stiffly as he ran to second base while two runs came home.

He had now driven home three of New York's four runs. He had twice made a contest of this game. He brought the Yankees up close enough to scare the daylights out of the Red Sox, until Joe's brother Dom hit one over the wall in the sixth.

Joe went on to make four hits in five times up, in his last game of the year. When he singled in the ninth, Bucky Harris sent Steve Souchok in to run for him. Maybe Bucky wanted the guy to walk off by himself, so he could get a personal tribute from the crowd instead of just going off, unnoticed, along with eight other guys. Because Harris thinks of things like that. Or, maybe, Bucky just wanted a sound runner on first base.

Anyway, Souchok went in and DiMaggio limped off, and the crowd stood up and yelled for the guy who had done more damage to Boston than any ten other guys they could mention. He tipped his cap and disappeared into the runway leading to the clubhouse.

That's all, except for one small story. Last night, Joe and his brother Dom dined together. Joe said, "You gave us hell today, but tomorrow I'll hit my fortieth home run."

His little brother said, "I don't think you will, but I'm gonna hit my ninth."

One of them had to be right.

—October 4, 1948

The Man Who Hates Ties

BOSTON—It was a large day for Bill Veeck, who can't abide ties. The young sachem of the Indians, with his throat bared as always in the frosty New England weather, sat in a Fenway Park box today and yipped and yowled and yammered like a common fan while his employees tore into tiny, tattered shreds the tie which had bound them to the Boston Red Sox.

Tromping along on their path of violence, the carnivorous Clevelands also destroyed the Sox and, in a belated burst of civic consciousness, brought to the home town its first baseball championship in twenty-eight years. They required, however, one day more than twenty-eight seasons to accomplish the deed, for after a campaign of 154 games, the vacillating American League still couldn't decide what to do with its pennant.

So they threw out everything that had happened to date as irrelevant, immaterial and incompetent, and let the whole business swing on a single game.

When at long last a decision was reached, Veeck jumped as though he'd heard someone say "Bob Hope is on the wire." Although he wears a machine-made leg in place of one which he contributed to the war effort, he couldn't have needed more than ten strides to get across the field and start thumping his wage slaves on their spines.

The wage slaves already had converged upon Gene Bearden, a comely but battered veteran of the unpleasantry with Japan, and flung his outsize torso up onto their shoulders, where he jounced and teetered in imminent peril of being dropped on his skull.

They would have given similar treatment to Lou Boudreau, their licensed genius, but he was otherwise occupied. As the final putout was accomplished, the Cleveland manager had made the swiftest dash his aching legs have managed in years. From his position at shortstop, he sped to the box where his wife sat watching, and while his operatives rushed off beating upon one another in jubilation, the maestro remained wrapped in his spouse's embrace, catching tears of joy on the first bounce.

It had been an afternoon dominated almost entirely by the genius of Boudreau and the brilliance of Bearden. It was, really, a considerably bigger game than a World Series game, for they play a World Series every year, but this was the only post-season play-off in the American League's forty-eight summers. And in a World Series there's always a fat consolation prize for the loser, but this was a case of life or death.

There never was a scale built in Toledo which could measure the weight of Boudreau today. His boss tried for a good part of last winter to fire him, because he wasn't Bill Veeck's idea of a manager. His team had blown a two-game lead in the last three games of the season. His pitching staff was used up, his club's morale was presumably shattered, and the Red Sox were on the crest of a wave, freshly reclaimed from the mortuary and confident of their destiny.

So this was Boudreau's chance to prove himself a manager. He started managing in the first inning. He came up with two out and nobody on base and he huddled down there at the plate in that funny, awkward crouch of his while Denny Galehouse threw two balls and a strike past him.

Then he whipped his bat around and drove the ball against the screen atop the left-field wall. His home run put Cleveland ahead, 1 to 0. It made him the greatest manager in the world. Connie Mack couldn't have done it.

In the fourth inning, Boudreau came up again, with the score tied at one-all. He was leading off. There is a theory subscribed to by many managers that when the score is tied it is a good idea to get some runners on the bases. So the manager managed a single to left field. Following his example, the Indians made four runs.

He came up again in the fifth with Cleveland in front, 5 to 1. Managing like mad, he hit another over the fence and made it 6 to 1. John McGraw couldn't have done it.

His next turn was in the seventh inning. The Sox had scored twice in the sixth and were back in the ball game. Now there were two Indians on base and one out. Joe McCarthy, a pretty good country manager in his own right, knew what to do in that spot. He gave the guy an intentional base on balls.

There remained only one more opportunity for Boudreau to make like a genius. He came up in the ninth with the Indians leading, 7 to 3, a runner on base and nobody out. Managing like a fiend, he whacked another ball into left field for a single, and in due course the Indians got their eighth run.

The manager had now made four hits in four times at bat, scored three times, driven in two runs and contributed to the scoring of another. He had handled six chances in the field without a flaw and taken part in two double plays. Not even Miller Huggins could have managed a club so well.

Meanwhile, Bearden was pitching with a single day of rest. On Saturday he had shut out the Detroit Tigers, 8 to 0. A lot of people thought it was reckless of Boudreau to pitch a left-hander against Boston's right-handed power in a park where the left-field wall casts its shadow across third base.

Moreover, this is a guy with physical handicaps. A Japanese torpedo blew him into the sea off the U.S.S. Helena. He was two years in a hospital, and he has a metal plate in his head and a metal hinge in his knee. But he held the robustious Red Sox to five hits.

That's all it took. With Boudreau's muscular management and Bearden's pitching, they gave Boston back to the Indians.

—October 5, 1948

Stock Market Report

CLEVELAND—A slight revision became necessary today in the business plans of Robert William Andrew Feller, Inc., the one-man mint. He will have to make a hurried trip to Boston to wind up baseball details for the year before undertaking his customary search through the shrubbery for loose dimes.

If he can find time between his prospecting expeditions and the opening of his winter baseball school, the chances are he will compose a couple of sequels to his popular book, "How to Pitch." Publishers began bidding frantically today for authoritative texts entitled, "How to Pitch to Bob Elliott" and "How to Pitch to Bill Salkeld."

Demand for these manuscripts developed in the fifth game of the World Series when Elliott got the Boston Braves four runs by whacking two of Mr. Feller's pitches out of Municipal Stadium, and Salkeld socked another that tied the score. When assorted parties took to clubbing him about

Bob Feller in his early days

the ears in the seventh inning, Robert William Andrew became the first double loser of the series, and the only Cleveland pitcher who has lost at all.

The most prosperous pitching property that baseball ever enriched took his lumps before the eyes of the biggest crowd that ever saw a baseball performance, single or double, night or day or twilight, domestic or foreign. The swag in the house was the richest of all time—$378,778.73, and not even the odd pennies go to the Feller Corporation.

As the celebrated commercial firm was dissolved by the Braves' bats, an explanation for the phenomenon occurred to some spectators. They realized Feller wasn't being paid for this day's work because the rules give participants no share of the loot after the first four games.

It was recalled that during the summer, Feller was nominated to the American League All-Star team. Ball players deem this an honor but get no material advantage out of playing in the annual All-Star Game. Feller not only declined to play; he wouldn't even show up and let the fans look at him.

Poets in today's crowd insisted that what they were watching represented poetic justice. Last Wednesday, in a game played for cash, Feller pitched a two-hitter and lost. This time he was flailed for eight hits, was bombed out in the seventh inning, and lost.

The odds on the game were 11 to 5. So was the score, but with the teams in reverse order.

There was more action, more excitement, more hitting, more scoring, and less pitching in this entertainment than in all the earlier games combined. There were more people in it, too, for when Feller went out everybody else got into the act. Characters named Ed Klieman, Russ Christopher, Satchel Paige and Bob Muncrief trooped in to pitch for the Indians and such names as Joe Tipton, Al Rosen, Hal Peck and Ray Boone bobbed up all over the box score.

All these are sterling characters, neither daunt nor trepid, but when they arrived they found the stable empty. Their affluent playmate was in the clubhouse and the game was in a Boston bag.

It is an ironic feature of Feller's great career that no matter how many games he wins or how many records he sets, the big ones always elude him. Away back in 1940, when the Indians and Detroit Tigers were fighting for the pennant, Feller was beaten by an obscure rookie named Floyd Giebell. On the last day of this season he lost, again to Detroit, in the game that would have given Cleveland the pennant.

The Indians finally won behind Gene Bearden in the American League play-off with the Red Sox, and reached match point with the Braves by winning three times in this series. Then Feller's turn came around again.

There was poetic justice, too, in the way he lost. Until today, Elliott had been having such a tough time that observers were picking him to become the first man ever to win the National and American League "most valuable" player awards in successive years.

Neither he nor his colleagues were transported with laughter by such wit. Cleveland's press and public, excited over the city's first World Series in twenty-eight years, have been crowing vociferously over their heroes and sneering that the American League's fourth best club could polish off the Braves.

The Braves have read, and cursed, pointing out that the Indians barely squeaked through in the games Cleveland won. It is not possible to estimate how much of the malevolence which the Braves exhibited today is chargeable to their reading matter. But they proved today that the only thing needed to put life in this series was a little lousy pitching.

And so we take our leave of romantic Cleveland, bearing in mind that Feller wasn't the unluckiest guy in the park today. That distinction belongs to a guy who showed up in the grandstand without a ticket or credentials but otherwise fully loaded, and informed a man, "I don't like you, and I'm taking that seat."

He is now languishing in the pokey. Out of 86,288 people, he had to pick on a cop in plain clothes.

—October 11, 1948

The City of Silences

BOSTON—And so, as the tranquil waters of the Charles close gently over the head of Sebastian Sisti, regretfully we say good by to beautiful Boston, always the most genteel of American cities and now, suddenly the quietest. 'Revoir, auf Wiedersehen, so long, and don't take any third strikes.

"I've never been in Boston before at this time of year," said Bob Feller. "Pretty, isn't it?"

Through most of this gray, unventilated afternoon, great echoing gobs of silence had risen from the crowd watching the sixth and final contest for the rounders championship of the universe. It was a smothered silence, depressed and dismal. It grew louder inning by inning as the Cleveland Indians chewed at the Boston Braves, achieving, at last, a lead of 4 to 1.

Then suddenly the crowd was screaming. Not just rooting or cheering or yelling, but screaming with a hungry passion. The Braves knocked Bob Lemon out of the ball game in the eighth inning, scored twice and put the tying run on third base, the winning run on second, before Gene Bearden could get them out.

Warren Spahn, who had struck out the last Cleveland batter in the eighth inning, struck out three more in the ninth. Spahn is the left-handed pitcher who was Cleveland's first victim in the World Series. The Indians beat him, 4 to 1, in the second game, but yesterday his relief pitching blinded them altogether. Yesterday he struck out five of the last six Cleveland batsmen, today he fanned the last four in succession.

Not even Stymie, not Snapper Garrison aboard old Malicious himself, could have finished like this. With every pitch the screams grew wilder.

The electric clock on the scoreboard showed 3:11 p.m. when Eddie Stanky led off in the Boston ninth. It was 3:13 when, with a count of three balls and two strikes, he walked.

All through the latter weeks of the season the Braves had been saying of themselves that they could be just as good as they had to be. Other people had begun to believe them, too, for although they cannot do well the things that champions are supposed to do, they had continued to do one thing superbly. They had beaten the Dodgers or the Cardinals or the Pirates when they had to. And yesterday, when the Indians had them teetering on the edge of obsolescence, they had beaten the Indians, too.

Connie Ryan replaced Stanky on first base and Sisti batted for Spahn. Sisti tried to bunt and popped up. Cleveland's elegant wicket keeper, Jim Hegan, caught the ball and threw to first for a double play.

It was 3:15. That's when silence fell, heavily, hugely, like a stricken ox. The earlier quiet had been spacious and intense. This one hurt the ears. It is still here, hanging around this deserted park like a fat, timid bum at the saloon door.

Maybe it's the contrast which makes this silence seem deep as a well and wide as a church door. Maybe it beats so fiercely only on ears that have lately been hauled here from Cleveland, the home of Bill Veeck.

As a matter of fact, chances are the entire course of recent baseball events stemmed from a plot to balk Veeck's plans for tossing a real victory binge in Cleveland. Probably a municipal plot, sired by Cleveland civic leaders who have had experience of Veeck's parties.

All summer long Veeck and Cleveland had been building up for a wingding. During the season, 2,620,627 fans rallied around him in Municipal Stadium to urge the Indians on toward their first celebration in twenty-eight years. On the last day of the season, 74,181 showed up in the stadium prepared to take the joint apart, piece by piece, the moment the Indians won the pennant.

For days Veeck had had the champagne on ice, the caviar on toast, the company silver polished and the napery agleam from the laundry. But not a cork popped that night on Sunday, Oct. 3. The Indians lost, the 74,181 went home to snap at the children, and Veeck had to bring the Indians to Boston to win the pennant.

He couldn't really celebrate in Boston. The city cramps his style.

So last week the Indians went home again, where 238,481 neighbors came clamoring around to see them win the world championship. Yesterday when the deciding victory seemed certain, there were 86,286 on hand with their sirens and cowbells. The champagne was cold again. Once more the host got stood up. Once more the Indians lost. Once more they had to win it in Boston.

Well, the Braves lost, as they were expected to do. But they made a run for it at the wire. They never were out of a single ball game. In the only game in which violence was done, they played rougher than the ruffians of the American League. They gave it the very hell of a try, and they sure loused up Veeck's party.

—October 12, 1948

One Sunny Afternoon

ST. PETERSBURG, FLA.—It was the fourth inning of a ball game between the Yankees and Cardinals on a quiet, amiable afternoon when the sun shone on Tampa Bay beyond the left field fence and sailboats lazed across the water and gulls and pelicans made figures in the sky. There had been only a moment or so of excitement.

Fan interest in St. Pete is lively enough but more academic than partisan. The average age of the customers here is a mite high for passion. Mostly the crowd comes out to loaf away a couple of leisurely hours, scarcely caring which team wins or loses but prepared to enjoy the work of a few stars as they might enjoy a fine painting or a symphony.

In the first inning there had been the usual sputter of applause when Stan Musial came up. His appearance always brings this response, which is more a murmur of appreciation than a howl of excitement. The fans seem to have a connoisseur's pleasure in just watching him crouch at the plate, slender and graceful and as complete a picture of menace as any pitcher would care to see.

On his first time up, Musial had lashed a double to dead center, a drive that hit the wall on the fly just above a sign reading 397 feet. That had brought a shout, of course. There'd been two bases on balls in the same inning but there was a double play, so the Cardinals didn't score.

Later Johnny Lindell tagged one. There was a Yankee on base when he got the fat part of his bat against one of left-handed Al Brazle's pitches. The fans in the small bleachers in left field looked up as the ball soared over their heads, then looked back to see whether it would clear the street beyond the fence and drop into the bay. That made the score, 2 to 0 for, the Yankees.

This was the score in the fourth when a kid named Jackie Collum took Brazle's place as the St. Louis pitcher. Collum is a little, left-handed guy no bigger than Murry Dickson. He isn't on the Cardinals' roster because he is not considered ready for the big league this year. They loved him in St. Joe last season. He won something like twenty-four games for the farm team and Eddie Dyer, the Cardinal manager, brought him along this spring as a reward for good work.

Against the Yankees, the kid may have been a little nervous. There was a hit, he walked a couple, and then the bases were filled with two out. Here came a real shout. Joe DiMaggio walked up to hit for the Yankee pitcher, Don Johnson.

A live spark snaked through the stands, DiMaggio had made his first appearance of the year the day before, coming in as a pinch batter and hitting a single and then retiring while another player ran for him. But this time the stage was set for melodrama.

"Here's what I came to see," said Harry Mendel, assistant matchmaker for Joe Louis's international boxing club who was over in this part of the state on fist-fight business. "This pays me back for the $13 it cost to fly up from Miami."

All through the first three innings Harry had been talking of Louis's promotional plans but all of a sudden that topic ceased to interest him. He was sitting up stiffly, watching the dark, tall man at the plate and the little rookie who faced him. So was everybody else.

The count went to three balls, two strikes. If this was a big ball game instead of a spring training exhibition and you were a dramatist writing a script for it, that's the situation you would create—bases full, two out, three-and-two on the hitter, and the kid out there looking past the tall man who stood stiffly with feet spread wide and bat high. The kid leaning forward from the waist, peering for the pitcher's sign.

In the brief pause between pitches, memory went back to a similar day last year. Then Joe McCarthy had his Red Sox here to play the Yankees, the first time in his new role as Boston manager that he led a team against the club he had handled for fifteen years. Chances are no managers ever wanted to win an exhibition game more earnestly than McCarthy and Bucky Harris did that day.

The Yankees, as the home team, had come to bat in the ninth inning with Boston leading by one run. They got a couple of runners on the bases and then DiMaggio came up, and the crowd had responded then exactly as this one did.

So Joe had poked one into the bay for that ball game. He had jogged as far as third base, by which time the winning run was in and the game was over. He didn't make the turn at third, but started for the dugout and the clubhouse. What was a home run to the old pro, in a spring exhibition?

But the other Yankees wouldn't stand for it. They had come pouring off the bench and were clustered around the plate, shouting and beckoning. At their insistence, Joe jogged on home, making the home run official. He came in, grinning and shaking his head with tolerant amusement, the old champ humoring the kids who were waiting to pump his hand and pummel his shoulders.

This time though, a year later, they used a new script. Young Collum threw the ball and DiMaggio swung. And missed. Almost before the ball reached the catcher, the kid was hiking for the dugout, not strutting, exactly, but kind of bustling along with short, confident strides, very erect.

Maybe there were a few faint boos mixed with the roar of the crowd. Fans like to boo for the fun of it, meaning nothing in particular. Joe was expressionless walking back to the bench. In this game you hit home runs sometimes and sometimes you strike out. His day's work was done.

"That wasn't what I came to see," Harry Mendel said. "But," he said, "it was nice, at that, wasn't it? For that kid, it was real good."

"Let's go back to the hotel," a fellow said. His companion wanted to wait until Collum finished pitching.

"What for?" the fellow said. "The balloon has gone up."

—*March 15, 1949*

The Object All Sublime

WHEN THE STORY broke, John Lardner, the essayist, said: "Did you see the game? He'll be acquitted." In one inning the Dodgers had scored eight runs before the Giants got anybody out. There are times when the manager of a baseball team is not only justified in using his knuckles for the purpose heaven intended, but is morally and ethically bound to belt somebody. Preferably a couple of his pitchers, but if such are not available, then the first chin offered.

The Dodgers had beaten the Giants, 15 to 2, and soon afterward a noisy Brooklyn fan named Fred Boysen was in a hospital, bearing a lawyer but no marks that the doctors or X-ray camera could discover.

Out of the confusion that ensued two points emerged clearly:

(a) If Leo Durocher, the Practically Peerless leader of the Giants, slugged and kicked a customer without sufficient provocation he deserves to get the book which Happy Chandler has been prepared, these last several years, to chuck at him.

(b) Of all the men in baseball, Durocher is the most vulnerable, the most likely prospect for a trumped-up charge.

This is Happy Chandler's chance to make the major leagues. He can prove himself as a commissioner if he moves swiftly but with caution, gets his facts straight and then acts with firm justice. And does it all in the open.

This will be easier than it sounds, for in this case the true facts will be made clear. Whatever happened, it took place in the open, in center field in the Polo Grounds with scores of witnesses present. Although the accounts of witnesses are confused and conflicting at present, as they always are immediately after an event, it will not be long before the truth is clearly established.

Thus far Chandler has done all right. His first statement on the case was one which the world has waited for four years to hear from his lips. He said: "I'll say nothing now." When, subsequently, he suspended Durocher pending investigation, he was not beating the gun or prejudging the case. This is proper routine as in the case, say, of a policeman who is relieved from duty until charges against him are heard.

These are points to be considered:

Physicians could find no evidence that Boysen had been hit, kicked or punished in any way. A man named Morris Golding told reporters he saw Durocher attack Boysen, that he took names of other witnesses, escorted Boysen to the hospital and called a lawyer. By yesterday, however, reporters at Golding's home were told he had left the city and had told his mother he knew nothing, had seen nothing, had done nothing.

Some men are fast with their fists, some are fast men with a dollar, and some are fastest of all with a lawyer.

Boysen said that during the game he had called Durocher names. One paper quoted him: "That's the fun of baseball." It is a debatable point. A man, who is prepared to debate it, says he sat behind Boysen, heard his remarks and did not consider them fun. "Vicious" is the word he used. "If he'd made those remarks to me," the man said, "I would have punched him." He said he saw Boysen run out after the game and grab at Durocher.

As a general business policy, it is unwise to punch customers, but it is a mistake to believe that nobody should ever be punched. Examples of candidates eligible for a slugging are sportsmen who believe the price of a grandstand seat entitles them to shout scurrilous comments about another man's wife, and politicians who run into print—before the facts have been established—with charges of "outrageous conduct," "downright intolerance" and "vengeful" acts, along with demands for expulsion of the manager and a racial boycott of the ball club.

There is nothing intrinsically wrong with whacking people, provided there is proper discrimination shown in the selection of the puncher and the punchee. Spectators at ball games have been belted in the past, with varying consequences.

Ty Cobb once climbed into the stands in New York to bop a fan and he got off with a short suspension. Moreover, although his playmates were not unanimous in considering Cobb a lovable character, they felt so strongly that justice was on his side that they called a strike in protest of his suspension.

On another occasion, the amiable John Lobert, then manager of the Phillies, rushed all the way up to the upper deck in Philadelphia's Shibe Park seeking to smack a client who had been shouting accusations that the Phillies were throwing the ball game. It was the illogical quality of the charge which offended Mr. Lobert, whose Phillies couldn't even throw the ball.

Leo Durocher, however, is not eligible to slug people because he is not a priestly character. There is a popular tendency to say "even if he didn't do it, the bum ought to be thrown out because he is bad for baseball." This sort of reasoning was officially applied against him in 1947. It falls short of perfect justice, for although a man might be banished because of his skill at gin rummy, at pool or because of a movie actor's amazing luck in rolling eights the hard way in some man's apartment, it is a disgraceful thing to convict him on a phony charge.

When punching needs to be done, it is especially unwise to elect Leo, because he hits too hard. A few years ago, a man named John Christian got a broken jaw, a black eye and head bruises out of not being punched by Durocher.

—April 30, 1949

Three Guys Depart

COVERING A BASEBALL game between the Red Sox and Browns in St. Louis, Burt Whitman collapsed and died of a cerebral hemorrhage. In South Bend, Ind., Jimmy Costin was fatally stricken by a heart attack. And in St. John's Hospital in St. Louis, death ended the illness of Sam Breadon.

Thus within the space of a comparatively few hours, our fraternity has suffered three losses we could ill afford. There were three fine guys, Burt Whitman, sports editor of "The Boston Herald," Jimmy Costin, sports editor of "The South Bend Tribune," Sam Breadon, the man who made the St. Louis Cardinals.

There is little that can be said of Sam Breadon which has not been said here before. When he sold control of the Cardinals after the 1947 season, it was a loss to baseball in general and, in particular, to the National League, whose competitive interests were served more successfully by Sam's teams than by any other in the last twenty years.

When he died, it was a loss both to his friends and to the cause of gaiety and good living, for there never was a man who added more to an evening's gathering or took more enjoyment out of it. Here was a man of high honor and exceptional ability, a boon companion, a dear friend and, probably, the worst tenor ever to flat the high notes of "Mother Machree." World Series gatherings of the future will be quieter without him, probably more harmonious, and certainly a great deal less fun.

Burt Whitman was one of those men who gave dignity to our sometimes raffish craft. He was an all-around newspaper man, a sincere fan and perhaps the most indefatigable bridge player east of the Mississippi River.

He was a reporter of integrity and a critic of mature, dispassionate fairness. Among the athletes he wrote about and the men who shared the pressbox with him, he enjoyed the respect that belongs to a gentleman and an honest craftsman.

The name of Sam Breadon was familiar to every baseball fan. Everyone who ever had any connection with major league baseball or with other sports in New England was a friend of Burt Whitman. Jimmy Costin wasn't known to the general public outside the circulation of "The South Bend Tribune." Yet there probably isn't a sports writer in America with more friends.

Jimmy was a little, gray guy whom you saw once or twice or three times a year, always on assignments involving Notre Dame. Indeed, to hundreds of sports writers he was Notre Dame, the unofficial host of newspaper men whose job took them to South Bend, an inexhaustible source of information about the university and its teams, a tireless evangel spreading the gospel of Frank Leahy—or, in their separate times, of Elmer Layden or Hunk Anderson or Knute Rockne—when he accompanied the teams on the road.

Jimmy and Burt and Sam. It has been a costly week.

The magic lantern is a mysterious and fairly terrifying development of modern science with which this department seldom has any truck. Recently, however, a group of baseball writers was herded together by a representative of Metro-Goldwyn-Mayer, fed intravenously and permitted to witness a set of animated slides entitled, "The Stratton Story."

This is the dramatized version of the true story of Monty Stratton, the excellent White Sox pitcher who lost a leg in a hunting accident, but managed a comeback on the mound in spite of his handicap. As viewed by a sentimentalist who can still weep over practically any page of "Little Women," it is a solid tear-jerker effectively performed by James Stewart and June Allyson, which commits no outrages when it deals with technical baseball.

The role of James J. Dykes is played by a mummer whose performance is a milestone in cinematic art. An actor name of James J. Dykes.

Another item concerning the world of make-believe is forwarded by Mr. Al Horwitz, a Philadelphia sportswriter who went square. Some years ago Mr. Horwitz abandoned the hopeless task of making the Athletics and Phillies seem credible and transferred to the almost equally unreal world of the cinema, where his creative work on expense accounts recently brought him a promotion to Universal's west coast headquarters.

Now he advises that Aaron Rosenberg, an All-America guard on the Southern California football team of 1933, has just finished his first picture as a producer, a semi-documentary about dope smuggling called "Partners in Crime."

Mr. Horwitz submits this to disprove the theory that when a guard has served out his period of athletic eligibility, he is put back in the bottle and never heard from again.

—May 12, 1949

Youth Movement in Dixie

AT THIS TIME of year, with the major league trading deadline coiled like a rattler in the path just ahead, managers and scouts and customers turn their wistful gaze upon that inexhaustible source of young talent, the minor leagues. Accordingly, attention is directed to a couple of Southern Association clubs, the Chattanooga Lookouts and the Birmingham Barons.

There is at hand an account of a recent double-header involving these teams. Chattanooga's starting pitcher in both games was a svelte young right-hander yclept Louis Norman Buck Bobo Newsom. He began with a seven-hitter but lost, 3 to 2, because the Lookouts made only five hits off a younker named Earl Caldwell, who won his own game with a home run.

Chattanooga won the second game but not until Bobo had departed, for reasons which will be made clear. Birmingham's starter was not present at the finish either, having made room for a stripling named Johnny Podgajny. The box scores include other names that seekers after raw material might well bear in mind—Jake Early, catcher; Tom McBride, outfielder; George Myatt, playing manager of the Lookouts; Pinky Higgins, boss of the Barons.

Presumably this is the Caldwell who celebrated his thirtieth birthday as a pitcher for the Browns in 1936; the same Early who was a pre-war catcher with the Senators; the same skinny Podgajny whom the old, old Phillies kept as a pet for the purpose of infuriating the Cubs, the one team he could whip; the same McBride whose tabs formerly were picked up by the Red Sox.

It goes without saying that this is the same Newsom who has, at various times, lent his gifts to the Dodgers, the Cubs, the Browns, the Senators, the Red Sox, the Browns again, the Tigers, the Senators, the Athletics, the Senators again, the Yankees and the Giants, not to mention teams in Greenville, S.C.; Wilmington, N.C.; Macon, Ga.; Jersey City, Little Rock, Albany and Los Angeles.

It goes without saying because there is only one Bobo Newsom.

"The season's largest crowd, 13,807, turned out," reports "The Birmingham Age-Herald," "brought no doubt by the prospect of seeing Bobo Newsom."

"Have you got speed?" an interviewer inquired.

"Speed? Why, Bobo, old Bobo is so fast the umpires are kickin' they can't call what they can't see."

"How's your curve?"

"Starts for third base and breaks over the outside corner."

"Control?"

"Bobo can brush the whiskers off'n a fly."

He was not asked about his hitting. An oversight. In the second game, Newsom singled. The report continues:

"Wooten also singled, Bobo stopping at second. Then Miranda singled and Bobo, taking it easy, pulled up at third. The Lookouts got confused because of Bo's sluggishness. Miranda went halfway to second, but nobody was covering first and he got back safely.

"Atkins pegged to second trying to get Wooten and the ball hit Wooten, skidding into the outfield and letting both Newsom and Wooten score."

The reporter describes the runs as "gifts," being too young to appreciate that the hallmark of a great base runner is his use of tactics calculated to drive the defense frantic. Cobb used to do it, too.

It is further reported that "Newsom injured his leg running (sic) out a double in the seventh and had to retire." There is the only false note. Could this be the real Buck Newsom, this weakling who would let a damaged gam prevent him from completing a double-header? It wasn't thus in the old days.

Once there was a Bobo Newsom who thrived on physical abuse. There was the day he didn't bother to duck and Ossie Bluege, his third baseman, broke his skull with a throw aimed toward first base. There was the time Oscar Judd bounced a line drive off his brow and the ball caromed into center field. Bobo went right on pitching.

There was the time he fell off a mountain and broke his leg. There was the time a mule ran over him at a horse fair in Columbia, S.C., breaking it again. There was the time—well, surely, everyone remembers the time he fielded that one against Earl Averill.

It was the second inning of a game in 1935, when Clark Griffith thought Washington was going to win a championship and got Bobo from the Browns as pennant insurance. He was pitching against Cleveland when Averill slammed one back against his knee, sweeping Newsom's feet from under him.

Bobo wriggled after the ball and threw Averill out. He went on pitching. After each inning, he returned to the dugout groaning.

"The dam' thing's broke," he said.

His playmates laughed.

"You big ape. You couldn't stand up on a broken leg."

So Bobo finished the game and lost, 2 to 1. That night he was encountered hobbling from his suite in Washington's Wardman Park Hotel, leaning on a cane.

"Gotta see a doctor," he said. "The dam' thing's broke."

It was, too. Shattered.

—June 14, 1949

Gentlemen's Night, with Homers

SOME EMPLOYEES OF the Phillies, guys named Andy Seminick and Del Ennis and Puddin'-Head Jones and Schoolboy Rowe, made five home runs in one inning the other night. It caused some commotion, which was natural enough, for it isn't the sort of thing that would be forgotten overnight by either the customers or the employees of the Cincinnati Reds, who happened to be pitching.

It was, as a matter of fact, only the second time this has happened in the major leagues. Five Giants—Harry the Horse Danning, Frank Demaree, Burgess Whitehead, Manuel Salvo and Joe Moore—did it against Cincinnati pitching on June 6, 1939. So it was natural enough for the bystanders to get into some sweat about it.

Trouble was, though, the rumpus got everybody so wheed up that the real story of the evening was missed. In no news account that has come to attention was there any mention of the real feature of the occasion. Nobody mentioned that this was Gentlemen's Night in Shibe Park.

This noble experiment by Mr. Bob Carpenter, the Veeckian president of the Phillies, is recommended for study by anyone with a sweet tooth for trends. Ladies' Day, of course, is an old baseball institution. It was inaugurated by some deep thinker who figured that if he let females into his park free once a week, a lot of them would get interested enough to come back on days when they had to pay their way.

Introduction of Gentlemen's Night suggests that baseball has come the full circle. In its early days as a professional enterprise, it was a raffish entertainment patronized only by sports of the flashier sort and females of dubious reputation. Now, apparently, it has become so genteel it is necessary to bribe masculine fans to enter the park.

Baseball has become the diversion of housewives. The gentle doves who formerly wept through the long afternoons over the misadventures of soap-opera heroines have become so bemused by the accents of Red Barber or Jimmy Britt or Byrum Saam or Franz Laux that they have crowded the men out of the grandstand.

Consequently, in a fairly desperate effort to reclaim the attention of males, the Phillies inaugurated Gentlemen's Night. On that evening, all males accompanied by wife, sweetheart, paramour or female guardian were admitted free on payment of tax and service charge (total, 50 cents). The broads, of course, had to pay the full tariff.

It is gratifying to see the single standard recognized in baseball. Or, more accurately, to see the double standard applied with reverse english. It is significant, though, that the innovation was tried in a night game, for in most cities tickets are at a premium after dark and there is no room for cuffers. Maybe the recession has caught up with the Phillies; if so, other clubs will feel it soon.

The Phillies' home-run hemorrhage recalled a story which Al Simmons tells as frequently as opportunity allows. Like most ball players, Al has a deep and abiding reverence for records. It is, for example, a source of real regret to him that he failed by a dozen or two hits to join the small company of guys who whacked 3,000 pitches safely. He often tells about the game of June 18, 1930.

"I and Jimmy Foxx and Bing Miller hit home runs in succession," he says. "That's the record, that's the most ever been hit in a row. Now we got a chance to set an all-time world record. Joe Boley is up. He can belt one now and then.

"So what does he do? He bunts. He bunts and beats it out! We're winning a mile. We don't need a bunt. I asked him afterward, 'Why and the hell did you do that?' He says to me, 'Why,' he says, 'they were playing back deep. They never looked for a bunt.' "

Well, students interested in trends might find some profit in studying the current passion for "percentages" among major-league managers. Unless the style changes, we've seen our last Joe DiMaggio or Stan Musial, because today's managers won't let a guy stay in long enough to become an all-around player. They consider it a mortal sin to let a left-handed batter swing against a left-handed pitcher, or a right-hander against a right-hander.

This slavish devotion to the "percentage" is all right when you win, but it can create gruesome situations. A manager starts all his right-handed batters because a left-hander is working for the opposition. Then a right-handed reliever comes in, and he changes all his hitters. The enemy switches back to a southpaw, and he's done. He has nobody left for the clutch.

It happens again and again. When the Dodgers were playing the Cardinals the other night, Burt Shotton sent in left-handed pinch-batters just as soon as St. Louis's Harry Brecheen, a left-hander, was replaced by the right-handed George Munger. A few minutes later Brooklyn had three left-handed outfielders batting against Howie Pollet, maybe the slickest southpaw in the league.

Managers can get too smart for their own good. Some of them should consider the 1949 record of the left-handed Stanley Musial. He has hit eight home runs this year. Two were off right-handed pitchers. The other six violated the rules of percentage. Maybe the rule should be repealed.

—June 15, 1949

Casey Didn't Say Anything

THEY WERE TELLING Casey Stengel that the Yankees were in, all right, although naturally you had to expect ball players as good as Pesky and Doerr to break up some furniture once in a while. But come October, somebody warned, and Casey would see some guys who wouldn't stand up there taking Joe Page's stuff for third strikes the way the Red Sox did on Wednesday night. Guys named Slaughter and Musial.

Mr. Stengel backed off a step or so. He passed a hand across his mouth in a gesture that is habitual with him, bringing it down to stroke his chin. There was a sort of wary humor in his eyes. He didn't say anything.

You knew he wouldn't say anything. To agree that October might find him looking at Musial and Slaughter across Yankee Stadium would be conceding that the Yankees actually were in, and the Cardinals, too, for that matter. In the same circumstances, Eddie Dyer wouldn't have said anything, either. Nothing terrifies a winning manager into silence in September like mention—even an oblique mention—of the World Series.

The curious thing is, World Series talk figures so boldly in managerial conversation from March until, say, August. There are always sixteen pennant winners in the spring. Under the separate rules of their separate lodges, the football coach must beat upon his sternum before his season begins, pulling the bedclothes over his head and wallowing in despair; the baseball manager must go about with buoyant step and beaming smile flicking dragons from his lapels. It is not until success comes within reach that the mention of success affrights him.

Probably there are basic differences between baseball and football players which require that the one must be told repeatedly that he is incomparable and the other assured that he smells. Something to do with the pituitary, no doubt.

"Anyhow," Bill Corum was saying, "the story of the Yankees this year is one of the most appealing I can recall in sports. These fellows really get you."

They do, too, and maybe this is the first time it has happened. For ever so many years, the Yankees have been a great club, prosperous and respected and feared and, in some quarters, hated. But they have not been greatly loved.

They have never, that is, won such an impassioned national following as the Dodgers have known. They have never so stirred the public imagination or inspired such genuine affection as some Cardinal teams have done, or as the Athletics would if they hit the top—although in that case it would be, primarily, affection for Connie Mack. Even in the roaring days of Ruth and Gehrig and Hoyt and Lazzeri, the Yankees evoked quite a different sort of feeling than did the Giants of John McGraw.

It is astonishing, and inexplicable, how often it is true that in spite of a constantly changing personnel throughout the organization, the personality of a team remains unchanged. For instance, the Frisches and Deans of the Gas House Gang are gone from St. Louis; Sam Breadon sold the club, died, and his successor sold out. Yet the Cardinals are still the exciting Cardinals. The flavor lasts, just as it often does with college football teams, where the turnover is much greater than in baseball.

Well, all these years the Yankees have filled the Stadium and drawn vast crowds on the road and smashed records and paralyzed the opposition. But never before this season would you have described them as "appealing." Perhaps they were too good. Maybe what their story lacked, the ingredient that is indispensable to a success story, is adversity.

If so, they lack it no longer. No team ever succeeded in the face of greater adversity than the Yankees have known this year, with their sixty-odd disabling injuries. To start a season without Joe DiMaggio and, perhaps, conclude it without Tommy Henrich, and still win—well, that alone makes a pretty fair yarn.

The old Yankees were a team of matchless skill. The current Yankees are a team of incomparable spirit. And that is the difference. Although they have been in front every day since the season began, they have never been easy front-runners. Every game has been a new problem for Stengel and a new challenge to the players; Mr. Stengel has faced and solved his and the players have risen to theirs.

People used to call the Yankees a team of businessmen ball players. They did a big business, and it involved approximately as much sentiment as the business of United States Steel.

These players are calling themselves a "team of destiny," which is as different from the old conception as it is corny. Still, it tells the story of the season up to now. Strange to hear Yankees using lines like that. And rather pleasant.

—September 10, 1949

Shadows on the Grass

MR. JOE DIMAGGIO, who has thrust a ghostly hand into the journalism of our town, made an interesting point in "The World-Telegram" yesterday. "The shadows the players curse," the most trenchant sports writer since Eddie Stanky vehemed in his spectral prose, "are creeping into the pennant race."

Joe's reference was not to the shades that operate typewriters. He referred especially to the American League race and specifically to the shadows that slant across Yankee Stadium in the autumn when the sun swings low, dimming the batter's vision, confusing the outfielder, making games and championships more difficult to win. No question but that he knows what he's talking about.

What he says about the American League must be true of the National, too. But it seems to an old Cardinal fan that the most troublesome and frightening shadows in the National League are not made by tall grandstands or slatted bleachers. They are those cast by guys named Jackie Robinson, Don Newcombe and Roy Campanella. And, going behind them, by the bulking figure of Branch Rickey.

Theirs are the shadows which stretch long across the turf of Sportsman's Park in St. Louis. They are the ones Eddie Dyer, the Cardinal's manager, must curse.

Because why, when you get down to it, do the Dodgers have a team good enough to contend with St. Louis for the championship? The question, and answer, are intriguing.

As everybody knows, Branch Rickey is the father of the farm system. He conceived the chain-gang idea in St. Louis and developed it there and then brought the original copyright to Brooklyn, where a former pupil of his named MacPhail had already forged a similar chain. Montague Street today is the center of the largest and most complex web ever spun in baseball.

Brooklyn scouts comb the world for raw material cut to the exact specifications dictated by The Master Planner. When Rickey tugs at a string, the net brings in hundreds of young men who can run and field and throw.

Down in Vero Beach, Fla., there is a vast factory where machine-tooled dies stamp out faceless ball players according to pattern and deliver them on a belt conveyor to the testing plant where machines measure and count and pack them for shipment.

Rickey has come closer than any other man to eliminating the incidence of human error from baseball, and the element of human sentiment.

So that's why he is successful?

Nope.

His club is battling for the pennant because he got there first and skimmed the cream of the Negro talent. The farm system had nothing to do with it. The fellows who will win the championship for Brooklyn—if anybody does—wouldn't have been allowed in the farm system while Rickey was developing it.

There is no more revealing example of how Rickey works. While his rivals were scrambling to catch up with him by developing chains of their own, he left them behind, walked into a field they didn't dare invade, and collared the talent they wouldn't touch.

Now there are other good Negro players in the majors, like Larry Doby and Henry Thompson. Some day they may be as good as the ones Rickey grabbed, but not yet.

It is altogether possible that Newcombe is the best pitcher in the world right now. (As this is written, he's due to pitch in Pittsburgh, but the returns aren't in yet and they wouldn't make any difference, anyhow.) There need be no argument about what Robinson has meant to the Dodgers, with his batting average of .347, his 117 runs-batted-in, his sixteen home runs, his threat on the bases.

Incidentally, who can explain why it is that when Robinson becomes a base runner, the game stops until he scores or the side is retired? He frightens the enemy into immobility, yet he never has stolen more than thirty bases in a season. In the days of Cobb and Eddie Collins, or even George Case and Walley Moses, the club secretary used to steal more.

Anyway, there is no disputing his value to the Dodgers, or Newcombe's, or Campanella's, with his dexterity behind the plate, his twenty home runs. Without these guys, not even Pee Wee Reese could have made the Dodgers a contender. And even Pee Wee, by the way, came out of the Red Sox farm system, not Brooklyn's.

Two or three weeks ago Stanley Woodward asked Burt Shotton, "If you were starting the World Series tomorrow, who are the three pitchers you'd depend on?"

"Newcombe," Burt said quickly, and hesitated. He tried again: "Uh—Newcombe, and, uh—" There was a longish pause. "Did I mention Newcombe?" Burt asked.

When he crossed the color line to get Robinson, Rickey denied that his purpose was, as expressed in Arthur Mann's song, "to triumph over prejudice—and the excess profits tax." He said he was not interested in pigmentation or in social causes.

"I don't care if a fellow is green and has fur all over his body and hands that hang to the floor," he said. "I want ball players who can beat the whey out of the Cardinals."

He may have been over-modest, a bedazzling thought. But if he does beat the Cardinals, it will be because of the colored guys he got.

—September 17, 1949

A Quarter-Inch Away

AT 5:18 P.M. yesterday, guys in gray flannels erupted from the Red Sox dugout and charged across the lawn of Yankee Stadium to beat upon Ellis Kinder's spine with jubilant paws. Johnny Pesky flung a headlock on Al Zarilla and hugged the outfielder to his small bosom in one of the great love scenes of modern drama. The Yankees walked off the field, and maybe out of the pennant race.

After three hours and eighteen minutes of frantic and untidy striving, the Yankees had lost a ball game by one run and a quarter of an inch; they had lost first place in the American League for the first time since the season opened last April 19; Ralph Houk, a former major in the Rangers, had lost a desperate engagement with the most sweetly forgiving umpires on earth; 66,156 witnesses had lost their voices.

The game that put the Red Sox in first place and the Yankees second turned upside-down on a line drive which failed by the width of Phil Rizzuto's little finger to become a triple play. Dom DiMaggio hit the ball in the eighth with two Bostonese on base, none out, and the Yankees leading, 6 to 3. Rizzuto leaped. The ball smacked the very tips of his gloved fingers, seemed to lodge there for a fragment of time, then tore loose and dribbled into left field for a single.

The count had been three balls, two strikes on DiMaggio, so both runners were away with the pitch. Both were far off their bases, could have been retired easily had Rizzuto held the ball. Instead, the inning lasted until Boston had scored four runs and won the game.

When Pesky slid under Houk with the winning run on a squeeze play, the Yankee pennant bubble and the Yankee catcher exploded. It is just barely possible that Major Houk saw more violent action in the Battle of the Bulge than that which followed.

Shrieking, he hurled himself from Willie Grieve, the plate umpire, and clawed at the honorable stomach. Joe Page, the pitcher, threw his glove aloft and rushed in, howling imprecations. White uniforms converged in a noisy swirl, and with them came Mr. Grieve's colleagues—Cal Hubbard, Charley Berry and Joe Paparella.

Mr. Hubbard, the largest peacemaker on the Eastern Seaboard, patted the major's breastbone with vast, placating paws. The major circled Mr. Hubbard, boring in upon Mr. Grieve. Mr. Berry, once an All-America end at Lafayette, over-shifted to the left and got a propitiating clutch upon the major's sleeve. Pigeons circled in affrighted flocks overhead, dropping olive branches.

At length something that might be loosely described as peace descended. Because their toleration is as great as their big, warm hearts, the umpires didn't chase anybody. The game went on and the last New York hope vanished when Zarilla, who had plucked a fly by Johnny Lindell out of the right-field seats in the second inning, made a running leap in the ninth and grabbed a drive that Tommy Henrich had aimed at a client's wishbone.

It will be written that the game was played in a bona fide World Series atmosphere. That isn't altogether true. During the more exciting moments, members of the Stadium Club who pay hundreds of dollars for season tickets stood at the bar and drank, listening to the game by radio. During a World Series, they sit at tables and play gin rummy.

There was something of the World Series attitude in the dugouts, though. The Yankees had all the carefree joviality to be expected of a team that had squandered a plushy lead by losing four of the last five games. The Red Sox grinned and Joe McCarthy, their keeper, relaxed in his office.

Casey Stengel had asked Henrich to try to play right field and Tommy, gently fingering the damaged vertebrae which he keeps wrapped in a straitjacket, had said, "I will for you, Case." Now somebody recalled the powerful throw with which Zarilla had retired Henrich at the plate Sunday in Boston.

"Did you ever see a better throw, Tommy?"

"I didn't even see that one," Henrich said.

McCarthy was laughing and spinning yarns in the small room which he used to occupy as manager of the Yankees. Casually he brought up a recent report in a Boston paper that he would be let out after this season, win or lose.

"He fired me," he remarked of the reporter who wrote the story. "There's just one thing I know; he won't get the job."

"Reminds me," he chuckled, "of Bill Dahlen when he managed Brooklyn. He's leaving the park one day when a fellow comes running up and says, 'Well, Bill, I hear you're losing your job.' 'I dunno,' Bill says, 'but you ain't gonna get it, you slob.' "

McCarthy shrugged, and started talking about prizefighting. His mind was on baseball, though. You could see that as he and Stengel jockeyed through the long afternoon all but clearing their benches. What their players' minds were on, nobody could guess. What they played wasn't baseball.

Well, the Yankees are down now. So are the newspaper men in the press box—down on their knees trying to find room to work. It would not be proper to say, compare the working press accommodations here to those which packers ordinarily provide for sardines, because the sardines are dead and seldom carry typewriters, anyway.

Yankee Stadium is the cathedral of baseball, a magnificent monument to the sport, the home of a club that has drawn 4,000,000 customers this summer. Its press box is altogether adequate for most series with the Browns.

—September 27, 1949

And Then It Was Over

By the time Cliff Mapes caught Carl Furillo's soft fly to retire the Dodgers in the ninth inning, Tommy Henrich, who had been playing first base for the Yankees, was halfway to the dugout. He couldn't wait to get to the bat rack.

A moment later, when the ball was still high in the misty air, Don Newcombe was halfway to the other dugout. He couldn't wait to get indoors for a good cry.

The first match between Brooklyn and New York for the rounders championship of 1949 was one of the strangest of all World Series games, and certainly the quietest since the one that was played for 6,210 customers in 1908. For eight and a half innings nothing happened because Allie Reynolds and Newcombe wouldn't allow it. There were no fielding plays of great distinction, no hits of special note, no moments of really great peril for either side, no remarkable deeds on the bases.

Humphrey Bogart and Baby Bacall sat looking on, as silent as the 66,222 other witnesses. They've put on more spectacular battles, and stirred more excitement, in El Morocco.

There was nothing to holler about except the pitching, and World Series fans don't holler much at pitching duels. And then, all of a sudden, it was over.

Spectators sat there, struck speechless before they'd had a chance to yell. They had seen Henrich whack Newcombe's third pitch of the ninth inning into the right-field seats but it took a moment for the meaning of the hit to sink in. In that moment, Newcombe started for the bench. Some in the stunned crowd thought, for just an instant, that he was taking himself out of the game in disgust.

Then they got the idea; Henrich had taken him out of the game. There was no place to go but home.

Henrich is the guy who hit a home run in the Yankees' first game of the season, when they went into first place; a home run in their last game of the season, when they won the American League pennant; and now the home run that sent them away ahead of the Dodgers, one game to none.

Between those first two hits, he hit a wall in Chicago and disarranged a string of vertebrae. They said then—this was Aug. 28—that he was through with baseball for the year and maybe forever. His injury was the most serious suffered by any of the patients in ward 4, the huge hospital wing formerly known as Yankee Stadium.

Ask Don Newcombe how Henrich is looking these days. He'll agree this is the most violent invalid on the Eastern seaboard.

This curiously peaceful affair was conducted in an atmosphere suggestive of the Forest Hills tennis matches, rather than a clash of teams whose ferocious struggles in their own leagues had drained the fans of emotion. Maybe that's why the crowd was so silent; maybe, after the pennant races, the public capacity for excitement was expended.

Unhurried crowds just strolled in, settling at ease while Guy Lombardo's band played "Sweet Mystery of Life" for Casey Stengel. (It's still a mystery how he got that team of his into the act.) It was a muggy, humid day with a threat of rain but before Happy Chandler had shaken more than three hundred hands the sun came out.

Nobody paid much attention to the chanteuse singing the national anthem while the flag was raised in center field. When the song ended, the spontaneous cheer that usually goes up wasn't heard. Scarcely anyone saw the first ball tossed out of a box seat. Pee Wee Reese, captain of the Dodgers, and generalissimo Stengel, of the Yankees, gabbed at the plate with the six umpires while fans gawked indifferently or ambled through the aisles. There were many empty seats when the game started, and some never were occupied.

No vulgar voices were raised. Everybody was cool and polite and uninterested, like a man saying no, it would not be possible to extend the loan.

Then the game started, and things got curiouser and curiouser. Here was big Newcombe, a rookie who'd never seen a World Series game before, slamming that hard stuff past the Yankees, who like to hit speed. Inning by inning, he crept closer to the strikeout record that Howard Ehmke set in 1929, when he struck out thirteen Cubs for the Athletics. Veteran ball players writhe with heartburn in a World Series, but after eight innings this big, shuffling kid had a four-hit shutout.

And here was Reynolds, the vanishing American, who had started thirty-four ball games for the Yankees this summer, and disappeared into the showers before thirty of them were finished. Not only did he keep a one-hitter going for seven innings, he kept getting better and better.

He didn't belong around there as late as he stayed, but there he was. He was mixing his curves beautifully, now throwing with a side-arm delivery, now coming over the top, now sneaking in with a fast ball, now shooting over a cross-fire pitch.

When the thing opened, Brooklyn's Burt Shotton had the advantage of being able to start his best pitcher, the guy he would depend on for three games in case the series went the limit. Stengel couldn't do the same thing because Vic Raschi had worked nine tough innings last Sunday while Newcombe was pitching only three in Philadelphia.

Casey got a victory and a complete game from an unlikely source, when Reynolds won for him. He didn't have to use Joe Page in relief, and now he has Raschi ready, with Newcombe temporarily disposed of. With that kind of luck going for him, chances are Stengel will get a week of rain now, and even Henrich will regain his health.

—October 6, 1949

1950s

The Revolving Thespian

CHARLES DILLON STENGEL, the great actor, was replaying the Boston series in the Yankees' dugout, simultaneously handling the roles of Joe DiMaggio, Joe Page, Dom DiMaggio, Larry Berra, Billy Martin, Ted Williams, Jerry Coleman, Casey Stengel, and the Red Sox fans.

As a Thespian, Mr. Stengel employs the revolving technique, embellished with squirms and wriggles and flourishes and pratfalls. He whirls from the bench to the dugout steps, impersonating Dom DiMaggio fielding a hit off the wall, spins back to his seat to whisper a husky confidence with a palm clapped tightly over his mouth, winks, nods, grimaces, leaps up and swings like Joe DiMaggio, reclines on his shoulder blades with hands clasped behind his neck to depict Manager Stengel thinking, finishes few sentences and almost never mentions a name.

The performance sounded remotely like this:

"I feel pretty good because I'll tell you why . . . you know last year we finished strong . . . Boston and then the Dodgers, two good clubs, and now this year those two games in Boston so that's eight out of ten for us against two good clubs, and these fellas have got the spirit.

"I always say I don't fear that little fella up there [Dom DiMaggio] because in that park all he can do is catch the ball off the wall like this and those legs of his don't do him no good. It's in this park I fear him because he'll run 500 feet and catch a ball off of you but those legs of his don't do him no good up in that park. . . ."

This sort of thing is wonderful to listen to, if you happen to know what Mr. Stengel is talking about, but this was a serious occasion in Yankee Stadium, being the opening of New York's American League baseball season and the triumphant homecoming of the World Champions.

It was, Mr. Stengel clearly felt, no time for comedy, so he devoted scarcely more than an hour before the game to swinging like Joe DiMaggio and fielding like Coleman and pitching like Page and booing like the Boston fans saluting Page ("he's lucky he don't get lynched by them Irish up there.")

Then, noticing a vast concourse of politicos and capitalists swarming over the field and hugging one another for the photographers, Mr. Stengel sighed, "Well, looks like I got work to do. Gotta pull up that flag."

"Cripes," Mr. Stengel said, "I get tired pulling up that flag after ninety years."

So he went out to join the mob on the field, which was approximately as large as the mob in the stands, and after they'd all got the flags hoisted in center field they came trudging back to the plate. Mr. Stengel was not required to sing the National Anthem because Lucy Monroe was present and he didn't have to remember any names because Mel Allen introduced everybody.

Although the sun came out later, it was a gray and fairly dismal day at this point, and the crowd seemed extraordinarily quiet for an opening day. Never even worked up a good sweat booing Happy Chandler when he was introduced.

At long last, Governor Dewey got finished summoning Yankees up to receive their World Series watches and rings, and Ed Barrow got a cheer tossing the first ball from a box seat, and the Yankees settled down to play the Washington Senators.

The Yankees weren't the only homecomers. Up in the new and commodious press box, wearing a new commodious mustache and striking a typewriter repeated blows, was Mr. Lou Nova, copyright owner of boxing's dynamic stance and cosmic punch, now world's most prolific columnist.

It was, Lou said, his first visit to the Stadium since he whipped Max Baer there in 1936. Before Tommy Byrne had pitched his first strike, Author Nova had filled two pages of copy.

"Got a deadline to make next Wednesday," he said, explaining his haste.

Quietest homecomer was Bucky Harris, the Washington manager, back in a Stadium dugout for the first time since he managed the Yankees in 1948. Practically immediately, familiar sights met his gaze. In the very first inning, the Yankees filled the bases and there was DiMaggio, feet spread wide and his big yellow stick waggling alongside his right ear.

Joe grounded into a double play though, and maybe Bucky wondered for a moment whether he hadn't got into the wrong park by some mistake. Yogi Berra, the kid whom Bucky had nursed along as a catcher, reassured him with a three-run belt into the seats, his first of four hits.

Later DiMaggio popped up with the bases filled again. But after Washington had tied the score at seven runs, Tommy Henrich walked and Joe dropped one in downstairs to win the game. Now Page was pitching for the Yankees, and now Henrich lashed a ball into the Yankee bullpen.

And now Bucky knew where he was, all right. He was in the right park, but on the wrong side.

—April 22, 1950

The Slightly New Musial

THE POLO GROUNDS gates were still closed and an assortment of cops, a lot of kids and a few cash customers drifted around in grubby Eighth Avenue while authorities scowled back at the misty skies and debated about trying to get in a ball game. There was a card game going in the Cardinals' clubhouse; players loafed in the warm room, half dressed and wondering whether to complete their change. Stan Musial, sitting in a corner, was pulling on his flannel rompers.

A visitor said, "Stan, from what I can read in the averages, you seem to have decided to pass up home runs this year and just go for base hits. Is that intentional?"

"Well," he said slowly, "I'm hitting more to left field."

"You've deliberately changed, trying to do that?"

"Yes. The first part of last season I was trying to pull every ball to right and I was popping 'em up or hitting nice easy grounders to second base. When you just try to meet the ball, the home runs come naturally."

"Eddie Dyer told me last year that you felt the fans wanted home runs from you and you were hurting your average trying to please them."

Musial smiled ruefully. "Well, the year before, I'd hit thirty-nine. That was the most I ever hit in my life." He sounded apologetic.

"Hitting is a matter of timing anyway, isn't it? Not a question of overpowering the ball."

"That's right," Musial said. "When you're trying to hit a home run, you never hit one. You're trying to meet the ball way out in front of the plate like this, and your timing, your swing, your stride, your eyes—everything gets off and you pop up."

"Have you ever got off to such a good start as this year?" (His average at the moment had plummeted to a mere .439, with two home runs.)

"A lot of it is luck," he said. "I've got some lucky hits this year." He turned to Martin Haley, a St. Louis newspaperman. "In my other good years, like 1946 and '48, I got a good start, didn't I?"

Haley nodded. "You were weak at the start of last season," he said. "I could see it in spring training."

"So many things have to be just right for a good year," Musial said earnestly. "You've got to be mentally sound and physically right. I had a lot of things on my mind. I'd had a tough winter." His father died that winter, just after Stan had bought a home in St. Louis and moved his parents out from Donora, Pa. "I hate to alibi," he said.

"You don't have to alibi," a guy said, thinking of his .338 average of last summer and his thirty-six home runs. "You had yourself a year, in spite of everything."

A fellow asked, "When you go around the league, which hitters do you like to watch at batting practice? Hitters always watch hitters."

Musial thought a longish time. "I like to watch any good hitters," he said at last. "But as for learning from their style, why, I hit so different from all of them, I don't think I try to study anybody that way."

"Have you always hit the way you do now, glaring around the corner?"

"Yes, ever since I came up. I feel natural and comfortable this way." He crouched forward as he does at the plate, tucking his chin against his right shoulder. "When I'm like this, it seems to me I've got both eyes dead on the pitcher. Other fellows facing the plate with their heads only half turned, it seems to me they're watching the pitcher with only one eye. I could be wrong, but my way seems right for me."

"He isn't wrong," Gabby Street said later. Gabby, who used to manage the Cardinals and now covers them on the radio, was in the press lounge upstairs. "He isn't wrong. He's as good a hitter as ever lived. You can pitch to some other good hitters. We used to pitch Chuck Klein tight, and you can pitch Johnny Mize that way, and remember how the Cardinals pitched Ted Williams on the fists in the World Series in '46?

"But you can't pitch to Musial when he's spraying them to all fields like this year. If it's outside, he hits it to left. Inside, he pulls it."

"He's right about not being able to hit a home run when you're going for a homer," Gabby said. "I often say, I'd like to see one guy hit the ball when he swings as hard as he can, but they never do. Paul Waner told me one time that maybe once in a game, when he was pretty sure what the next pitch would be—the fast ball, the money pitch—he'd go for a home run. If he didn't get it on that swing he'd forget about it for the day."

"I know of only one intentional home run," a fellow said. "Not counting the one Babe Ruth called in Chicago, that is, if that gesture that we all saw really meant he was calling one. I've never been really sure about that.

"But there was one season about twenty years ago when the Senators were challenging the Athletics and went to Philadelphia for a Memorial Day double-header. Al Simmons won the first game with a home run but hurt his knee and it swelled up so badly the doctor said he couldn't play the second game.

"'Can I hit?' Al asked. The doctor said yes, on one condition, 'You can't run,' he said. 'You've got to strike out or hit a home run.'

"So in the second game Simmons went up as a pinch-hitter and won it with a home run. Just obeying orders."

—May 25, 1950

It Never Happened Before

FOURTEEN YEARS, THREE months, one week and two days ago, a slender, dark haired kid played in the outfield for the Yankees against the St. Louis Browns and made three hits in six times at bat, including a triple off Elon Hogsett. The Yankees won, 14 to 5.

Since that date, May 3, 1936, the Yankees have won nine American League pennants and eight world championships. Since his first game in the major leagues he wasn't able to play during the first two weeks of that season because his ankle had been burned under a sun lamp in the training room Joe DiMaggio has walked alone, comparably and indisputably the finest baseball player of his time.

Night before last, with the Yankees playing the frowzy Athletics, DiMaggio was benched. Nothing like that ever happened before. Over the years, DiMaggio has missed many Yankee games, because of injuries or illness or military service. This was the first time a manager ever looked down a bench, looked past a hale Joe DiMaggio, and said, "Mapes, you play centerfield."

In the seventh inning Cliff Mapes hit a home run with a playmate on base and the score tied at 5-all. DiMaggio's substitute won the game, 7 to 6.

DiMaggio was taken out of the line-up so he could rest. This wasn't the end. He will be back and he will win a great many more games for the Yankees. Nevertheless, it was something that never happened before. Casey Stengel benched him.

Ted Williams with Joe DiMaggio in 1948

The rest of this space could be filled, easily, by the statistical record of DiMaggio's contributions to the Yankees—his 1,552 American League and World Series games, his 2,090 hits, his 344 home runs, his unexampled feat of hitting safely in fifty-six consecutive championship games.

But that would make dull writing and duller reading and it's an old story, anyway. The little things which a fellow remembers furnish a clearer idea of what he has meant to the Yankees than the record books ever could. A fellow remembers, for instance, a remark Bill Terry made fourteen years ago.

The Yanks had run second three times in a row before DiMaggio joined them, but in 1936 they won the pennant by nineteen and a half games. The rookie hit .323 that season and batted in 125 runs. In the World Series with the Giants he batted .346 and in the sixth and deciding game he made an unbelievable catch, racing back past the Eddie Grant monument in the Polo Grounds to the foot of the clubhouse stairs to grab a fly by Hank Leiber.

It was the last putout of the series. Joe kept on running as he caught the ball, mounted a step or so up the clubhouse stairs, then remembered and stood at attention until President Roosevelt left the park. As his car rolled through the center field gate, the President lifted a hand in salute to the ballplayer there on the steps.

A little later in the Giants' clubhouse, when the newspaper men had run out of questions, Terry volunteered a statement.

"I'd like to add one thing," said the manager of the defeated team. "I've heard about how one player made the difference in the Yankees this year, made a championship club out of a loser. I never understood how that could happen, until today. Now I know."

It was not, you see, a coincidence that the Yankees, who won four pennants in the eleven years before DiMaggio joined them, won eight in his eleven active seasons with the team.

Once a newspaper man did penance for his great sins by ghost writing a magazine series called "My Greatest Thrill," as told by assorted athletic heroes. He started, naturally, with DiMaggio. "Champ," he asked, "what was your greatest thrill?"

Joe started talking. He told about how, when he was a kid in high school in San Francisco, they had a teacher who would bring a radio to class during a World Series and tune in the game, and how he had sat there listening and dreaming of playing in a World Series and hitting a home run. At that time, Joe explained, he was just a sandlotter, but after a while he got into organized ball and finally he was in the Coast League and, he felt, coming closer to realization of his dream.

As he talked, he kept filling in the background with small details, a better newspaper man than the guy who was interviewing him. He told about coming to the Yankees and getting into a World Series in his first year. He had a great series, but he didn't hit a home run. He waited another year and got into another World Series, and he had to wait until the very last game of that one before he hit the big one.

That was it, he said. "That was my biggest thrill." He paused a moment, and then he said, "Hitting in fifty-six straight games, that was no slouch, either. What I remember, when I broke George Sisler's record of forty-one games in Washington, our whole club ran out of the dugout to congratulate me. And when I broke Willie Keeler's National League record of forty-four in a game against Boston, they all came running out again. That's what I remember, the way the guys on the club acted."

This was a shy and lonely guy talking. He is still, after all these years, a shy and lonely guy. They have been saying lately that he wasn't taking his decline gracefully. There have been pieces written criticizing him, and pieces defending him. He needs no defense and there'll be nothing like that here. Just one last item:

He came downtown the other evening, after a game when he'd got no hits and the Yankees lost, to cut a record for his weekly radio show. The program began with Joe answering questions mailed in by fans, and one of the questions concerned the popular practice of switching right-handed and left-handed hitters against left-handed and right-handed pitching. How did the guy who was taken out of the batting order feel about that?

"As far as his feelings are concerned," Joe said without hesitation, "it doesn't matter. His job is to help the club win." Anybody got a better answer?

—August 13, 1950

The Vacant Chair

HALF AN HOUR before the people giving an automobile to Lefty McDermott threw out the first polysyllable, amplifiers outside Yankee Stadium were warning the crowds that all reserved seats were exhausted. This was erroneous. During the first game of the itsy-bitsy World Series between the Yankees and Red Sox, the seat reserved for Casey Stengel remained unoccupied. It was Casey that got exhausted.

Before the game, the doughty field marshal of the Yankees did deign to sit down, if you can call his posture sitting. While the players warmed up he assumed a characteristic pose, in which the only part of him in contact with the bench was a spot on the back of his neck about the size of a silver dollar. Disposed thus in defiance of all natural laws, he plaited his legs into a long braid and, folding his arms, hugged himself tightly, as though wrapping himself up in himself against the afternoon's gray chill.

It was Yogi Berra who called attention to the weather. His comely features were unshaven and somebody remarked about the thick shrubbery on his jaw.

"I'm wearin' it to keep warm," Yogi explained sensibly. "I got a little cold."

Physicists were still studying this when Ed Lopat went to work on the pitching rubber. Thereafter, Marshal Stengel covered more ground than both DiMaggios. A witness watching nobody but Casey could have told pretty accurately what was happening on the field.

When Dom DiMaggio opened the first inning for Boston by cowtailing a fraternal triple over the head of J. DiMaggio in center field, Casey clutched for support and got hold of an upright supporting the dugout roof. He stood frozen. So did Dominic as Lopat retired Johnny Pesky, Ted Williams and Junior Stephens in order.

Nobody knew it then, but that brotherly belt of Dominic's was to be the only loud hit off Lopat all day. It was almost as loud as the boos which welcomed Sir Williams on his first time at bat in the Stadium since early July.

In the Yankees' first inning, Berra's beard hissed in the breeze as he rushed down to first base in time to beat a double-play throw which would have retired the side. Then Joe DiMaggio took one pitch for a ball and sliced a fly into the first row seats in right field. Joe's hit traveled about 310 feet, his kid brother's approximately 450. The big guy got two runs, junior got exercise. In baseball, there is no substitute for experience and savvy.

As the ball leaped from Joe's bat, Mr. Stengel leaped from the dugout. His cap was off and he was springing about in such a whirling frenzy he looked like several Hopi Indians in a tribal sun dance. He swung his cap again and again in an encircling gesture that said: "All the way around! All the way!"

In the second inning, Bobby Doerr tied into a pitch and lashed it on a line over second base. Clean, stand-up double, one would say as it started. Joe raced in on a long angle to his left, thrust out his glove, palm up like a landlord taking a pay-off under the table. The ball snuggled into the pocket.

Casey stood on the dugout step, his face blankly agape. His chin, which is fairly long in repose, touched his breastbone.

In the third inning, Joe charged into left field, reached up and plucked a drive by Dominic out of the air. Casey shoved his paws into his hip pockets and strutted the length of the dugout, his chest out. A few minutes later he was straining across the bat rack, his jaw waggling so fast it was a mere blur. Joe Paparella, the plate umpire, had called a strike against Bill Johnson and Mr. Stengel was offering a suggestion.

Johnson walked, Phil Rizzuto doubled and Joe DiMaggio was purposely passed, filling the bases. John Mize hooked a single into right for two runs. This flushed Yankees out of the dugout like a covey of quail, but this time Mr. Stengel indulged in no theatrics. His manner was that of a commander whose operations were proceeding precisely according to plan.

He responded similarly when Hank Bauer followed with a double good for the fifth New York run. Casey popped up the steps so he could follow the ball's flight into right field, then relaxed, planting an elbow on the dugout roof and leaning there at peace with the world.

By this time early returns were in from Cleveland and the scoreboard recorded the beginning of Detroit's ordeal out there. With the Tigers headed for defeat and Lopat breezing along on a five-run cushion, just ambling toward his fourth shutout of the season, Mr. Stengel was relatively content.

As the afternoon darkened and New York prospects brightened, he did a good deal of pacing, shouting, wigwagging and leaping about. But his carriage was jaunty now, with just the proper touch of swagger for the manager of a club leading its league by a game and a half, with a three-game bulge on the Red Sox.

If he frowned, ever so slightly, it was in concentration, thinking of today's game.

—September 24, 1950

Tomorrow in Brooklyn

IF BRANCH RICKEY'S decision to sell his quarter share of the Dodgers means the end of his administration as general manager, then Brooklyn baseball is losing more than a whipping boy for a few fish wives who posed as sports writers. In the absence of official announcement on Rickey's plans, it is conceivable that he might remain as an employee of the Dodgers even after he has ceased to be a part owner. This seems more than improbable though. It is downright implausible, and the betting is that he will, in spite of denial, wind up in the office of the Pittsburgh Pirates.

If that's what happens, Brooklyn will lose and Pittsburgh will gain the ablest baseball administrator now in circulation. In our time there have been two baseball executives whose all-around ability set them far apart from all the rest. The other is Ed Barrow, who built the Yankees into the mightiest empire baseball has known and then retired.

It is not expected that this estimate of Rickey will be universally accepted. It will be disputed by the noisy minority of the press that has made a career of pitching journalistic dusters at the Rickey skull and by those fans who have been influenced by the guy's unfavorable press.

There remains, however, a question which the dissenters would find difficult to answer: If you owned the Dodgers, where would you go to find a successor for Rickey?

This is not to suggest that Rickey's departure, if it comes about, must necessarily be followed by a baseball decline in Brooklyn. He has built a strong organization there. The squad in Ebbets Field and the minor league farms he cultivated to feed the parent club are so rich in playing talent that a good many seasons could pass before famine set in. On the momentum he has provided, less gifted men may keep the Dodgers rolling for a long time.

It has taken time, for example, for the effects of Rickey's departure from St. Louis to show. He quit the Cardinals after they won the world championship in 1942. In the eight seasons since then St. Louis has won three pennants and two World Series and never finished worse than second until this year.

But the cracks have been getting wider and more noticeable each year, and now the Cardinals have busted open. They're going to finish in the second division for the first time in thirteen years.

Rickey conceived the chain-store idea in St. Louis. He made the Cardinal farms the most richly productive in baseball, able to furnish St. Louis with enough top-grade talent to dominate the league with a profitable supply left over for sale to other clubs.

When he departed the farms went to seed. Sam Breadon had always left the minor-league organization to Rickey. Sam's interest always was and continued to be concentrated in Sportsman's Park. Later, efforts to rebuild the network were begun by Bob Hannegan and have been continued by Fred Saigh. But their results have not, up to now, come close to repairing the damage.

The simple fact is that the Cardinal farms have not produced an outfielder of note since Stan Musial came up, not an infielder of distinction since Red Schoendienst. Both were, of course, Rickey's boys, as were Enos Slaughter and Marty Marion and all the others who kept the Cardinals on top until this year.

Even the players who are thought of as young Cardinals, members of the post-Rickey crop, like Joe Garagiola and Eddie Kazak and Rocky Nelson and Tommy Glaviano and Del Rice, were brought into the Cardinal chain during Rickey's administration, although most of them hadn't progressed as far as St. Louis when he moved to Brooklyn.

This is no effort to set Rickey up as a plaster saint. He is responsible to a large extent for the unfavorable press he has had. Because he is wordy and loves to make speeches and frequently combines his eloquence with a pomposity of manner, many listeners have marked him down as a rush of wind in an empty corridor.

Because he has stayed away from the ball park on Sundays he has been pictured as a sanctimonious fraud, although anybody interested enough to look below the surface might have discovered that this practice didn't necessarily connote religious scruples of his own. When he set out as a kid ball player he promised his mother that he would refrain from Sunday baseball, and he lost at least one job and jeopardized his career to keep his word.

There is little actual evidence to support his reputation for parsimony, yet he is the one chiefly responsible for that reputation because he has an incurable passion for horse trading and is constitutionally unable to pass up a chance to haggle in any deal.

In argument he can be so specious, in conversation so prolix and vague, under questions so evasive that not even those most favorably disposed toward him can resist the temptation to make fun of him and his manners of speech. Those less favorably disposed simply write him off as a phony.

Yet put him to work on a baseball problem or a social or political problem for that matter, and his thinking is as direct as a right cross, his arguments brilliant, his action unhesitating. He is a man of great intelligence, extraordinary perception, uncommon originality and inexhaustible vitality. These are facts. But facts are a thin defense against personal gibes. That's the way the world is.

—September 26, 1950

Off the Highest Board

THE TALLEST, STEEPEST, swiftest, dizziest, dare-devil, death-defying dive ever undertaken by a baseball team came off with a rich and fruity climax yesterday when the Phillies toppled headlong into the World Series.

For thirty-five years, the Phillies struggled to win a National League pennant. For the last twelve days they battled mightily to lose one. Then in the tenth inning of the 155th game of their season, all snarled up in a strangling tie with the team that had closed eight laps on them in a fortnight, they were knocked kicking into the championship by the bat of Dick Sisler.

George Sisler, probably the greatest first baseman who ever lived, whose .400 hitting couldn't get him into a World Series, sat in Ebbets Field and saw his big son slice a three-run homer which shattered the pennant hopes of the Dodgers, whom George now serves.

Sisler's hit won the game, 4 to 1. Minutes earlier, lustrous pitching by Robin Roberts had saved it, after the Dodgers had come within a dozen feet of the victory which would have closed the season in a tie and brought Philadelphia and Brooklyn together for a playoff.

"There hasn't been such a finish," said Mr. Warren Brown, the noted Chicago author, "since sporting British officials carried Durando over the line in the 1908 Olympic marathon."

On Sept. 19 the Phillies had the pennant won in every sense save the mathematical one. They were seven and a half games ahead of the Boston Braves, and Brooklyn was third, nine games off the pace. The Dodgers won fourteen of their next seventeen games, the Phillies three of their twelve. So when they showed up yesterday before Ebbets Field's largest gathering of the year, the Phils' lead was exactly one game, with one game to play.

They had neither won nor lost the championship, but they had qualified handsomely for off-season employment—substituting for the diving horse in Atlantic City.

They had also brought gold pouring in a bright yellow stream into the Brooklyn box office. Instead of leasing out their park for family picnics this weekend, the Dodgers sold 58,952 tickets for the last two games, many of them to customers who stood outside the bleacher gates all Saturday night.

By 4 a.m., cars were pulling into parking lots near the field. By 6:30, there were 5,000 or 6,000 persons in line. By 1 p.m., all gates were closed and nobody without a reserved seat ticket was admitted. Cops estimated that 25,000 were turned away. It was bigger than many World Series crowds in Brooklyn, and properly so, for this was bigger than a World Series game, where even the losers gather much loot. The losers of this game got the winter off.

In spite of everything, the Phillies managed a surface appearance of confidence. Before the game the Philadelphia manager was asked to name his pitcher for the first playoff game today.

"That's one thing I never do," he said mildly. "Announce my pitcher for the day after the season closes."

For what seemed an interminable time, though, there was reason to doubt that the season ever would close. Big Don Newcombe was rocking back on his hind leg, waggling a big spiked shoe in the Phillies' beardless faces and firing his service past them. They had at least one base runner in every inning after the first, but these Phils are kids still damp from the nursing bottle and this was hard stuff Newcombe was serving.

Roberts, who passed his twenty-fifth birthday watching the Phillies lose on Saturday, was pouring an even more poisonous potion. In seven innings, the only Dodger to hit him was Pee Wee Reese, who was to make three of Brooklyn's five hits and the only Dodger run.

This was the run that tied the score in the sixth inning when Pee Wee sliced a ball which jammed in a chink on the top of the right-field wall, at the base of the screen which surmounts the wall. Ground rules specify that a ball lodging where this one did remains in play for an Oriental homer.

To say tension was growing is to abuse the mother tongue. Things reached such a pass that when a bug flew into the eye of Mike Goliat, the Phillies second baseman, Mr. Babe Alexander, of Philadelphia, cursed. "Those Dodgers," he said, "have adopted germ warfare."

But shucks, things were practically lethargic then compared to the Brooklyn ninth, when the Dodgers put their first two batsmen on base and Duke Snider lashed what had to be the deciding hit into center field. Richie Ashburn fielded the ball on one hop, threw swiftly and superbly to the plate, and Cal Abrams, coming home with the winning run, was out by twelve fat feet.

Nobody ever saw better pitching than Roberts showed then. With runners on second, third, and one out, he walked Jackie Robinson purposely to fill the bases, then reared back and just threw that thing through there. Carl Furillo popped up. Gil Hodges flied out.

Ken Heintzelman and Ken Johnson ran all the way from the bullpen to shake Roberts's hand. Eddie Sawyer patted Robin's stomach. Those were gentle hands. Sisler and Roberts felt others later.

Sawyer watched his operatives pummel this pair when their great deeds were done. Then he announced that the Phillies would take today off. Most of them to rest. Roberts and Sisler to anoint their bruises.

—October 2, 1950

A Game for Boys

PHILADELPHIA—After thirty-five years, three hours and fifty-six minutes, the Phillies scored a run off American League pitching today, and such excitement swept this town you'd have thought the British were coming again. They weren't. DiMaggio was.

If the second game of the World Series proved anything to the 32,660 witnesses yeeping and bawling in Shibe Park this afternoon, it demonstrated that baseball is a young man's game. For nine innings the elderly gentlemen who work for the Yankees hit pusillanimous pop-ups against the wonderful pitching of the Phillies' young Robin Roberts.

On fourteen separate occasions the field agents of Casey Stengel tottered up to the plate and gave what Uncle Wilbert Robinson once described as brilliant imitations of men hitting out of a well. It was a bad day for low-flying ducks.

Again and again, feeble little bloopers spiraled skyward and descended into the gloves of Philadelphia infielders. On five occasions, the New York batter missed the ball altogether, striking out.

Doddering Joe DiMaggio, who'll hobble into his thirty-seventh year next month, was the feeblest of them all. On his first time at bat, he popped to the second baseman, on his next, he popped to the second baseman. On his third, he popped to the third baseman and a small cheer went up among a knot of his friends.

"He's pulling the ball now," they exulted. But on his fourth trip Old Joe popped to the first baseman.

Then he came up again in the tenth inning with the score tied at 1-all, Roberts threw him one pitch. Joe said later that it was a slider, and Roberts said it was a fast ball. There'll be bad blood between them until the issue is settled, so let's not be drawn into the quarrel. Whatever it was coming, it was a fast ball going.

It streaked over second base on a rising line. Richie Ashburn, playing center field for the Phillies, turned and started toward the double-decked bleachers. He ran a few yards, stopped and watched. He saw a customer several rows back in the upper stands rise, catch the ball and sit down.

It was an old gentleman's hit, an old professional gentleman's. The old professional gentleman went creaking around the bases, and the Yankees got ready to catch a train for New York, where they will endeavor to beat the Phillies for the third and fourth time tomorrow and Saturday.

As a matter of fact, Joe may have saved the game in his elderly, professional style a few minutes before hitting the home run that won it. With one out in the ninth inning, Granny Hamner—whose name suggests a sweet old lady smelling of lavender but who used to rack balls in a pool hall in Richmond, Va.—racked up a ball served by Allie Reynolds.

It was a long line drive that whistled out on a flat trajectory between center and right fields, and if it had got through the New York defense it would surely have been a triple and possibly the home run that would end the game. DiMaggio, starting when the ball did, loped over to his left, fielded the hit like a shortstop, and stopped Hamner at second base.

What followed did not suggest that the Phillies could have scored Hamner, even from third base. But nobody ever can tell about that. The way it went, Professor Eddie Sawyer, the licensed sorcerer of the Phillies, chose Dick Whitman to bat for Ken Silvestri, and Casey Stengel, the Yankees' resident djinn, advised Reynolds to put him on first base. Mike Goliat then grounded into a double play, retiring the side.

By contrast with the Phillies' demonstration of how not to hit Vic Raschi in the first game, this was lively entertainment. Philadelphia kept rapping Reynolds for extra bases and managed to tie the score in the fifth inning. Roberts and Reynolds, both pitching elegantly, managed to keep it tied until DiMaggio loosened the stays.

With both teams frequently threatening, excitement grew. At one point Happy Chandler, baseball's little king, came right up out of his box seat and visited the Phillies dugout, presumably to ask the score. His action was generally approved, on the principle that a fellow ought to know the score at least once in five years.

Afterward it was said that the fans who waited since 1915 for their Phils to get into a World Series no longer seemed to care if they had to wait thirty-five years to see it happen again. This was unfair. They were still whooping for their heroes in the home half of the tenth when a walk and sacrifice put the tying run on second base with one out.

Reynolds threw something small, blurred and white to Richie Ashburn, who popped up. He threw more of the same to Dick Sisler, who started to swing at a third strike, checked himself halfway around and learned from Bill McGowan, the umpire, that the game was over.

McGowan walked toward the dugout. Yogi Berra and the Yankee infielders ran toward the mound to salute Reynolds. Sisler stomped behind McGowan, saying things. Nobody listened. He hurled his bat away and a customer leaped aside, dodging.

Mr. Stengel smiled and spoke behind his hand in the manner of a conspirator. "I am," he confided hoarsely, "getting good work from my help."

—October 6, 1950

Scandal in the Day Nursery

THERE ARE NOW sixty-four shopping days until Christmas.

A mistake begun thirty-five years ago was brought to its horrid consummation before 68,098 eyewitnesses in Yankee Stadium yesterday when the Phillies lost a World Series game for the eighth consecutive time. On Oct. 8, 1915, the Phillies won an engagement from the Boston Red Sox, this being their first victory over an American League team since the game of rounders was devised. That was thirty-five years ago today—and for the Phillies there is no today.

Casey Stengel, a gentleman of great age and infinite wisdom, sent a kid on a boy's errand in the fourth and final match of the struggle for the pitch-catch championship of the world. To combat the precocious moppets of Philadelphia whose youthful ardor had enabled them to lose three times by one-run margins in three days, he selected as the Yankees' pitcher a tot of twenty-one named Ed Ford.

What Ford did to Eddie Sawyer's beardless pupils was a scandal in the day nursery. Although they had managed to score three runs in twenty-seven innings against the elder statesmen of Stengel's pitching corps, the Phils scored nothing on their own merits against the babe of Casey's woods.

At no previous time in the series had they seemed so immature and futile, so hopelessly beyond their depth in a man's game, as they did against the blond boy graduate of the Yankees Kansas City prep school. He had them shut out, 5 to 0, and the World Series was over when Gene Woodling, playing left field, botched up a fly ball and let two Philadelphia runs come home.

Casey Stengel is a wise old gent. Back in the World Series of 1941, when Hugh Casey was beating the Yankees for the Dodgers until his catcher, Mickey Owen, failed to catch the strike that should have ended the game, a crazy panic swept Ebbets Field. In the shrieking excitement, nobody had the sense to go out and remind the pitcher that he still had the game won, that there were two out and a runner on first base and all he had to do was retire one more batter. Everybody went frantic that day, and in the confusion the Yankees made off with the ball game.

Now, before the crowd was through shouting about Woodling's error, Stengel was out on the mound telling Ford the score. It was still 5 to 2, Casey said, with one man on base. Casey just stood there in the middle of the hubbub talking quietly to the kid, patting him briskly on the rear of his lap until Bill McGowan, the umpire, moved in from his station at second base to break up the kaffeeklatsch.

Maybe Ford was upset in spite of Casey. Or maybe he was tired. Or perhaps Mike Goliat was due to get a hit then, anyhow, Goliat did hit and Casey walked out again and patted Ford's stern some more and prodded his bosom with a gnarled finger and talked some more. But now he was apologizing to the kid for what he had to do. He had announced his decision and two umpires, Charley Berry and Jocko Conlan, were signaling the bullpen to send in the right-hander.

Allie Reynolds came striding in lugging his glove and a windbreaker, and Ford walked to the dugout, pulled on a jacket, got a long drink at the water cooler, and stayed to watch the finish.

Know what Casey had said to Ford when the manager took him out? Casey said, "There's a stinkin' little ground ball between third and shortstop and it's my fault. I should have had Rizzuto over there but he didn't see me waving at him."

That was a lie, of course, from a very considerate liar.

Well, Reynolds threw four pitches past Stan Lopata and struck him out. Yogi Berra caught the last strike, leaped approximately twelve feet straight up, brandished a fist with the ball clutched in it, and ran around in small circles looking for somebody to embrace.

Ford started out of the dugout on the run, stopped suddenly as though remembering that this day he had become a man, and walked sedately back toward the tunnel to the clubhouse. Behind him, running to beat the crowd, came Eddie Sawyer on his way to give a loser's congratulations to a winner.

Mr. Stengel then summed it up for the visiting press:

"I hated to take that kid outta there but sometimes you hafta do it because you fellers hafta get home."

So then everybody went home, after a World Series that could have been one of the best but was only routine. The Phillies played well, kept all the games close, and weren't good enough. The story of the Phillies this year was a story of bright kids. The story of the final game is the story of an extraordinary kid.

This extraordinary kid, Ford, might have had butterflies in his bosom when he opened his first World Series game by walking the first man he faced and yielding a double to the third. But he pitched out of that first inning, and never allowed another base on balls. He was as cool as Joe Kuhel, his Kansas City manager, had been saying he was.

"When he gets a guy or so on bases," Joe had been saying, "you can see him set his teeth and start pitching. And what pitching! Other times he's good fun. He's a wise-cracker on the bench, and all the rest of the time he talks baseball. In the hotel or on the train he plays a game. 'Who won the 1940 World Series?' He'll ask the other players. 'How many home runs were hit? Who pitched the last game?'

"It's a quiz game he plays, and he's wonderful at it. And it's never about anything but baseball."

"Watch him," Mr. Stengel said, "next year."

—October 8, 1950

Connie J. Dykes

WEST PALM BEACH, FLA.—The strangest sight in Florida is Wright Field without Connie Mack sitting on a little hard funeral-parlor chair in front of the dugout. The Philadelphia Athletics are courting health here, and it is the first time in fifty-one years that they have done so without Connie on the playground. As manager emeritus in his eighty-ninth year, he watches the exercises from the grandstand. (An exception was yesterday, when gallantry called him to the tomato-growing community of Dania, Florida, to crown a comely little tomato as Miss Tomato of Tomatoes of 1951.)

"You ought to see him," said Lou Brissie, the pitcher. "He looks younger and livelier than he has in two or three years. I think it's been a relief to him to quit managing. I know that if I'd been managing this club last year, I'd have shot myself."

The chair was standing, unused, in front of the dugout.

"I'm disappointed," a visitor said to Jimmy Dykes, the boy manager. "I took it for granted you'd be sitting there wearing a high, hard collar and waving a scorecard. So you're not. All right, tell us about the Athletics."

"The Athletics," Mr. Dykes said, "represent Philadelphia. Connie Mack is the president. Roy F. Mack is executive vice-president and treasurer. Earle Mack is vice-president and secretary. Arthur H. Ehler—"

"No," the guy said, "tell us about the ones who sweat."

The boy manager complied, speaking as well as conscience permitted about the team that started last season as a dark-horse contender for the

American League pennant, came all unstuck in a welter of front-office dissension, and wound up a miserable last. It is not so bad a team as it looked last fall, and it is not so good as it seemed last spring.

But Mr. Dykes has them running and throwing and swinging and he will have them mentally and physically sharp when they go north, and when he gets them to Shibe Park he will know what to do with them. He will not, for example, temporize with a pitcher who is losing his stuff.

"When I was playing with the A's," Dykes said, "Rube Walberg was pitching for us, and he was staggering in the ninth inning. From the bench Mr. Mack waved me in from second base to check up on the Rube. 'I'm great,' Walberg told me, 'I feel fine.' The sweat was pouring off his face and he was gasping.

"I said: 'The boss wants to know. He thinks you're tired.' Rube said: 'I'm great. I'll strike this guy out.' I waved okay to the bench and started back to my position. I took about three steps and I heard the crowd go: 'Oooh.' I turned around and here's Walberg lying on his face. The poor guy had collapsed.

"When I went out managing, Mr. Mack told me never to listen to the pitcher when I thought I should take him out. There never was a pitcher in baseball who couldn't strike out the next hitter. The first experience I had was with Milt Gaston. That big Pepper, of the Browns, was up, and I walked out to take Milt out of there, and he told me he could get Pepper—he could always get Pepper. I just got back to the bench in time to see Pepper hit the wall in right center for the ball game.

"The next time was with Ted Lyons against Cleveland when Bob Feller had a lead of 1 to 0 on us. They got men on second and third with two out, and I wanted Lyons to walk Ray Mack because Feller was up next. Ted said he could get Mack out. I said maybe he could, but first base was open and it was a cinch he could get Feller. Ted said: 'They'll put in a pinch-hitter,' and I said: 'Fine, we can't hit Feller. Either Oscar Vitt tries to hit with Feller or he takes him out and maybe we can do something with the next guy.' But Ted says he's sure he can take care of Mack, and finally I say okay, he can go ahead.

"I'm not even back to the dugout when I hear: 'bong.' And it's a triple by Mack and now we're licked good. Afterwards I'm walking out and I'm burning, and I hear Lyons behind me. 'Skipper,' he's saying, 'you were right again.' So that's how I learned to make up my mind and stick to it."

"The first guess," said Dave Keefe, the coach. "I don't know how many times I've heard Mr. Mack say: 'If I'd only acted on my first thought.'"

"That's right," the boy manager said, "but sometimes these pitchers awe you. I had that Xavier Rescigno in Hollywood. Whenever there was a blooper single against him, he'd look straight up at the sky and start to yell.

'Oh, God,' he'd yell, and everybody in the ball park could hear him, 'oh, God, why are you always mad at me? Why don't you ever get mad at that batter, just once?'

"They tell me he had a catcher out there on the coast one year named Camelli, and when those two got together it was something. Camelli would be giving him the sign and Rescigno would be shaking him off, and finally Rescigno would yell: 'No. No. No, I will not throw my curve!"

"It was an act, they tell me, but how can you know? My owner in Hollywood was giving me hell for not lifting my pitchers soon enough, and one day I started Pinky Woods and he walked the first four men in a row. So I walked out there. 'Pinky,' I said, 'the boss says I'm too slow changing pitchers. You're through.' He says: 'Jimmy I'm just barely missing the corners.'

" 'You've missed sixteen times,' I told him, 'and that's enough for me. On your way.' "

—March 7, 1951

Happy Landings

ST. PETERSBURG, FLA.—Nothing that Happy Chandler did in his six unquiet years as Baseball Commissioner became him so well as his leave-taking. He has not, to be sure, actually departed as yet, but that was a swan song which the Sweet Singer of Versailles, Ky., warbled in Miami yesterday, and even the Good Humor Man, himself, must have recognized it as such.

Happy has been an indifferent Commissioner, but he is a pretty fair ham actor, and his farewell performance was one of his best. Not many men can achieve an air of perfect nonchalance when they have been publicly divested of their pants, but the unfrocked Commissioner carried off his part with a jaunty swagger.

Strutting into the conference room to open the meeting at which his employers were to vote down his plea for a new lease on the baseball trough, he strode through a gauntlet of newspaper men and advised them airily:

"The condemned man ate a hearty breakfast and took steps toward the guillotine."

He opened the meeting, turned the chair over to Warren Giles, of Cincinnati, and withdrew to let the club owners have their say. In spite of all his campaigning and maneuvering during the last three months, in spite of uncounted rumors that he had picked up a vote here and lost one there, the count on this ballot was the same as that of last December—Happy needed the endorsement of twelve of the sixteen owners to hold his job, and he was backed by only nine.

A. B. "Happy" Chandler as Commissioner of Baseball

John Galbreath, of the Pittsburgh club, left the meeting to inform Happy of the verdict, and when they returned to the conference room Chandler knew he was licked, yet he marched in, beaming as though he were receiving news of a smashing victory. Even when he came out, repudiated by his bosses for the fourth time (they took three ballots in St. Petersburg in December), he still had a broad and meaty smile all over his complexion.

"I can't complain," he said, "because I fought 'em on my own grounds and—" he smoothed the lapels of his natty gray haberdashery—"I wore my Confederate suit."

So it must be said to his credit that when he had to take it, he took it well. Admittedly, it would have been a more graceful act to step out the first time he was asked. It can be argued that the office of Baseball Commissioner ought to be a position of dignity which should not be undignified by such public wailing and unblushing toadying as Happy has done since his repudiation in December.

But to a politician there is nothing wrong with campaigning for a place on the payroll. By his own confession, Happy loves baseball and his actions never have betrayed any deep loathing for a wage of $65,000 a year plus expenses. Fighting for that worthy cause, he did, as he said, fight on his own grounds and with every trick learned in the back alleys of politics.

As recently as yesterday morning, owners who were known to be opposed to Chandler were receiving telephone calls from field agents who told them, "Look, Happy has thirteen votes lined up, so it's in the bag. Why don't you come over and make it fourteen for the sake of appearances?"

The stratagem didn't fool anybody but it might have, for the owners arrived in Miami in a state of feather-brained bewilderment, with only the vaguest notion of what they were there for. The four-man screening committee had, presumably, been seeking a successor to Chandler for three months and still had nobody to recommend.

Advised that the committee had accomplished nothing, members of the two major leagues met separately on Sunday and voted to consider only one candidate—Chandler—in yesterday's elections. To men who had come from as far off as Catalina Island, it must have seemed fairly silly to be flying across continent just so they could do again what they'd already done three times last December. Some of them might very well have been in the mood to say, "The hell with it," and take Happy as they might take castor oil, just to get an unpleasant job over with.

However, Happy himself had eliminated this possibility by overcampaigning. He had made it, as far as baseball was concerned, a battle to the death with men like the Cardinals' Fred Saigh, the Yankees' Del Webb and the Braves' Lou Perini. He had operatives digging up dirt about their private lives and there was at least a suspicion that he was the source of whispering campaigns charging them with piracy on the high seas, wife beating and spitting on sidewalks.

Obviously, these men were not going to risk their millions in a game administered by an employee who served them by peeping through their keyholes, and on their own time, too, when they were paying him to shake hands and sign autographs. If Happy were to stay, there would be at least three franchises for sale cheap.

According to reports, Happy squeezed these concessions out of the owners: A unanimous vote against appointing Walter Mulbry, who was Chandler's Man Friday, but appears to have lost the Little King's favor, to the advisory board of the majors; an agreement to demand Mulbry's resignation as commission secretary on the ground of "disloyalty to the Commissioner"; assurance that the members of Chandler's staff will be taken care of.

Presumably, Happy's campaigning is now ended, which should be a comfort and a relief, unless he changes his mind again. But meanwhile, baseball is in the foolish position of paying $65,000 for a Commissioner who can no longer commish. Maybe that's what baseball really wants at the top—a vacuum.

—March 14, 1951

The Red Sox? Not Again

SARASOTA, FLA.—BILL Wight was sitting in the lobby of the Sarasota Terrace Hotel when Dom DiMaggio entered, walking like a .328 hitter. Bill Wight used to view the world through the bright eye of a Yankee pitcher, then he saw the seamy side of life with the Chicago White Sox and now he is a member of the Cadillac convertible set, or Boston Red Sox.

DiMaggio disappeared into an elevator, and through the front door came Bobby Doerr (runs batted in, 120). In a minute Billy Goodman entered (batting average, .354). Then Ted Williams (.317), then Walt Dropo (.322).

Wight stole a glance at the clock.

"Wow," he breathed, "this club gets stronger by the minute."

Somewhat later Mr. Joe Cronin, general manager and treasurer of this covey of coupon-clipping capitalists, was chatting with some strays in the Boston play pen. With more courtesy than curiosity he asked what they knew and one of them said redundantly, "Nothing. We were up in Clearwater the other day and Eddie Sawyer said second place was the proper spot to pick for his Phillies."

"He asked us," another guy said, "if we were picking the Red Sox in the American League."

"And we," said the first, "told him, 'Jeepers no. Not again.'"

Mr. Cronin smiled with the warmth of a brave man having splinters thrust under his fingernails.

"And yet," a fellow said, "when you come down here and take a look around—"

"I know," said Mr. Jerry Herne, the Boston strong boy of American letters, "say no more. Late last season, in September some time, we were out in St. Louis where those snarling savage Browns won two games out of three. I took a blood oath that night. I'd just cut my finger and I made a big red X on a sheet of Western Union copypaper—that never again in my life would I pick the Red Sox to win a pennant.

"And then—and then—well, you come down here and you got a touch of sun, probably, and a touch of scotch, certainly, and the first thing you know you're thinking—"

"It's looking at these brutes that does it to you," a guy said. "It's not the sun nor the scotch. It's seeing all those muscles."

"Perish forbid," Mr. Herne said. "Not me. I don't dare look at 'em. If I ever did, I wouldn't be picking them for a pennant. I'd have 'em in Cooperstown."

Just the same, the visitor does look and all around him he sees people named Williams and DiMaggio and Dropo and Doerr and Johnny Pesky and Junior Stephens and Goodman.

"You," Jimmy Dykes told a rookie pitcher about to make his first start for the Athletics last year against Boston in Fenway Park, "are just like a mouse in a cage with nine cats."

There are all those muscles and this year, in addition to pitchers like Mel Parnell and Ellis Kinder and Lefty McDermott, there are the very good workmen, Bill Wight and Ray Scarborough, to comfort the Irish heart of Steve O'Neill, of the baseball O'Neills, of Minooka, Pa.

Around this genial Irisher there is an aura of camaraderie that infects the whole organization. Sometimes in the past there has been an air of tension in this camp, which was understandable enough because the Red Sox have been overtaken at the wire in so many pennant races that they were bound to be haunted by a feeling that they were being followed.

But under the management of Minooka Steve they are, at least, relaxed. Which may be a good thing for them and may not, but is, in any case, the way ball clubs are that play for O'Neill. The visitor stands around and gabs with the manager, who seems placidly pleased with his guys and the way they've been playing and a dark, slender fellow comes along and Steve says, "You know Lou, of course."

Here is a guy who has to finish one-two in any contest to select the greatest shortstop that the American League has known in its half-century of existence. Never the swiftest runner in the world, he always played the hitters so astutely and got such a jump on ground balls that it was next to impossible to hit anything past him. Not blessed with the strongest arm in baseball, he could get his throw away so quickly he always got his man. For years the pitchers called him the smartest hitter in the league, a guy who couldn't be outguessed and who hit the ball where it was pitched, pushing the outside ball into right field, pulling the inside pitch into the left-field seats.

Boudreau's legs aren't what they were when he played for Steve O'Neill in Buffalo in 1939 and his arm isn't what it was. At the moment he has a bruised hand, but he is physically fit, as always, and mentally alert, as always, and he is only thirty-three, a year older than Phil Rizzuto and two years older than Pee Wee Reese.

All this and Boudreau, too, a guy thinks looking around, but all the while, a guy knows he can't pick the Red Sox.

"Even when Lou isn't playing," says Eddie Mayo, Boston's third base coach, "he'll make everybody else hustle just by being around threatening their jobs."

"He may not play," a guy says, "but he'll scare hell out of some people so they'll play twice as well as they did before."

"Twice as well?" another guy says. "For some of you guys, that's all they need to be major leaguers."

—March 16, 1951

Opening Day, Yankee Stadium

AN HOUR AND a half before the New Year dawned, Mickey Charles Mantle—he was christened Mickey, not Michael, after Mickey Cochrane, whose name is Gordon Stanley—was standing on the top step of the Yankees' dugout looking back into the stands where a kid in a bright windbreaker brandished a home-made sign fashioned from a big pasteboard carton. The sign bore a photograph of Phil Rizzuto, cut out of a program, and crude lettering read: "C'mon, Lil Phil. Let's go."

Sitting on the bench, Casey Stengel could see his newest outfielder only from the chest down. The manager grunted with surprise when he noticed that the sole of one baseball shoe had come loose and was flapping like a radio announcer's jaw. He got up and talked to the kid and came back shaking his head.

"He don't care much about the big leagues, does he," Casey said. "He's gonna play in them shoes."

"Who is he?" a visitor asked.

"Why, he's that kid of mine," said Mr. Stengel, to whom proper names are so repugnant he signs his checks with an X.

"That's Mantle?"

"Yeh. I asked him didn't he have any better shoes and he said he had a new pair, but they're a little too big."

"He's waiting for an important occasion to wear new ones," the visitor said.

Casey is not unaware of the volume of prose that was perpetrated about this nineteen-year-old during his prodigious spring training tour, when he batted .402, hit nine home runs and knocked in thirty-one runs.

"How about his first game in a big league park?" a kibitzer said.

"Saturday in Brooklyn, when he got only one single. What was wrong?"

"My writers," Mr. Stengel said, "had an off day."

Mr. Stengel told about Mantle asking him how to play the right-field wall in Ebbets Field.

"It was the first time the kid ever saw concrete," he said. "I explained how the ball hits the wall like this and bounces like this and how you take it as it comes off the wall. I told him, 'I played that wall for six years, you know.' He said, 'The hell you did!' "

"He probably thinks," Mr. Stengel said, "that I was born at the age of sixty and started managing right away."

A couple of newspaper men were talking to Bill Dickey. About Mantle, naturally.

"Gosh, I envy him," one of them said. "Nineteen years old, and starting out as a Yankee!"

"He's green," Bill said. "But he's got to be great. All that power, a switch hitter, and he runs like a striped ape. If he drags a bunt past the pitcher, he's on base. I think he's the fastest man I ever saw with the Yankees. But he's green in the outfield. He was a shortstop last year."

"Casey said that out in Phoenix he misjudged a fly and the ball stuck on his head."

"It hit him right here alongside the eye," Bill said. "He's green, and he'll be scared today."

"If anybody walks up to him now," a newspaper man said, "and asks him if he's nervous, Mantle should bust him in the eye. Golly, Bill, do you realize you were in the big league before he was born?"

"He was born in 1932," Dickey said, "and that was the year I played my first World Series."

"And I'd been covering baseball years and years," the guy said. "What's been happening to us?"

After that there was a half-hour relentless oratory at the plate, and then Whitey Ford, the Yankees' prize rookie of last year, walked out in his soldier suit to pitch the first ball, and then the season was open and it was New Year's Day.

Mantle made the first play of the season, fielding the single by Dom DiMaggio which opened the game for the Red Sox. He broke his bat on the first pitch thrown to him and was barely thrown out by Bobby Doerr. He popped up on his second turn at bat.

When he came up for the third time the Yankees were leading, 2 to 0, with none out and runners on first and third. Earlier, Joe DiMaggio had started a double play with an implausible catch of a pop fly behind second, as if to tell Mantle, "This is how it's done up here, son." Now Joe, awaiting his turn at bat, called the kid aside and spoke to him.

Mantle nodded, stepped back into the box and singled a run home. Dickey, coaching at third, slapped his stern approvingly. When the kid raced home from second with his first big-league run, the whole Yankee bench arose to clap hands and pat his torso. He was in the lodge.

—April 18, 1951

History in the Making

A CONGREGATION OF 1,789 dolls, stirred by the same macabre curiosity that moved the sisterhood who knitted beside the guillotine, took their needlework and their clear, rippling trebles to the Polo Grounds yesterday. Like the morbid molls of Paris, they saw history made.

That is, they saw the Giants hit three home runs off Warren Spahn and take a lead of 3 to 1 over the Boston Braves, the only baseball team they have beaten in a championship game since September, 1950. At that point history, appalled at its own unorthodox behavior, got repetitious to the point of banality. The Braves, also hitting three home runs, extended the New York's promising young losing streak to nine games.

This did not entirely eliminate the possibility of memorable accomplishments by the Giants this year. They are still four defeats short of their own all-time record for sustained ineptitude, having lost thirteen in a row in 1902 and again in 1944. And much farther ahead of them, a beckoning will-o'-the-wisp, is the National League's mark of twenty-three consecutive lickings sustained by the Pirates in 1890.

Much remains to be accomplished.

New York is a naive town. You can always draw a crowd here by jumping from a tall building, provided, of course, you don't do it so often as to spoil the novelty. Thus there were, in addition to the Jennies who got in free, 6,981 citizens who bought tickets.

Chances are they had a double motive for attending. Some were incredulous, felt they had to see for themselves what was happening to a club that had opened the season as a prime pennant contender, and to seek their own explanation of the riddle. Some just wanted to see what Leo Durocher, the monkish manager, would do next.

On the preceding evening he had taken several measures. He had benched Eddie Stanky, considered the key man of the team, and started Artie Wilson, a rookie, at second base. He had installed himself on the coaching line at first base, replacing Fred Fitzsimmons, on the theory that maybe he could think more effectively on his feet.

This time he experimented with a bolder hand. He chose Ray Noble, another rookie, as his catcher; sent Jack Maguire to right field in place of Clint Hartung, who ordinarily replaces Don Mueller when a lefthander like Spahn is pitching; assigned Jack Lohrke to third base instead of Henry Thompson; returned Stanky to the infield and gave his own intellect another chance to operate from a standing stance.

To be sure, the Giants' first-base coach was destined to have few pupils to coach during the afternoon, yet he made his presence on the field felt as early as the third inning. In that inning, Jim Hearn was called out on a close play under the manager's nose, and there wasn't so much as a mumble of protest from the coaching line. Had Leo been sitting on the bench, where he does his best umpiring, the ladies would have been late for supper.

Other effects of leaders' strategy became evident as the entertainment progressed. Having no employees to talk to at first base, he cupped his hands and shouted, "C'mon, kid, you can do it," to his batters. And sure enough, the very individuals whom he had selected for the purpose did do it. Noble, Maguire and Stanky all hit home runs.

Subsequently the Braves made three successive singles off Hearn with nobody out. One of the balls they hit might conceivably have been employed in a double play, but it wasn't. Hearn had been pitching effectively up to then, but Durocher's current state of mind is not, understandably enough, distinguished by patience.

He directed Hearn to the shower bath and Sheldon Jones to the pitching mound. A moment or so later, the Braves were in front, 6 to 3. One of the balls hit off Jones might have been a double play, too, but wasn't.

What had started out as a lovely summer afternoon had turned unaccountably chill. The dolls in the stands left off their yelping and went back to their knitting. Shadows crept across the turf, long and dark and dismal.

The leader held his ground, a small, lonely figure, expressibly forlorn. Not so lonely, though, as Herman Franks. Herman coaches at third base.

Not so forlorn, either, as Horace Stoneham, the Giants' president. It was Horace's forty-eighth birthday. One could picture him out in his top-floor office beyond center field, celebrating the anniversary all alone, quietly hanging by the neck.

—April 28, 1951

How Colorful Can They Get?

THE BROOKLYN DODGERS, whom the colorful Red Barber frequently describes as a colorful baseball team and who certainly are the best to represent the National League since the 1942 Cardinals, went the polychromatic limit yesterday in Columbia Broadcasting System's first color telecast of a ball game. On a twelve-inch screen in an air-conditioned studio in C.B.S. headquarters, the Dodgers and Boston Braves all came out as spectacularly beauteous critters, except for Roy Campanella, who had neglected to shave.

The reproduction was excellent, striking, and only faintly phony. That is, the grass had just a touch of the unreal sheen that used to be seen at the Army-Navy game in Philadelphia when it was the practice to paint the December turf green. The athletes looked only a wee bit too athletic, being endowed with magnificently bronzed complexions glowing with not quite believable health. You would have thought that painters had freshened the orange and blue trim of Ebbets Field within the last hour.

Like a picture postcard, everything was just the least little bit brighter, more colorful, neater and prettier than life itself.

"A new era," Mr. Jack Collins, Brooklyn's business manager, told Mr. Barber and the audience, "has been born."

Although the camera intensified all colors to the edge of overemphasis, it created contrasts which made for a sharper image than black-and-white television provides. The white ball, for instance, was much easier to follow against the background of green.

Mr. Barber was also wittier than in black and white, although it would require either an engineer or a psychiatrist or both to explain why this should be. At least, the man outside the studio door said he was wittier. The game had already started, and the man said to late arrivals. "You ought to hear Barber. He's funny as hell."

Very soon thereafter Mr. Barber responded to this billing as follows:

Mr. Collins, having announced the birth of a new era, added that some equally delectable entertainment was in store for next Monday night, when the Dodgers would observe "musical appreciation night."

"Musical appreciation?" Mr. Barber said. "Or depreciation?"

The first play witnessed by a tardy viewer was an error by the Braves' first baseman, Earl Torgeson, who muffed a pop fly. The camera followed the ball closely and when it squirted out of Torgey's mitt the studio audience saw it and emitted the same grunt of amused astonishment that the microphone picked up in the grandstand. At that moment, at least, the studio audience forgot it was watching a scientific experiment and became fans watching a ball game.

"Here's big Hodges," Mr. Barber said a moment later when the Brooklyn first baseman came to bat. "See those muscles ripple?"

You could see 'em, too, although they were encased in a pelt of somewhat lovelier tone—about the shade of roast beef medium—than Gil wears in real life.

With only two color cameras working, the crew had to switch lenses constantly to change from close-ups to wide-angle shots embracing a considerable portion of the field. It was a small screen, too, so that in the wide-angle scenes the outfielders were mere specks against the distant walls. Thus when Sid Gordon hit a home run for Boston in the second inning, the ball was just too small for the studio audience to see.

There was some slight running of colors. When Charley Dressen, the Dodgers' resident djinn, stood on the bare base path to chat with one of his runners, his white uniform was as immaculate as a prom queen's gown. But the camera followed him as he returned to the coach's box beside third, and against this background of turf he turned green, like cheap jewelry.

Light blues ran a good deal, too, washing across the picture. The Braves' gray traveling uniforms took on an unnatural bluish cast, and when the camera swept the shirtsleeved crowd one had the impression that all the customers had been laundered together with too much bluing in the water. The dark blue of the Dodgers' caps, however, remained fast and true.

If you watched intently while a batsman swung in a close-up, you saw a regular rainbow of bats of varying colors. For a fraction of an instant, the moving bat became a big Japanese fan.

And after you had stared at the screen for a minute or so, you saw a retinal image in basic colors when you looked away. This, plus the strange sensation that all the players had been bathed in a powerful skin tonic for the occasion, made the viewer feel curiously uneasy.

Altogether, though, the colors were about as good as in Technicolor, and the view of the game was as fine as it can be through a camera, which can show only part of the action on any play.

Mr. Barber said morosely that he had lain awake all Friday night planning his costume for this historic occasion and might just as well have worn a plain white shirt because the lens hadn't been aimed at him even once.

The camera then picked him up in a shirt of such splendid and new design that words haven't yet been invented to describe it. This showed how swiftly science marches. It also gave a hint of horrors to come, when color television will inspire broadcasters to overdress even more barbarously than they do now.

—*August 12, 1951*

American Indian Day

AFTER ALL THESE years, the Yankees just had to find a new way to make sure of finishing in first place. Since they got the habit in 1921 they've been in a rut, just pennant after pennant, championship after championship, season after season—eighteen times in thirty years. The dreary, weary, yawning ennui of it all!

This, though, was laying it on a little too thick. This was showboating of the most vulgar and ostentatious sort. Here it was, American Indian Day according to the "Farmers Almanac" and out there was the noble redman, Allie Reynolds, pitching the first game of a double-header, pitching the game the Yankees needed to guarantee a tie for the title, at worst.

The only no-hit pitcher ever born to the Creek nation—he won that distinction against the Cleveland Indians last July 12—was working against the Boston Red Sox, malevolent leaders of the American League batting lists and prime contenders for the pennant until a few days ago. These were the guys whom Jimmy Dykes described to a rookie pitcher about to make his first big-league start for the Athletics in Boston: "You are just like a mouse in a cage with nine big cats."

So now it was the eighth inning and the Yankees were leading, 8 to 0, and Reynolds had not allowed a hit. He came up to bat, walking through a tunnel of noise, and paused beside Phil Rizzuto, who was kneeling in the chalked circle where the next hitter waits.

"Stengel says," he told the Yankee shortstop, "that if I get away with this one I can have the rest of the season off."

This was the only time he hinted that he was going for his second no-hitter in a single season, a feat brought off only once in history and never in the American League. While pitching his no-hitter in Cleveland he had horrified Yogi Berra by mentioning it in defiance of the superstition which forbids speaking of such matters while the game is on. Afterwards he got letters from fans scolding him for "tearing down baseball traditions," so this time he wasn't talking.

Now it was the ninth inning, three putouts to go. Every time he threw the ball, the crowd screamed. A pinch-batter named Charley Maxwell grounded out. Dominic DiMaggio walked. Johnny Pesky took a curve for a third strike. Ted Williams slouched up; his pale bat looked as long as he is.

Berra walked out to the mound, waddling under his catcher's armor. "Take it easy, now," he said. "What do you want to throw to him?"

"Anything," Reynolds said, and Yogi went back behind the plate to call the pitches. Rizzuto, shifted a little to the right of second base for the lopsided defense against Williams, was talking with Charley Berry, the umpire.

"Holy Cats," Phil said, "let's walk this guy and work on Vollmer."

"Naw," says Berry, courageous as a fight manager. "Allie's got good stuff. He can throw it by this fella."

"Charley's cool," Rizzuto said later. "He's got it all figured out—and I'm fainting!"

The first pitch to Williams was a called strike. Williams hit the second straight up, a towering foul behind the plate, and Reynolds dashed in to give help if Berra should need it. A draft swept the ball back over Berra's head and Yogi lunged backwards for it, missed and fell at Reynolds's feet. Allie tripped over him but didn't fall. Instead, the pitcher bent to help the catcher up, patted his back, spoke in his ear. Yogi didn't want to get up. He wanted to keep going down, into a hole, out of sight. The game should be over, and now, if Williams should get a hit on this second chance—

One wondered how Williams was feeling. The Red Sox weren't going to win, no matter what he did, but he was hitless for the day and he is a hitter. The crowds in Yankee Stadium always boo him, just for living. If, on this undeserved last chance, he should ruin Reynolds's no-hitter they'd curse every breath he drew into his old age.

"Allie had Williams, two strikes and nothing," Bill Dickey said later, "and now he can work on him. So what does he do? He rams the next one right through there."

It was another strike, and again Williams lifted a foul, over in front of the Yankee dugout this time. Berra went over and Reynolds went with him. "Lots of room!" Tommy Henrich cried from the bench. ("There was about three feet of room," Tommy confessed afterward, "But it looked like a lot to me right then. If Yogi falls in the dugout, we'll catch him.")

Yogi caught the ball and Reynolds caught Yogi. Everybody on the Yankee bench sprang out and caught the pair of them. Henrich, on the fringe of the knot dived up onto the top of the mob, cracking heads together as he clawed toward Reynolds.

After a while things got quiet in the clubhouse. There was still one more river to cross this side of a pennant, but nobody doubted that it would be crossed, as it was within three hours. Reynolds was quietest of all, crouched in his locker, answering questions.

"Come back in about two hours," he said apologetically, "and I'll give you some better answers."

Art Patterson, of the Yankees' office, told him about the "Farmer's Almanac" designating this as American Indian Day.

"Does it say anything about Creeks?" Allie asked.

—September 29, 1951

Call Out the Reserves

THE BRIDGE WAS closed at 11 p.m. Friday and an hour later John Cashmore, borough president of Brooklyn, called members of his Cabinet from their beds for an emergency meeting to ban the sale, transportation and possession of ropes, knives and firearms in the city of churches. Early yesterday afternoon when Willie Mays walked, stole second, stole third and scored on Don Mueller's single, civil defense squads fanned out to confiscate all belts and suspenders in Flatbush, Greenpoint, Bay Ridge and Brownsville.

Alarmists demanding Brooklyn's immediate and permanent withdrawal from organized baseball, as a measure of public safety, were persuaded to wait for this afternoon's final returns from Philadelphia and Boston.

Independent estimates of the number of bodies floating in the Gowanus were repudiated as irresponsible and, probably, exaggerated. The courts entertained seventeen applications to change the names of newborn boys from Charley to Branch or Leo.

Things will be quieter tomorrow. Meanwhile, no matter who wins the National League pennant, it is time to salute the Giants for the most heartwarming exhibition of resolution, determination, spirit, backbone, mettle, pluck, spunk, perseverance, doggedness, intransigence—go it, Webster. Come on, Roget—within modern memory.

From the beginning, it was a myth and an illusion. On Aug. 12, when the Giants began to cut into Brooklyn's thirteen-game lead with a winning streak of sixteen games, all right-minded citizens realized that this was an empty gesture. To be sure, other teams in the past had closed wide gaps and come on to win a pennant. The Braves of 1915 were last in July and first in October. The Red Sox of 1948 came from seventh place to tie the Indians on the last day of the season, and lose in a play-off.

But they were teams of a quality equal, if not superior, to the opposition. When a club comes out of the ruck to win, it is because that club is fundamentally the best in its league but was slow to settle into stride. There never has been a case of the best team losing a thirteen-game lead in a league which is clearly outclassed.

So as the Giants crept closer and closer to the Dodgers, everybody knew their stretch run was meaningless, though admirable. You might catch an inferior team that had gotten in front by luck. You couldn't overtake one that was away out there on sheer merit.

Everybody conceded the Dodgers' superiority. Position by position, they come pretty close to constituting a National League All-Star squad. As to the Giants with their two-man pitching staff, the questionable quality of their catching, with retreads at first and third base, an aging Eddie Stanky at second, and an erratic Al Dark playing shortstop—well, no odious comparisons, please.

It couldn't happen, but it did. Friday night the Giants and the Dodgers were tied. Yesterday afternoon New York was ahead, though not necessarily to stay. Whether they stayed or not, the Giants had accomplished the impossible. How? Upon what meat did these, our Caesars? Simply an effort, on will and, one must believe, on leadership.

It doesn't matter whether you admire Leo Durocher's taste in haberdashery or not; you needn't applaud his diction or concur with his views on world affairs or approve of his social graces. You must accept him as the manager and leader of the team that has brought off this magnificent coup.

He always said they could do it. It is not possible to believe that he believed it. But he never confessed the doubts he must have had, and his ball players never gave up.

Neither have the Dodgers given up, of course. They shouldn't. But it would be a more agreeable world to live in if the cult of Dodger worshippers were just a mite less vociferous in their protestations of idolatry. Some fairly appalling examples of Dodger-worship at its worst were the savage attacks, oral and written, upon Frank Dascoli after that umpire tossed Roy Campanella out of Thursday's game in Boston.

Published accounts of the incident suggest that Dascoli may have been hasty in hoisting the imperious thumb the instant the Brooklyn catcher flung his mitt to the ground in protest of a decision at the plate. "Let's all keep cool" is a good working principle for everybody under the stress of a pennant race like this one. One still remembers with respect the example of patient self-control set a couple of years ago by the American League's Willie Grieve when Ralph Houk was bulldogging him around Yankee Stadium and other Yankees were reviling him for calling Johnny Pesky safe with an important run for the Red Sox.

On the other hand, if it is a rule in the National League that a player who throws his glove goes out of the game on June 2, then the rule still applies on Sept. 27.

In any event, the name-calling, door-kicking tantrums which ensued, on the part of the Brooklyn players and the Brooklyn idolators, were a simple disgrace.

—September 30, 1951

Last Chapter

Now it is done. Now the story ends. And there is no way to tell it. The art of fiction is dead. Reality has strangled invention. Only the utterly impossible, the inexpressibly fantastic, can ever be plausible again.

Down on the green and white and earth-brown geometry of the playing field, a drunk tries to break through the ranks of ushers marshaled along the foul lines to keep profane feet off the diamond. The ushers thrust him back and he lunges at them, struggling in the clutch of two or three men. He breaks free and four or five tackle him. He shakes them off, bursts through the line, runs head on into a special park cop who brings him down with a flying tackle.

Here comes a whole platoon of ushers. They lift the man and haul him, twisting and kicking, back across the first-base line. Again he shakes loose and crashes the line. He is through. He is away, weaving out toward center field where cheering thousands are jammed beneath the windows of the Giants' clubhouse.

At heart, our man is a Giant, too. He never gave up.

From center field comes burst upon burst of cheering. Pennants are waving, uplifted fists are brandished, hats are flying. Again and again, the dark clubhouse windows blaze with the light of photographers' flash bulbs. Here comes that same drunk out of the mob, back across the green turf to the infield. Coat tails flying, he runs the bases, slides into third. Nobody bothers him now.

And the story remains to be told, the story of how the Giants won the 1951 pennant in the National League. . . . The tale of their barreling run through August and September and into October. . . . Of the final day of the season when they won the championship and started home with it from Boston, to hear on the train how the dead, defeated Dodgers had risen from the ashes in the Philadelphia twilight. . . . Of the three-game play-off in which they won, and lost, and were losing again with one out in the ninth inning yesterday when—Oh, why bother?

Maybe this is the way to tell it: Bobby Thomson, a young Scot from Staten Island, delivered a timely hit yesterday in the ninth inning of an enjoyable game of baseball before 34,320 witnesses in the Polo Grounds. . . . Or perhaps this is better:

"Well," said Whitey Lockman, standing on second base in the second inning of yesterday's play-off game between the Giants and Dodgers.

"Ah, there," said Bobby Thomson, pulling into the same station after hitting a ball to left field. "How've you been?"

"Fancy," Lockman said, "meeting you here!"

"Ooops!" Thomson said. "Sorry."

And the Giants' first chance for a big inning against Don Newcombe disappeared as they tagged him out. Up in the press section, the voice of Willie Goodrich came over the amplifiers announcing a macabre statistic: "Thomson has now hit safely in fifteen consecutive games." Just then the floodlights were turned on, enabling the Giants to see and count their runners on each base.

It wasn't funny, though, because it seemed for so long that the Giants weren't going to get another chance like the one Thomson squandered by trying to take second base with a playmate already there. They couldn't hit Newcombe and the Dodgers couldn't do anything wrong. Sal Maglie's most splendorous pitching would avail nothing unless New York could match the run Brooklyn had scored in the first inning.

The story was winding up, and it wasn't the happy ending which such a tale demands. Poetic justice was a phrase without meaning.

Now it was the seventh inning and Thomson was up with runners on first and third base, none out. Pitching a shutout in Philadelphia last Saturday night, pitching again in Philadelphia on Sunday, holding the Giants scoreless this far, Newcombe had now gone twenty-one innings without allowing a run.

He threw four strikes to Thomson. Two were fouled off out of play. Then he threw a fifth. Thomson's fly scored Monte Irvin. The score was tied. It was a new ball game.

Wait a moment, though. Here's Pee Wee Reese hitting safely in the eighth. Here's Duke Snider singling Reese to third. Here's Maglie, wild—pitching a run home. Here's Andy Pafko slashing a hit through Thomson for another score. Here's Billy Cox batting still another home. Where does his hit go? Where else? Through Thomson at third.

So it was the Dodgers' ball game, 4 to 1, and the Dodgers' pennant. So all right. Better get started and beat the crowd home. That stuff in the ninth inning? That didn't mean anything.

A single by Al Dark. A single by Don Mueller. Irvin's pop-up. Lockman's one-run double. Now the corniest possible sort of Hollywood schmaltz—stretcher bearers plodding away with an injured Mueller between them, symbolic of the Giants themselves.

There went Newcombe and here came Ralph Branca. Who's at bat? Thomson again? He beat Branca with a home run the other day. Would Charlie Dressen order him walked, putting the winning run on base, to pitch to the dead-end kids at the bottom of the batting order? No, Branca's first pitch was a called strike.

The second pitch—well, when Thomson reached first base he turned and looked toward the left-field stands. Then he started jumping straight up in the air, again and again. Then he trotted around the bases, taking his time.

Ralph Branca turned and started for the clubhouse. The number on his uniform looked huge. Thirteen.

—October 4, 1951

The Alarm Clock Rang

THEY BUNDLED UP the charms and amulets, the love philters and voodoo powders, the shrunken skulls and soggy old tea leaves and crystal balls and magic wands, and pitched 'em into the Harlem River yesterday. The Yankees don't believe in miracles or ghosts. They only believe in Santa Claus (pronounced Hank Bauer).

Magic and sorcery and incantation and spells had taken the Giants to the championship of the National League and put them into the World Series. Their flying carpet had carried them as far as the ninth inning of the sixth game. But you don't beat the Yankees with a witch's broomstick. Not the Yankees, when there's hard money to be won.

With the score, 4 to 3, against them, two men out and the tying run on second base, the Giants called Sal Yvars in from the bullpen to hit. The third-string catcher hurdled the bullpen gate and came running. It was only his forty-second chance to bat since this scatter-brained rigadoon began last April.

He lashed into the first pitch and drove a hard liner into right field—straight for the yawning glove of Bauer. The outfielder's feet shot from under him as he made the catch. But he held the ball, and as his bottom hit the turf, the bottom dropped out of the hasheesh market.

For the fourteenth time, the Yankees were baseball champions of mankind. Theirs is a charm nobody breaks.

It had to be that way. Somebody had to restore public faith in this sport. One more climax dreamed up in a joss house by an alcoholic Hollywood script writer would have finished everything. So they put it up to Bauer, a tough ex-Marine as starkly realistic as "The Naked and the Dead."

His three-run triple won the world championship. His sliding catch kept it won.

Well, the nonsense had gone far enough. It began in the spring when the Giants went romping off to an eleven-game losing streak. It carried through sixteen consecutive victories in August, went on through September as the team cut away Brooklyn's thirteen-game lead, and on the last day of the season the pennant was won in Boston, then lost on a railroad train.

So it had to be done over again. So the Giants did it over, in a three-game play-off with the Dodgers that ended when Bobby Thomson transmuted a 4-to-2 defeat into a 5-to-4 victory with a home run in the ninth inning.

Now, of course, the dream would end. The Yankees would put a stop to witchcraft and hexes and curses in four straight games. But it didn't end. No metal could touch the Giants. They won the first World Series game, lost the second, won the third.

Then it happened. They lost on Monday. They lost on Tuesday. Here came Bauer, and now they were losing on Wednesday. There'd be no game Thursday.

Nobody told the Giants, but it was all over. The handwriting was plain in the seventh inning when Willie Mays and Bill Rigney opened with singles that knocked out Vic Raschi. If victory were in the cards for the Giants, they would have rallied then. But in came Johnny Sain, and out went three batters in order. The score was still 4 to 1.

Still, maybe the Giants can't read handwriting. Maybe Leo Durocher, the Little Shepherd of Coogan's Bluff, hasn't taught them to play cards. For in the eighth inning they filled the bases with two out. Those three runs would tie the score.

Up came Rafael Noble, the second-string catcher. He represented the winning run. The Black Pearl of the Antilles glowered at one strike, swung at another and missed, stared stonily at a third.

That had to be the end. Great as the Giants have been, no team could rally in the face of such miserable failure, nobody could decline to surrender now. But the first man up in the ninth was Mr. Edward Stanky, a competitor. Durocher has a phrase for guys like Stanky.

"He came to play," Durocher says, meaning he wasn't here to look on.

Stanky singled. Al Dark bunted safely. Whitey Lockman singled. Here came Monte Irvin, batting star of the series, co-proprietor of a record of eleven hits for a six-game struggle.

With the bases filled, nobody out and two right-handed batters due at the plate, Casey Stengel took a long time to make up his mind. Then he gestured with his left hand, and the left-handed Bob Kuzava marched out of the bullpen. Curious strategy, but maybe the Yankees' manager can do a few card tricks, too.

Irvin hit a long fly that scored Stanky and advanced the other runners. Here came Thomson with the tying run on second base, exactly where it was exactly a week earlier.

"Casey," said Rud Rennie in the press box, "is playing for three long flies. That scores two runs and ends the game."

So Thomson flied out, scoring Dark. So Yvars flied out. It had to be that way. Got a reefer, Mac?

—October 11, 1951

The Real Amateur

ONE OF THE very few very great pros of professional sports issued a statement yesterday to the press and to the public. It was the statement of an amateur, in the best sense of the word.

"When baseball is no longer fun," said Joe DiMaggio, "it is no longer a game. . . . And so, I have played my last game of ball."

That is the amateur view. It is the feeling which prevents a great commercial enterprise like baseball from ever becoming a commercial enterprise exclusively. Joe DiMaggio made a great deal of money playing baseball. Most of all, though, he played for fun, and now that it is no longer any fun, he isn't gong to play any more.

Back in the days when Babe Ruth drew $75,000 or $80,000—which was more than any other ball player had received before him or has received since, if you allow for inflation and taxes—it used to be said that Babe was the truest amateur in the game. That is, he played baseball because he loved baseball, and the money was a mere by-product. He would, if necessary, have played without salary or have paid for the privilege of playing.

The same has been true of Joe. The same was true of most of the others who were the best and who won the greatest rewards, including that affluent old gentleman, Ty Cobb. Through salary and investments, Cobb made a million dollars. Yet when others were playing for money, he was playing for the game's sake.

"Of all the guys I have known," Al Simmons said one time, "Cobb was the only one who played as hard after he got rich as he ever did when he was hungry." There was the true competitor talking of the true amateur.

This is a meandering way of approaching the simple, flat fact that the greatest ball player of our day and one of the greatest of any day quit baseball yesterday.

It was by no means unexpected. As far back as last spring, DiMaggio revealed that the thought of retirement was in his mind. He said 1951 might very possibly be his last year as a player, and when he said it the Yankee bosses were upset. They knew, of course, that the time of decision must eventually arrive, but they didn't want to believe it must come so soon.

When the World Series was over, Joe again made it clear that he wanted to give up. Again the Yankee owners stalled for time, hoping that a couple of months' rest would recharge Joe's battery and he would come to believe that there was at least one more good season left in him.

Then yesterday, when the whole town knew that a press conference had been scheduled and the irrevocable decision would be announced, the whole town was talking about it. Wherever you went yesterday in the early afternoon, the waiters and captains and cab starters were asking the same question: "What about Joe?"

It would have done Joe good to know how the waiters and captains and cab starters were talking yesterday. Not that they could have or would have helped him to make up his mind, or would have changed his mind for him once it was made up.

"It was my problem, and my decision to make," he pointed out. And, of course, it was. Had he said the word the Yankees would have handed him a contract willingly. Yes, eagerly. It was for him to say, and he realized that as he has always realized it, for all through his adult life he has been a lonely guy who had to chose his own path and walk it alone.

When he came to New York from San Francisco he was scared. He'd been fed a lot of fiction about what a hard-boiled town this was, and he believed at least part of it.

"Forget it," said his San Francisco manager, Lefty O'Doul. "It's the friendliest town in the world."

Joe found that out. If New York was hard-boiled, he soon cracked its shell. But it was a long time before he could come out of his own, this shy, silent guy.

One night he was in Toots Shor's with a crowd that included Lefty Gomez. This was years ago, when Lefty was still pitching for the Yankees. Table hoppers kept coming to say hello and try out their newest, most studiously rehearsed wisecracks, and Gomez had the quick and easy and affable retort for all of them.

Joe listened for a long time as Lefty batted the badinage about. Then he turned to the guy beside him. "I'd give a million dollars," Joe said, "if I could do that."

So he would have been pleased, although he wouldn't have shown his pleasure, to know how they were talking about him yesterday around this town. Maybe it would please him to know that they approved his decision.

They hate to see him go, but they know and understand why he decided as he did. They know he's quitting because he cannot stand mediocrity in anything, and least of all in himself. They couldn't stand it either, not in Joe. On him, it couldn't look good.

—October 12, 1951

The Williams Deal

THROUGH THE EARLY weeks of winter, the Boston Red Sox talked and talked of trading away Ted Williams. All they wanted in exchange was "the guts of a ball club," Lou Boudreau said with simple elegance. Now at long last a deal is in the works, but the Sox are taking no bows for it. When and if Williams rejoins the Marine Corps, all they'll get out of it is an aching void.

It has been a sorry year for hitters. Tommy Henrich, Charley Keller, Bobby Doerr, Joe DiMaggio, Joe Louis—they're all gone, and now apparently Williams is on his way.

It would be difficult to overestimate Boston's loss if Williams goes. Hitters like him cannot be replaced because there aren't any hitters like him at large. In the American League there aren't any hitters like him, period.

Because of a somewhat capricious temperament, Ted has always been the subject of adverse criticism, even when he was batting a dandy little .406. There have always been some ready to argue that the Red Sox would be better off without him, but that is an argument which neither the pitchers nor the managers of other American League clubs have espoused.

There's a line in his record which reflects the opinion that pitchers have of him. It reads: "Broke major league record for most consecutive years, 100 or more bases on balls." As for the managers, when Williams comes to bat and they wrench the defense all out of shape to confound him, they don't do it just to tease.

There was a well-remembered game last summer when Paul Richards, the White Sox manager, paid Williams as pretty a compliment as a hitter could receive. A right-hander was pitching and winning for Chicago when Williams, who'd already made several hits, came up for the last time. Richards shifted his pitcher to third base just long enough for a left-hander to come in and retire Ted, then the original man returned to the mound and finished the game.

Richards was openly declaring that he considered his pitcher good enough to whip the rest of the Red Sox, but not good enough to face Williams. Obviously Richards agrees that Ted's departure would be good for the Sox, provided the sox are white.

Ted passed his thirty-third birthday in October. It was fourteen years ago that he made his first trip to a Boston training camp. In his only full season of professional baseball he had caused some Pacific Coast League pitchers to wake up screaming in the night, but his talents as an outfielder had not been polished to a dazzling brilliance.

In fact, the representative of one major league team had watched him play for San Diego and shuddered violently. "He's another Buzz Arlett," the man said, employing a standard of comparison that still causes strong men to turn pale, although it has been many years since the muscular Buzz plodded across major league outfields.

Anyhow, Boston was taking a chance and the kid was bound for Florida with several other players. Al Horwitz, a Philadelphia baseball writer visiting the camps, encountered them on a train and sat down to chat. They talked, naturally, about hitting.

"You'll see some pretty fair hitters with the Red Sox," Horwitz said, "Joe Cronin, Mike Higgins, Jimmy Foxx—"

Young Williams said he'd already seen some good hitters, out on the Coast.

"I know," Horwitz said, "but wait till you see Jimmy Foxx hit."

The rookie gazed out the window dreamily. His fingers gripped the handle of an imaginary bat.

"Wait," he said, "until Foxx sees me hit."

Nobody had to wait long. Ted's lifetime average against major league pitching is barely under .350. It's anybody's guess how high it might be if he could have played through World War II and swung against the guys they were using instead of pitchers in those years. He was twenty-four years old and at his loftiest peak as a batsman when he went into the service for three years.

If he has to serve seventeen months this time, he'll be in his thirty-sixth year before his hitch is finished. By that time, he could be finished, too. Not necessarily, however. John Mize celebrated his thirty-ninth birthday the other day. He celebrated by signing a contract with the Yankees.

—January 11, 1952

Babes in Kiddieland

MESA, ARIZ.—It was ten or a dozen years ago and the Chicago Cubs had returned to the continental United States (pronounced Southern California) after some preliminary physical culture among the mountain goats and prawn divers of Catalina Island. They were accompanied by Mr. Ed Burns, the amiable baseball authority of "The Chicago Tribune."

"What's your ball club like this year?" Mr. Burns was asked.

"The Cubs?" he said, "fine boys. They're all fine boys. They're the nicest bunch of kids you ever saw. In all my years, I've never traveled with nicer kids."

For a moment or possibly two, he was silent.

"They faint at the sight of blood," he said.

Of all the names on the Chicago roster then, only one remains. That is Philip Joseph Cavarretta, part manager and part first baseman, the club pro. Yet the impression on viewing the Cubs is that only the personnel has changed. They're still nice lads, agreeable and inoffensive.

It is no accident that when he is at home in Dallas during the winter, manager Cavarretta operates an amusement park called Kiddieland.

Chicago has some bright young pitchers and some who've been left out in the weather for quite a spell now, like Dutch Leonard and Willie Ramsdell and Joe Hatten and Walt Dubiel. In fact, Leonard has been throwing knuckle balls for pay since his wise old leader, Cavarretta, was a wise old moppet of thirteen.

Biggie Smalley, the shortstop, can play ball. So can the third baseman, Randy Jackson, and some others. But with the exception of Hank Sauer, brutality is foreign to them. They are kind to women, animals, and pitchers.

In all this pleasant desert town there is only one man who, observers believe, might collaborate with Sauer to lend a small streak of meanness to the Cubs' attack. That is an outsized package of gristle named Jack Wallaesa.

Back in 1942, a leggy, scrawny puppy of a shortstop, showed up in the Athletics' sweat shoppe in Anaheim, Calif. At twenty-one, Wallaesa looked like a beardless and overgrown fifteen. He was 6-feet 4-inches tall with the girth of a rainspout. He had managed to get a uniform that was too small for him, and the skintight pants, reaching barely down to his knees, gave the effect of a masquerade costume.

He was as graceful as a Newfoundland pup or a two-day old colt trying to discover what legs were for. He'd get his feet crossed going after a ground ball. Trying for the double play, he'd trip over second base and sprawl on his face. When he did get a throw away, the ball would trail plumes of smoke, but no life was safe within thirty feet of first base.

First time he walked up to the plate you'd have given 9 to 2 that a fast ball would knock the bat clean out of his hands. Yet in his first exhibition game he drove a home run out of the small park in Fullerton, Calif. And as one day followed another, his improvement was beyond belief.

Everybody in camp fell in love with this pink-cheeked, eager kid.

Everybody knew he was unprepared for big-league baseball, yet his daily development was such that the correspondents couldn't keep him out of their stories; he got more attention than any five regulars combined.

He also got more instruction. Al Simmons, a coach with the A's, worked on Wallaesa's batting style in camp. The club went to Los Angeles, where Babe Ruth was making a movie. The Babe hadn't been in the park five minutes before he had a bat and was telling Wallaesa, "Look, kid, the way you're striding, your body's ahead of the swing. You want to get your weight behind the bat, like this."

Up in San Francisco, Lefty O'Doul said, "Who is that big kid at shortstop? I could make a hitter out of him." He invited Wallaesa out to Seals Stadium mornings, tied a long rope around the kid's waist and tethered him to break a habit of lunging at the ball.

The Athletics went to Oklahoma City where Rogers Hornsby was manager, and the Rajah joined the faculty temporarily, trying to smooth out the boy's swing.

By the time the club got home to Philadelphia, Wallaesa was a composite hitter—one part Al Simmons, one part Babe Ruth, one part Lefty O'Doul, one part Rogers Hornsby. Baseball never had seen a combination like that, a potential 1.500 batter, and baseball didn't see this one for long. In practically no time, Army rolls bore the name of Pvt. John Wallaesa.

Carrying a musket, the pupil had no time to practice what his fabulous faculty had preached. Since the war he has wandered, to Toronto, to Philadelphia, to the White Sox, to Newark and to Springfield, Mass., where he was shifted to the outfield last summer.

He's a big boy now, a muscular 205 pounds. The other day when the milk-and-water Cubs were torturing the Giants, he made three hits, drove in two runs, threw once to the wrong base, letting two runners advance. After all these years, it's just barely possible. . . .

—March 14, 1952

Lefty O'Doul and the Peanut-Hater

SAN FRANCISCO—This is a sparkling and glorious town, perhaps the loveliest of American cities, especially on a day like this when the sky is unblemished blue and the sunshine is breathtaking on the tumbled hills that flank the bay. It is a strange town, though, without Lefty O'Doul.

It is odd to come back to San Francisco and not see Lefty. Used to be you'd see him everywhere—in Seals Stadium teaching some kid ball player to hit, in his own cheerful joint on Powell St., where all the murals are left-handed, in the press club.

For seventeen years he was manager of the Seals and the city's finest good-will ambassador, both here and in the Orient. You'd sooner pass up a drink at the top of the Mark or lunch out at Seal Rock or a trip to Fisherman's Wharf than come to San Francisco and miss a visit with Lefty.

After last season he got fired. He got fired by one Paul I. Fagan, a man who hates peanuts. Mr. Fagan didn't bother telling Lefty he was fired. He waited until O'Doul was in Japan and then told the newspapers. This year Lefty is managing the San Diego club.

This Paul Fagan is, relatively, a newcomer to baseball. Maybe he knows as much about the game as St. Louis's Fred Saigh does, maybe not. He wasn't exactly a pauper in his own right and he suffered no financial damage by marrying into the great Crocker banking family.

A few years ago he bought in as a one-third partner of Uncle Charley Graham and Dr. Charles Strub, the horsey dentist of Santa Anita. Charley Graham continued to run the club, as he had since the dawn of human memory around here, and O'Doul continued to manage it.

Uncle Charley was a practical baseball man, one of the best, and Lefty was his boy. They made a superb team. In 1946 and 1947 the Seals did a soaring business and everybody was happy.

Mr. Fagan contented himself with dolling up the park, polishing up the men's rooms and installing $50,000 powder rooms for the ladies, patterned after the Taj Mahal, only fancier.

Then Charley Graham died and Fagan became head man. Up to this time, the new magnate had nothing against peanuts or, if he had, he had not come out into the open as a goober-hater. Crunch and let crunch had been his policy.

However, in a chat with one of the sweepers after a ball game one day he discovered what all proprietors of ball parks and horse parks and sports arenas know—that the meanest litter on earth to clean up is peanut shells, cracked and scattered and ground underfoot. They adhere to concrete as a small, sticky child clings to white woodwork.

Learning that the cost of sweeping up peanut shells was greater than the profit on goobers, Mr. Fagan issued a proclamation. Henceforth the nutty fruit would not be offered for sale in Seals Stadium.

Well, sir, the response was exactly what you'd expect, and twice as loud. The fans screamed like wounded catamounts. Baseball without peanuts? Hell's bells. . . . Pretzels without beer. . . . a honeymoon without a bride. . . .

Spokesmen for the peanut interests denounced Fagan as a destroyer of the most sacred American institutions, a despoiler of youth and traducer of everything the public held dear. Fans vowed they would buy peanuts outside the park and would carry in two sacks for every one they had previously consumed, crunching the shells more maliciously and scattering them more widely than ever before.

Under the bludgeoning of city-wide wrath, the peanut-hater surrendered and restored the goober to its proper place in the concession booths and human hearts.

After firing O'Doul, Fagan hired Tommy Heath as manager. Heath would get a chance to inspect the playing talent, the owner announced, and any additional players whom he deemed necessary would be purchased instanter.

Three days later, Mr. Fagan declared that the club was set and no new material would be added. No more deals, no purchases. Even if the Seals could get a fellow like Joe DiMaggio, they wouldn't bother. In the future foreseen by Fagan there would be no room for such dotards as DiMaggio.

Now the Seals are playing exhibition games in their stadium. Customers have discovered that there are peanuts for sale, but the price has been raised to fifteen cents a sack. Howls of rage are echoing from Twin Peaks to Sausalito across the Golden Gate.

The goober-lovers are mobilizing again. Soon the vigilantes will ride by night. This is war.

—March 23, 1952

Begging Mr. Sullivan's Pardon

THE MAJOR LEAGUE baseball season—which means, translated, the annual struggle for the gonfalon in both the senior circuit and the Harridge loop—opens today. It is an occasion which affects various individuals in various ways. It has impelled two normally law-abiding citizens to trespass upon a field legally posted by Mr. Frank Sullivan, the Sage of Saratoga, curator of clichés, platitudes and bromides for the American Museum of Iniquitous Antiquities.

Somewhat surprisingly, the poachers are not baseball writers, or even baseball broadcasters. They are horse race reporters fetlock deep in turf lore, and each is better than a green hand with an inept aphorism, himself.

They have submitted the following record of an interview, presumably overheard, between an applicant for a job as baseball writer and a sports editor who wonders whether the candidate can make the grade, fill the breach and carry the ball:

Question (by sports editor): What is baseball?

Answer: The national pastime.

Q.: Good, very good. Now, what is the game played with?

A.: The horsehide and ash.

Q.: Excellent. And what else?

A.: The sphere, hassocks. . . .

Q.: Yes, yes, I see you have the idea. And what is the game played on?

A.: It is played on the velvety sward.

Q.: Identify the home team.

A.: Our heroes.

Q.: And they oppose?

A.: The hated visitors.

Q.: Now, where do both teams go in the spring?

A.: They head for sunny climes.

Q.: Where do they go on road trips?

A.: To the hinterlands.

Q.: Fine, fine. What is another name for umpires?

A.: The arbiters, the men in blue, or, collectively, the Three Blind Mice.

Q.: What is a rookie?

A.: A rookie is The New Dazzy Vance, The New Babe Ruth, The New Ty Cobb, in special circumstances The Left-Handed Dizzy Dean.

Q.: What does the rookie who is The New Ty Cobb run like?

A.: A deer.

Q.: What has he for an arm?

A.: A rifle.

Q.: On days when he doesn't run like a deer, what does he run like?

A.: The wind.

Q.: Anything else?

A.: A gazelle.

Q.: Corking, corking! What is the manager?

A.: The Gallant Skipper, The Silent Strategist, The Tall Tactician, The Brain. . . .

Q.: Fine, that's enough. What is the president of the club?

A.: The prexy.

Q.: And prexies as a group?

A.: Magnates.

Q.: What is a pitching arm?

A.: The old soupbone.

Q.: What sometimes happens to old soupbones?

A.: They get chips.

Q.: Where do the chips go?

A.: To Johns Hopkins.

Q.: What happens after they are removed?

A.: GIANT HOPES SOAR AS JANSEN PREDICTS 20 WINS.

Q.: What is the name of that type of headline?

A.: Set and hold for spring.

Q.: Describe a man who has played baseball for five years.

A.: An old pro with know-how.

Q.: With anything else?

A.: With diamond savvy.

Q.: What is the Eddie Stanky type?

A.: A holler guy.

Q.: What else?

A.: A take-charge guy.

Q.: Can you elaborate?

A.: He is a sparkplug.

Q.: What does the sparkplug do?

A.: He keeps the pennant machine rolling along.

Q.: What is it when a man hits the ball out of the park?

A.: A four-master, a round-tripper, a circuit clout. . . .

Q.: Good, good, you're doing splendidly. Now, let me ask you this: What do you call it when two men are retired on one play?

A.: A double play.

Q.: A double play! A double play! Anything else?

A.: Well, a—er, rippling double play?

Q.: Think boy, think! Isn't there—uh—say, a twin answer to the question?

A.: A twin answer?

Q.: Yes, twin, twin, t-w-i-n.

A.: I'm sorry, sir, it's just a double play to me. I can't think of anything else to call it.

Q.: Well, son, maybe I'm being a bit hasty about this. Maybe I don't need a new baseball writer. Tell you what I'll do; I'm going to put your name on the list. Leave your address here and I'll drop you a line if anything turns up.

—April 15, 1952

Through Cranberry-Colored Glasses

"THE DAILY WORKER," whose enthusiasm for American sports is not noticeably greater than its affection for the American capitalistic system, nevertheless makes a concession to decadent Western tastes by publishing a sports column entitled "On the Scoreboard," by Lester Rodney. It is written with approximately the same carefree gaiety and spritely wit that characterized the Communist manifesto of Marx and Engels, court trials in Moscow and trainloads of happy excursionists bound for Siberian salt mines.

Recently the author peered through his cranberry-colored glasses at baseball and was saddened by the degenerate ethics of the game. More in sorrow than in anger, he commented upon the moral slackness of ball players who, mistakenly ruled safe at the plate with the winning run, do not arise in dusty robes of honor to correct the umpire.

Subsequently there appeared in "On the Scoreboard" a letter from Prof. Howard Selsam, director of the Jefferson School of Social Science and something of a student of Marxist ethical theory.

"You finally admitted," Mr. Selsam reminds Mr. Rodney, "that there was a basic lack of ethics in the situation in baseball in which a player would not correct the umpire when he ruled erroneously in his favor—when the player knew he was out, for example, but the umpire called him safe.

"At the same time, you agreed that if a player were to declare the umpire wrong, when to do so would go against his own team, he would be regarded as 'nuts' and would be out of the game for the rest of his life. You further admitted that you feared you yourself would be unable to act in such an 'ethical' way in a baseball game. . . .

"I think that you . . . missed the distinction between the type of game governed by mutually accepted moral standards and the 'mass production' games, such as American football, basketball and baseball, which are basically professional and in which the sole possible goal is to win, by no matter what means."

Brooding at considerable length upon the subject, Mr. Selsam inquires "How is it that this great game has become so commercialized and corrupted and so played to win at any cost that all other considerations are thrown to the winds?"

Asking the question, "How can such approaches to athletic contests be eliminated?" he decides the solution is "not contradicting the umpire to the detriment of your team, but fighting for socialism under which all sports appear in their true light as valuable and significant forms of human activity and recreation."

Well, kids, this points the way pretty clearly. There can't be much doubt that the capitalistic system, the profit motive, is to blame for the appalling moral standards in sports. Why is a ballplayer like Phil Rizzuto, who seems such a decent, honorable little fellow when you meet him on the subway, reluctant to call himself out when the umpire thinks he is safe?

Why, it is because the rules do not require him to do so, and Phil wishes to be as successful as possible within the rules and help his team win as often as possible, so he can earn large, coarse sums of dirty old repulsive money and maybe grow up to be a fat and loathsome capitalist with a silk hat and great vulgar yellow diamond studs in his sloppy shirt front.

In a truly democratic society (i.e., socialist state), no such low and selfish motives would prevail. Comrade Stanislavov Musial, of the Louisgrad Cardinals, would not strive to hit line drives against Comrade Maxim Surkont, of the Bostonik Workers, because all men would be brothers and Comrade Musial would not wish to do injury to his fellow man.

A comrade going from first to second base would not slide into the comrade shortstop to break up a double play, because that would be playing to win and, besides, sliding is hard on the worker's behind.

If Comrade Leon Durocher realized that the umpire had erred in calling Comrade Willie Mays safe at third, he would instantly halt play and say, "Let us all be patient, Comrade Dascolivich, and strive to improve. My man was out."

We know that happy ideal would be achieved because we have the example of Russian athletes, who care so little about winning that they usually decline to enter competitions where the result is in doubt, and if they are defeated, they patiently change the rules to reverse the decision.

"We must struggle to create the kind of society," writes Mr. Selsam, "in which all athletics, all sports, will be forms of creative activity and not commercialized spectacles controlled by big-money interests. Only under socialism can all sports and their participants be governed by ethical principles."

Perhaps Mr. Selsam would be encouraged to know that we are closer to the goal than he thinks. When Rogers Hornsby was serving his first hitch as manager of the Browns, he applied an automatic $100 fine against any pitcher who did not waste the third pitch when the count was two strikes and no balls. In such a situation one day, the St. Louis pitcher lost control and clipped the outside corner for a called third strike.

The batsman, a good citizen, acknowledged the voice of authority meekly, but everybody in the park could hear the scream of protest and supplication from the pitcher.

"No, no, no!" he cried, rushing toward the plate. "Please Bill, the ball was a foot outside!"

—April 27, 1952

A Chapter Closes

IT WASN'T THE end of the story, but a chapter was coming to a close. It began —well, of course it really began three or four years ago when Willie Mays was a high school kid playing at nights and on weekends with the Birmingham Black Barons when the club was at home, but hardly anybody got to read any of it until a little more than a year ago.

Then Willie, who had moved swiftly up in the Giants' chain through Trenton, N.J., to Minneapolis, started hitting about .250 for the Millers. As Tom Sheehan, the Giants' chief scout, recalls it: "We pick up the papers one week and say, 'Hey, Willie's hitting .300.' Next week we look and it's .350. Another week and it's .400. Finally, holy mackerel, Willie's up to .477, which has to mean he's going at something like a .600 clip, after that slow start. So he's got to come to New York.

"When the Giants called him up, Tommy Heath, the manager out in Minneapolis, told me over the phone, 'Tom, you'll think I"m crazy but this is the only guy I ever saw can bat .500.' "

It was just one year ago yesterday when Willie Mays went to bat for the first time in the Polo Grounds. He had joined the Giants on the road and had gone up twelve times without a hit but now, in his first appearance in the park that was to become his home, he got hold of a pitch by Boston's Warren Spahn.

It cleared the fence in left. It cleared the seats in the lower deck. It cleared the tall upper deck. It cleared the roof above that, and disappeared.

"That," said Spahn after the game, "Was one of the best curves I ever threw in my life. It must've broke a foot."

So now, a year later, Willie was in Ebbets Field wearing the gray flannels of the Giants for the last time in—a year? Two years? Eternity? Nobody knows.

This morning Willie reports to the Army Induction Center in Whitehall St. and when they fit him with a soldier suit his future becomes something nobody in the world can predict. The story may not be done but the chapter is ended. New York had whipped the Dodgers twice and taken first place away from them, and on any other occasion the Giants would have been replaying those victories before this game and chattering jubilantly about Sal Maglie's four-hit shutout of Tuesday night. Instead, they were talking about Willie.

Leo Durocher, who has become a genius among defensive managers —with Willie playing practically his whole outfield—was saying how he wished the Army would take him and leave Willie. Maybe he wouldn't hit with Willie in camp games, the manager was saying, but he could rack up pool balls in the PX and do K.P. and pick up waste paper in the area and handle other such soldierly chores in Willie's stead.

Up in the stands, a Brooklyn fan was saying, "He plays the outfield like he's there all alone. A ball is hit and he flaps his arms like a bird."

In the press box a man said, "Leo's instructions to Willie are to catch anything he can reach, in left or center or right. He has top priority on all fly balls and it's up to the other outfielders to get out of his way."

Another man said, "Somebody down on the field was saying that if the Giants think Don Mueller and Henry Thompson are slow, wait till they see that outfield without Willie and they'll learn what the word 'slow' really means."

When the batting orders were announced, there was a fine, loud cheer for Willie. This was in Brooklyn, mind you, where "Giant" is the dirtiest word in the language. And the Giant they were talking about and cheering is a baby, only one year old in the major leagues, a child who is only learning to play baseball.

As it turned out, the Giants made it three straight for the Brooklyn series, stretching their lead to two and a half games, with only a modicum of help from Willie. They didn't need his aid because Jim Hearn pitched a four-hitter, digging his own way out of difficulties created by some shoddy fielding, and young Dave Williams hit two doubles and a home run.

Willie took a third strike, flied out, grounded out and lined out on his four turns at bat, and his only play in the field was on a line drive by Carl Furillo, which Willie charged so hard the collision would have been fatal if he'd missed the catch.

The score was 6 to 1 and Brooklyn fans had given up when Willie came to bat for the last time. Suddenly the playground bubbled with noise, everybody in the place howling, clapping, yelling for a farewell hit.

Willie took a mighty swing, topped the ball so that it cracked down on his left foot, sprawled across the plate, and the cheers went on unabated. He took another fierce riffle, and missed. Then he lined low and hard and straight to Pee Wee Reese at shortstop. Cheers followed him to the dugout steps, where he tipped his cap hurriedly.

He was standing with arms folded in center field when the game ended. As he jogged toward the dugout, all four umpires purposely cut across the diamond to wave goodby. He caught up with the victorious Hearn, offered a hand, and hesitated at the dugout, where three or four kids were pushing score cards and autograph books toward him.

Then he disappeared in the tunnel to the clubhouse, where his playmates gave him a portable radio and he got a tie clasp, suitable for dress uniforms, from Leo and Laraine Durocher.

On the organ, Gladys Goodding played, "I'll See You in My Dreams."
—*May 29, 1952*

Monstrous Infant

HELSINKI—They played a ball game here last night, and if there's a stone left upon a tomb in Cooperstown today it's an upset. What the Finns did to the game which Doubleday did not invent shouldn't happen in Brooklyn, not even under its Finnish name "Pesapallo."

Although Pesapallo is only about thirty years old, it is a monstrous infant that has grown up to be Finland's national sport. It was invented by Lauri Pihkala, a professor who wears a hearing aid and believes his game was modeled on baseball. Somebody must have described baseball to him when his battery was dead.

"Well," explained a tolerant Finn, "he took baseball and, ah—." He paused to grope for a word meaning adapted, "—and, ah, mutilated it," he said.

Somebody then performed the same service for the English language while composing program notes to explain Pesapallo to foreigners.

"The batsman, or striker,' wrote this Helsinki Rud Rennie, "must try by power of hit of his own and teamfellows to run from base to base with home-base as final objective. The striker is allowed three serve; i.e., a serve rising at least one-half meter above his head and falling, if not connected by the bat, within base-plats with a diameter of 60 cm."

If that doesn't make you see the game with vivid clarity there seems little use of further elucidation. Stick around, though, if you've nothing better to do.

Pesapallo hasn't yet achieved Olympic status and was presented merely as an exhibition for about 25,000 spectators in Olympic Stadium. Two nine-man teams came trotting in from the outfield in single file, converged in a "V" at home plate and removed caps. Their captain stepped forward and shook hands with the referee, a joker in cinnamon brown carrying a bat, possibly in self-defense. The players wore baseball uniforms, white for one team, malevolent red for the other.

Four other jokers in brown did a lock step on to the field. These were "assistant controllers" or base umpires. A tasty shortcake in gay peasant costume threw a ball out to the referee and dropped a deep curtsy. The referee fired the ball—which is about the size and weight of a 10-cent "rocket"—to the server, blew a long blast on a police whistle, the game was on.

A Pesapallo field is a lopsided pentagon 278 feet long and 131 feet wide at its broadest. The pitcher stands across the plate from the batter and tosses the ball straight up like a fungo hitter. Base runners all act like Dodgers gone berserk.

That is, they start for third base and then get lost. First base is just where Phil Rizzuto likes to place his bunts; in Yankee Stadium it would be between third base and the mound. If Finns didn't use chalk lines instead of fences, second base would be against the right-field wall. Third is directly opposite, on the left-field boundary. The route from there home is a dogleg to the left. The plate is a trash can cover, two feet in diameter.

The pitcher may fling the ball as high as he chooses but if it doesn't drop on the garbage can lid it's outside the strike zone. Two successive faulty serves—they must be consecutive—constitute a walk, but the batter goes to first only when there are no runners aboard. Otherwise the runner who has advanced farthest takes one more base.

The batter gets three strikes but nobody is required to run on a hit except on the third strike. Players are retired only on strikeouts, pick-offs or throws that beat them to a base. On a fly that is caught, the batter is only "wounded"; he is not out.

A wounded man just stands aside and awaits his next turn at bat. One who has been put out may not bat again in the same inning; if his turn comes around, they skip him. An inning ends after three putouts or after all nine men have batted without scoring a run. (This can happen if enough men are wounded.)

That's about all, except that over the fence would be a foul ball if there were a fence. Hits must bounce in fair territory. A Ralph Kiner would be a bum in Pesapallo; a Leo Durocher whose fungo stick is a squirrel rifle that can brush a fly off an infielder's ear, would be a Finnish Willie Keeler.

This game progressed at bewildering speed with the ball practically always in motion. There is no balk rule. The server would fake a toss for the batter and whip the ball to a baseman on an attempted pick-off. The baseman would fake a throw back and try the hidden-ball play. Infielders, outfielders, and the pitcher-catcher, they heaved that apple around with the sleight-of-hand of the Harlem Globetrotters.

They played the hit-and-run, with the batter clubbing the ball into the earth like a man beating a snake, then standing still at the plate while the base runners sprinted across the landscape. Everybody show-boated frantically. Base umpires lifted cardboard signs to signal "safe" or "out" and the referee announced decisions on his whistle in a sort of morse code of dots and dashes.

Finally a guy named Eino Kaakkolahti slapped a bounding ball past one infielder, through a second infielder, and past an outfielder, with one runner on base. It was a triple, which counts as a home run in Finland. That was as much as one foreigner can take.

—*August 2, 1952*

The Appearance of Evil

THE SINGLE BASIC purpose of all the rules governing the operation of professional baseball clubs is to guarantee equal, fair and honest competition. The rules are written with that end in view, they are administered to serve that goal—and then the men who create the rules and hire the men to enforce them go off and rack their brains seeking ways to evade, nullify and contravene their own regulations.

This is true, no matter how eloquently the Yankees' Dan Topping may dispute it, of the rule forbidding exchanges of players among major-league teams after June 15. If club owners like Dan Topping appreciated what damage their trespasses against this rule do to the public faith in baseball, they would take the pledge.

Guys like Dan Topping do not know the damage they do because they are obsessed—as perhaps they should be—with winning. The only fans they meet are those who swarm through the Stadium Club following a winner and applauding every Yankee coup. The noise made by these fair-weather friends drowns out the suspicious and discontented muttering of the millions who are genuinely important, the real baseball fans.

To put it as bluntly as possible, the real baseball fans—or, at least, a great many of them—feel the Yankees are stealing the pennant this season and have been doing so for years. It isn't particularly important whether they are right or wrong. The vital thing, for baseball, is to cease giving them cause for suspicion.

It is a wise rule which provides that major-league clubs may not sell or trade players to one another after June 15. Certainly it is a liberal rule. It gives an owner and manager all winter, all spring and two months of the championship season to tinker with their team and get it set for the race.

After that, the teams are supposed to fight it out on their merits. The rule is intended to make it impossible for a rich club to go out in August or September and outbid less affluent rivals for the one man needed to bring off a championship.

Each summer for several years now, the fans have seen the Yankees reach out when the struggle got hot and pluck out of the National League a Johnny Mize or Johnny Hopp or John Sain or Ewell Blackwell. The fans have concluded that the rule against exchanging players during a pennant race applies to the poor, but not the rich. They think championships are being decided not on the field, but on the auction block.

It's bad enough when the fans come to believe this is so. It is worse when they are right. And they are.

It would be unwise and unfair to put an absolute freeze on every club roster on June 15 and permit no changes of any sort thereafter. Consequently, a club is permitted to bring up help from the minors and dispose of useless major-leaguers by the waiver method. This simply means offering the expendable player to all other clubs in the league for $10,000. If nobody claims him at that figure, he can be sold to the highest bidder in any other league.

In recent years, National League clubs have contrived to get waivers on players whom the Yankees wanted so the players could be sold to the Yankees at prices far above the waiver figure. On the surface this is entirely legal. Topping is telling the truth when he says that the Yankees have not violated the letter of the rule in these deals. He is mistaken when he says there has been no violation of the spirit of the rule.

By flashing their fat bankroll, the Yankees have baited National League clubs into evasions of the rule. The clubs employ devious devices to get waivers on players they want to sell.

Sometimes they do it by asking waivers repeatedly and withdrawing the request whenever there is a claim, until their seven lodge brothers despair of getting the man for $10,000 and don't bother to enter claims. Sometimes they load a waiver list with the names of all their best players, creating such an absurdity that nobody attempts to claim a lot of guys they know aren't for sale. Sometimes there is collusion among the owners, with favors given now on the promise that similar courtesies will be returned later.

It is ridiculous to rail at the league presidents, Will Harridge and Warren Giles, or at the baseball commissioner, Ford Frick, and say they ought to put a stop to this sharp practice. Under the rules, they can't put a stop to it unless they have supportable evidence of collusion in the granting of waivers. Harridge and Giles and Frick can't change the rules; that's the owners' prerogative.

The remedy lies with the owners, who must either abide by their own rules or revise and tighten them.

Hank Greenberg, of the Indians, has suggested that a club wishing to dispose of a player be required to get waivers from both major leagues instead of just its own league. This would make it more difficult to manipulate player contracts, but not impossible.

Another remedy, and perhaps a better one, would be to abolish the right to withdraw a request for waivers. The majors tried out something approaching this a few years ago. They provided that waiver requests could be withdrawn only once; if waivers were asked a second time and a claim was entered, the player had to be sold at the waiver price.

This rule didn't last. It took all the fun out of hanky-panky.

—September 3, 1952

The Forgotten Men

HALF A DOZEN baseball players sat in a wretched huddle in the darkest corner of a midtown hash house. They were silent, glum, staring miserably at the plates before them. It was a tableau to wring tears from the most stony-hearted onlooker, for these were the forgotten men of the national game. Nobody, but nobody, had offered to shoot them.

It must be a humiliating experience for a ball player to go through this summer playing day and night, running and hitting and fielding and throwing to the limit of his ability, without receiving a single death threat in return.

Everybody who is anybody in baseball is getting threatening letters this season. It is the hallmark of success, the accolade of fame, setting the great apart from the faceless failures.

Consider the identity of those whose anonymous correspondents have promised to plug them on sight. They are either the best or the richest. The slobs get nothing but adoring fan letters, signed with name and address and sometimes enclosing stamped envelopes.

The roster of those who have been dignified by the promise of a sudden and violent end reads like a roll of honor—Ralph Kiner, Bobby Shantz, Warren Spahn, Joe Black. The committee of baseball writers appointed to select the "most valuable" players of the American and National League wouldn't go far wrong if they confined their attention to this select group.

To be sure, it wasn't merely because of Kiner's ability to massage a curve that the big Pittsburgh outfielder was honored. A coarse commercial note crept into his letter from a correspondent who demanded money under threat of making Nancy Chaffee a widow.

It must have made Ralph feel like the heiress who can never be sure whether she is loved for herself or her old man's pelf. Still, Ralph can console himself with the thought that if he weren't able to beat a baseball out of shape he wouldn't be rich, so his was a kind of roundabout compliment, at that.

If Shantz doesn't walk away with the American League's most valuable player award, somebody had better demand a recount. At this writing the little lefthander of the Athletics' pitching staff has received three threatening letters and is lengths ahead of the field.

Spahn, of course, has been eligible for years to be drilled by some Dodger or Giant fan, and if Black hasn't stirred homicidal notions wherever the Dodgers have traveled it was not for want of trying.

Outside of the Post Office and the Department of Justice, where officials take a rather humorless view of threatening letters, the fad has got to be a poor joke. It could not, however, have seemed altogether hilarious to Kiner, the first to be designated as a clay pigeon.

In spite of a written reminder that his broad and muscular back would offer a tempting target in left field, he went out and played errorless ball, and also slugged a home run. One can imagine him standing with his back to the bleachers reassuring himself over and over that nobody who wasn't completely deranged would try to get away with target practice in such a public place.

"But suppose," he must surely have asked himself, "suppose the cluck that wrote that letter really is as nutty as he sounds. Suppose he's sitting up there behind me drawing a bead right now."

The thought must also have occurred to him that Forbes Field hasn't been an especially public place this summer. The way the Pirates have been drawing, a guy could be rubbed out in left field and the body might not be found for weeks.

Even so, it is better to be scared a little than not to be noticed at all. Ralph may have had some uncomfortable moments but his distress was nothing compared to the despair of a guy who never encounters anybody except shrieking idolators clamoring for his autograph, never feels a small, hard pressure against his spine or hears a voice in his ear rasping, "Okay, Mac, keep walking and no funny stuff, see?"

If it is any comfort to those who have been threatened and those who have been ignored, the history of organized baseball records no instance of a player being knocked off by a fan during an actual game. Some have been skulled by glassware flung down the stands or pelted with decadent vegetation, and a few were seriously injured.

On the whole, however, people who throw things from the stands seldom have much in the way of control, or Durocher would have them down on the field pitching for the Giants.

As a matter of fact, physical violence or threats thereof always have been the sincerest form of flattery. It was so away back in 1922 when Whitey Witt, playing center field for the Yankees, had his sconce dented by a pop bottle hurled from the bleachers in St. Louis.

Although badly hurt, Whitey recovered in time to read some of the most flattering prose ever written about any athlete. It was composed by Mr.

Buck O'Neill, a righteous man who was a tenant of the press box that day, whom the incident stirred to a perfect froth of creative inspiration.

"When you throw a pop bottle at Whitey Witt's head," Buck wrote in a foam-flecked paragraph of indignation, "you are throwing a pop bottle at the foundation stone of our national game!"

—September 6, 1952

Dept. of Emotional Reactions

WHEN CARL ERSKINE was a kid pitcher in Montreal he was personally scouted by Branch Rickey, then the principal indoor genius of the Dodgers. Watching with broody gaze from under the dark tangle of his brows, Rickey saw the young man win a two-hit shutout, tossed away the cold carcass of his cigar, and took himself back to Brooklyn alone.

Rickey journeyed north again for the same purpose and Erskine responded by winning another, 2 to 1. The great man pulled his circuit rider's black slouch hat lower over his eyes and returned to his lair in Montague St., alone.

It happened again and again. Rickey made four, maybe five trips to Montreal just to look at Erskine, and not once did the International League hitters get more than one run off the kid.

"What in the holy name of A. Doubleday," Erskine was asking himself, "does the man expect me to do? Have I got the wrong idea about this game?"

There came at length a night when Rickey sat in the stands as Erskine struggled and scrambled through a game to win, 6 to 5. That's when Rickey took him for Brooklyn. He didn't bother to clear up the young man's bewilderment until much later. Then he told him:

"Carl, I was waiting to observe your emotional reaction in a game when you didn't have your best stuff."

Students of emotional reactions had 70,536 of them to ponder yesterday in Yankee Stadium while Erskine labored all through the sunny afternoon and into the sultry dusk to win the fifth game of the World Series for the Dodgers, 6 to 5, in eleven tremendous innings.

Customers expressed their emotions by wild animal cries, by boos and cheers for a California politician named Richard Nixon—first Republican to be jeered by a World Series crowd since Herbert Hoover got it in 1931—and, in one instance, by slugging an usher earnestly upon the mandible.

But if young Mr. Erskine felt any emotion himself he didn't show it until he had thrown a third strike past Yogi Berra for the game's last putout.

Then, grinning like a billiken, he suffered himself to be thumped and hugged and patted and mauled by all such Dodgers as were able to lay a paw upon him.

Those who couldn't get through the pack around Erskine ran out to intercept Duke Snider and beat upon him. Snider had won the game once with a two-run homer which put the Dodgers in front, 4 to 0, then tied it with a one-run single after John Robert Mize had sent the Yankees ahead, then won it again with a one-run double in the eleventh.

Erskine is an agreeable young man with good habits and an equally good overhand curve. He does not drink, does not smoke and does not choke in the clutch. On out-of-town business trips, while his playmates sit in the hotel lobby waiting for somebody to discard a newspaper, he visits art museums.

He was a no-hit pitcher against the Chicago Cubs on June 19 and no pitcher at all against the Yankees last Thursday, when New York batted him out of the second game and beat him, 7 to 1. That day his father may have wondered whatever gave him the idea of traveling from Anderson, Ind., to Brooklyn to see his son pitch. Yesterday Erskine pere's doubts were dispelled.

Until the fifth inning, the only hit against Carl was a bunt by Mickey Mantle. There were four hits in the fifth, including a home run by Mize. Erskine must have been fairly beside himself after that destructive blow. At least, he was beside the Yankees, with both hands at their throats.

He retired the next nineteen batsmen who faced him. No others came up.

Unlike some men who forget their wedding anniversaries, Erskine is a dutiful husband. He was married five years ago yesterday.

Erskine, Snider, Mize and Nixon—these were the featured actors of the most lurid entertainment yet offered in baseball's big show. Arriving late, waving and bowing, exchanging salutations with the Dodgers' Jackie Robinson, signing autographs, posing for pictures eating hot dogs, posing drinking pop, the Senator proved himself the most gifted grandstand performer since Happy Chandler.

Not even Republicans, however, hailed him as boisterously as they did Mize. When John Robert socked that three-run wallop for his third World Series homer in three successive days, the whole joint trembled. When he reappeared from the dugout to play first base, a noisier tumult saluted him; when it was announced over the public address system that the hit was his 2,000th against big-league pitching, eardrums split. The announcement was witless, for the figure includes hits made in World Series and All-Star games. No such figure will appear in the record books until Mize makes fifteen more hits in regular league games.

However, he deserved the applause. After all, he's older than Nixon, been around longer.

—October 6, 1952

Curtain Calls

EARLY IN THE game Arthur Patterson, the Yankees' trumpeter, walked through the press box asking, "Will you come to our victory party if we win?" Frank Graham Jr., the Dodgers' dean of American literature, came later and his tone was more wistful. "If we should have a victory party, will you come?" he asked, emphasizing the first part of the sentence.

After all, these celebrations had been going on for forty-nine years and the Dodgers never had tossed one. They still haven't. A couple of citizens named Mickey Mantle and Bob Kuzava saw to that yesterday. Abetted by sundry playmates, this pair won the seventh and deciding game of the World Series, 4 to 2, putting an end to the liveliest baseball show in eighteen years.

Not since the Dean family's brother act in 1934 has there been an entertainment to compare with the one that closed at 3:54 p.m. yesterday in Ebbets Field. It wound up with all the stars and supers on stage taking curtain calls—Joe Black, Preacher Roe, Carl Erskine, Ed Lopat, Allie Reynolds, Vic Raschi and even Kuzava, the specialist whom Casey Stengel keeps around exclusively for pitching in final games of World Series.

The only guy who wasn't there was Ralph Branca, who was invited out by Larry Goetz, the plate umpire, for overdoing eloquence in the Brooklyn dugout. Last year Ralph was invited out by Bobby Thomson, of the Giants.

Kuzava is a Polish name that sounds like some kind of melon.

Anyhow, that's how it sounds to the Yankees, who cut up thirty-four slices worth $6,360 each last night.

A year ago in the final game the Yankees were three putouts short of their third successive world title when the Giants filled the bases with none out. Casey Stengel called in Kuzava to protect Johnny Sain's lead of 4 to 1.

Monte Irvin flied out on Kuzava's first pitch, scoring a run. Bobby Thomson flied out, scoring another. With the Yankee lead reduced to 4 to 3, Sal Yvars lined out and the Series was over.

Yesterday the Yankees were leading, 4 to 2, when the Dodgers filled the bases with one out in the seventh inning. Stengel, who couldn't have visited his pitchers oftener if they'd been rich inlaws, went calling again. With one hand he reached to pat Raschi's lofty bottom consolingly, with the other he beckoned to the bullpen.

Kuzava came in to pitch to Archduke Snider, of Brooklyn's royal family. With the count three balls and two strikes, the best-loved Flatbush entertainer since Henry Ward Beecher popped up. Jackie Robinson got two balls, two strikes. Then he popped up.

The ball that Robinson hit bore, in addition to Warren Giles's signature, the name of Joe Collins. It was the Yankee first baseman's to catch but with the sun slanting into his face across the grandstand roof, he couldn't see where it was. He stood gazing curiously aloft, wondering about life. Billy Martin, the second baseman, stood gazing curiously at Collins, wondering about him.

For what seemed a full week, nobody moved. In fact, Collins still hasn't. Martin did, though, and fast. He moved forward, broke into a jog, then stretched into a full run as the wind carried the descending ball away from him toward the plate. He ran harder and harder, ran himself clear out from under his cap, and managed at the last instant to get his glove under the ball.

That closed the inning and put an end to the last real chance the Dodgers ever had to win a world championship. Since Brooklyn got a baseball franchise in 1890, there have been six opportunities to beat a team of American League champions.

The Brooklyn-Cleveland series of 1920 went seven games but in those days a club had to win five and the Dodgers got only two. In 1947 they beat the Yankees three times in another seven-game match. In neither of those years, however, did they play so well or have anything like the opportunities to win that they enjoyed this time.

This time they weren't playing Yankees named DiMaggio and Henrich and Keller and Ruffing. They weren't even playing Indians named Smith and Sewell and Wambsganss and Uhle and Speaker or Red Sox named Hooper and Hoblitzel and Lewis.

This was a series in which neither team looked good enough to win more than one game. The Yankees ran off with that game, 7 to 1, but in no other contest was either club able to take charge. A team would get a one-run lead and the opposition would get it back the same inning, or the next.

They pulled and mauled and wrestled around and it took a guy named Kuzava, one of the most obscure of Yankees, to wrap it up. When the last pitch of the series was batted by Pee Wee Reese into the glove of Gene Woodling, the whole Yankee squad spewed out of the dugout or rushed in from the field to pelt Kuzava around, mauling him, knocking his hat off, pounding lumps all over him.

Meanwhile Woodling was running in from left field, flinging his arms about and leaping like a man with a hernia.

—October 8, 1952

A Bus Named Adolphus

ST. PETERSBURG, FLA.—August Adolphus Busch Jr., the new president of the Cardinals, is a chubby gentleman called Gussie, about the size of a St. Louis brewer. He has horn-rimmed glasses, a zillion dollars and an air of pleased bewilderment. He rides to the hounds and travels by bus.

The bus is named Adolphus, after Gussie's grandfather. It is a plush job that looks like a Greyhound wearing white tie and tails. It has a paneled interior, sleeping accommodations for eight, and several footmen out on the front porch.

If Adolphus carries Gussie through towns in the Cardinals' minor league chain this summer, chances are his well-shaped ears will be assaulted by hoarse, gasping cries of thirsty citizens. When the clubs were taken over by Anheuser-Busch, a firm that has specialized for generations in moistening the palates of this nation, the immediate result was to remove beer from the minor league parks.

The laws of many states forbid breweries to own or operate saloons, even indirectly. It doesn't apply to Sportsman's Park in St. Louis, where beers are sold, including Griesedieck, whose manufacturer spends $600,000 a year on the Cardinals' radio broadcasts to advertise his product in competition with Busch's Budweiser.

However, because the Houston, Rochester and Columbus clubs now are in the same stable as the brewer's big horses, beer of any brand will be illegal in those parks.

Comes the hot summer and fainting fans will be heaped in windows in the grandstands clawing at their neckties and crying piteously for sustenance—"Buns! Hot dogs! Beer! For the love of Heaven!"

The arrival of Gussie and Adolphus here this week was reminiscent of a story told about a similar occasion when Powel Crosley, having just bought the Cincinnati Reds, made his first visit to their training camp. Crosley was due to arrive for the opening of the exhibition schedule, and nervous lackeys attached to the club stalled around scanning the skies until his red plane hove into view.

The new owner was gathered up, tenderly convoyed to the ball park by a fleet of scurrying junior executives, and eased into a box seat. One vice-president slid a cushion under the presidential stern, another placed a scorecard in his lap, a third thrust a bottle of pop into one nerveless hand, a fourth produced a sack of peanuts.

"Now, Mr. Crosley," they told him, "our boys are the big fellows wearing red stockings. That's first base over there, second there, third, and that white thing is home plate. It's quite simple; the man with the stick, called a bat—"

The first hitter for the visiting team slashed a shrieking drive that lifted the Reds' third baseman bodily into the air, performed an appendectomy on him, and bounced crookedly into left field.

There was a strained silence in the presidential box, or so the story goes. More in sorrow than in anger, the new owner shook his head.

"Tch-tch-tch," he said. "Errors, so early in the season."

A similar air of taut expectancy was discernible here when Gussie, preceded into town by a public relations expert, rolled up in Adolphus accompanied by assorted executives. Scarcely anybody connected with the Cardinals knew the new boss, for the sale of the club had been a hurried deal.

When it became necessary for Fred Saigh to dispose of his stock, Busch remarked idly to a vice-president that it would be a shame if the Cardinals were to leave St. Louis. The vice-president construed this as an order; inquiries were made and Saigh said he was about to accept an offer of $4,100,000 from a Milwaukee group.

In rapid negotiations, brokers' commissions were waived and cut off the purchase price, other details were arranged such as having Saigh put $1,000,000 in escrow to discharge any tax obligations which the club might have, and Anheuser-Busch bought the Cardinals for $3,750,000, subject to approval of the brewery stockholders. Holders of 1 per cent of the stock voted no.

Aware of the boss's interest in St. Louis's Bridlespur Hunt Club, the Cardinals half expected him to arrive on horseback wearing a pink coat and blowing a horn. Instead, he showed up wearing a woolen shirt of burgundy hue and the bemused expression of a fox hunter whose horse had dumped him into a thicket of newspaper men, photographers, television cables and newsreel cameras.

"How many ball games have you seen?" he was asked.

"Not a hell of a lot," he said.

He said his elderly associate, Mr. Anheuser, was overjoyed in the new role as club owner, because he'd been a kid third baseman sixty years ago.

From the field, the players stared with faint apprehension, hoping the front-office enthusiasm for bus riding wasn't catching.

—*March 15, 1953*

A Real Rough, Lovely Guy

BILL CISSELL WAS a rough, tough, go-to-hell guy out of the cavalry who served a ten-year stretch in American League infields with a couple of years off for bad behavior. The White Sox paid a good chunk of gold for him as a rookie in 1928 and he should have been a great star, but he drank.

He drank with the White Sox and the Indians and the Red Sox and he never made any secret about it because he was a dead honest guy. In the autumn of 1936 Connie Mack drafted him from Baltimore and Al Horwits, who was a Philadelphia baseball writer then, said: "He is a good ball player and he has had a couple of years down in the minors and the chances are he has learned his lesson."

"Yes," Connie said, "I understand he is not drinking in the daytime now."

This story isn't primarily about Bill Cissell but in order to make a point it is necessary to explain what sort of guy he was. It has been ten, maybe eleven years since Ciss was last encountered and that was out in California and he had a number of teeth missing. Not from age; probably from knuckles. He was a real rough, honest, lovely sort of guy.

Once he told a story about the first time he ever saw Ty Cobb. It was his rookie year with the White Sox and Cobb was an elderly gentleman playing out the string with the Athletics. Cobb went into third base, Ciss related, and Willie Kamm was in the way so Cobb upped with his spikes and cut Kamm out of the way.

All the White Sox were enraged because they were fond of Kamm, the quietest, most inoffensive guy on the ball club. None was more furious than Cissell, the rookie at second base.

Next time Cobb reached first base and started for second, Cissell got the ball and, holding it in his bare first, tagged Cobb squarely between the eyes. Then he invited Cobb to make something of it if he chose.

The ensuing dialogue, as Bill repeated it, eludes memory but the substance was this: Cobb, getting to his feet and dusting himself off, expressed willingness to meet Cissell under the stands after the game if Ciss insisted. But he managed to make it clear that he did not resent Cissell's energetic tactic and that he had used his spikes on Kamm without malice. Cobb had sought to reach third base and Kamm had endeavored to prevent it, and somebody had to lose.

Next day Cobb was out early giving Cissell a few pointers about playing ball.

There is another story which Grantland Rice tells about an evening in a hotel room with two retired ball players, Ty Cobb and Nig Clarke, the old Cleveland catcher.

Clarke was describing a technique he had perfected for retiring runners at the plate when there were two out. He'd catch the ball, make a sweeping gesture at the runner sliding home, roll the ball out toward the mound and walk to the dugout. Half the time, he said, he'd never tag the runner but it enabled him to dodge spikes and the umpire seldom knew the difference.

"I probably got you out ten or fifteen times," he told Cobb, "without ever laying the ball on you."

Cobb came out of his chair and across the room and he had Clarke by the throat when Granny pulled them apart.

"I'll kill him!" Cobb was screaming. "He cost me ten or fifteen runs off my record!"

This, mind you, was years after Cobb and Clarke had retired.

The point is, that's the way guys used to play ball. Today they make a Federal case of it when a guy named Martin belts a guy named Courtney and a ruckus ensues on the field.

Maybe the old guys were wrong and the young guys are right. Perhaps the Browns' Clint Courtney shouldn't provoke the Yankees' Billy Martin by sliding into Phil Rizzuto with his spikes showing.

Maybe Sal Maglie shouldn't pitch high and tight to Carl Furillo, and Furillo shouldn't retaliate by throwing his bat at Maglie. If that's the case, the Dodgers' president, Walter O'Malley, certainly should not reward Furillo with a $50 bonus.

It is difficult to say which attitude is the wiser. Today a fellow runs a considerable risk if he gets his features mussed up trying to win a ball game. It may cost him a remunerative post-game appearance on television. Meanwhile, attendance at the games declines.

—May 7, 1953

Year of Decision

IT IS HIGH time that doubts about the legality of the baseball industry's operating methods be resolved, once and for all. Three bush league lawsuits have been appealed to the Supreme Court and in the autumn the court will decide whether baseball is or is not interstate commerce subject to Federal anti-trust laws.

If the answer is yes, then the courts will be in position to rule on the question of whether anti-trust laws are violated by the "reserve clause," which is not a clause at all but a set of interlocking rules affecting player contracts. These are the rules that require a player signing his first contract to relinquish the right to pick his own job in the future.

Baseball men are not notably happier about the situation than any other business men would be about being dragged into court. However, for the ultimate good of the game and the business, there's got to be a decision.

There's a great big cavity in baseball's tooth. A slug of whisky held in the mouth for a time and then swallowed might give temporary relief. But sooner or later there must be a visit to the dentist's chair. The sooner the better.

In all probability the Supreme Court will rule that baseball is interstate commerce. This view is suggested by almost every precedent since Justice Oliver Wendell Holmes took the opposite position in 1922.

Holmes submitted that a ball game was essentially local in nature and that interstate travel of players, shipment of equipment and so on were only incidental to presentation of a local entertainment.

Since his day the view of interstate commerce has broadened immensely. It has been ruled, for example, that a window-washing firm which washed the windows of a company engaged in interstate commerce was itself engaged in interstate commerce.

When Danny Gardella brought suit in Federal District Court five years ago, the judge told him in effect: "Under the ground rules I am bound by Holmes' ruling and must dismiss your suit. But if you take it upstairs, I am pretty sure the Court of Appeals will reinstate the case."

He was right. The Court of Appeals did reinstate the case, on the grounds that interstate broadcasting and telecasting of ball games had altered the situation since 1922. In fact, Judge Jerome Frank called the Holmes precedent an "impotent zombie."

To be sure, the suits now in the Supreme Court could be settled without a decision, as Gardella's was. Two factors, however, make a settlement appear improbable.

For one thing, if there were a settlement at this point, the next Congressional investigation of baseball might nail all persons involved as possible parties to a conspiracy.

For another, baseball simply can't go on buying off every complainant who comes along. Payment of hush money only postpones the inevitable showdown.

In the Gardella case the Court of Appeals did not rule formally on the reserve clause, but Judge Frank remarked upon some "shockingly repugnant" aspects of the clause. With regard to salaries received by baseball's "quasi-peons," he said "only the totalitarian-minded will believe that higher pay excuses virtual slavery."

The same point could have been made with equal clarity in the

Mickey Jelke case, i.e., that a question of morality cannot be judged according to the price scale.

What has been said before must be said again: If the reserve clause is immoral, then it is up to baseball to find another way of protecting investments in player talent and preserving the major-minor league structure of the game.

Baseball men have realized this for a long time, but baseball men are curious creatures. Most club owners are outstanding successes in business, extraordinarily able in their own fields. But offer them a vexing baseball problem and their solution almost invariably is: "Let's pay no attention and maybe it'll go away."

Several years ago Louis Carroll, attorney for the National League, advised his owners to go home and think up some workable substitutes for the reserve clause. They returned at the next meeting empty of hand and head.

In their hair and ears and eyes were quantities of sand.

—May 27, 1953

The Great Unloved

A TOURIST RETURNED from the Middle West brings home a trove of souvenirs—a sign wired to the bumper reading: "Jesse James' Hideout, Meramec Caverns," a baseball autographed by Stan Musial, a postcard photo of a two-headed calf seen in Ohio—and a new understanding of the breadth and depth of this country's dislike for the New York Yankees.

Just as it is necessary to travel abroad to sample the envious resentment which many people feel toward rich America, so one must visit the lands beyond the Hudson to appreciate the antagonism roused by the wealth, the success, the swagger, the arrogance and the complacency of baseball's strong-arm tyrants. And like the noisy tourist abroad, the Yankees are not blameless.

At the start of July, the New York club's losing streak was, as it should have been, the top news on most sport pages. As defeat followed defeat and the team's long lead dwindled, more and gorier details were published, frequently under a headline that reflected the undisguised glee of the copyreader who had written it.

Everybody tried his hand at diagnosing the Yankees' ailments, and the tone of these essays was more like that of the mortician than the physician. As often as not the Yankee decline was seen not as a slump but, hopefully, as disintegration and total collapse. The hunting cry of Paul Richards, whose White Sox were closing in, echoed through the press.

The Yankees righted themselves, leveled off and slowly regained headway. Now the voice of the pack changed. Instead of the eager, joyful baying of the hunt, there came a yapping carping chorus.

Casey Stengel, one paper announced, had lost his sense of humor and was whining now about how everybody hated the Yankees. He complained bitterly, the author reported, that rival American League clubs saved their best pitchers to work against and torment his team. Did he expect the enemy to help him toward his fifth straight pennant by pitching ushers against him?

As a matter of fact, Casey and all other successful managers learned long ago that the leaders must always expect to face the opposition's best. He has remarked upon it often in the past, with a wry sort of pride, appreciating it for the compliment it is. Now they were reading a whimper into his familiar statement of a fact.

More recently the Yankee manager observed that Mickey Mantle might be more valuable to the team if he would only swing naturally instead of trying to pull every pitch for a record home run.

Chances are this was simple, dispassionate analysis of Mantle's batting form, but it came over the wires as a "peevish" complaint about the young star. A Midwestern paper ran the story under a three-column head declaring: "Casey Bites Off Tough Words at Golden Boy."

Wherever you go you hear fans say what a healthy thing it would be for baseball, what a pleasant touch of poetic justice, if Milwaukee were to win the National League pennant. It is difficult to find anybody to agree that the Yankees' effort to set a new record with five straight championships has the makings of an exciting sports story.

They can't get excited about the Yankees, and they don't want to. This is, in part, a natural human reaction against the rule that "them as has gets." Nobody gets a great emotional kick out of the spectacle of the rich getting richer. In part, however, the New York organization contributes to the ill-will it meets out of town.

The Yankees do swagger, not individually but as a team. Stengel almost never lets a challenge go unanswered.

For example, when it was written that the White Sox brainbund had discovered hitherto unsuspected flaws in the team and had broadcast the discoveries through the league so that all could play according to Chicago's "book," Casey snorted a rebuttal.

If the White Sox were so smart, he demanded, why didn't they write a "book" on the Philadelphia Athletics, who had been whipping Chicago regularly? This was a good enough answer, but no answer at all had been necessary.

A disposition to take quick offense and give back more is typical of the organization. Somehow the Yankee bosses seem always to be on the defensive; their corporate skin is the thinnest in baseball.

They do not appear able to realize that they occupy a position where they must always be a target. Constant criticism is part of the price of success, but the Yankees never want to pay the price.

They are forever issuing statements defending some club action or policy reproving the press, calling attention to their greatness. They would be more popular champions if they could understand how well a certain modest reticence becomes a champion.

—August 9, 1953

To the Losers, the Spoils

IT HAS BEEN written that Charley Grimm and Paul Richards probably will be knighted as "managers-of-the-year" this autumn, partly because of the excellent baseball which the Braves and White Sox have played, and partly because the electorate—i.e., the baseball writers—will be disinclined to vote for Charley Dressen and Casey Stengel.

This seems to suggest that because their teams have played well, Richards and Grimm have earned loftier professional esteem than Stengel and Dressen, whose teams have played better. Those who hold this view will rationalize it thus: Milwaukee under Grimm and Chicago under Richards, probable runners-up in the major leagues, have accomplished more than was expected of them when the season began; the Yankees and Dodgers were considered most likely to succeed in the first place, and have done no better than they should.

So here we go again with that seamed and creaking dispute. Who deserves the credit for success—the manager or the players? If a man is to be denied homage on the ground that he has good players, shouldn't the Browns' Marty Marion and the Pirates' Fred Haney stand elected by acclamation? They have the poorest players.

Sixteen managers were hired to win. Two are going to succeed. Now we are told that success disqualifies a candidate for canonization. We are to write off those who accomplish the job they were hired to do, and seek a purer excellence among those who fail.

As a manager—as student, teacher, leader and dean of men—Paul Richards has no warmer admirer than the voter in this booth. In thirty-four years since the 1919 World Series scandal, the White Sox have had thirteen managers and never has the team caused the commotion it has raised under Richards except, occasionally, in Jimmy Dykes's administration.

The manager's influence is reflected in the work of his men—in the pitching of Billy Pierce and Virgil Trucks, the hustle of Nellie Fox, the proficiency of Minnie Minoso, who is the league's most valuable player in this book.

Yet if Casey Stengel's Yankees win their fifth consecutive championship under his direction, how could anybody consider ranking another manager ahead of him? How could any manager in all the history of baseball be ranked above him, considering that no team in history has won five straight?

John McGraw never made such a record, nor Connie Mack, nor Frank Chance nor Miller Huggins nor Joe McCarthy. In their time, as in Casey's, there was a disposition to give all credit to the players and none to the leader. McGraw, they said, won by despoiling other teams of their talent; Connie had his "$100,000 infield"; Huggins had Ruth and Gehrig; McCarthy was the "push-button manager" of a troupe of robots.

Yet theirs are the names that are honored today, and all had better teams than Stengel's. If the play of the White Sox reveals Richards's fine hand, then there must be a little of old Casey in the Yankee picture.

Dressen's credentials do not match Stengel's—nor do any others—so there is more room for argument in the National League than in the American. However, the Dodgers' manager has converted a lot of non-believers this summer.

It was he who insisted, from the outset of spring training, that Junior Gilliam would be Brooklyn's second baseman. It required more than small faith to remove one of the game's finest from that position to make room for the kid. Gilliam has become a bona fide star.

When the season opened there was confusion at third base and in left field and Gil Hodges was suffering spiritual boils but the team was basically sound, except for its pitching. There some difficulty was anticipated, and even greater problems developed.

Joe Black was not the Black of 1952. Preacher Roe was wearing out. Ralph Branca was no help. Of the four top names on the staff, only Carl Erskine measured up. Until the end of June, Brooklyn's pitching staff was shabby as a reporter's wife.

Lacking quality, Dressen settled for quantity. His numbers game has paid off. Instead of one Joe Black he has used three men—Jim Hughes, Bob Milliken and Clem Labine—to furnish relief for his starters. Today Erskine is an ace. Johnny Podres and Billy Loes are solid winners. They do not always finish what they start, but there are always plenty of guys around to take charge when necessary.

Comparing the jobs done by Dressen and Grimm, two major differences are noted.

One is that Dressen began with a pennant winner, a team of established players, power hitters and gifted fielders, whereas Grimm moved into a new city with the remnants of a seventh-place club and a great raft of strangers. Instead of familiar names like Robinson, Snider, Campanella and Reese, the Braves' roster bore what looked like aliases—Bruton, Adcock, Mathews, Dittmer, Logan.

The other difference is that Dressen is going to win the pennant and Grimm will finish second.

—August 22, 1953

This Is Progress

THE CLASSIC EXAMPLE of a thick-head is the Brooklyn cop who found a dead horse on Kosciusko Street and dragged it around to Reid Avenue because he couldn't spell Kosciusko in his report. So he was stupid? Well, the intellectual giants who own the American League have been carrying a dead horse on their backs for years and are determined to go on toting it indefinitely because they can't pronounce "Veeck" without spitting.

At least, that was their expressed intention yesterday, though there was another meeting scheduled for last night and some faint hope existed that maybe a little sense could be batted through their skulls at that session.

With their St. Louis franchise dead and partly decomposed, the league's best brains assembled on Sunday to discuss disposal of the body. They sat and talked for nine hours and then voted to do nothing, tossing the problem back to the Department of Sanitation.

In the course of the wrangle, Baltimore was killed off as a possible home for a major league team and, probably, was ruined for minor league baseball as well.

This is progress.

Obviously, some of the owners who do not approve of Bill Veeck's taste in neckties are determined to drive him out of the game by blocking every move he tries to make to repair his rickety franchise. Obviously they do not care how much damage they do if they can achieve their ends.

On Sunday four of Veeck's seven lodge brothers voted down his proposal to move the Browns to Baltimore. The Yankees' Del Webb, who led the opposition, got one more vote than he needed to block the move. It is understood he was joined by the delegates from Boston, Philadelphia and Cleveland, at least one of whom was supposed to have promised Veeck his support.

Perhaps the Baltimore move would not have been ideal. A fifth Eastern club would throw the league out of geographical balance and there would be, as Webb pointed out, a heavy concentration of baseball between New York and Washington.

As compared with a hostile St. Louis, however, Baltimore's attractions are compelling. The sixth city of the country with a population of 1,000,000 and a potential of 2,000,000 in the metropolitan area, Baltimore offered a floodlighted stadium seating 51,750 for baseball, partially sheltered by an upper deck, with parking space on the grounds for 4,000 automobiles.

The city was enthusiastic over the prospect of returning to the majors and local capital was prepared to give Veeck the financial backing he needs.

It is a mystery what happens to smart, able, successful business men when they employ their talents in baseball. Here's Del Webb who'll take a multi-million-dollar contract to build a new city in the Arizona desert, and will get it built. Yet when action is called for on a proposition that was up before the owners away back in March and has been under examination ever since, Webb says, "Let's wait another thirty days and think about it."

Mayor Thomas D'Alesandro, of Baltimore, quite properly said nuts to that. Baltimore had been pushed around long enough and the fans wouldn't hold still for any more stalling. Either accept the proposition now or forget it.

The geniuses dealt with the problem by forgetting it.

They said they would look further into invitations from Los Angeles, San Francisco, Kansas City and Minneapolis. Strangely, nobody has come up yet with a bid from Las Vegas.

When Veeck attempted the switch to Baltimore in March, a St. Louis attorney named Jerome Duggan started yipping about going to law to keep the Browns at home. He and some friends showed up here at Sunday's meeting to vilify Veeck as a detriment to baseball and St. Louis.

Veeck has a lot of dizzy ideas, some of them unpalatable to the baseball brass and some altogether indigestible. Yet he wasn't a detriment to baseball in 1948 when he was festooning Cleveland dolls with orchids, employing baby-sitters in the stadium and otherwise whooping up a promotion that set an all-time baseball attendance record of 2,620,627. The owners of seven visiting clubs who shared the swag found nothing detrimental about profits.

He was not a detriment to St. Louis when he moved into the town and began pumping life into a moribund franchise, delighting the citizenry and driving Fred Saigh to distraction with the lively competition he gave Saigh's Cardinals.

What made him detrimental was that he went broke trying to promote baseball in St. Louis. That's unpardonable.

—September 29, 1953

Dodgers Defeat Yanks, 3–2, as Erskine Fans 14

THE LATE LAMENTED stirred fitfully yesterday, twitched, moaned softly and got shakily to their knees, helped up by a plump old gentleman with a busted paw and a young accident case of two days earlier. Yesterday the Dodgers was dead. Today they is weak and gasping for breath, but the breath is still in them.

Two days after he tripped, fell and was mangled by the Yankee juggernaut in one cruel inning, Brooklyn's Carl Erskine pitched a six-hit ball game in which he broke the famous World Series strikeout record established twenty-four years ago. Two days after a pitched ball smashed a knuckle on his right hand and rendered him apparently useless as a batter, ample old Roy Campanella wrapped his aching fist around a bat and slugged a home run that won for Erskine and the Dodgers, 3 to 2.

After one of the most grandly exciting games since rounders became a national religion, the Dodgers still must win three of four games to achieve their first world championship. Trailing the Yankees, two victories to one, they aren't in what you'd call boisterous health, but at least they aren't three games behind.

That they would surely be if it weren't for Erskine, Campanella and Jackie Robinson, aided by a curious balk committed by the Yankees' fine pitcher, Vic Raschi.

It was a brute of a ball game. It was stiff with tension from the first pitch until the last one was batted gently back into Erskine's glove by Joe Collins, with the issue even then undecided. A peddler of pills for the pale and nervous could have found 35,270 buyers in Ebbets Field.

Erskine, of course, is the story. Brooklyn's only twenty-game winner started the first game on Wednesday and was ruined in a four-run first inning. Yesterday he had a no-hitter for four innings, yielded a one-run lead in the fifth which the Dodgers immediately erased, lost a one-run lead in the eighth, and never had another pitch batted out of the infield.

Of all World Series records, possibly the one which has been talked about most often was established on Oct. 8, 1929, when Connie Mack flabbergasted even his own Philadelphia players by starting beat-up old

Howard Ehmke, in the first game against the Cubs, whereupon Ehmke struck out thirteen batters.

Yesterday Erskine fanned Joe Collins four times, Mickey Mantle four times, and had twelve strikeouts when Don Bollweg opened the ninth inning as a pinch-hitter. Down went the rookie swinging and the record was tied. Up came John Mize, whose pinch-hits mutilated the Dodgers last year.

Mize took two called strikes, fouled off the third pitch, swung at the fourth and missed. The old record was dead but the Yankees were still alive. Irv Noren, a third pinch-hitter, walked.

Now Collins could tie the record that a Yankee pitcher, George Pipgras, made in 1932 by striking out five times, or he could win the game with a two-run homer. He tapped gently to Erskine who brandished the ball in a triumphant fist and tossed it to Gil Hodges at first base for the last easy play.

It was pretty nearly the only easy play of the afternoon. Among those that will be remembered longest, the most curious occurred in the home fifth after Jackie Robinson doubled with one out. Raschi, conscious of Robinson on base behind him, hesitated in his pitching motion and Robinson called the balk himself, the umpires concurring.

Robinson trotted to third, whence he got home on Billy Cox's squeeze bunt, tying the score. Possibly Cox might have batted him home from second or maybe Erskine, who singled after the squeeze, would have knocked the run in. Maybe not, too.

Now melodrama thickened. With none out and runners on first and second, Campanella tried to bunt in the sixth because it seemed certain he couldn't hit. He popped out to Raschi.

This was the fourth time since he was hurt that Campanella had come up with big runs on the bases, and he hadn't gotten a ball out of the infield. He did not look like a man who would deliver the winning hit.

Before the sixth inning ended, Robinson singled home a run which put Brooklyn ahead, but in the eighth the Yankees made trouble again. Hank Bauer singled with one out and for the second time Erskine hit Yogi Berra with a pitch, bringing applause from fans who boo when a pitch crowds Brooklyn's batters.

Up came Mantle, three times a strikeout victim. He stood still for two strikes. Casey Stengel burst from the dugout, furious. He swung an imaginary bat in a gesture of rage: "Swing, dammit!" Then, leaning against a post at the dugout's mouth, he stood glowering. His posture has already been described:

"With neck out-thrust, you fancy how,
  Legs wide, arms locked behind

As if to balance the prone brow
Oppressive with its mind."

Obediently, Mantle swung and missed. The manager turned his back as the young man returned to the dugout regarding his own toes as though he'd never seen them before.

Gene Woodling's single then tied the score again, but that was all except for Campanella—a considerable exception. Incidentally, Robinson and Campanella had led the Dodgers in a special batting practice session at 10 a.m. They have been practicing batting all their lives.

Maybe those few extra minutes were just what they needed.

—October 3, 1953

Tale of One Pitch

AT 1:50 P.M. yesterday, Russ Meyer started warming up in the Ebbets Field bullpen while Johnny Podres took his exercise on the center court down in front of the grandstand. For an hour and five minutes, Meyer threw baseballs to Rube Walker. At 3 o'clock he walked to the mound and threw one to Roy Campanella. It didn't get there.

High in the upper stands in left center field, there was a sound of furniture splintering. Joe Collins, Hank Bauer and Yogi Berra, whom Podres had left on base, trotted around to the plate and waited there for Mickey Mantle, the fourth man in World Series history to hit a home run with the bases filled.

Berra, straddling the plate, flapped his fins like a circus seal applauding his own cornet solo. They leaped upon Mantle as he arrived, and struck him repeated blows. Jubilantly they convoyed him to the dugout where the whole Yankee squad had come boiling out onto the lawn to maul and pummel the young man. Two days earlier they'd studiously shown him the back of their necks when he walked to the bench after striking out.

These were the blasé Yankees to whom world baseball championships are mere routine. Even to them, though, this was somewhat better than a poke in the eye with a sharp stick. Mantle's hit meant a lead of 6 to 1 in the fifth game and from there it was all downhill to their third victory, 11 to 7.

With two more chances for the one victory now needed for their fifth consecutive championship, the Yankees are in a commanding position. Having got by with Jim McDonald, a pitcher from the second echelon, Casey Stengel now has his big guys available—Ed Lopat, Vic Raschi and Whitey Ford.

Charley Dressen has Preacher Roe, who has rested since Thursday but never started more than one game in a World Series in his younger days, and Carl Erskine, who worked one painful inning on Wednesday and nine tough ones on Friday.

It begins to look as though the Dodgers, who died and arose from the dead, is dying again.

The Yankees played this one as though two straight defeats had brought out the beast in them. They mangled the Dodgers cruelly, and the spectacle had only a morbid interest except as an example of how one pitch can turn a whole series upside down.

Brooklyn was the betting favorite in the fifth game and even money to win the championship. After Meyer's first pitch, Brooklyn was a populous borough located on the western end of Long Island.

For psychological reasons, the noted psychologist, C. Dressen, made yesterday's pitching assignment a secret. After the game started it was a puzzle to him. Four Brooklyns worked and all got slugged. McDonald had the Dodgers under control until they got rowdy in the eighth. Then Bob Kuzava quieted them for a time and Allie Reynolds finished the job.

Reynolds's aching back did not appear to handicap him as he pitched to Jackie Robinson, who ended the game by grounding into a double play. Sound or not, Allie probably can give more help if needed.

Because Podres is a rookie who only turned twenty-one last Wednesday—opening day of his first World Series—Dressen has usually not notified the kid that he was working until the day of the game, lest Podres lose sleep over the prospect. Yesterday Johnny said he had slept well Saturday night, adding that perhaps he wouldn't have if he had known for sure he was going to start.

He was calmly hopeful before the game, chatting about his boyhood in the little Adirondacks iron mining village of Witherbee, N.Y., where his righthanded father pitched for the town team and Johnny was playing with grown men when he was thirteen.

No kid of his age ever got a less reassuring baptism in World Series play. He threw three pitches to Gene Woodling, the first hitter, and then Woodling lined the fourth into the seats in dead center field.

Podres got safely through the rest of that inning, though, and an unearned run tied the score in the second. He would never have got into trouble in the third except for an error by Gil Hodges which gave the Yankees one run and kept the inning alive.

The error, a hit batsman and a walk filled the bases, and here came Meyer, who is older than twenty-one but doesn't always act it. Meyer pitched twice for the Phillies in the 1950 World Series, both times in the ninth inning. Things are worse in the third, he discovered.

An eternity or so later, it all ended. The crowd departed and in the darkening stands workmen took down the pretty drapes of red, white and blue bunting. On the scoreboard stood the figures describing the situation before Reynolds's last pitch to Robinson: "Two balls, one strike, one out." They needn't be changed before spring.

—October 5, 1953

Martin's Hit in 9th Wins Yanks 5th Series in Row

THE MORGUE DOORS yawned yesterday, snapped shut, then swung open again, and as they carted the remains away a man in the press box gazed thoughtfully at the knot of Yankee baseball players at first base tossing Billy Martin aloft like a beanbag. "You wouldn't think," said Mike Lee, the man in the press box, "that they could—get so mercenary over a lousy $2,000."

The fiftieth World Series was over and this time the Dodgers really and truly was dead, beaten 4 to 3, in the sixth and final game after Carl Furillo had snatched them to temporary safety when they were only four strikes away from destruction.

In a florid finish that stretched dramatic license to the breaking point, Furillo saved the Dodgers from routine defeat by tying the score in the ninth inning with a two-run homer with one out and a count of three balls, two strikes on the scoreboard. Then Martin lowered the boom.

The gray and chilly day, suitable for funerals, had thickened into grayer, chillier twilight and some of the Yankee Stadium crowd of 62,370 had departed when Martin walked to the plate in the rusty glow of the floodlights. Hank Bauer was on second base, Mickey Mantle on first and Yogi Berra had been retired. Clem Labine, Brooklyn's best pitcher, threw once for a called strike.

He threw another and Martin slapped a ground single over second base into center field. Duke Snider fielded the ball but didn't trouble to throw as Bauer went ripping home with the winning run.

The Dodgers trudged to their dugout behind third base, looking over their shoulders toward first, where the Yankees were spanking Martin. It was a sight worth at least a backward glance. Never again, perhaps, will it be possible to look on a baseball team that has just won the championship of the world for a fifth consecutive year. It never was possible before, never in any age.

Martin's single was a mercenary stroke, worth something like $2,000 to each Yankee, this being the approximate difference between winner's and loser's shares. On the holy pages of the record books—and these are sacred writings to a ball player—it represents a good deal more, for the blow broke a noteworthy World Series record.

It was Martin's twelfth hit of the six games. Nobody ever made more, even in an eight-game series, and nobody ever made so many in six. Twelve hits had stood as a record since Washington's Sam Rice made that total in seven games in 1925, and the Cardinals' Pepper Martin did the same in 1931.

Those Martin guys. Pepper personally took the Athletics apart in 1931. Billy was a rookie star against the Dodgers last year and this time the brash, combative, fist-slinging little hellion tortured them as a child might pluck the wings from a fly. His namesake needn't be ashamed of yielding his share of the record to a ball player like this.

It is an extraordinary achievement which the Yankees have brought off and the manner of its completion was so outrageously melodramatic that witnesses were shrieking senselessly at the end. Even so, it was a Dodger crowd. Even in the Yankee fortress, the alien cries for Furillo were wilder than the cheers for Martin.

"How can you root for the Yankees?" an actor named Jimmy Little had asked a friend earlier in the series. "It's like rooting for United States Steel."

"Do not forsake us," the page-one bannerline of "The Brooklyn Eagle" had implored yesterday following the Dodgers' third defeat. They weren't forsaken in enemy territory. They were only defeated in splendid competition.

For a show with such a taut ending, the last act began limply. The Dodgers made three errors in the first three innings, and the Yankees three runs in the first two. Even the incomparable Billy Cox booted one, and he's the man who, Casey Stengel says, should be required in fairness to the opposition to play third base in chains.

Whitey Ford, who is really pinker than he is white, allowed the Dodgers only one run in seven innings, confirming Stengel's conviction that there's a future in this Ford. Carl Erskine, making his third start for Brooklyn, went out for a pinch-batter after four innings and might have departed earlier except for Ford's overdeveloped sense of sportsmanship.

In what should have been a big second inning, Ford was on third with the bases filled and one out when Berra hit a long fly to Snider. Ford tagged up, started home an instant before the catch. Twenty feet down the line his conscience overtook him. He started back, saw Joe Collins arriving from second base, turned toward the plate again, and was an easy half of a double play ending the inning.

This was light comedy. They came on with the corn in the eighth. First

Allie Reynolds appeared unexpectedly, tramping in from the bullpen with purposeful stride, like a players' delegate come to make demands on the owners. He made demands, but chiefly on the Brooklyn hitters. Striking out Roy Campanella to close that inning, the Indian was really pouring that kickapoo joy-juice.

With two out and two on in the Yankee eighth, the crowd put in a pinch-batter. Joe Collins was up for his turn, but from everywhere came cries of "Mize! Mize!" Yielding to popular demand, Stengel sent John Mize up to howling applause for what John and the fans agreed would be his last time. He grounded out.

Silence fell, but not for long. It has only returned just now, as these last lines are written. Down in the clubhouse, Ford has had the last word.

"I felt bad when Casey took me out," he said. "Then I thought, 'Well, he hasn't been wrong in five years.' "

—October 6, 1953

Clean, Refined Fun

JACKSONVILLE, FLA.—Between New York and Miami the opportunities for clean, refined amusement and instruction are practically unlimited. If you're weary of looking at the tumble-down shacks which Al Jolson couldn't possibly have seen before he sang so affectionately of them, you can memorize the Burma Shave ads or savor the rhapsodic prose of the roadside signs describing the creamy rich pecan-filled divinity fudge that can be purchased only thirty-three miles ahead from B. Lloyd or Stuckey or J. Woodall or Horne.

Or else you can play the game of "B" teams. You do this by saying, "Let's pick an all-time all-star baseball team of guys with names starting with 'B.' I'll take Roger Bresnahan behind the plate." "Well," the other guy says, "how about Jim Bottomley at first base?" You go on like that, and when you've got good men in every position with maybe six or nine pitchers and a couple of reserves for the infield and outfield, you suddenly discover that you overlooked Home Run Baker at third base.

You'd be surprised how easy it is to pick an outfield of Jackie Robinson, Ed Roush and Pete Reiser, and not realize inside the next thirty miles that you didn't mention a pretty good fielder with a great throwing arm, named Babe Ruth.

"Now let's take 'S,' " you say. "I've got the outfielders—Enos Slaughter, Socks Seibold and Amos Strunk." Timidly the other fellow says, "Would there be any room on that team for Tris Speaker? I wouldn't want to force Duke Snider on you, but could you possibly find a spot for Al Simmons?"

Next thing you know, you're recalling the days when the Athletics trained in Fort Myers, Fla., which was also the site of a laboratory where Thomas A. Edison was experimenting with synthetic rubber. For reasons which were not crystal clear at the time and are much foggier now, Mr. Edison paid a visit to the ball park and was accorded the privilege of an introduction to Al Simmons.

They didn't have a tremendous lot to say to each other, Mr. Edison being approximately as well informed on baseball matters as Mr. Simmons was regarding development in synthetic rubber.

"Ah, what is your position, Mr. Simmons?" the inventor managed to ask.

"I'm an outfielder, Mr. Edison," Al said.

"Is that so?" said the father of the incandescent lamp. "I thought you was a batter."

Well, that's the point where you start picking guys because you know stories about them, instead of selecting them on ability alone. You get working on a "Z" team—how far can you go past Heinie Zimmerman at third base? Well, you're working on this "Z" team, and you come up with Rollie Zeider.

Why? Well, not because Zeider was wonderful, but because his name recalls a story now forty years old.

A way back, then, the Yankees were managed by Frank Chance, the peerless leader, who got justifiably burned up at his first baseman, Hal Chase, and traded him to the White Sox for Zeider, a third baseman, and Babe Borton, a first baseman.

Compared with the incomparable Chase, Borton was strictly for Emporia, Kan., and Zeider developed a bunion on his foot and couldn't do the Yankees any good. There was a baseball writer in those days named Mark Roth, later road secretary of the Yankees. He kind of summed it up, to the delight of all New York.

"Chance," he wrote, "traded Chase for a bunion and an onion."

As the game goes along, you find yourself remembering guys on account of the stories you remember. You've got an "S" outfield, for instance, of Simmons, Speaker and Slaughter, but you want Wes Schulmerich in there somewhere. Not because he could play ball with the others, but because of the remark the Giants' Freddy Lindstrom made the first time he saw Wes playing for the Boston Braves.

"He's built," Lindstrom said, "like a bag of nuts and bolts."

Same thing happens when you're working on a "C" team—which doesn't figure to be bad when you start with Mickey Cochrane, Ty Cobb,

Eddie Collins and Jimmy Collins. You take Chase at first base, regretfully passing up Chance and Rip Collins, and then you think of Marty Cavanaugh, who played first for the Tigers.

You want Cavanaugh earnestly, not because he was as good as those others, which he wasn't, but because he was maybe the nicest and perhaps the homeliest guy around in his time.

Nick Altrock was even then a coach with the Senators. Various people told Nick that the Tigers had a player who was even homelier than he was. "I don't believe it," Nick said.

First time Washington played Detroit, Altrock visited the Tigers' bench. "Where's Cavanaugh?" he asked. "Here," Cavanaugh said. Nick peered at him closely, possibly with some envy.

"You win," Nick said at last.

—February 19, 1954

Bob's Public Eye

THERE ARE NOT many infielders better than Granny Hamner of the Phillies, but there've got to be more accomplished gumshoes than the too, too public eye whom Bob Carpenter put on his second baseman's tail. Hired by the Phils' president to find out where and how the athletes were passing their time after business hours, the hawkshaw followed Hamner home from the ball park but let his quarry spot him and call the cops, who flung the shadow into pokey.

This demonstration of the fine art of tailing recalls the late Wilson Mizner's critique of a certain pickpocket: "He couldn't dip his hand in the Hudson without knocking over the Palisades."

In the dick's car, cops found two heaters, a .32 caliber revolver and a .38 pistol. It is not clear what manner of mischief was suspected of Hamner, but the Falcon evidently was prepared to cope.

The notion here is that Carpenter has had his bloodhounds following the wrong spoor. They ought to be out tracking down some hitters who could help Robin Roberts, Curt Simmons and Murry Dickson win ball games. However, the Phillies' boss is correct when he says this isn't the first time a club has sic'ed sleuths on its hired hands.

Readers of Frank Graham's baseball histories, "The New York Yankees," and "McGraw of the Giants," know the practice was old before Granny Hamner was born. There was, for example, the amiable young stranger in St. Louis who introduced himself to Wally Schang, the Yankees' catcher in 1922.

Kelly, this fellow said his name was, and he had a technique that Mr. Carpenter's shamus could have studied with profit. He had charm. He also had tips on horses that won. He also had sources which the 18th Amendment had not dried up. The Yankees liked him and he went war-whooping around the league with them, to Chicago, Detroit, Cleveland, Washington.

A baseball writer named Marshall Hunt, new to the Yankee assignment and a stranger to the players, was on the trip. "A writer, eh?" Kelly told his roistering pals, "you know what I think? I think he's a detective. Take it easy when he's around." For some time thereafter, the players wouldn't even lend him a match.

At a big beefsteak party in a Joliet, Ill., brewery, the players posed for a photograph, beer mugs aloft, and Kelly had them autograph the picture as a souvenir. In Washington, Babe Ruth had a hunch.

"I think that guy Kelly is a detective," the Babe told the pitcher Carl Mays.

Mays hooted, and took Ruth's offer of a $100 bet. It was on the next stop, Boston, that Kenesaw Mountain Landis, the baseball commissioner, appeared unexpectedly in a clubhouse meeting. He had been called in after the club received Kelly's report.

Judge Landis read aloud from a lengthy document. Everything was there—names, dates, places and the quantity and type of refreshments consumed. There was also a photograph.

"Is there any one of you who wishes to deny," the Judge asked, "that this is his signature under his picture?"

Now the Judge really lifted his voice, and when at long last he set it down, the meeting was adjourned. Ruth sidled up to Mays.

"All right, sucker," he said, "I'll take cash or a check."

All this happened five years before Hamner was born. More than a dozen years earlier than that, John McGraw had a pitcher named Bugs Raymond on the Giants. Raymond was a man with magnificent stuff who never touched milk.

Reporting at the Polo Grounds one day, Bugs found McGraw waiting for him, a document in hand. "You made six stops on your way home from the park yesterday," the manager said, and began to read:

"In the first place, you had two beers and went to the lunch counter, where you ate three onions. In the second place, two ryes with beer chasers, some cheese and crackers and three onions. In the third place, one rye, two beers and an onion. In the fourth, two ryes, two onions and—"

"That's a lie!" Bugs roared. "I didn't have but two onions all evening!"

—May 21, 1954

Surrender

THERE IS IN our house a small radio whose transparent plastic construction reveals everything inside except the color of Connie Desmond's vowels. Several days ago a large spider, evidently hard of hearing, crept in through an air hole in the back and settled down for the finish of the National League pennant race. Yesterday morning the spider began spinning a web from the condenser. A Dodger fan.

An hour before Monday night's ball game, George Shuba greeted a visitor to the Dodgers' dugout in Ebbets Field. "Hi, done any fishing lately? I'm going to Canada next week for bass and pike."

There were a lot of newspapermen on the bench and a member of the club's office staff was saying: "Saw the lights on at the wake and decided to drop in, eh? Were you friends of the deceased?"

When they started playing, the Giants got two runs right away. The lead didn't look like much when Sal Maglie walked the first two Brooklyn batters. Then Duke Snider grounded into a double play and Gil Hodges gazed with loathing upon a third strike.

Formal surrender wasn't long in coming. In the second battle of Brooklyn, Sir Leo Durocher met meeker opposition than Sir William Howe encountered in the first.

In the ninth inning, Roy Campanella tapped the last pitch back to Maglie. The Giants started for the clubhouse where Piper-Heidsieck waited, together with other appurtenances of a championship such as news photographers, radio and television men, microphones and cameras. A man with a mike said to his director, "Say when, and I'll start talking."

Larry Jansen, the pitcher-turned-coach, appeared in the doorway where Willie Goodrich, of the Giants' press department, tried to hold him back for a grand entrance. Jansen pushed on in and the man with the mike started talking: "Yi, yi, yi, yi, yi! Here they come, hey yi, yi, yi, yi!"

The spontaneous, unrehearsed enthusiasm of photographers and radio men exploded with a violence that drove the quiet players reeling back against their lockers. Clamoring cameramen clambered over trunks and stools and people, shoving, shouting. "One more! One more! Hey, Walter, over here!"

On instruction from a photographer, Johnny Antonelli clutched Dave Williams's head, Williams clutched Antonelli's and they mauled each other, rub-a-dub-dub. The flash bulb failed. "That figured," Antonelli said, and they waited and then did it again. They did it six times hand running.

Again and again Tiger Arch Murray, part Princeton man and part sports writer, led a cheering section of players through the Princeton "locomotive" while perspiration dripped from his face. All over the room there were cigars sticking out of young faces and glasses clutched in sweaty hands.

"I had somebody hold my drink," said Horace Stoneham, the Giants' president, "and it's gone." A photographer pushed him aside.

While tumult piled on turmoil, Willie Mays backed off into a corner to peel off his uniform, removing two pairs of drawers, took his shower and started getting into street clothes. He was the first one dressed. His expression was melancholy, his eyes downcast; he kept shaking his head with what seemed inexpressible weariness.

"Willie looks plum tuckered out," a man said.

"He's not tired," another said, "he's fuzzy after one glass of champagne."

For the seventeenth time since 1888, the Giants were champions, and nobody could say they hadn't earned this pennant. They beat every opponent oftener than the opponent beat them. Through the last month they barely kept ahead of the sheriff, yet when challenges came they braced and beat them down.

Last time the Dodgers ran at them in the Polo Grounds, the Giants whipped 'em two out of three. Then the Braves moved in and were slammed for three straight. When the night of decision arrived, it found the Giants at their best.

Last time they won a pennant they did it with a wild stretch run and a post-season play-off decided by Bobby Thomson's home run. This time they have substantially the same team, plus Mays and Antonelli, that finished thirty-five games back of Brooklyn in 1953.

They don't win as often as some, but when they do they put a flourish into it.

—September 22, 1954

A Gomez Never Fails

LEFTY VERNON GOMEZ, who won six World Series games for the Yankees, was gratified that Ruben Gomez won his game for the Giants. It is a point of family pride that no Gomez ever has been beaten in a World Series. Lefty approved the well-stroked drive which Ruben lashed to Larry Doby in deep center field as a typical Gomez clout, although there are authorities who contend Señor Vernon could have swung a Louisville Slugger in a subway without bruising one old lady.

"As a matter of fact," the Señor insisted, "when I came to the Yankees

I was a hitter of the Don Mueller type. Sprayed line drives to all fields. Then Joe McCarthy tried to make a pull hitter out of me, and ruined me."

The Yankees were forever tampering with Gomez, trying to remold him nearer to the heart's desire. One recalled when they were trying to fatten him up with a milk diet.

"In my first full season in New York," Lefty said, "I won twenty-one games and lost nine. I was a pale, skinny kid. 'If you weighed twenty pounds more,' they told me, 'you'd be a good pitcher.' First thing they did, they sent me to a dentist who pulled all my teeth so I couldn't eat anything and had to stay skinny. The next year I won twenty-four and lost seven.

" 'Son,' they told me, 'if you weighed twenty pounds more, what a pitcher you could be!' I was the bashful type. Since they hadn't noticed it for themselves, I didn't like to call attention to the fact that I was a rookie who'd won forty-five games for them in his first two full years.

"Anyway, now the Yankees send me to a health farm where it's in bed every night at 9, and I have to drink at least six quarts of milk a day. I drank so much milk I couldn't walk past a cow or a goat without bleating.

"I put on about eighteen pounds. In the spring, Ed Barrow told me, 'Now, it cost us $1,200 to keep you on that health farm, so don't be losing any of that weight. Take it easy.'

"Down in St. Petersburg I'm sitting down, following orders, and Joe McCarthy hollers at me: 'Gomez, you think this is a rest home? Get out there and run!'

"O.K. Now I'm running. I'm running and running, and I run past where Col. Ruppert is sitting with Ed Barrow. 'Hey, Gomez,' they hollered, 'all that money we spent building you up! Sit down!'

" 'Run!' says McCarthy. 'Yes, sir.' 'Sit down!' says Barrow. 'Yes, sir.' They built me up into a sixteen-game winner."

A man said, "Lefty, Phil Rizzuto told me that when he joined the Yankees in 1941, you were the only one who spoke to him in the first week. He supposed most of the Yankees resented him and Gerry Priddy coming on to take jobs away from Crosetti and Gordon."

Gomez grinned. "I used to tell Fred Logan in the clubhouse to give Rizzuto a stool he could stand on in the shower, so the water wouldn't be cold by the time it got down to the little runt.

"The first time Phil played in New York was in the city series, the spring exhibition series with the Dodgers. I was pitching. They got the bases filled against me and I turned and called Rizzuto in from shortstop.

" 'What do you want,' he asked me.

" 'Nothing,' I told him. 'I just want to talk with you for a while.'

"'Gee,' Phil said, 'I better get back out to shortstop! Mr. McCarthy will—' You know that little Dennis Day voice of his.

"'Stick around,' I told him, 'and talk to me. You can't play shortstop until I start pitching again.'

"He started, 'I better get—' and I asked, 'Phil is your mother here watching the game today?' 'What?' he said, 'my mother? Yes, I guess so. Why?'

"'Well,' I told him, 'how do you think she's feeling now? Know what she's saying to the people with her?'

"'Look at that!' she's saying. 'The first time the great Gomez gets in trouble, who does he call on for advice? My little Phil!'

"'I'd better get back to shortstop,' Phil said."

—October 5, 1954

A Is for Antiquity

THREE YEARS BEFORE Connie Mack was born—and he is rising ninety-two—there was a baseball team in Philadelphia whose members wore upon their flanneled chests the curly Gothic A of the Athletics. Long before the world heard of Rube Waddell or Eddie Plank or Eddie Collins, the Athletics had stars named Al J. Reach and Lip Pike and Cap Anson. Before Mickey Cochrane or Al Simmons or Jimmy Foxx or Lefty Grove was born, Uncle Wilbert Robinson was the Athletics' catcher. (In Robbie's day the team had a ladies' auxiliary that chestily called itself the "Big Bosom A Gals.")

The Athletics were a ball club before there was such a thing as a baseball league. They were pennant winners in the first professional league, the National Association, and charter members of the National League when that grew out of the association. They played in the American Association and the Eastern League before the American League was created.

Almost from the beginning, Philadelphia has had the Athletics. Now they are done, even if the projected transfer to Kansas City falls through. The American League has conceded. Even stubborn Roy Mack will have to concur.

If Arnold Johnson buys the team, perhaps he will take the name along to Kansas City, but that won't make them the Athletics. For fifty-three years, copyreaders have been calling them the Macks in headlines. From now on, presumably, they will be the Johns.

Something like this had to happen. To many observers, financial failure seemed inevitable from the time Roy and Earle Mack put the club in hock to buy control from their half-brother, Connie Jr. and Ben MacFarland, the grandson of Ben Shibe. Outsiders realized then, if Roy and Earle didn't, that in today's economy a major league organization cannot be operated on a shoestring, as their father was able to operate in his time.

When Connie moved from Milwaukee to Philadelphia in 1901, he got his quarter-interest in the club for nothing. Chances are the original park at 29th Street and Columbia Ave., in what Philadelphia called Brewerytown, didn't cost much more than a high school pitcher of today expects for signing a contract.

Bystanders saw Roy and Earle borrow the money to buy control, and said to one another: "Here's the story of the old Phillies all over-borrowing, then selling off stars, then the finish. Stick around a few years, and there'll be a big league franchise to be picked up cheap."

In this they were mistaken, being unable to foresee what economic changes the years would bring. In 1945 the mighty Yankee empire was sold for something between $2,500,000 and $3,400,000, and that deal included Yankee Stadium, the ball parks in Newark and Kansas City, the franchises, players and possessions of the whole great chain. The Athletics have scarcely anything but debts in Philadelphia, little except bills in the minor leagues, and their price is $3,375,000.

In addition, if Johnson gets the club he must indemnify the American Association and Kansas City's Yankee landlords for invasion of their territory and expand the park from a capacity of 16,000 to 35,000 at current building costs.

He'll be starting with a nut of at least $4,000,000 in a relatively small city (population 456,622 by the 1950 census), with a dreary ball club whose farms have offered small promise for the immediate future. If he can make this venture go, baseball will stop referring to the Milwaukee phenomenon as a miracle.

Perhaps baseball mentalities are not as gravely retarded as they sometimes seem, but the gift of original thinking is not a distinguishing characteristic of the brass. For half a century club owners parroted the dictum of some forgotten authority that it was impossible to move big league franchises. Then the Braves moved to Milwaukee, and now the boys take it for granted that travel will automatically cure all financial ills.

The Kansas City project is much more like the Baltimore experiment than like the Milwaukee adventure. Artistically, the Athletics are about on a level with the Browns, who went to Baltimore. The transfer from St. Louis is neither a success nor a failure, yet. The Orioles did far better business than the Browns, but Baltimore enthusiasm diminished as the summer wore on, and already the management has been changed in the office and on the field. Immediate improvement is imperative.

The Braves, on the other hand, took a good young team to Milwaukee. Lou Perini had believed it would be a good team, and that's why the move had to be forced on him; he wanted to take one more shot in Boston with an improved club. Some of the other factors that worked in the Braves' favor may be present in Kansas City.

The prairie population is accustomed to driving several hundred miles for a football game and might do it for a baseball game as willingly as Wisconsin fans do. Like Milwaukee, Kansas City isn't much of a theater town, has no horse racing or other sports to compete with baseball.

Perini, though, owned Milwaukee territorial rights in the first place and got the ball park free. It cost him nothing to move but express charges on the trunks. Arnold Johnson is going for fresh greengoods.

—October 15, 1954

Sans Wings, Sans Halo

HIGH ON THE list of items that hold no interest whatsoever for the baseball fan is the identity of the team's owner. Nobody has yet bought a ticket to see the club president arrive in his box, sit down and hold his hands across his abdomen. To the fan, the most sincere and amiable sportsman in the world is a creep if his team doesn't win and the most miserable skinflint alive is a credit to the race if he owns a champion.

Probably it shouldn't be that way, for if the fan paused to reflect he would realize that the most important man in the organization is that guy behind the mahogany desk. Managers come and shortstops go, and across the years a team succeeds or fails because of the policies dictated by the man who owns the store. The history of every club in the game proves that this is so.

The New York baseball writers, who annually distribute an assortment of hardware among individuals in the sport, have chosen Horace Stoneham, president of the Giants, as recipient of the William J. Slocum Award for services rendered to baseball over the years.

No effort will be made here to measure Horace Stoneham's graying sconce for a halo or to fit his tailored shoulders with wings. He is as prone to human folly as any of us. It says here, nevertheless, that he is one of the very few club owners to whom the writers could, in conscience, accord this recognition.

Let's put it this way: How many other owners of big league clubs are themselves proven big leaguers? Boston's Tom Yawkey? Yes, he is a bonafide fan who was drawn into baseball by a genuine enthusiasm for the game and has paid dearly, and cheerfully, for everything he has got out of it.

Washington's Clark Griffith? Yes, in spite of all the indictments drawn against him. In sixty-eight years he has known no life outside of baseball. It is his living and it is also his religion, even if the game never has produced a hero he could admire as devoutly as he worships his radio idol, The Lone Ranger.

Detroit's Spike Briggs? Probably so, although he is a relatively young one. He was brought up in an organization that made a fetish of playing it the big league way, and as between automobiles and baseball there never seemed to be any doubt about where his interests were.

The rest are mostly carpetbaggers looking for a fast buck, industrial princes who use the game for advertising and tax purposes, or Johnny-come-latelies who have not been around long enough to establish their form. If the baseball writers had to confine themselves to club owners when they awarded the Slocum Trophy, it would have gone out of circulation before now.

To get back to Stoneham, there is a foggy recollection that years ago Bill Corum wrote a piece about Charles Stoneham coming home late one night, rousing his young son from sleep and telling him, "Son, I bought the Giants for you today." Or something to that effect, unless memory is playing tricks.

That would have been a long time ago, back around 1919 when it was still possible for somebody to come in late enough to rouse Horace from sleep. Whether it happened or not, the fact is that Charles Stoneham did buy the Giants and Horace did grow to manhood in the knowledge that some day he would be head of the club of John McGraw and Christy Mathewson and Joe McGinnity, Larry Doyle and Art Nehf and Frank Frisch and Dave Bancroft.

You have to remember what the Giants were in Horace Stoneham's boyhood to appreciate what it meant to be heir to that team. They were the kings of baseball, the swaggering rooters who were—or believed themselves to be—bigger big league than all the rest.

It says there that Horace Stoneham, brought up in the big league tradition, has remained faithful to it. He has made as many mistakes as the next man, but he has never chiseled or cut corners or thrown down any man who had proved himself a proper Giant. It seems here that whenever there has been some question about how to handle a proposition, he has asked himself, "Which is the big league way?" and then chosen his course.

An incident comes to mind, a small thing perhaps but characteristic. Probably the greatest day the Giants have known in Horace Stoneham's time was Oct. 3, 1951, when Bobby Thomson whacked the home run that won the pennant in the third game of the post-season play-off with the Dodgers.

Since then the Giants have won another pennant and cleaned up a World Series in four straight games, but that was only remarkable whereas the other thing was impossible—that wild, careening stretch run of theirs and the final triumph in a game they'd already lost to the rival they hate most dearly.

There were 34,320 witness in the Polo Grounds when Thomson flogged that ball, and there were two others on the premises who didn't see it happen.

One was Sal Maglie, the Giants' starting pitcher, who had been taken out for a pinch-batter in the eighth inning with Brooklyn in front, 4 to 1. When Maglie trudged out to the clubhouse in center field, Horace had quit his post at the window in the office one floor above and gone down to talk to him.

When Thomson hit the home run, Maglie and Stoneham were sitting in front of a locker and Horace was saying, "Okay, Sal, so we've lost this one, but you are the guy who did the big job for us all this summer, and I want you to know I appreciate it."

—January 13, 1955

Straws in the Pasture

MIAMI, FLA.—This could be nothing but coincidence, the merely happen-so, but this is how it is. On the drive south this year, not a single game of baseball or softball or one o'cat was seen anywhere along the 1,500-mile route from New York to Miami. Never before, over a period of years that has got much longer than a fellow would care to mention, had this happened.

Often enough in the past, there'd be snow on the ground when you left New York, as there was this time. Generally you get out of the snow on the first day's drive, but for a while there may be rain and mud and fog. Then you get down into the Carolinas and then Georgia, and always in past years there were kids playing ball on the school yards and in pasture lots.

It was always good to see. It was the surest harbinger of spring, and it took a fellow back to his own boyhood and the lazy, happy summer days on cow-pasture diamonds which, it has always seemed here, were the real source of the love so many of us feel for the game of baseball.

Perhaps a one-paragraph digression may be taken to labor this point.

The only reason baseball is our national sport, instead of cricket or soccer, is that practically all American males play baseball or its equivalent—stickball on the city streets, softball on the school yards—when they are young. When they grow up they go watch the games, not so much to enjoy the thrill of appreciation that anybody must feel seeing a Phil Rizzuto scoop up a grounder and get rid of the ball in one fluid motion, but more because the spectacle restores their youth, warms them with nostalgic memories of the fun they had as kids.

It follows that if the kids aren't playing ball now, they're not likely to flock to the big league parks in great numbers tomorrow. Maybe they are playing, but they weren't on the route down here. Kids were shooting baskets on the playgrounds and in one lot there was a football game going on, but not a baseball was seen.

There was another discovery to be made on arrival here. It seems that in 1955, for the first time since World War II, there will be no organized baseball in Miami. There will be no professional baseball at all in southern Florida, and it may be that this situation hasn't existed since Ponce de Leon came barnstorming through these regions.

Perhaps that doesn't seem important up North, but it is important. For many years, Florida has been a breeding ground for ball players and baseball fans. Big league clubs have been training here for half a century; the state has been the hub of pre-season operations for more than thirty years. If there is any place where the game ought to be booming, it is here.

Already there are guys playing pitch-catch all around here. It's entirely unofficial, because there is a rule against teams starting training before March 1. All the clubs do is lend uniforms, bats and balls to fellows like Roy Campanella and Don Newcombe, who wish to entertain themselves on their own time. Their employers realize that they simply can't keep boys from playing baseball in a free country.

Next week Florida will be flooded with big league players, and for the next month there'll be games everywhere. Then the teams will start north, and that will be the end of it. Summer will come on, without baseball.

There's something wrong about this. In recent years, Miami—just to mention one town—has had some pretty exciting times, even if the baseball was minor league stuff. The incomparable Pepper Martin was operating here as a manager, and livening things up by trying to choke an umpire.

("When you had your hands on that man's throat," Pepper was asked by Happy Chandler, who was baseball commissioner then, "what were you thinking?"

"I was thinking I'd kill the —!" Pepper said, being a dead honest guy.)

That's the way it was around here only a few years ago, and now it has ceased to be that way. Miami is a big city. If towns like Richmond, Va., Havana and Charleston, W. Va., can support teams in Class AAA ball, so can Miami. There's a splendid ball park here, and plenty of money.

However, the Florida International League collapsed last year. A town that ought to be able to support Triple-A ball isn't going to have any ball at all.

George Trautman, boss of the minors, was around the other day saying the minors were in pretty good shape. He said it was unfortunate that there would be no baseball in southern Florida this year, but he said maybe this would make the consumers hungry for the stuff and encourage them to bring it back in 1956.

You can't even excuse this by calling it wishful thinking. Absence doesn't make the heart grow fonder of baseball. The only thing that can stimulate baseball interest in any area is baseball itself. When the men who make a living from the game let it die in any part of the country—as it has died in the whole of New England—they are simply banging themselves on the sconce, and not with a hammer. They are using an ax.

—February 24, 1955

School Days

VERO BEACH, FLA.—In the "string area" of the Dodgers' baseball foundry, a baby pitcher named Sanford Koufax was throwing, with Joe Black on one side of him and Joe Becker on the other. Joe Black is, of course, the pitcher who was rookie of the year in 1952, a bust in 1953, and an exile to Montreal in 1954. Joe Becker is Brooklyn's new coach of pitchers, successor to Ted Lyons.

The "strings" are a vestigial reminder of the days of Branch Rickey, who created this sweaty assembly line and, if he had remained in charge of Brooklyn operations long enough, eventually would have had machines here to do everything ball players can do except hold out for more money. In the string area are wooden gibbets like soccer goalposts; within this framework cords are strung taut to outline a vertical rectangle representing the strike zone.

Koufax is a big lefthander with a big fast ball. He was nervous and worked hurriedly, and now and then Becker murmured bits of advice. "Toe in, now," and, "take it easy." When the kid had the range his pitches whistled through the lower corners but now and then the ball got away from him. One wild pitch sailed over the catcher's head and smacked high against the backstop. "Oh, nuts," the kid said.

"That's all right," Becker said. "Just take it easy."

"Everybody throws 'em there," Black said. "I know a fellow used to throw 'em over the backstop."

"Sure," Becker said. "His name was Feller, wasn't it?"

On his next delivery, Koufax winced and grunted. He had pulled a muscle in his side. He started lobbing the ball to the catcher, and Becker said, "Don't throw if it hurts you. That's enough, now. Don't throw any more." Koufax shook his head and kept throwing gently, said he thought the soreness would work out.

"Have you had Doc rub it?" Black asked. The boy shook his head again.

"He works for you, too, you know," Black said.

"How about that?" a spectator muttered. "Is Black a coach, too?"

"He's just waiting his turn to throw," another said. "But why shouldn't he give advice? He's had enough so he must have plenty to spare."

Koufax got loose again, threw a few more hard ones, and then Black took his place while Becker watched with undisguised approval.

"Black looked good," the coach said later. "He had his curve breaking in there low. Couple of fellows told me he never threw that hard all last year."

Joe Becker is a tall, rather lean man out of St. Louis with sunburned features boldly cut. He is a former catcher who has been around, up and down and across the baseball map. As a player he worked in the Cardinals' organization, the Indians', the Giants' and the Dodgers' and for a raft of independents. The forefinger of his right hand makes a right-angle turn at the top joint, a souvenir of the season when he caught men like Bob Feller and Mel Harder with the finger broken.

At one time he and Whit Wyatt, later to become a Dodger hero, were traded to Milwaukee. Another year Becker was shipped from Montreal to Baltimore for Dixie Howell, who is a thirty-five-year-old rookie in this camp, signed to a Montreal contract.

Becker was manager in Sioux City, Jersey City, Toronto and Charleston, W. Va. In Sioux City he won a pennant and lost in the play-offs to Walter Alston's Pueblo club. In Toronto he clashed again with the Dodgers' manager, who noted that even Becker's weaker teams seemed to have strong pitching. So when the departure of Lyons made an opening in Brooklyn, Joe was invited in.

If there's a change for the better in Don Newcombe this year, Becker will share the credit. Recently he sat in on movies here which showed Newcombe pitching against the Yankees in the 1949 World Series and in another game last summer.

"You wouldn't believe it was the same man," Joe said. "In that game last summer, Newk was coming down with a jolt on the heel of his front foot at the end of his delivery, breaking off the follow-through. Other times in the same game he'd finish with his right foot crossed over toward first base and the mound over here behind him. He was hopelessly out of a position to field a ball then, and why the other team didn't bunt him crazy I can't imagine.

"Alston has spoken to Newk and he says he was pitching the same way last summer that he did before he went into the Army. I know he believes that, because lots of times a man doesn't realize that he's changed his style. The catcher can tell, though, and that's our job here in camp—to stop 'em when they do something wrong and point it out."

"When a pitcher is five runs ahead or five behind," Joe said, "he may get a good hitter out on something less than his best pitch. He'll think, 'Now I got his number,' and next time in a tight spot he'll try the same pitch and get belted. You try to explain to pitchers the importance of making good hitters go for their best pitch, their 'out' pitch.

"The good ones listen and learn. The others have a big hole in the head that starts at this ear and goes right through."

—March 5, 1955

Fans Underground

IN A CHICAGO restaurant near Tribune Tower, a handful of conspirators meets once a week to talk in hoarse whispers about The Cause. They are baseball fans, but not Cubs fans or White Sox fans, and that's what has driven them underground. They are dedicated to the proposition that the St. Louis Browns shall some day rise again.

This week, with American League baseball under way in such outlandish places as Baltimore, Kansas City, Washington and New York, a task force will travel from Chicago to the deserted home of the Browns, flaunting souvenir pennants, chanting the battle cry, "Are We Downhearted? No, We're Brownhearted!" and bearing a floral wreath complete with ribbon declaring, "The Browns Will Rise Again."

A sense of delicacy has altered the original plan to lay the wreath on the grave of Chris von der Ahe, the saloonkeeper who founded the Browns in 1881. Instead it will be affixed, probably under the cover of night, to the door of what used to be the Browns' office in Sportsman's Park, now called Busch Stadium by infidels.

Among the pilgrims will be Eddie Gaedel, the midget whom Bill Veeck smuggled into baseball for one turn at bat as a pinch-hitter for the Browns in 1951. Batting for Frank Saucier, he drew a base on balls and was replaced by a pinch-runner. The Browns, naturally, didn't score. Eddie is now a three-foot seven-inch messenger for "The Daily Drovers Journal" in Chicago. At thirty, he is still young enough to help the Kansas City Athletics.

The St. Louis Browns Fans of Chicago originated in the bleachers in Comiskey Park, where the founding fathers went regularly to root against the home team. Because the Browns required more rooting than other visitors, they won a special affection.

In those happy days Satchel Paige occupied the bullpen in front of the bleachers. He would gather pebbles, fire them accurately at Minnie Minoso, the White Sox centerfielder, and disappear behind the canvas wall of the bullpen before Minoso could discover who was peppering his posterior. Other times he'd turn a fine spray aloft from the groundskeeper's hose and stand under this soft, refreshing shower in full uniform, watching the game.

"You couldn't hate a team with a man like that," testifies Bill Leonard, corresponding secretary of the St. L. B. F. C.

On the closing weekend of the 1953 season, twelve members went to St. Louis for the Browns' last games. They had a twenty-foot banner reading, "First Annual Tour, St. Louis Browns Fans of Chicago," and many St. Louis Browns pennants. (The Comiskey Park concessionaire sold out his stock with almost vulgar alacrity.) The Browns lost on Saturday night and again on Sunday afternoon. "We returned," Mr. Leonard writes, "unsurprised and undaunted."

With a new season opening, Mr. Leonard graciously submits a progress report, on brown stationery, with corrections penciled in brown:

"A news story last Feb. 14 told how the reservations manager at the Hotel Cleveland, where the Browns stayed for fifteen years, had written Charley DeWitt, former Browns' road secretary, inviting the team to stay there this season and wishing the Browns the best of luck in 1955. We happily took this to mean that the tidings 'The Browns will rise again' had reached Ohio, and wrote inviting the reservations manager to become an honorary member, but heard nothing from him. No progress there.

"Another story reported that the Baltimore Orioles had staged a ceremonial burning of the Browns' old uniforms. We asked Dick Armstrong, Baltimore public relations director, the date of the bonfire so we could make it a day of mourning. He replied that the Orioles wouldn't do anything so foolish when they could recondition the old flannels.

"To make matters worse, he wished our club luck. We had intended hating the Orioles and Mr. Armstrong confused the issue momentarily with his friendliness, but we decided to go ahead and hate them anyway. No progress there.

"We have completed our stirring song, 'The St. Louis Browns Victory

March.' The lyrics are pretty bad ('You will arise to play another game, and once again recapture your old fame') but the melody is stirring enough to empty the restaurant. Our treasury, built on dues, profits from our own bar, poker pots, etc., is richer than the Browns were when they left St. Louis. Some progress there.

"Members attending the American League Christmas party in Chicago were introduced to Will Harridge, the league president, as believers that 'the Browns will rise again,' and Mr. Harridge said, 'Migod, I hope not!' Definitely no progress there."

The weekly meeting, or Brown Study, is held in the Brown Room of Ray's Famous Steaks and is devoted to the drinking of toasts in nut-brown ale. The last two articles of the constitution merit attention. They read:

"It shall be a tenet of the club that the Baltimore Orioles are for the birds.

"Employees must wash hands before returning to work?"

—April 12, 1955

Leaden-Stepping Hours

BEATING BALTIMORE, 7 to 5, in eight and a half innings, the Yankees consumed three hours, twenty minutes. In Brooklyn the Phillies contrived to overcome the Dodgers, 5 to 3, in two hours, forty minutes. Time of the New York-Pittsburgh game the same night (Giants, 6; Pirates, 3) was 2:16. Here's one, though: In Chicago, a character named Arthur John Ditmar pitched a two-hitter for Kansas City and the White Sox were shut out, 1 to 0, in one hour, thirty-nine minutes.

Before Ford Frick gets too much preoccupied with the research firm he is hiring to find out what's good and bad about baseball, he should have Arthur John Ditmar stuffed and mounted for Cooperstown. Then let the commissioner's inquiring pollsters ascertain, if they can, the fans' true sentiments about the tempo of modern games.

The researchers should not be content merely to sound out the customers in major league cities. Let them also make inquiries among fans in the Pacific Coast League, if they can find any fans out there. Elapsed times for three recent games between San Francisco and Sacramento were 1:22, 1:52 and 1:31, the first being a seven-inning opener of a night double-header.

Frick's plan for a quasi-scientific survey of baseball's problems seems sensible enough. There is probably no other business field where so many free-hand thinkers arrive at snap judgments, pontificate upon them publicly and reiterate the opinion until it is accepted as fact. If the researchers get nothing more than some straight answers about the pace of today's ball games, they'll have earned a substantial fee.

This is an old argument which nobody has resolved because nobody really knows how the fans feel about it. Sports writers, representing themselves as spokesmen for the public, are eternally harping that games are too long. Dissenters like Warren Giles, the National League president, retort that the only complaints they hear come not from customers but from newspapermen who are bored with their jobs.

Ford Frick has opposed unnecessary delays, but sometimes he inclines toward Giles's view. He says he seldom sees many customers quit the park before the ninth inning.

Both sides, it seems here, are slightly off the target. It isn't that the games are too long, but that they are frequently too slow; it's the pace that counts, not the number of minutes consumed.

A three-hour game is not too long if it is a good game, briskly contested, offering three hours of sustained suspense. A two-hour game is an abomination if it consists of only one hour of entertainment.

The Coast League is mentioned because Claire Goodwin, the new president, is bribing the teams to keep the show lively. He raised a $20,000 endowment to be distributed, $2,500 at a time, in monthly awards for hustle beyond the call of duty.

Money makes the mare go, and it also encourages flanneled lardbuckets to move on and off the field with more than wonted celerity. Though the San Francisco-Sacramento games mentioned may not be typical, more games are being completed under two hours than formerly.

Observers on the Coast profess to sense a new urgency in the play, a more nearly unanimous disposition to get the show on the road and keep it moving. There are fewer time-wasting arguments, fewer instances of deliberate dawdling.

What few customers the league has been drawing seem to have caught the spirit. Where they used to jeer the umpire, they are now booing the frustrated ham who tries to make a Shakespearean tragedy of each small disagreement. Emboldened by support from stands from upstairs (there's a $2,500 Umpire-of-the-Year award on Goodwin's prize list), the umpires give stallers a quick brush.

Attendance has been discouraging. Chances are this is due to a variety of factors—unfavorable weather until recently, too much loose talk about major league baseball moving west, San Francisco's chilly night fogs, maybe a smothering oversupply of Eastern baseball on the radio all day.

However, if Goodwin's new crackle-snap-pop-and-bustle policy hasn't improved business, it can't possibly hurt it. It keeps the performers alert.

Recently three managers, Tommy Heath, Lefty O'Doul and Clay Hopper, called on the league president. In the outer office, Heath took a hitch in his ample waistline.

"You guys open the door," he said, "and I'll do a belly-slide up to his desk. We'll show the bums some hustle."

—April 22, 1955

The Last Frontier

OFTEN WHEN THERE'S a ball game on the television screen or the car radio, a numbness settles upon the senses. Limbs grow heavy, there is a tightness at the base of the scalp, eyelids droop, consciousness swims hazily. At such times it is realized that practically the only place left today where it is possible to escape the smothering avalanche of inanities that passes for baseball reporting on the air is the ball park itself.

Lately it has been discovered, with a tingling shock of alarm, that not even the grandstand can be considered safe. Through the complicity of a couple of club owners, the relentless syllables of the broadcaster now pursue victims all the way out the left field line and clear upstairs into the top deck behind third base.

In certain sections of Chicago's Wrigley Field and Philadelphia's Connie Mack Stadium are amplifiers through which is piped the regular radio description of the game, complete with commentaries, feeble jokes and commercials.

There the customer who has paid for the privilege of watching with his own eyes sits helpless while a disembodied huckster plucks at his sleeve, bludgeons him with advice, burdens him with statistical trivialities, embarrasses him with autobiographical revelations, hectors him to buy beer or cigarettes.

Living has become increasingly difficult in our living rooms. Tranquility fled the salon when the cathode ray tube arrived. Now the sanctuary of the grandstand is menaced. Soon there will be no escape anywhere this side of the Styx.

This latest ordeal-by-audio is the fiendish work of Phil Wrigley, a twentieth-century Torquemada who owns the Cubs. He decided some months ago that radio and television fans were getting more information about the games than the cash customers in the stadium.

In this respect, of course, he was right. Though hits and errors are flashed on the scoreboard, there are other decisions of the official scorer—

on wild pitches and passed balls, for example, and other sources of information like the latest hospital bulletin regarding an injured player—which go out over the air but not over the public address system.

Had Mr. Wrigley reasoned just a bit further, he might have concluded that some fans were willing to make these small sacrifices in order to escape the appalling flood of balderdash that issues from their receiving sets along with the tidbits of information.

Instead, he installed loudspeakers in several sections of Wrigley Field, with the volume theoretically modulated so as to reach only the 1,500 or so occupants of those sections. Subsequently Bob Carpenter, owner of the Phillies, seized upon the idea and made similar provisions in Connie Mack Stadium.

In Chicago, only two full-blown commercials are piped to the victims in the grandstand during one game, but of course the system also carried all the parenthetical sales pitches with which the running descriptions are larded: "Glockenspiel Beer pouring it all to ya," etc.

In Philadelphia no provision is made to screen out the sponsor's persistent plugs. The upper-deck customers behind third base get the full treatment, without even the privilege of tuning out. They're a captive audience, and the chains that bind them are stout.

Incidentally, the engineers have had some minor difficulties adjusting the volume and keeping it constant. At times in Chicago, the pear-shaped tones of Jack Brickhouse, the announcer, burst upon the fans like a summer thunderstorm. At other times he speaks in a conspirational whisper, straining attention to the snapping point.

In the early days of radio, the sportscaster's cardinal principle was: "What they can't see won't hurt them." Confident that his audience was safely out of view of the actual play, he babbled along as his mood dictated, unhampered by slavish fidelity to fact. Then it was literally true that a man who happened to be sitting at the game within earshot of the broadcaster found himself attending a double-header—the game he saw and the game he heard.

Time and television have wrought some changes. Today's announcers are better reporters than the pioneers, although they do cling to the preposterous fiction that they can recognize a slider or a screwball from the broadcasting booth, and many find it difficult to believe that their auditors would rather hear the score than personal reminiscences.

However, they do of course, commit errors of fact, being approximately human, and this, it seems here, can cause repercussions among their captive audiences. Some day there may be a major error, a wild discrepancy between the thing seen and the thing heard. Auditors will doubt either their ears or their eyes, since it will be impossible to believe both. Panic will stalk the stands.

—August 22, 1955

All Guys Finish at Last

THE BRIDGE AT 155th St. still spanned the Harlem yesterday. No part of Coogan's Bluff had crumbled. The seismograph was quiet at Fordham, and along Eighth Ave. not one numbers bank collapsed. The departure of Leo Durocher was a sensation, but the earth didn't tremble.

Speaking of sensations, they varied. In some quarters there was regret, in others relief, here a sigh for the past, there a hope for the future. In no case where the name of the Giants means anything was there indifference.

It wasn't a shattering surprise when the Little Shepherd of Coogan's Bluff hung up his crook. Since June it had been evident that this must be a year of decision for the Giants. The defending champions of the world were not only third in their league, but also third in their town, which is far more important from a business point of view.

There is a hard core of Giant fans, mostly members of the Old Guard, who never were reconciled to the presence of Durocher in the seat formerly occupied by John McGraw, Bill Terry and Mel Ott. The team's dramatic success in 1951, last year's front-running race and four-game conquest of Cleveland won new followers and brought in fresh business to counteract earlier losses. This year those Johnny-come-latelies deserted to the Yankees and Dodgers, and the old dissenters still held out.

The problem had to be faced, and everybody knew it. Nearly everybody assumed it would be tackled as Horace Stoneham has attacked it—by reshuffling the deck for a new deal.

If nice guys finish last, what sort of guys finish third?

Well, in this case, it is a controversial guy, and that may be the understatement of the decade. It has never been easy to characterize Durocher either as a man or as a manager, not because he is an especially complex personality, but because so much depends on where you stand when you view him.

Regarding him as an athlete and competitor, there is no room for disagreement. He was a first-rate ball player and he is an altogether intractable antagonist, obsessed with winning, a stranger to physical fear. He will fight anybody any time for anything.

Leo Durocher as manager of the New York Giants

Combative, quick-witted and knowledgeable, he was truly the practically peerless leader on the field, a superior gambler with a nice balance of calculation and recklessness. Like any good gambler—horse player, card expert or pool shark—he has the gift of absolute concentration. Half an hour after a long double-header he can recite every detail of the eighteen innings, play by play. An hour or so later he has forgotten it all.

As a director of tactical operations, then, he was as good as a manager can be. As a leader of men—that's something else again.

He is ambitious, brassily assertive and impatient. Though he can be gracious when he chooses, instinctive regard for others is not ingrained in him. Some players responded to his goading, played better for him than they would for another man. Others found him impossible to live with, and these weren't necessarily congenital sulkers.

Durocher did play favorites, he did indulge in personal dislikes, he was swayed by enthusiasm and prejudice, he could be outrageously unreasonable. Some of the Giants will rejoice in his departure and perhaps flourish under more temperate leadership. Some will miss him.

In his first couple of seasons as manager in New York, the personnel of the Giants changed rapidly. Leo wanted, he said, "my kind of ball club." What that appeared to mean was that he wanted the team staffed with men just like himself. Chances are there aren't nine major league ball players just like Durocher, let alone twenty-five. This is not an unmixed evil.

However, he did get enough of "his kind" to win two pennants and a World Series.

That's got to be a major item in any accounting of his stewardship. Some felt from the beginning that it was a mistake to bring him across the river from Brooklyn. From July 1902 to July 1948, none but a Giant had ever managed the Giants. Now Stoneham brought in an alien, and one of the most devoutly detested enemy aliens ever to invade the Polo Grounds.

Those who insisted the fans never would stand for Durocher were partly correct. Some never did. Yet the Giants, who had not won a pennant in eleven years, won two in the next six. It's in the records.

Long before the decision was officially made, Durocher's successor had been selected and was waiting in the wings. It was taken for granted everywhere that when a change was made, Bill Rigney would become the Giant manager. He's a Giant, personally popular, and he has been successful on the Minneapolis farm. He's going to take over a team that isn't good enough. No miracles need be expected.

—September 26, 1955

Is There a Doctor in the House?

DR. JOSEPH PAUL DIMAGGIO, the noted diagnostician, gave it as his considered opinion recently that if the Dodgers were going to play rounders again with the Yankees they'd better consult a good psychiatrist first. After getting slapped bubble-eyed in five World Series with the bullies of the Bronx, Dr. DiMaggio thought, there must be distinct symptoms of kakorrhaphiophobia (fear of failure).

Yesterday they made a head-shrinker's couch of the emerald and sand-red lawn of Yankee Stadium. It was a skull-rapper's picnic as the Yankees squeaked through 6 to 5, and the heroes of Jersey City-on-the-Gowanus left the starting gate in reverse, as they have invariably in any exercises begun on an American League playground.

For five-and-two-thirds innings Don Newcombe suffered from acathisia, a dread of sitting down, but in the sixth Dr. Billy Martin administered a three-base hit and the patient shuffled to a seat.

Kleptomania laid its grip upon Jackie Robinson in the eighth inning, complicated by a touch of basophobia, or hysterical fear of standing up.

Dashing himself violently onto his stern, he slid under Yogi Berra and stole home. When the umpire signaled "safe," Berra was overcome by trichotillomania, or hair-plucking.

There were noted only superficial symptoms of the baseball manager's occupational ailment, sophomania (delusions of omniscience). That will come later, and the way matters are shaping up for them the Dodgers are in for a siege of skopophobia, which is paranoidal fear of spies and foreign agents.

The first three-way World Series game every played—among New York, Brooklyn, and Jersey City—was a stunning triumph of matter over mind. It turned on the supple muscles of a man who is physically unwell but mentally hale—Joseph Edward Collins, the Sick Man of Scranton, Pa.

Wearing a shinguard to armor a phlebitic leg and taped bandages over a strained muscle in his groin, Collins put his battered torso into two home run swings. The first gave the Yankees a lead and the second made it safe.

One of the most popular of the Yankees, the gracious Collins is a top-drawer athlete who would be an entire first baseman on almost any other team. Under the platooning system of C. Stengel (suggestive of Philoneism, or obsessive interest in fads), Joe is only one-third of that, having shared the work all summer with Bill Skowron and Ed Robinson.

For all of that, it has been an eventful summer. First, an attack of virus influenza laid him up, aggravated by tonsillitis. Then phlebitis developed in a badly bruised right leg. He came out of Lenox Hill Hospital in time to save a stranger's life with a tenth-inning home run in a night game.

The stranger was watching the game on television in his home in Long Branch, N. J. When Collins broke it up, the man switched off the set and went into the kitchen. Moments later a runaway automobile came hurtling in from the street and shattered the television set.

Collins didn't get a Carnegie Medal for that, but for saving the Yankees yesterday he may wind up with a winner's purse around $10,000. His second homer was a prodigious hit that cleared the wall and bleacher railing in right center field. Duke Snider chased it, leaped and hung himself high on the auxiliary scoreboard—where the number on his shirt looked like four runs for the Dodgers—but caught only vertigo at that height.

Even so, this wasn't necessarily the mightiest hit of the day. Snider may have produced that with a home run into the gaping maw of a ramp deep in the third tier beyond right field. Duke's hit was one of several which set the experts to mumbling in confusion.

When Stengel chose the left-handed Whitey Ford and Tommy Byrne to pitch the first two games, experts explained that he did so because the Dodgers' preponderantly righthanded power would be somewhat muffled in the Stadium, where the leftfielder can catch flies that would be home runs in Brooklyn.

So it turned out that with the exception of a triple by Jackie Robinson, all Brooklyn's scoring power was in right or center field. Carl Furillo sliced a home run to right in the second inning, Snider's went that way in the third, and before Robinson stole home in the eighth, Furillo got around on a single to center, an error and a fly to center.

In fact, Robinson's triple would have been a home run in Ebbets Field, so would a triple by the Yankees' Billy Martin in the sixth, but Collins's first homer was a line drive that would have bounced off the wall in Brooklyn.

Not that the score would have been altered importantly. The experts figure these matters out with staggering profundity, and then a sick man gets up from his bed of pain and settles everything with one stroke.

—September 29, 1955

Cross Over the Bridge

IN THE EIGHTH inning, with Phil Rizzuto on third base and the tying run on first, Hank Bauer struck out on a high, hard pitch. With a wild cry, witnesses sprang to their feet, fists brandished high. Johnny Podres started for the dugout beyond third base and Gil Hodges, overtaking him, flung a dare at fate. Surreptitiously, Gil patted the pitcher's bottom and trotted past.

It was too soon. The sixty-third inning of the World Series was still ahead. Three monstrous putouts lay between the Dodgers and the impossible—the fourth and final conquest of the Yankees which would accomplish the thing that had never happened, which perhaps never could happen in this world.

Scoreless in their half of the ninth Brooklyn took the field for the last time, Podres pitched to Moose Skowron—a ball, a called strike, a second ball, another called strike, then Skowron swung. The ball came back hard to the pitcher, stuck in his glove as he and the batter raced toward first. "Throw!" The shout came from thousands. In the last instant, Podres wrenched the ball free and threw. One out.

Bob Cerv up. A called strike. The pitcher's shoulders lifted and sagged in a mighty sigh. Ball one. A second called strike, then a high fly to Sandy Amoros in left.

Now Elston Howard. Podres's right leg kicked high, a strike came through that only Jim Honochick, the umpire, saw clearly. A curve hung high for ball one. Howard swung and missed strike two. Gingerly, with just his fingertips, Podres lifted the rosin bag and dropped it, tugged at his cap, brought a flanneled forearm across his brow. Ball two was high. The pitcher pumped three times, stopped and sighed again as Howard stepped back from the plate. Fast ball, fouled back; fast ball, also fouled; then a gentle ground ball to Pee Wee Reese, and there it was.

There it was, but what was it, exactly? It was a baseball game, the seventh and last of the fifty-third World Series, very well played, close and exciting; won by the Dodgers, 2 to 0, on the magnificent pitching of a muscular, quiet country kid from an obscure Adirondacks village.

If he never pitches again, Podres will still be the only man on earth who ever started and won two games for Brooklyn in one World Series. If he ever does pitch again, it will be a miracle, for when Reese's throw had smacked into Hodges's mitt and ended it all, the pitcher's playmates set out to make a litter case of him.

All of a sudden he was lost from sight in a howling, leaping, pummeling pack that thumped him and thwacked him and tossed him around, hugged him and mauled him and heaved him about until Rocky Marciano, up in a mezzanine box, paled at the violence of their affection.

Now there was mufti in the swirl of gray flannel as kids materialized from nowhere and adults swept down onto the field behind them, and it seemed that Podres, caught in the eye of this hurricane, could never be brought through to the sanctuary of the dugout. At length the last uniform disappeared, but the crowd stayed on, reluctant to leave the scene where the deed was done. Even as this is written kids are running the bases, boys measure their small feet in the depressions dug by Podres's spikes, and their elders stand staring in at deserted benches.

One has to pause a moment and consider, before the utter implausibility of this thing can be appreciated. First, the Dodgers had never won a World Series, and especially they had never won one from the Yankees, not in five meetings over fourteen years.

Unprecedented to begin with, it became impossible after the Yankees won the first two games. No team in history had ever recovered from such disaster within the limit of seven games. Then after the Dodgers accomplished the wildly improbable feat of taking the lead, three games to two, the Yankees ground them down again.

If hope wasn't stone cold dead in the marketplace, faith certainly was when yesterday arrived. This one, though, was meant for Brooklyn. That wasn't evident in the early stages as Tommy Byrne began with three hitless innings, but slowly signs and portents appeared.

In the third inning, the Yankees had Rizzuto on second base and Billy Martin on first with two out when Gil McDougald bounced a fair ball toward third so slowly that he seemed sure to beat any play to first base. Rizzuto, coming over, slid into the batted ball for the third out. The fates that rode so long on Yankee battle wagons were hitching a ride to Brooklyn.

In three other games played in Yankee Stadium, Roy Campanella had not made a hit. His first there was the biggest of his life, a double in the fourth inning that enabled him to score the only run Podres needed.

With Reese on first in the sixth, Duke Snider bunted to Tommy Byrne, who threw to Bill Skowron, who had moved in off first. Although Skowron spun around and tagged Snider out, the ball somehow wriggled out of Skowron's mitt and Snider was safe. That made the second run possible, unearned but beautiful.

Now the Yankees threatened again, putting runners on first and second with none out. Yogi Berra sliced a fly out the line in left, far out of reach of Amoros, who was properly playing Berra well over toward center. By the time McDougald discovered that the ball wasn't really out of Sandy's reach, the outfielder had caught it and doubled Gil off first.

That's how it went because that's how it was meant to go.

—October 5, 1955

Curtain Call

CONSIDERING THE NATURE of the team's performance over the last decade, it might be said that the Pittsburgh Pirates have hired the wrong Joe Brown. When Branch Rickey, the greatest of all double-talk monologists, withdrew to the wings, the role as his successor cried aloud for Joe E. Brown rather than the comedian's serious-minded son. Who'll do the entertaining now, unless Bing Crosby sings for his fellow-directors?

Since Rickey relinquished the general manager's swivel chair to young Joe L. Brown and backed off into a never-never land identified as "an advisory capacity," practically everybody has been trying to call the score on his fifty-eight years in baseball. It can't be done. The man confounds arithmetic as easily as he confuses an audience.

This inept mathematician undertakes the task knowing in advance that it's impossible. Add Rickey up? How? As a player, manager, executive, lawyer, preacher, horse-trader, spellbinder, innovator, husband and father and grandfather, farmer, politician, logician, obscurantist, reformer, financier, sociologist, crusader, sharper, father-confessor, checker shark, friend or fighter?

As Rickey said, wilted by a salary debate with a rookie named Dizzy

Dean, "If there were one more like him in baseball, I'd quit the game." If there were one more like Branch—well, Judas priest!

Rickey is inimitable, but that doesn't mean he hasn't had plenty of imitators in addition to Arthur Mann, whose parodied impersonation of the master has convulsed audiences for many years at the annual baseball writers' show in New York. Junior executives learning the baseball business under the great man have tried to adopt his methods, not always with unmixed success.

When Al Gionfriddo was chattel of the Dodgers, he made a winter visit to the Brooklyn office to plead his financial case. He was intercepted in an outer office by a subaltern who undertook to soften him up for the Old Man.

Gionfriddo brought forth all his carefully rehearsed arguments for a wage commensurate with his ability. The subordinate replied as he fondly imagined the Maestro would have done.

"You don't know anything about baseball," he told the player. "You're a rotten base-runner, haven't the first idea how to steal a base. Look, this is the way to steal."

He sprang from his chair, hurled himself across the room, and slid into a wastebasket.

Gionfriddo walked over and stood gazing moodily down upon the apprentice magnate, prostrate on the rug.

"What base were you stealing?" he asked softly.

"Second!"

"You're out. Hooked the wrong way into the bag. Lemme see the boss."

Most players dreaded to approach Rickey at contract time, fearing that after ten minutes under the spell of his persuasive eloquence they would emerge minus salary increase and underwear. If Gionfriddo had been as good at belting baseballs as at bearding lions, he wouldn't be a star outfielder today for Visalia in the Class C California League.

Yet there are players and managers and scouts and pensioners, men in baseball and out of it, who have worked for Rickey and will say of him sincerely, "All that I am and hope to be, etc." in terms that make Mother Machree a fishwife by comparison.

There is no doubt here that Rickey brought into baseball the finest, liveliest, most inventive and resourceful mind the game has attracted. To hear him speak, in public or private, is to be allowed a glimpse of that mind's operation. When the topic is one he wishes to consider, he goes directly to the heart of the matter, sorting out, analyzing and cataloguing each point in beautiful order. When he chooses to avoid a direct statement, he numbs his listeners with rhetoric and leaves them bound hand-and-foot in circumlocution.

He has built many monuments in baseball. The farm system that he devised brought about the greatest single change of this century in the business structure of the game. By breaking the color line, he revolutionized the social structure of baseball and, in a lesser degree, the nation.

It is the notion here, however, that when he looks back on what he has accomplished, he does not consider first the social progress made. More important than that, to a baseball man, was tapping a great pool of talent that had been dammed up and ignored. He is a baseball man first, and that was his proudest achievement.

—October 28, 1955

No More Ten-Dollar Days

AFTER EIGHTEEN YEARS as an umpire in the American League, Willie Grieve has worked his last ten-dollar day. That's a private joke and not an especially good one, but the lively, gray-haired man whose retirement was announced yesterday will know what it means.

Back in the last days of the depression before World War II, American League umpires barnstorming with clubs in the spring exhibition season received an expense allowance from the league based on a sliding scale, though it didn't slide as far or fast as, say, Pepper Martin. When there was an overnight stop involving lodging in a hotel, the allowance was $10; if the night was passed in the team's Pullman traveling to another city, walking-around money was cut to $5.

One spring Willie Grieve mentioned this arrangement to newspaper men who thereafter gave tongue to witticisms they might better have saved for the typewriter. "Hey, Willie!" one of them would bray from the press coop in Yuma, Ariz., during a lull in the action. "You got to bear down in this one; it's a $10 day!"

Some of the more pompous members of the clan would have been outraged, perhaps properly, by such public bawling about their income, but Willie was amused. He'd turn, grinning, toward the source of the bellow, acknowledge it with a genial sweep of his mask, and turn back to his work. It was this friendly equanimity of his that made his path smoother than the one most umpires travel.

Ability to keep his temper is a priceless attribute in an umpire, perhaps as necessary as normal vision, courage of his convictions and some inkling of the rules. The guy who bows his neck when challenged invites trouble. There comes to mind an instance when Willie Grieve's deportment in trying circumstances entitled him to special applause; whether he got it is something else.

In the closing week of the 1949 race the Yankees and Red Sox were playing in New York with first place at stake. In the eighth inning Johnny Pesky slid home on a squeeze play with the run that put Boston in front by a full game.

Ralph Houk, the Yankees' catcher, gave one of the most stirring impersonations of a homicidal manic since the original Lon Chaney. Joe Page, the pitcher, flung his glove aloft, inviting immediate dismissal. Casey Stengel came heel-and-toeing out of the dugout to rub waistcoats with the umpire, a crime tantamount to parricide in baseball.

Willie would have been justified in unfrocking the three of them on the spot and recommending fines or suspensions. Instead, he reached for the whiskbroom and dusted the plate, a fair and patient man who was not going to handicap either contending team in order to save face before the big crowd.

Later an obscure outfielder named Cliff Mapes confronted Grieve under the grandstand and, with a fine blend of bush-league effrontery and repartee, demanded: "How much did you have on the game?"

Even that bit of scurrility didn't bring reprisals from Willie, who may have been inured to abuse during his hitch as a Republican assemblyman from Westchester County. Lacking conditioning in politics, Will Harridge, president of the American League, slapped a $200 fine on Mapes and demanded telegraphic apology.

Another incident is recalled in which Willie was involved in absentia. There was a vastly complicated play which created a knotty problem for the umpires in a game between the Athletics and Indians in Cleveland. It doesn't matter now what raised the argument, and the chances are Willie never heard of it, for he was nowhere near Ohio that day. Anyhow, while the debate raged Connie Mack thrust his head from the dugout and waggled a finger for permission to speak. Joe Rue, who was working the game, scampered in to hear his suggestion.

"Don't you agree, Mr. Grieve," Connie began, and went on with his version of the play. It was Connie's special gift that he could, in one breath, get the decision right and the umpire's name wrong. Being in a friendly mood, he'd naturally think of a friendly name.

It was, as a matter of fact, Willie's ability to get on with people that led him to professional umpiring in the first place. He had a home and family in Yonkers and was picking up an extra buck working high school and college games in baseball and basketball. In the fall, big league players would come barnstorming through Westchester and a number of them, having seen

Willie work, said: "Why don't you try organized ball? You'd make the majors in two or three years."

Willie held out a while, but at length got a job in the Northwestern League. The pay wasn't big enough to keep him going on the road and support the Yonkers establishment, too, so Mrs. Greive packed up the two kids, moved out to join him, and they lived in furnished rooms.

"I know you'll make the big league," she said, "and the children and I aren't going to stand in your way."

She was right, but the ball players who had advised him weren't. It took Willie four years to get to the top.

—January 12, 1956

Connie, as Ever Was

IT IS NOT for mortals anywhere to suggest that another has lived too long, yet for those who knew and, necessarily, loved him it is difficult to regard Connie Mack's last years as part and parcel of a life that was a beacon in our time. Toward the end he was old and sick and saddened, a figure of forlorn dignity bewildered by the bickering around him as the baseball monument that he had built crumbled away.

That wasn't Connie Mack. Neither was the bloodless saint so often painted, a sanctimonious old Puritan patting babies on the skull and mumbling minced oaths and platitudes. As long as he was Connie Mack he was tough and human and clever. He was tough and warm and wonderful, kind and stubborn and courtly and unreasonable and generous and calculating and naive and gentle and proud and humorous and demanding and unpredictable.

Many people loved him and some feared him, everybody respected him and, as far as I know, nobody ever disliked him in the ninety-three years of his life. There may never have been a more truly successful man, for nobody ever won warmer or wider esteem and nobody ever relished it more.

Only the most fortunate men can appreciate their own success and enjoy it fully. Connie entered professional baseball when it was a game for roughnecks. He saw it become respectable, he lived to be the symbol of its integrity, and he enjoyed every minute of it.

He had an innocent vanity that could delight those who knew him. He liked going places and, of course, he was recognized everywhere. To see him introduced, say, at a fight in the Hollywood Legion Stadium was something to remember: He would spring through the ropes as nimbly as a preliminary boy and draw himself erect, hands clasped overhead, acknowledging the spontaneous cheers.

There were unexpected demonstrations of the affection felt for him in far places. It could be in Dallas or Houston or Fort Worth just before an exhibition game in the spring. All of a sudden, in the lull between infield practice and the first pitch, applause would go rippling through the stands, swelling to a roar, and the customers would be on their feet and here Connie would come hiking from dugout to dugout with his bouncy, long-legged stride, his scorecard waving high. For a moment, swallowing would be difficult.

He could laugh at himself. One winter he obtained title to the renowned orator and pitcher, Bobo Newsom, and brought Bobo up to Philadelphia for a formal signing. When the press was admitted to the tower office in Shibe Park, Connie was on his feet and Bobo relaxed in the swivel chair behind the desk, a big cigar in his face. A little later Newsom stepped outside to take a phone call and Connie dropped absentmindedly into the boss's seat.

As the door opened for his employee's return, Connie sprang up in mock alarm, reinstalling the great man with wonderfully exaggerated humility. Bobo was quite nice about it.

It is the little things one remembers most happily, the small foibles of his great humanity, like his sudden flash of real anger one day in San Francisco. It was a nippy morning and one of Connie's companions suggested closing the windows of a car that was taking them to San Quentin for an exhibition. He was astonished when his solicitude infuriated Connie.

"Dammittohell!" the old man exploded. "Don't worry about me! Dammit, everybody's always worrying. Mrs. Mack says, 'Con, wear your overcoat; Con, don't forget your rubbers!' So I put on my dam' coat and my dam' rubbers and go out to the drugstore to get medicine for her!

"And that Blackburne!" Lena Blackburne, coach with the Athletics, had a leg infection that had kept him in bed in Anaheim, California, when the team broke camp there. "That Blackburne!" Connie said. "It's 'Boss, are you comfortable? Boss, are you warm enough? Sit still, boss, and I'll get it for you.' And where's Blackburne? Down on his tail in Anaheim, dammit!"

So many little things. He could fight a player for the last dime at contract time and win. Yet he confessed that after fifty years two jobs still made him miserable—haggling with a player and telling a kid from the minors that he had to go back.

Little things. His unfailing gift for getting names wrong, from the day of the pitcher Addie "Josh" to the time of the young Cleveland manager

"Mr. Bordiere." "It is a great pleasure," he told fans in Long Beach, California, before an exhibition game with Gabby Hartnett's Cubs, "to be here in Long Branch playing my old friend, Pat Hartnett."

His Athletics are gone. Memories are his monument, and small things like the elevator built for him in Shibe Park before the place was renamed Connie Mack Stadium. The elevator was tailored to measure, eight feet tall and narrow as a phone booth, and there was an old press box attendant named Smitty assigned to take the lift to the ground floor each day in the eighth inning and hold it so Connie could ride up to his office directly after the game.

One day in 1945, the score was tied 1-all when Smitty went down in the eighth. It was still tied when the game was called after the twenty-fourth. Smitty stood with his foot in the door for sixteen innings.

—February 1956

Mr. Stengel Plays It Back

ST. PETERSBURG, FLA.—When the Yankees' daily chores are done, Casey Stengel and his coaches gather with the newspaper men in a mezzanine room in the Soreno Hotel where William, maitre de press room in Yankee Stadium, serves refreshments. If a visitor minds his manners and is pure of heart and does good deeds, he may be rewarded with a dissertation on baseball by the incomparable, the inimitable, the unmitigated Mr. Stengel.

This was such a day. Talk meandered aimlessly for a while, touching on Mr. Stengel's threat to play nine shortstops occasionally this year just because he has nine shortstops in camp, moving on to the six-man and seven-man infields which Branch Rickey experimented with a few springs ago, and all of a sudden the meeting was hips-deep in a discussion of offensive tactics with special reference to the final game of the last World Series.

That was the Game of the Wonderful Double Play which Brooklyn won, 2 to 0, behind Johnny Podres. The Yankees couldn't score on Podres but they were about to score when Yogi Berra sliced a fly to left field with none out and runners on first and second. Sandy Amoros, going faster and farther than Wes Santee, rushed from left center field to the foul line, caught the ball and fired it to Pee Wee Reese, whose relay doubled Gil McDougald off first base, then Hank Bauer rolled out ending the inning and saving the world's championship. It was a game whose details remain vivid in Casey's memory and probably always will because he'd never lost a World Series before.

Now he replayed it.

"I didn't make too many excuses because how can you get mad at that fella for pitching so good and everybody keeps talking all winter about the seventh game but where I lost the series was in the third, fourth and fifth games because all I got to do is win one of them and there ain't no seventh game. I win the first two games and if you win the first two games of a short series like that you figure to take the series and all I wanted was one of those three games in Brooklyn but I lost three there and after being ahead in one, 6 to 1.

"Now, they ask me would I bunt with Berra in that situation with two men on base and I say, yes, I would bunt with Berra but let me remind you of Charley Dressen a couple years before. He bunted with Campanella but I got a man there behind the plate built like a wrestler, you'd say, and a pretty good hitter too. And that fella jumped out there in front of the plate and got the bunts and th'owed men out at third. All the writers said wow, it was close, did the umpire blow the play maybe, but Mr. Berra made the play and the umpire said out.

"Now, you compare catchers, if you can compare American and National League, and I don't think Campanella, the great catcher that he is, could get out there for that ball quite as fast as the wrestler. Ask me a catcher that can th'ow a little better than Berra sometimes and I have to give you Mr. Campanella. Or you want a fella can do a job for you with that stick on a ball up here, Mr. Campanella is a batsman that gets better with age. He will hit that ball for you and Berra will hit some of them, too.

"All right, maybe I could bunt with Berra but baseball today is the greatest rush act I ever saw in the seventh, eighth and ninth innings. The first baseman charges you and the third baseman charges you and when you got runners on first and second base they can make a force-out at third.

"Suppose Berra does bunt and move those runners over, are they going to bring the infield in now and give the next batter a chance to get a base hit on a ground ball? With the score 2 to 0, they are not. That fella over there who I think did an amazing job because he kept his mouth shut and handled some men that were maybe a little tough to handle, he will have his infield back for the double play and concede me that run on third base.

"Maybe I could get that run home but the way that fella was pitching we didn't look like we were going to score because we had other chances and didn't score. Do you know how many innings I went without scoring? The day before, I won, but I didn't score after the first inning so it was seventeen innings I didn't get a run in those two games and then I went to Honolulu and I didn't score in my first three innings there. That's twenty innings and I'm not used to going that long.

"No, I figure I got a man up there at bat built like a wrestler that can pull a ball into the right field seats pretty good and if we're going to score at all against that pitcher this might be the time. Remember, I need two runs to tie and I can't give up Berra on a bunt.

"I figure Berra might pull the ball to right field and so do they, because if they were pitching outside to make him hit to left, why was their outfield playing all the way over in right field? Because it's a right field hitter that's up.

"But Berra hits to the foul line in left and with the leftfielder way over towards center that's going to be a two-base hit nine times out of ten. McDougald runs past second base and I don't blame McDougald because he's looking to tie the score from first base the way our club can do sometimes. McDougald ain't dumb and he runs the bases pretty good.

"If I was the runner on first base I would do the same thing as McDougald because he is the tying run. If that ball drops in there, they wouldn't of had a chance in the world to get McDougald at the plate, I don't care how good the relay is.

"But the ball don't drop in, and I'm ruined."

—March 7, 1956

Pity the Poor Umpire . . . Drs. Frisch and duRocher

THIS IS A sort of "get well" message to one Patrick Badden, a supervisor of umpires for the National Baseball Association. Under a headline announcing, "Umpire Sick With Remorse," an item out of Brazil, Ind., reported that Mr. Badden, stricken with a bellyache, had made the diagnosis himself: "I must be suffering because of all the bad decisions I've made in my life."

Now, Mr. Badden is no acquaintance of this bystander but the heart goes out to him in his hour of pain. If he thinks he's nauseated now, wait until he starts hearing from friends. "At last," ball players all over the nation must be saying, "an umpire who has managed to turn his own stomach!"

Chances are a lot of fans merely glanced at the headline, asked themselves what was so unusual about that, for the love of Augie Donatelli, and went on to read about Robin Roberts. This merely indicates loose thinking on their part.

To be sure, umpires are subject to many of the same ailments that attack humans, but usually these seizures occur on the playing field with specialists in attendance on both benches, ready to diagnose the case and recommend remedies. Mr. Badden fell ill while traveling, presumably alone, without medical advice.

It is to be hoped that he will have recovered completely before these lines get into print. If not, attending physicians might be advised to call into consultation the distinguished Bavarian specialist, Dr. Franz Frisch, B.Sc., Fordham; M.D., Heidelberg; Ph.D., Pilsen-with-an-egg-in-it.

Though he is not now in active practice, Dr. Frisch is recognized as the world's foremost authority on the afflictions of umpires, and his sprightly monograph, "Psycholepsy in Psychasthenic Individuals and Its Effect Upon the Neurospongium or Inner Reticular Stratum of the Retina," is regarded as the definitive work in this field.

When he was Chief Resident in Sportsman's Park, St. Louis, and subsequently in Wrigley Field, Chicago, and Forbes Field, Pittsburgh, Dr. Frisch was especially noted for his brilliantly rapid diagnoses, particularly in cases involving myopic astigmatism. On one occasion, musing in the dugout, he employed some abstruse medical terms in a ringing tone that reached the ears of the umpire behind the plate.

The umpire whipped off his mask and whirled to face the great scientist. "What did you say?" he demanded truculently.

"Himmel!" said Dr. Frisch after a shocked pause. "Don't tell me you're deaf, too!"

Almost equally renowned in this field is the French scholar, Dr. L. Ernest duRocher, D.D., West Springfield Seminary, NBC-TV, famed especially for his work with anxiety neuroses and sophomania, or delusions of omniscience. He, too, has temporarily retired from active practice to the west coast, where he is engaged in research experiments with apes.

Umpires who consulted Dr. duRocher complained occasionally of his brusque bedside manner and insisted that the treatments he prescribed were worse than the ailments they suffered. Dr. duRocher's professional colleagues, however, say he has a heart of gold, mostly Horace Stoneham's.

In any event, Mr. Badden should be warned against any attempt to treat himself with home remedies. When the late Bill McGowan was an umpire in the American League, he cited the tragic case of an umpire named Mike with whom he had worked in the Eastern League.

Like Mr. Badden, Mike had a conscience; like him, Mike called some bad decisions in his time; these led, inevitably, to periodic fits of depression. After one particularly untidy rhubarb, he was inconsolable. This, he told Bill in the dressing room, was the end. The league president's patience had worn thin, anyhow, and there'd surely be a telegraph of dismissal in the morning.

Deaf to Bill's words of comfort, Mike went out that night and applied medication. He continued to apply it right on through the darkness and into the dawn, and when he reported for work the next afternoon it required no specialist to diagnose his condition.

There were only two umpires assigned to a game in those days but Bill told Mike to go back to the hotel and let him work alone. No, Mike said, if Bill would just lead him to the foul line he could find his way out the stripe to his position at first base.

Bill complied and Mike assumed his stance near the bag, arms folded and chin outthrust. On the very first batter there was a hairline play at first base. Mike didn't twitch.

"What is he, Mike? Out or safe?" There was no answer. First baseman, coach and runner converged on the umpire. He stood statuesque and immobile, his eyes fixed on a point somewhere beyond the horizon.

"Mike! Mike! What is he?"

"What is he!" Mike roared. "Hell's bells! *Where* is he?"

—April 1956

Over the River

JERSEY CITY—Ten years ago Jackie Robinson played here, and in 1948 Duke Snider was bombing these fences for Montreal. In this same Roosevelt Stadium, Walter Alston broke in as first baseman for Rochester. On the long, rough haul through the bushes, half a dozen other Dodgers served time in this garden spot of the marshes. Then Brooklyn beckoned, and they thought they had reached the majors. That's what they thought. Today they found out.

In gray and windy cold, a few cars crept through the Holland Tunnel, negotiated the traffic of Journal Square and groped on across the flatlands past rubbish heaps and industrial plants, following the oldest established permanent floating franchise in baseball to its home-away-from-home.

Outside the gates, newsboys hawked papers whose headlines heralded the historic event; "Jersey City's Dodgers Open Major League Season."

It was the start of Walter O'Malley's ignoble experiment—baseball's return, on a part-time, piecemeal basis, to the town which the International League deserted six years ago—but Jersey City wasn't exactly beside itself. Indeed, Jersey City still wasn't beside anything but the pig farms of Secaucus. The first of Brooklyn's seven home games abroad drew 12,214 desperadoes to an abandoned auto race plant that can accommodate 25,000.

A wind howling off the Hackensack River stiffened flags on the grandstand roof, pointing them rigidly toward a muddy barren beyond right field where workmen tearing up the auto track had left a bandshell uprooted. Also in the mud, fenced off from the playing field by a low temporary wall, stood the flagpole where Eddie Fisher and a Marine color guard were to soil their boots ceremoniously.

Eddie sang and an American Legion band tooled while flags went up—first the Stars and Stripes to tell the barnstormers what country they were in, and then a pennant hauled over from Brooklyn to remind the Dodgers that they were champions, even here.

Possibly the most appropriate touch, in view of the weather, was a big football scoreboard.

Near home plate, photographers made shot after shot of Jocko Conlan, the third-base umpire, brandishing a mask and crying, "Play ball!" It wasn't Jocko's mask, for Augie Donatelli was working behind the plate, and umpires in the majors never actually shouted, "Play ball!" But, then, major league teams never play championship games where they don't belong, either.

While bands marched and both teams were booed impartially as they straggled out for the opening ceremonies—after all, both are strangers here—a new baseball was entrusted to Mayor Bernard S. Berry. When the public address system announced that the Mayor would now toss out the first ball, his honor was chatting with voters. Frantic joggling of his elbow won his attention.

"Mr. Mayor! The ball! The ball!"

"The ball?" said Mr. Berry. "I gave it to some kid."

Well, the first major league pitch in New Jersey history was a strike thrown by Carl Erskine and called against the Phillies' Richie Ashburn. The first play with real Jersey flavor was a collaboration by Philadelphia's Willie Jones and Granny Hamner. Jones fell down backing up for a pop fly and knocked himself out of the game while Hamner stood tranquilly at his side and let the ball drop safely.

It was by no means the last play of this sort. Before the last horrid deed was done, the whole business looked like a conspiracy to stink baseball out of the state.

Del Ennis dawdled after a drive by Gil Hodges in the first inning and converted it to a three-run double. Then while Robinson played cat-and-mouse between first and second base, Hodges tried unsuccessfully to sneak home from third and killed off the Dodgers' only scoring inning against Murry Dickson.

Due chiefly to boots by Robinson and Carl Furillo and a wild pitch by Erskine, Philadelphia tied the score in the third inning. In the tenth, Philadelphia went ahead, 4 to 3, whereupon Roy Campanella retied the score by doubling Snider home.

At long and gruesome last, Rube Walker got Zimmer home with a fly ball, and the Dodgers had their first official victory since Oct. 4.

They had waited for it 197 days. Jersey had waited since the dawn of civilization. It required two hours, forty-three minutes, ten innings and eight errors. As the fellow says, you can take the boy out of the bush, but—

Far off on the gray horizon, a ray from the setting sun touched the towers of Manhattan. They were a million light years away.

—April 20, 1956

Farm Kid from Iowa

THIS WAS EASTER Sunday, 1937, in Vicksburg, Miss. A thick-muscled kid, rather jowly, with a deep dimple in his chin, slouched out to warm up for the Indians in an exhibition game with the Giants. He had heavy shoulders and big bones and plowboy's lumbering gait. His name was Bob Feller and everybody had heard about him.

This was the farm kid Cy Slapnicka had dug up in a town named Van Meter, Iowa. In a night exhibition in Cleveland the previous July, he had struck out eight Cardinals in three innings, though not every pitch had found the strike zone. One had shattered a chair in the grandstand. In August he had struck out fifteen Browns in an official American League game, and three weeks later he had fanned seventeen Athletics. With a dead ball or live one, no American League pitcher from Cy Young and Rube Waddell through Walter Johnson and Lefty Grove had struck out so many in a nine-inning game.

All this the Giants had heard, but they had not seen the young man. They were taking their pre-game exercises when the kid kicked his left foot high and delivered his first warm-up pitch. All over the field, action ceased.

Nobody said anything. Everybody just stood still and watched. Twenty baseball seasons have passed, and that small tableau remains vivid in the memory of witnesses. Those who were there do not tire of describing the scene. "That day," they say, as though telling of a personal achievement, "I saw a pitcher."

Last spring the Giants came barnstorming east from the Phoenix, Ariz., training camp in company with the Indians, as is their habit. Arriving in New York just before the season opened, one of the party said, "You're going to be astonished when you see Feller this summer. He's got the fast one back again, somehow. For three or four innings, I'll swear he's good as ever."

As it turned out, there was little occasion for astonishment because

American League fans didn't see much of Feller. He is coming now to the end of his eighteenth season—there were, in addition, forty-four months in the Navy and eight battle stars. He has pitched forty-nine innings, lost three games and won none.

You could call it the end of an era, probably, for if there is another player active in either league who was there as early as 1936, his name does not come to mind. At any rate, it's the end of a career.

Hank Greenberg has said he would talk to Feller soon and "be guided by whatever decision he makes" regarding the future. He said he didn't feel that Feller was "doing justice to himself to stay on the team without working. There's something wrong with the picture of him warming up in the bullpen."

Of course the picture is wrong. So are those figures: no victories, three defeats. It always seems wrong when this happens, though there never could have been a moment's doubt that the year would come when Feller wouldn't win a game. When Slapnicka led him off the Iowa sandlots, he started the boy toward this year.

Reviewing the seasons that lay between, one must take exception with the record books, which usually offer a reliable measure of ability. Feller, for example, will never join the tight little group of twelve pitchers who won 300 or more games in the big leagues.

He should be No. 13, but his total is 266 and the thirty-four victories he did not score will forever be beyond him. In the three seasons before he joined the Navy, he won twenty-four, twenty-seven and twenty-five games. He was away more than three seasons, far more time than he would have needed to win thirty-four games against the strongest opposition. Against the squatters who homesteaded the American League during World War II, he might have won thirty-four in a single summer.

To be sure, there is meat enough in Feller's record to feed any man's pride. In 1938 he struck out eighteen Tigers in nine innings. In 1946 he fanned 348 batsmen, smashing a record that Rube Waddell had held for forty-two years. He pitched three no-hit games. In one four-year span, he struck out 1,007 batters in 1,238 innings.

He was, simply, the greatest pitcher of his time. Curiously, the biggest victories almost always eluded him. In 1940 a stranger named Floyd Giebell beat him, 2 to 0, in the deciding game of Cleveland's pennant race with Detroit. In 1948, he pitched a two-hitter in the opening World Series game with the Braves, and lost to Johnny Sain, 1 to 0. Trying for Cleveland's fourth victory in that series, he was knocked out before the biggest crowd that ever saw a baseball game.

All the same, he was a pitcher whose like is seldom seen. One winter a Cleveland newspaper man scoured through the records and then telephoned Feller. "There is," he said, "just one regular player in the league whom you've never struck out. Did you know you'd never fanned Birdie Tebbetts?"

"No," Feller said, "but I will."

He did.

—September 24, 1956

Water-Winged Victory

IF THE DODGERS win the National League pennant by, say, one game, theirs will be a phony championship, though not through any fault of their own. There is a strong feeling that this has been written here before, in the same words, in the same circumstances, maybe three or four or five years ago. Certainly it will be written again, possibly by Bill Corum in his next edition.

When the pennant race is over, it may very well be possible to look back to Sunday's operations in Pittsburgh and say, "That did it; that was the day of decision." If that's how it turns out, then nobody can pretend that the Dodgers won a baseball championship, because that wasn't baseball they were playing.

Early in the afternoon, a sudden, violent electrical storm drove groundskeepers to cover before they could get the tarpaulin over the field. Play was interrupted for an hour. Had this been June, the umpires would have declared the field unplayable.

This is September, though, and these games must be completed and there isn't much time. Also, the crowd was the biggest ever assembled in Forbes Field since the joint was built in 1909. A postponement would have meant almost 45,000 rain checks would have to be redeemed later. Black earth was shoveled into some of the larger lagoons on the infield, and play was resumed. What followed was a humorless travesty.

Pittsburgh's Jack Shepard lost his footing rounding second base and was unable to reach third on a slowly bounding single to center. Lee Walls, swinging at a pitch, fell down in the batter's box.

Converging on a bunt by Roy Campanella, Pirates slipped and floundered and couldn't make a play.

"When you see those fellows skidding and sliding and scrambling," Vin Scully observed to the television audience, "I mean, it isn't a normal game, not under these conditions."

"Here's another bunt," Vin said a little later, "down Mud Alley."

This was a baseball game? A ball game on which a championship might depend?

"The field," Vin Scully said, straining understatement to the snapping point, "is not in very good shape at all." He said it looked more like a scarred battlefield than a baseball diamond. On television, it looked like an advanced case of acne.

Rain fell heavily again with the Dodgers at bat in the top of the sixth. They had scored one run in the inning and were leading, 4 to 3, with one out, the bases filled and Duke Snider at bat. Play was suspended for the second time.

Weigh the burden on the umpires. If the game were washed out at this point, the score would stand at 3 to 3, as it was when the fifth inning ended. The Dodgers would lose the run they had made in the sixth, they would lose this opportunity for Snider to drive in a gang of colleagues, and—most important of all—a starting assignment for Don Newcombe would be squandered. Newk was on his way to victory but now the game would have to be replayed without him.

So, of course, the umpires didn't call the game. The news will come as a surprise to some, but umpires are human. They waited another hour, while the television camera prowled the stands, picking up shots of fans holding umbrellas and newspapers and seat cushions and top coats and sodden pasteboard cartons over their heads to ward off the rain. There's nothing so sadly forlorn as a baseball park in the rain, except maybe last summer's tattered circus poster flapping in a January wind.

They rolled back the tarpaulin and used brooms to sweep water away from third base. "Boy," Vin Scully said, "the infield is really a mess!"

A ball plowed into the earth and an attendant had to bring a towel to swab mud off the face of the Pirates' catcher, Shepard. Lee Walls couldn't run hard for a foul fly because, Vin Scully said, he was afraid of falling down. Tom Gorman, the umpire, dropped his cap in the mud, had to wring it out and clean it with a towel. They brought towels to scrub off the plate.

Curfew rang with the Dodgers still at bat in the ninth, but leading by a comfortable margin. The game would be completed later and they'd probably win, but could anybody say it was a ball game they were winning?

Bill Corum has been yipping about this for years. He has pointed out that there is a lot of air in the season's schedule and it would be no trick at all to tighten the program and leave a week, if necessary, at the season's end to play off games "weathered out" in the late stages of a race. Vital games should not be played under unplayable conditions, he says, and he is so right.

The men who own baseball will say, "Pittsburgh's biggest partial concession is the National League ruling that games bearing on the championship shall be played off after the season if they can't be completed earlier, but this doesn't go far enough. If the umpires knew there was a clear week available if needed, they wouldn't feel it necessary to tolerate games in intolerable circumstances."

The men who own baseball will say, "Pittsburgh's biggest crowd sat through it all. The fans didn't go home. Doesn't that prove they were satisfied?" It does not. It only proves that business was real good in Forbes Field, and rain checks won't have to be honored. To the men who own baseball, this is a business. To the Commissioner of Baseball it ought to be a sport.

—September 25, 1956

Damyankees

ON THE DAY before the 1949 baseball season ended, the Red Sox led the American League by one game and had two to play in Yankee Stadium. The Yankees had to win both games to take the pennant. That day, Joe DiMaggio spoke. The Yankees had played 152 games that summer and heard nothing from Joe, but this day he addressed them all as they started out of the clubhouse.

"All right, gentlemen," he said, "let's give it a little extra today."

They won that day and the next, of course, and beat the Dodgers in the World Series.

In 1937 the Yankees signed Tommy Henrich as a free agent, gave him $25,000 and sent him to Newark. He had played only seven games there, and was batting .440, when New York lost two straight to Detroit. In the clubhouse Joe McCarthy chewed them out.

"Hell's bells," grumbled Roy Johnson, the outfielder, as the manager stalked out, "that guy wants to win every game!"

He didn't intend that McCarthy should overhear, but Joe did. Without glancing back or breaking stride, the manager marched directly to the telephone. That's how Henrich became a Yankee and Johnson a member of the Boston Braves.

Several years before that, the Yankees trampled the Milwaukee Brewers by something like 19 to 0 in a spring exhibition in Palmetto, Fla. As the players waited on the bus for St. Petersburg, McCarthy climbed aboard, tossed one black look around and sat down next to a player who hadn't known him long.

"Well," the young man said brightly, "pretty good today, eh? 19 to 0?"

Savagely the manager turned on him.

"Pretty good? Against these bush league humpty-dumpties? We should beat 'em 29 to 0."

In a clubhouse meeting before the 1941 World Series with Brooklyn, McCarthy asked whether any of the Yankees knew how to pitch to Jimmy Wasdell. Henrich knew Wasdell could be fooled by a change-of-pace, but Wasdell was his friend. They had come up together, more or less, through the minors, and Tommy wasn't going to blow the whistle. He and the rest were silent.

"Saw him four years ago in Chattanooga," McCarthy said. "Looked to me like he might have trouble with a change."

"Wasdell," Henrich told himself, "is a dead duck."

McCarthy is gone now, and Henrich and Wasdell and Roy Johnson and DiMaggio, and maybe these tales haven't any bearing on developments of the next few days in Ebbets Field and Yankee Stadium. Then again, maybe they have. Maybe they suggest, in their small way, what it is that makes the Yankees the Yankees. Maybe they hint at the nature of the task that faces the Dodgers.

Joe McCarthy did want to win every game, not entirely out of greed for victory but for a sounder reason reflecting the basic philosophy which has guided the Yankees for years. He believed that every baseball man's job was to play the game better than anybody else. If you lost a game, that meant something was wrong. Better find out what was wrong, and remedy it.

That is exactly the way Casey Stengel looks at it, the way George Weiss does, and Ed Barrow did before him. Like McCarthy, Stengel remembers what he saw in Chattanooga four years ago, and in Aurora, Ill., four decades ago.

People ask what makes a Yankee. Part of the answer, at least, is there in that attitude, deeply ingrained in every one of them. Going for the championship of the Bronx, Flatbush and Jersey City's Journal Square, they expect to win every game. By their reckoning, any World Series is a four-game series. If it takes longer, it's a mistake. If they don't win at all, it's a scandal.

This is an important reason why professional price makers install the Yankees as favorites in any World Series, even against a club that whipped them the year before. The professionals can make mistakes, of course. Mistakenly, they liked the Red Sox over the Cardinals in 1946 and they thought Cleveland would smash the Giants in 1954. Curiously, with each Giant victory in '54 the Indians became stronger favorites for the next day's game. It was all over before anybody could accept the notion of four straight for New York.

Scarcely anybody will quarrel with the statement that the Dodgers won their pennant against sterner opposition than the Yankees met this year. That's one consideration. Another is that Brooklyn has some hot-and-cold guys, like Duke Snider and Gil Hodges. Hot, they might win it all, but baseball as the Yankees play it, is a chilling business.

The Yankees in six, it says here. Brooklyn gets two tokens for the subway.

—October 3, 1956

Feat Against Dodgers First in Any Series

THE FIFTH GAME of the World Series had been finished for forty-five minutes but the crowds didn't want to go. They moved slowly through the stands like files of army ants. In front of the visitors' bench a throng swelled steadily, packing more and more tightly around a man who stood pinned against the dugout corner, signing programs with stiffening fingers.

Dear diary! It was exciting! They were getting Ed Sullivan's autograph.

Upstairs a stray thrust a scorecard into the press box, interrupted a newspaper man at work, and asked for *his* signature. The interruption didn't matter, for there was no story to write. The Dodgers hadn't got any hits.

Down in the catacombs where the Yankees bathe and dress, a big man sat and sweated. His name is Don Larsen. He is a pitcher, the first who ever lived to pitch a no-hit game in the World Series, the first in thirty-four years to pitch a perfect game anywhere in the major leagues.

Nobody asked him to sign anything. From San Diego to Baltimore, Bourbon drinkers arose and lifted glasses in a solemn, silent toast.

Let's make it simple, this: Behind Larsen's strong pitching, the Yankees defeated the Dodgers, 2 to 0, yesterday for their third victory and now require only one more for their seventeenth world championship. They made five hits off schoolboy Sal Maglie, including a home run by Mickey Mantle.

Now, then. When Don Larsen was born in Michigan City, Ind., Aug. 7, 1929, seven years had passed since the last big league team played nine innings without getting a man to first base. Charley Robertson, of the White Sox, pitched that perfect game.

Larsen grew up big, six-feet-four and 225 pounds. He came to the American League with the Browns, where his pitching equipment and his power at bat set the more excitable scholars babbling about a second Babe

Ruth. Then the Browns became Orioles, and although Baltimore isn't exactly a nine o'clock town, it couldn't hold Donald. One of the first orders Paul Richards received as manager was to get rid of Larsen.

Dealt off to the Yankees, Larsen was sent down to Denver for a while, came back and helped pitch New York to the 1955 pennant. This year he did nothing spectacular until September, when he won four games and discarded his windup.

During his next-to-last game this season, in Boston, he experienced blinding intellectual flashes. If hitting was all a matter of timing, he reasoned, why couldn't a pitcher unsettle the batters' rhythm by leaving out the big motion they were accustomed to seeing? Since then he has just bowed from the waist, straightened up and thrown.

"I still say," a Brooklyn fan insisted yesterday when the deed had been done, "that the big stiff throws like a girl."

From the beginning, this was the best game in a struggle that has been getting better and better. It was just five years to the day since Maglie, as a Giant, had lost a World Series game to the Yankees, yielding a home run to Mantle's predecessor in center field, one Joe DiMaggio. It was thirteen days since Sal himself had pitched a no-hitter against Philadelphia. It was five days since he had beaten the Yankees in the opening game of the World Series.

He had better control in this second start, this swarthy and poisonous descendant of the Borgias, but he had Larsen against him and Larsen had Yankees behind him. When Don didn't take care of the hitters, his playmates did. A savage line drive by Jackie Robinson, a bitter ground ball hit by Junior Gilliam, a long fly by Gil Hodges, all became putouts.

From the seventh inning on, 64,519 witnesses screamed with every pitch. As Larsen completed each hitless, runless inning, they howled hoarsely. When he walked to the plate to lead off the Yankees' last turn at bat, they rose in salute, beating their palms and emitting wild animal cries. Then in the ninth—

Well, Carl Furillo fouled off two pitches, took a ball, fouled twice more and flied out. Roy Campanella fouled once and grounded out. Dale Mitchell, batting for Maglie, took a ball, a called strike, swung and missed, took another ball, hit another foul. The last pitch came in. Mitchell leaned forward, twitched, and took the final strike.

Yogi Berra plunged out to intercept Larsen, wrapped arms about his head, put a leg-scissors on his middle, and swung ponderously off the ground. He might have pulled even that tower of gristle to earth, but now the other Yankees closed about the pair. Larsen vanished in the middle.

In the confusion, Benny Weinrig won $9. Benny is pressbox steward in Ebbets Field. Whenever the Dodgers or their opponents are hitless for three innings, somebody starts a pool on the first hit. If nobody wins, Benny gets the swag.

Benny loves the Dodgers. To him, this was blood money.

—October 9, 1956

Boom-Boom Is Back

OGDEN, UTAH—It isn't really when you see the Statue of Liberty that you know you're home, nor is it the sight of Golden Gate Bridge. It's getting to read the cheerfully familiar headlines again—"Nab Doctor as Cat Burglar," "Zoo Has New Rhino, Needs Name," "Cracker Crunching Killer Smiles," "Missing Girls on Hike."

Here's one that announces, "Senators Sign Boom-Boom Beck"—and talk about sour familiar lines. One strives in vain to recall how many times over how many years he has read the same tidings in practically the same words, with only the name of the ball club changed. "Browns Sign Boom-Boom Beck," "Boom-Boom Comes to Bums," "Beck Inks Pact With Tigers"—hiring Walter Beck is an old American custom which has its roots deep in the soil.

At first glance, the reader assumes that Washington has employed Beck as a pitcher, which seems a sound move toward strengthening Charley Dressen's staff. After all, Boom-Boom is only fifty-two and he can talk English without a Latin accent, which should make him a sensation in Griffith Stadium.

On closer inspection, however, it turns out that Walter is to assist Mr. Dressen as coach of the pitchers, filling a vacancy created when Joe Jaynes was promoted to vice-president in recognition of his ability, his years of loyal service, his inspirational qualities, and his marriage to one of the Griffith girls.

Boom-Boom will make a fine coach. Nothing will surprise or dismay him. There is nothing that can befall any of the pitchers, even Washington pitchers, that hasn't already happened to Walter Beck.

Also, there is no sweeter guy in sports than this tall, friendly, four-eyed gentleman of the painfully descriptive nickname. As pet names go, "Boom-Boom" is eminently suitable for a drummer boy or an accomplished wingshot of a fist fighter or even a home run hitter. For a pitcher, it has connotations that cannot be construed as complimentary, yet Walter is a man of rare amiability who accepted the cognomen without protest.

There is, in fact, only one case on record in which Beck lost his patience in public. The particulars of that incident are perhaps as widely known as any in baseball; whenever baseball yarns are being swapped, this tale inevitably is told. It is just barely possible, though, that there are some subscribers young enough to be unfamiliar with the story, for it goes way, way back.

It goes back to the piping times of peace and depression in the 1930s when the Dodgers were bums in fact as well as in name and included on their roster some of the oddest characters ever exhibited in flannel rompers. Not the least of these was Mr. Hack Wilson, a little round man with big muscles and thirst to match.

It was remarked a few paragraphs back that Boom-Boom Beck once lost his temper in public but this is not strictly accurate, for the incident took place in Philadelphia's antique Baker Bowl where ball players were assured of privacy if nothing else. This ancestral home of the Phillies was a squalid well of loneliness, studiously avoided by cash customers but beloved by lefthanded hitters whose feeblest pop fly would rebound thunderously from the tall, tin-faced fence that cast its shadow upon first base.

Walter Beck was pitching for the Dodgers against a Philadelphia batting order of unexampled ferocity—Chuck Klein, Lefty O'Doul, Don Hurst, Spud Davis, Pinky Whitney, Dick Bartell. Those guys swung so hard that when they missed a pitch it was generally scored as a two-base hit off the wall.

It wasn't one of Walter's best days. He would throw and Klein would swing and—karroom. There was a whirling white projectile caroming off the fence with stubby-legged, potbellied Hack Wilson in panting pursuit.

It wasn't one of Hack's best days, either, due in part to the fact that the evening before had been one of his very best nights. Head throbbing and legs protesting, he patrolled right field with such fortitude as he could muster while drive after drive whistled over his head and rebounded past his ears.

Memory suggests that the manager of those Dodgers was Max Carey, though it could have been Casey Stengel. Whichever it was, he endured the horrid spectacle for an inning or two, then trudged out to change pitchers. Walter, though, had set out to do a job and was in no mood to leave it unfinished. Earnestly he pleaded for another chance; reluctantly his leader assented.

Volley followed volley. Thunder pealed and echoed. Here and there Hack Wilson raced, gasping and wheezing. Wearily the Brooklyn manager made his way to the mound once more. This, he told Walter, was the end, positively and beyond debate. He signalled to the bull pen.

Walter argued. He pleaded. No, his skipper said firmly, and held out his hand for the ball. Rage and frustration overcame Walter Beck. He spun and threw the ball, hard as he could, toward the right field fence.

At that moment, Hack Wilson was catching a breath. Feet wide, hands on knees, he stood bent with head hung low trying to shake the cobwebs from his brain. Something crashed against the wall behind him.

He straightened. He whirled. The ball came back to him on one bounce. Pivoting, he fired a strike to second base. It was his finest play of the day.

—December 14, 1956

Spit and Polish

EARLY IN THE training season, Charley Dressen split his squad down the middle and the two halves—designated in the box score as the Have Nots and Haven't Eithers—played a ball game that ended in a tie. "The Senators this year," wrote Bob Addie in the "Washington Post," "are so bad they can't beat themselves."

Since then Dressen's disciples have contrived to beat themselves in some games and the opposition in others, same as all the clubs do during the muscletone season. No effort has been made to check the records, but dispatches from the camps have left the impression that there has been an uncommon number of extra-inning games and low scores this spring.

If that is so, then some original thinker is going to declare in the paper one of these mornings that, "the pitchers are ahead of the hitters." After championship play starts the hitters will catch up, Mickey Mantle will lose a ball in Westchester County, and the inevitable cry of protest will arise about the lively ball.

It happens every year, so maybe now is as good a time as any to propose a remedy. When the pitcher is being subjected to cruel and unusual punishment, the rules ought to permit him to retaliate against the batter, i.e., to spit in his eye.

The suggestion is put forward in all seriousness. If, as some believe, emphasis on hitting has knocked the game out of joint, then the rulemakers could take a long step toward restoring balance between offense and defense by returning the spitball to respectability.

Because spit is a horrid word, misconceptions have grown up regarding the irrigated delivery. Authors who should know better have written that it was ruled out because it was a dangerous pitch, difficult to control and a menace to the batter's life and limb. In the popular mind, the spitter is not only unsanitary and illegal but intrinsically dishonest, a cheating device to be employed only by a low, unprincipled cad.

Actually it is an effective pitch when mastered, no more difficult to control than any other. Leaders of the saliva set like Red Faber, Clarence Mitchell, Bill Doak and Burleigh Grimes were no wilder than their arid playmates, and if the records were to show that Grimes potted more batsmen than some of his contemporaries, that should be attributed to his combative disposition, not his moist delivery.

The only thing wrong with the spitter is that it has been illegal since 1920. Its use was prohibited that year, except by pitchers already employing it in the majors. Faber continued on his slobbery way through 1933 and Grimes was still drooling in 1934, but when they departed that was the end of sanctioned expectorations.

There are qualified baseball men who believe that legalizing the spitter would do more than arm the pitcher with a weapon which he needs. There is at least some ground for a belief that it would mitigate the plague of sore arms which is an occupational hazard blighting many young lives.

All the evidence indicates that the pitch was easy on the arm, for Faber was still with the White Sox at forty-six and Doak, Mitchell and Grimes all pitched into or past their fortieth year.

When they departed, spitting didn't cease all together, though only Ted Williams has done it openly. Preacher Roe has confessed that he slipped in a wet one now and then when he pitched for the Dodgers, Lew Burdette is accused of it, and Nelson Potter got caught at it.

The records credit Potter with nineteen victories for the pennant-winning Browns of 1944 but with a little more guile he could have made it twenty. He was winning another game that summer when the umpire detected more on the ball than the A. J. Reach Co. had put there. "Shame!" cried the umpire, "Begone."

In 1920 the growing popularity of Babe Ruth made fans and club owners home run conscious, and trick deliveries were outlawed to aid the batters and draw more customers. The profit motive sired the rule and it is for personal profit that pitchers occasionally violate it, moistening fingertips with the tongue or with a smidgeon of perspiration from brow, neck or forearm.

They aren't necessarily evil characters. There is a classic tale about the estimable Tommy Bridges, Detroit's wonderful little curve ball pitcher, struggling to protect a one-run lead over Washington with menacing Stan Spence at bat.

He got Spence on three dipping strikes whose erratic behavior brought loud protests from the batter and his manager, Ossie Bluege. Spence, Bluege and Bill Summers, the umpire, trooped out to the mound where Summers put the question bluntly: Had Bridges thrown a spitter?

Tommy was deeply hurt. This, he told Summers reproachfully, was tantamount to a charge of cheating. As the delegation turned away, defeated, Bridges cupped his glove to his mouth.

"Hey, Bill," he called in a stage whisper, "wasn't that last one a sweetheart?"

—March 29, 1957

Men Who Drink and Those Who Don't

BEFORE THE GAME, the Yankees were in third place and had scored fewer runs for the season than any other club in the major leagues. It needs a moment for the full horror of that to sink in. It means New York has scored less than the Pirates, less than the Cubs, less than the Senators. In six starts since coming home to the Stadium the Yankees had made fifteen runs, six in one game, which means they got nine in the other five.

"I know you'd be just as well pleased to be five games in front," a visitor said to Casey Stengel, "but for us fans this is more fun."

The Yankee manager was watching the White Sox in batting practice. "I know," he said, nodding. He understands that the customers enjoy the illusion of a pennant race, but he doesn't pretend it is fun for him.

"We been having it tough," he said. "I never had so many good players all bad at the same time. My men that drink and my men that don't drink."

Casey was on his feet in the dugout, swinging an imaginary bat.

"Skowron," he said, "he never takes a drink, so he's looking off here and swinging there and the ball is in the dirt but he can't stop himself and he swings. They pitch him up here and he swings and you say he don't know the strike zone, but you know he does."

"Mantle," Casey said, and now he was swinging lefthanded. "They're fighting him and they say we'll walk him and he gets madder'n hell and madder'n hell and they say we won't walk him, just pitch him inside. So they throw a couple in here and he's madder'n hell, and he jumps back and swings and goes out.

"Then he wants to kill himself, which would be a hard thing, making the kind of money he is and so young."

A man had come through the tunnel from the Yankees' clubhouse and, catching the manager's eye, signaled that he was wanted on the phone. Casey walked his way, talking over his shoulder as he went.

"To kill himself so young," he said. "He oughta wait till he starts getting pains in the neck. He don't have to give himself a pain in the neck."

He disappeared into the tunnel. Thus endeth the text for the day. Thus starteth, pretty soon, the season's fifth meeting of Yankees and White Sox.

In the next couple of hours, all the experiences ordinarily reserved for the drunks befell the Yankees—the ones who drink and the ones who don't. The Sox ran them dizzy, the Yanks threshed and floundered in a mystifying haze, and fortune, smiling on Chicago at the outset, was laughing like a loon at the end.

Speed and a bad-hop single gave Chicago a one-run lead but in the fourth inning Yankee hitting made the score 3 to 1. These were the first runs scored in twenty-two consecutive innings off Jim Wilson, proprietor of the most awesome earned-run average in the big leagues.

It seemed then that the Yankees had found the answers for Wilson, but now something happened which isn't seen once in a decade in Yankee Stadium. With Luis Aparicio on base, Minnie Minoso sent a tall fly to left center. Elston Howard approached it with confidence, Mickey Mantle with great resolution. Due to natural laws, this required them to approach each other. When a tangle of arms and legs had been sorted out, Aparicio was home and the Yankee lead was only 3 to 2.

That was only the beginning. In the sixth, a line drive deflected by the pitcher hid itself under Billy Martin's sprawling torso. It was called an error. Mantle looped out for a long drive by Nellie Fox, moving at the relaxed, unhurried gait that bespeaks an easy catch. The ball went over his head for three bases and they called that an error, too, an unbelievable one.

In the confusion, Johnny Kucks went to the showers. He was still soaping his pelt when he heard the voice of his reliever, Art Ditmar. "Move over," Arthur said. Chicago now had five runs for the inning and the score was 7 to 3. Later on it was 8 to 4, the final.

"Radio Liberation," a note from the Yankees' publicity office reported, "is taping parts of the game plus interviews in Russian for re-broadcast beamed to Russia."

It's not going to help. If the Soviets hear this one they're going to say, "That's ain't the game we invented."

—May 23, 1957

A Wake for the Giants

IN THE SIXTH inning the Pirates scored their seventh run and Bill Rigney walked out to call for a new pitcher. The crowd booed the Giants' manager, and this was the first time its voice was loud, though there had been decent applause before the game for Mrs. John McGraw and some of the old players.

Probably it is fanciful and sentimental to suggest that the quiet was that of the wake. Of course, it was a wake. There were 11,606 customers for a game between the Giants, moored in sixth place, and the Pirates, tied for seventh. If it hadn't been the very last that New York's oldest team would play in the hallowed Polo Grounds, the count might have been closer to Saturday's 2,768.

When they were simply the New York Club in 1883, they played down at 110th St. It was there they received their name from their first manager, James Mutrie, who wore a top hat and frock coat and carried a gold-headed cane. "My big fellows!" he cried exuberantly. "My Giants!" It was 1891 when they took over Brotherhood Field and renamed it the Polo Grounds.

Here Amos Rusie fired the fast ball that inspired a line which batters still use, probably believing they are coining it: "You can't hit it if you can't see it." Here a kid out of Brooklyn, Willie Keeler by name, broke in as a third baseman, not very good. Buck Ewing was good, though. Saloons all over town displayed a garish lithograph of "Ewing's famous slide."

There was a pretty fair cheer for Bobby Thomson when he went to bat the first time. He got a single but wandered off base and was doubled on a fly ball. He was playing third base.

That's where Thomson was playing that unforgettable day in 1951, and he was having a time of it then, too. He messed up a promising inning by stealing second with a playmate already there, and when the Dodgers scored the runs that seemed to sew up the pennant play-off, it was through Thomson's position that their big hits whistled.

Then Bobby swung his bat, and the Giants were champions of the National League. Maybe they'll win other championships, some day, for San Francisco. Surely there'll be other home runs hit at timely moments, but will there ever be another scene like that? The season was over but the fans wouldn't leave. Thousands stood cheering beneath the clubhouse windows in center field, singing, sobbing, calling again and again for the heroes to show themselves. Twilight deepened, and still the clubhouse windows blazed with the flashes of photographers' lamps.

Yesterday's customers were equally reluctant to leave. Most of them sat it out as the Giants dragged wearily to defeat. Pigeons kept circling overhead, as though impatient to move in, and one could fancy Robert Moses, blueprints of a housing project in hand, waiting to pounce.

These Giants played as though they couldn't wait to get to San Francisco. They couldn't hit the ball or catch it, pick it up or hold it, and Rigney kept calling the bullpen for another bull.

One day John McGraw handed Bugs Raymond a new ball and sent him out to warm up for relief. When Bugs got into the game he was loaded. Leaving the bench, he had hiked right past the bullpen to a gin mill across the street, and traded the ball for three shots of rye.

Pitchers with the old Giants got knocked out, too. After Rube Marquard arrived here as the "$11,000 beauty," it wasn't long before they were calling him the "$11,000 lemon." Rube Schauer had to relieve Ferdie Schupp so often that Sid Mercer wrote in "The New York Globe," "it never Schupps but it Schauers." And there was even a Giant manager who tried Christy Mathewson at first base and shortstop and in the outfield because he said Matty couldn't pitch. Horace Fogel was the name of that genius.

In the ninth inning a Pirate named John Powers hit the last home run that will ever be struck in the Polo Grounds. It went clear over the roof and stirred scarcely a murmur. When Joe Jackson hit one there, it was a sensation.

The crowd shouted for Willie Mays on his next-to-last time at bat, when he beat out an infield single, and stood up to cheer him on his last, when he grounded out. A thunder of boos responded when it was announced that "after the game, patrons will not be permitted on the field until the players have reached the clubhouse."

The instant Dusty Rhodes hit a grounder for the last putout—remember the World Series of 1954 when he did everything but walk on water?—hundreds of kids rushed onto the field and Giants ran for their lives, fending off souvenir hunters who snatched for caps and gloves. Adults followed the boys.

Kids tore up the bases, clawed at the mound for the pitchers' rubber and dug for home plate. Boys scooped earth from the mound into paper bags and pulled outfield grass which they stuffed into pants' pockets. They ripped the green canvas from the scene behind home plate, gouged sponge rubber from the outfield walls, tore the roof off the bullpen bench in right field.

A man took a photograph of the plate. Another pried the number tag from the railing of a box. A woman walked off carrying a big cake of sod from beneath the plate. Below the clubhouse windows, a forlorn throng lingered. Somebody out there held up a sign. It read: "Stay, team, stay."

—September 30, 1957

Mr. S. Plays It Over

MILWAUKEE, WIS.—At 3:26 p.m. yesterday Hank Bauer forced Bobby Richardson at second base and the World Series score stood at one victory each for the Yankees and the Braves. As this is written just about twenty-four hours later, the Yankees are leading, two games to one. Their beloved leader, Mr. Casey Stengel, re-played the second one in Bedroom E, Car Y-2, on the train that hauled them from New York to this Queen City of the Cheeselands. Casey won going away.

"That ball Shantz hit," Mr. Stengel said, "It went pretty fair, didn't it?" This was a drive to left field which Milwaukee's Wes Covington caught with a splendid backhand stab in the second inning when the score was tied and there were Yankees on first and second base.

"Two out and everybody running," Mr. Stengel said, "if that fella don't ketch it maybe two runs can score and that pitcher is out of there. Well, about him being out of there I don't know because if I say he is then I'm managing the other team but he might be. His control [Lew Burdette's] wasn't any too good early but he started throwing the ball low and kept getting better and better."

"Now," Mr. Stengel said, and paused, and there was silence in the room. After all, Covington had caught the ball and then there had been home runs by Johnny Logan and Hank Bauer which offset each other, and then Milwaukee had won it in the fourth inning. With Braves on first and second Covington had fouled off two bunts and then popped a soft hit to left field and two runs had scored when Enos Slaughter's throw got past Tony Kubek at third.

"Now," Mr. Stengel said, getting into that fourth inning as everybody knew he would, "we had some tough luck on the bunt. The first time, he [Covington] dropped it in front of the plate and Berra jumped out for it but it took a backspin and bounced back foul. I wish it was fair because Berra was right on it and he'll get somebody, maybe go to third and then first for the dee-pee.

"But it's foul. I got Shantz pitching and I don't take him out because the fella is up to bunt, which I agree—a lefthand hitter and a lefthand pitcher—and Shantz is a pretty cute fielder. He'll handle the bunt if he gets it. So this time the fella rolls it along the first base line. I think maybe he could of got him at first, which moves the runner over, of course, but Shantz yelled, 'Let it roll,' and it went foul again.

"I would have to say I still had some doubt but that he might still be bunting, but all the reports say [Covington] is a pretty good hitter and you can't play him shallow in left field. So he's hitting but he don't hit it good and Slaughter has to run in for the ball.

"Now, in justice to Slaughter, I had him playing in the hole in left center and he did make a couple of ketches there, didn't he? But I think he might of forgot who was the runner.

"The fella on one leg didn't get a good start because McDougald was bluffing him back—you know how, making a break for second. McDougald wasn't sure the fella [Covington] wasn't bunting on third strike, either. Being lefthanded he [Bobby Shantz] can do that pretty cute, looking around like maybe he's going to make a play there [a pick-off at second].

"When the runner [Adcock] gets to third he [Connie Ryan, Milwaukee coach] don't know whether to send him in but the fella that was on first [Andy Pafko] is coming around second and if he don't send him in we're going to have two runners on third. I guess when Slaughter saw him running he thought, 'Oh-oh, the play's at third.'

"Now, if you're pitching and men on first and second, where do you go? Behind the plate, don't you, to back up for the catcher? I would have to say that's where I'd go if I was pitching. And I don't blame the kid at third [Kubek] for coming in to take the cut-off and then having to get back fast because that's the play. Men on first and second, the third baseman comes in for the cut-off, and the shortstop covers third, but McDougald was looking for a play at third.

"I didn't see how the ball got past Kubek because I was watching the fella on one leg coming home and I thought we could get him. The ball went through and nobody backing up because Shantz expected the play to be at the plate. So two runs score.

"Now, we get the runner at the plate it's one out or even if he stops at third, the bases are filled and no runs in. Then I can switch on the catcher [call in righthanded Art Ditmar to pitch to righthanded Del Crandall, Milwaukee's next batter] and maybe he don't hit because he didn't. Two out, and the pitcher is up and maybe we can get out of the inning."

After the two runs scored, Mr. Stengel did call in Ditmar. Crandall popped up, Burdette popped up, Red Schoendienst grounded out and the side was retired. It was great the way the Yankees won it, except for those two runs.

—October 5, 1957

Braves Dethrone Yankees as World Champions

TONY KUBEK, the brightest recruit in Casey Stengel's command, left the stockade gate unlatched yesterday, and in poured a party of war-whooping Redskins, looting, pillaging and burning. Led by the fierce and bloodthirsty Chief Rubber Arm Burdette, Milwaukee's bold and warlike Braves raided Yankee Stadium, the impregnable fortress of baseball, which palefaces doubted they would dare to enter, and put the torch to the Yankees' pretensions as champions of the world.

Scoring their fourth victory in seven games, 5 to 0, the demigods of the midlands laid violent hands on the title that metropolitan New York had monopolized for nine years, claiming it for the youngest franchise now operating in the National League. It was a triumph fairly earned and richly merited, though marred in the artistic sense by shoddy play uncharacteristic of Yankees in the decisive game.

Save for a wretched throw by Kubek on a double play chance, four of Milwaukee's runs need not have scored. However, the Braves did get an unsullied one on a drive by Del Crandall, the catcher, to the seats beyond left field, and that was all the help Lew Burdette needed.

It was the third victory for Chief Rubber Arm—to enemy batters he is known as Chief Slobber on Stitches—and his second successive shutout. After the third inning of the second game, which Burdette won, 4 to 2, the Yankees never made a run against him. Alternately embraced and abused by his ever-loving playmates, he departed with an unfinished string of twenty-four consecutive scoreless innings.

It is necessary to go back more than half a century, to the World Series of 1905 and the princely Christy Mathewson, to find a record of better pitching under pressure. That year Matty pitched three shutouts, twenty-seven scoreless innings in a row. Last man to start and win three games in a World Series was Cleveland's Stan Coveleski against the Brooklyn Robins of 1920, though the Cardinals' Harry Brecheen beat the 1946 Red Sox three times, once in relief.

Along with a winner's share of the loot, Burdette received a sports car as the outstanding player of the competition. Not even the Yankees could have begrudged it, and by the time he was done it seemed that every member of the crowd of 61,207 was giving him the acclaim he deserved.

Decidedly pro-Milwaukee, or perhaps just anti-Yankee, the witnesses began screaming Burdette's praises when he went to bat in the third inning. By the time he made his last appearance at bat in the eighth, the scalp-raising howls would have turned a Comanche pale as the Baker's blonde daughter. So transfixed by Burdette's skill was Bill McKinley, the umpire, that he remembered only once to call for the ball and scrutinize it for the casual moisture; he detected none.

When Bill Skowron—salvaged from sick bay along with Mickey Mantle for the final struggle—forced Jerry Coleman at third base for the last putout, Burdette had allowed twenty-one hits and two runs in twenty-seven innings. As Ed Mathews scooped up the ball and took a step or two to the bag, Crandall made it from plate to mound on the run and clutched the pitcher to his bosom. Mathews sprang upon Burdette from the rear. Between them, they pressed their playmate like spam before the other Braves moved in to dismantle the remains.

It had been a splendid series, thrice tied in games, with only one downright loathsome production (the third game) and one that was exciting as baseball can get (the fourth). Though the Braves went into the last game with a team batting average of .199, individual members of Burdette's supporting case enjoyed a fine series, notably Hank Aaron, Mathews, Frank Torre and Johnny Logan.

Playing like champions, they took the Yankees apart, and as soon as the customers departed, workmen started taking the Stadium apart. A displaced person in the press box, exiled from Ebbets Field and the Polo Grounds, looked up startled to see crews digging holes in the infield for football goal posts. "Gad!" he moaned. "Is Bob Moses getting his hooks into this place, too?"

Matched with a team whose habit of winning is deeply ingrained, and over-matched in the judgment of many, the Braves had to come from behind twice, after losing the first game and the third. When, having struggled to the front, three games to two, they were beaten in the sixth game, their prospects took on a dull gray tinge, for now the Yankees seemed to have a big advantage in pitching.

With Warren Spahn ill, Burdette had to work with only two days rest, a prospect that dismayed everybody except the pitcher himself. He'd done the same thing two years ago, he pointed out, and had grown "bigger, stronger and dumber" since.

The Yankees' starting pitcher, Don Larsen, had enjoyed four days of rest, which may have been unwise. On the early-to-bed-early-to-rise issue, Donald and poor Richard do not see eye to eye.

Not that Larsen or Morpheus was to blame for what happened. If Don's infield had handled the double play chance offered by Logan in the third inning, he would have shed no blood then. As it was, the inning didn't end until he was in the bath and the Yankees over the barrel, 4 to 0.

Even for the ingenious Mr. Stengel, there was no recourse save to echo Custer's dying words: "Too damn many Indians."

—*October 11, 1957*

Nice Guys Finish

WHEN THE gallant skipper, Walter O'Malley, gave orders to abandon ship in Brooklyn, there issued from the office of Warren Giles, president of the National League, a paragraph or so of singularly rancid prose which received less attention than it merited chiefly because ears were deafened at the time by applause for Lew Burdette.

"The National League," its chief executive crowed, "has again demonstrated that it is a progressive organization—," at which time this reader asked permission to leave the room. Thus did the guiding genius of the senior major league gloss over the despoliation of two of baseball's most valuable franchises, the abject surrender of the world's greatest market, the boldest step backward since the league was born in 1876.

Warren Giles is an old friend and a nice guy. Unless they can make some vestige of sense, nice guys should finish speaking, but immediately.

The departure of the Giants and Dodgers from New York is an unrelieved calamity, a grievous loss to the city and to baseball, a shattering blow to the prestige of the National League, an indictment of the men operating the clubs and the men governing the city.

It is difficult to apportion the blame because so many must share it. Horace Stoneham sat still for twenty years watching the deterioration of the wonderful organization he had inherited. When at long last the noose had tightened around his neck, he cried, "All is lost!" and scuttled for San Francisco.

O'Malley, operating like a dealer of three-card monte, made threats and half-promises, blew up smoke screens, played one city against another, took millions of dollars out of Brooklyn and then took Brooklyn's ball club in order to latch onto a big chunk of property near the heart of Los Angeles.

Los Angeles and San Francisco are major league towns where major league ball probably will enjoy great success, for a while at least. Yet suppose you manufactured ladies' garters and your sales manager said: "I can't do business here among 15,000,000 consumers. Let me go sell to San Francisco's 1,000,000 or Los Angeles' 2,000,000 and I'll show you some real business." You'd fire him, wouldn't you?

Outside of New York there are six owners of National League teams who sat on their hunkers last summer and voted permission for O'Malley and Stoneham to abdicate the New York territory. Some of them regret it now. Even while his team was winning the championship of the world Milwaukee's Lou Perini was telling everybody he encountered: "We must have a team in New York, even if it means a nine-club league."

Where was he three months ago when the deed was done? If a single dissenting voice was raised in that meeting in Chicago, the fact was not reported to the newspapers.

As to those dim bulbs in the city administration maybe the Greeks have the word for them. This edition has to go through the mails.

If they don't know what major league baseball means to a town, financially and in prestige, then they're alone in their ignorance among all the municipal authorities of the nation.

If they weren't aware of what was going to happen unless they took steps to avert it, then they are blind or illiterate, for the warnings were published in the papers no fewer than a hundred times.

An inescapable comparison forces itself into attention. Last spring a party of political space cadets headed by Los Angeles' Mayor Poulson flew into the Dodgers' training camp in Vero Beach, Fla., to bid for the Brooklyn franchise. The mayor mouthed a lot of Hollywood malarkey about "thinking big," but he also said, in practically these words: "It is our duty to go all out to get a major league team for the entertainment and pleasure of our citizens."

New York's Mayor Wagner has said a number of things, too. After the city had lost both the Giants and Dodgers, he said that "in a few days" he would appoint a committee of businessmen to inquire into the possibility of getting a nonexistent National League team to come and play in a park that's never been built and probably won't be.

So go ahead, put the blame where you feel it belongs. An incredibly stupid thing has been done. Some of the men responsible are stupid and some are not. All must share the discredit.

A hundred years ago, give or take, a man named Browning wrote a toast that seems to fit the occasion still. All together now:

Just for a handful of silver he left us,
Just for a riband to stick in his coat.

—October 15, 1957

Rhubarb del Caribe

SAN JUAN, P.R.—Fifteen thousand baseball fans walked away from a World Series game last night with the score tied in the bottom of the ninth inning, the bases filled and nobody out. Though it was almost midnight, it wasn't that they were in a hurry to get home. For more than half an hour they had hung around throwing chairs and things at the umpires. It was unutterably lovely.

It was the first meeting of Puerto Rico and Cuba in the round-robin series for the championship of the Caribbean. Puerto Rico's unbeaten Caguas team was leading the competition with two victories. The Marianaos, of Cuba, had split two games with Venezuela and Panama and could tie the leaders by winning this one.

There wasn't a vacant seat or a square foot of standing room unoccupied in Sixto Escobar Stadium. The night was hideous with shrieks and sirens, hoots and whistles, clattering cowbells and the hoarse and ceaseless braying of an old Klaxon horn. Looking on from a sort of hen coop high up under the roof behind first base was His Excellency Muñoz Marin, Governor of Puerto Rico.

The Governor is a large man with a smallish mustache. He sat with his hands folded on his stomach, a brooding area of heavy calm like the eye of a tropical hurricane. He yawned frequently. Sometimes his head drooped and heavy lids closed. He looked like a statesman wearied by the burdens of office, doing his duty when he would much rather be hacking at a golf ball in Augusta, Ga.

In the first inning Puerto Rico made two runs and Cuba, batting second because this was its turn to play as the home club, scored once. In the fourth inning Cuba went ahead, 3 to 2.

With two out and two on base in the seventh, Felix Mantilla, a chattel of the Milwaukee Braves, hit a ball that eluded the centerfielder and rolled to the wire fence for a triple, putting Puerto Rico in front, 4 to 3.

Going into third standing up, Mantilla took a step or two past the bag and the third baseman, Milton Smith, stabbed at him with the ball as he hopped back. The ump signaled safe. While Smith screamed and kicked up clouds of dust, a fan sprang out of the stands, took a flying leap high onto Mantilla's bosom and hugged him warmly about the ears.

The Governor, who had stood up obediently at the start of the seventh, sat with his palms on his knees, tapping with his heels. Two and a half innings more, and he could get some sleep.

Puerto Rico still led, 4 to 3, when Cuba came to bat for the last time. José Santiago, who used to pitch for Cleveland, was tired and when he walked the first batter he was replaced by Marion Fricano, of Philadelphia and Kansas City. Rafael Noble, the former Giant catcher, singled and Fricano hit the next batter with a pitched ball.

Bases filled, nobody out, and a righthanded pinch-batter named Orlando Leroux up. Out went Fricano and in came Juan Pizarro, the Braves' lefthander who is the greatest thing on this island since Ponce de Leon.

Leroux sent Marcial Allen back for a long fly to right. Allen got the ball in his glove and stumbled to one knee. Smith scored the tying run after the catch and both other runners advanced. When the ball got back to the infield, Leroux was halfway between first and second. He scrambled back like a base runner. The infielders paid no attention, assuming he had flied out, but Leroux held his place on first base.

Now it developed that the umpire at second base, an arbitro named Burns representing the Cuban League, was ruling that Allen had dropped the ball and Leroux was safe. From the stands it was impossible to see the ball drop. Up to now, no player has been found to testify that it was dropped, yet Allen himself didn't come in to protest until playmates ran out to right field and summoned him.

For a while the crowd was too mystified to make much commotion. Gradually the climate changed. At first it was something sensed in the air, like the oppressive stillness before a storm. Then it was something heard, a sullen growl in anger. Then came the rain—beer cans, bottles, wadded paper and refuse. The great chant swelled: "Pillo! Pillo! Pillo! Thief! Thief! Thief!"

Dozens of players milled about, arguing with the umpires, arguing with one another. Scurrying photographers fired away; an exploding flash bulb sounded like a shot. Allen, the little outfielder, trotted from one umpire to another, jabbering and flinging both hands high. Fans began filtering onto the diamond. The umpires drew together near the mound, head to head like a covey of quail.

One cop ambled out to first base, casually kicking bottles aside. A wooden chair, one of those folding funeral-parlor jobs, sailed through the air and crashed in foul territory. Several more followed. After a while there were about two dozen cops on the field gazing idly toward the stands while glass and tinware sailed over their heads. They made no move toward the marksmen.

The infield area was a rubbish heap. Groundskeepers starting loading the debris into wheelbarrows but were driven off by a fresh barrage. Bottles began crashing in the front boxes. Spectators there folded chairs flat and held them on their heads as shields.

Miraculously, nobody was injured. Obviously, a forfeiture was in order but just as obviously a real riot would follow any announcement. Followed by managers, players and civilians, the umpires made several trips to the grandstand screen to consult George Trautman, head of baseball's minor leagues, who occupied a box seat. Upstairs, the Governor, who had moved to the rear of his hen coop for a quick getaway when Cuba went to bat, was sitting down again looking on in mild silence.

Flanked by police, the umpires pushed out through a packed areaway. While players gathered up bats and gloves, Trautman's Solomonic decision was announced. The game was suspended on account of unplayable grounds; it would be resumed tonight from the point of suspension, bases full, none out, scored tied. The crowd dispersed slowly. Up to now in this series there had been a double-header each evening. Tonight there will be just one game.

—February 12, 1958

History in the Raw

SAN FRANCISCO—For gents of the outdoor type, a local haberdasher recommends the Big Leaguer, "a new hat inspired by a great moment in California sports history."

Giant values are promised by a distributor of radios. The manufacturer of a hearing aid guarantees that with his gadget, "you'll hear the crack of the bat again." If you buy a certain automatic dishwasher, "she can go to the games with you." A store selling phonograph records has a "Welcome Giants Sale" featuring a special double-header bargain. A grog shop boasts of its Giant line-up of star-studded liquors, and—well, that's the general idea.

As Ralph Henry Barbour used to put it, the day of the big game dawned bright and clear. For the first major league game ever played west of Pecos, San Francisco turned out glittering weather with a fresh summer breeze whipping in from the Golden Gate and not a cloud above the roofless, single-decked stands of Seals Stadium.

Though the newspapers here have insisted that the city was beside itself with excitement, the customers took their cool and leisurely time about showing up. Most of the early arrivals were New Yorkers like the Toots Shors and Mrs. John McGraw who had to travel 3,000 miles to see baseball on opening day.

Ultimately the former playground of the Pacific Coast League filled to its capacity of 23,448 but it was still half empty when ceremonies began a half-hour before the game. As the golden voice of Duster Mails issued from the public address system—Duster is the old pitcher who now makes speeches for the Giants—a long two-by-four dropped from the roof of an auxiliary press box and skulled a citizen.

Led by a Marine Corps color guard, a band shuffled in from left field playing, "San Francisco—open your Golden Gate . . ." At the plate the Giants' manager, Bill Rigney, and the Dodgers' Walter Alston introduced their players alphabetically and the deities lined up on the baselines flanking a walloping big floral display, a red horseshoe, yellow bat and white ball.

"There they are, ladies and gentlemen," Rigney said. "They're all your San Francisco Giants."

After sundry other introductions, the Mayors of San Francisco and Los Angeles, George Christopher and Norris Poulson, corned it up painfully. With Poulson at bat, Christopher pitched from the mound. The first ball drove Poulson out of the batter's box but he swung and fouled it. Christopher bounced the next in front of the plate, muffed Valmy Thomas's return toss, heaved one behind the batter, finally flung another inside that Poulson tapped, backing away.

The first citizen of the Dodgers' new home then dashed for third base.

For an eerie moment, veterans of the baseball beat had the uneasy feeling that they'd never left Brooklyn.

History was being born, and the labor pains consumed 30 minutes. Not a moment too soon, the Giants' Ruben Gomez reached the mound and faced Gino Cimoli, the only native of San Francisco on either team. On the chance that civilization will cease to be unless these facts are preserved for posterity, it should be recorded that:

The first major league pitch ever delivered on this side of the Rockies was a strike which Cimoli fouled off.

The first big league play registered in a California box score was a strikeout.

The first base hit was a line single to left by Charley Neal leading off for the Dodgers in the second inning. Dick Gray, the Dodgers' third baseman, followed with another single but Gomez pitched strongly to escape damage, getting Carl Furillo on in infield grounder and striking out Rube Walker and Don Drysdale.

The first run was scored for the Giants by Danny O'Connell, the second baseman, in the third. He got home on a sacrifice fly by Jim Davenport, the third baseman, which Furillo grabbed at the top of his reach.

For two innings Drysdale's evil sidearm speed had disposed of the Giants in order but starting the third he walked O'Connell and Valmy Thomas and Gomez bounced a ball to third base which hung so long over Gray's head that the bases were filled when it came down. Then O'Connell scored on Davenport's fly; Jim King, the rightfielder, singled Thomas home, and Willie Mays and Willie Kirkland flied out.

Once more, haunting memories of Brooklyn were revived on Kirkland's fly to right center. Running for the ball, Cimoli tripped and fell, pulled up erect on his knees and made the catch.

For the first time, crowd noises became noticeable. Unlike the burghers of Milwaukee and the Latins of Puerto Rico, these people brought no sirens or cowbells. They sat quietly attentive and cheered with decorum as the home club took its two-run lead.

In the fourth inning Daryl Spencer lined a big league home run into the crowd halfway up in the bleachers in left, more than 375 feet away.

The Giants went on to score three more runs in that inning and knock out Drysdale. The fans shouted happily but they weren't coarse about it.

The Dodgers played poorly, getting only six hits off Gomez. By the time the score had grown to 8 to 0, they had heard California jeers for the first time. Sounded familiar.

—April 16, 1958

Uncle Will's Platoons

BILL VEECK SAID it didn't really matter whether Will Harridge and Lew Fonseca had rocks in their heads or not. He conceded that their idea for free substitutions in baseball might be sillier than buying the St. Louis Browns—Bill Veeck once bought the St. Louis Browns—but he found it immensely heartening to discover somebody in baseball with an idea, even a bad idea.

Veeck was one of a group sitting with Fred Haney in the Braves' dugout during the Giants' recent visit in Milwaukee. Nobody dissented from his opinion. Any time there are signs of breathing in the baseball hierarchy it is exciting news, and when some member of the waxworks goes so far as to propose tampering with the sacred body of the playing rules—well, if that can happen, man can reach the moon, probably without rockets.

"Just the same," one man said, "the suggestion sounds pretty goofy to me, if I understand it. The way I get it, the idea originated with Fonseca, and, of course, Lew used to manage the White Sox, so that may explain everything. He brought it up with Harridge and Will thinks enough of it to take it to the owners. Is that right?

"Okay. It is proposed, then, that a man who is taken out of the game doesn't have to remain out, but may be put back in the line-up any time after a lapse of one full inning. You can pinch-hit for your pitcher and then, after waiting an inning, put your pitcher back in. Now, can you re-employ that pinch-hitter later in the game?"

"Certainly," he was told. "As long as a man has been out for one inning, he's entitled to re-enter the line-up."

"Wow!" the man said.

"Roy McMillan," Haney said, "wouldn't get to bat twelve times a season." Cincinnati's McMillan may be the best defensive shortstop in baseball but he haunts the dreams of few pitchers.

"You'd get another glove along with him," Haney said. "Somebody like Miranda. You'd play McMillan an inning or two, let Smoky Burgess hit for him, play Miranda until McMillan was eligible again, hit for him again with Burgess, then bring Miranda back, then McMillan—"

"No," somebody said, "not all the stories made this clear, but I understand you couldn't use a man more than twice in a game. The second time he came out, he'd stay out. Still, you could get pretty near all the way through a game alternating a fielder and a hitter."

"It's been suggested," Veeck said, "that under such a rule you wouldn't need twenty-five men on a team because you could keep on using the same ones over again. Do you suppose it was proposed with the idea of spreading out the manpower, so the majors could expand to ten-club leagues?"

Under a rule, like that, Haney said, "we'd all want more men than were allowed now. We'd want specialists for everything."

"Baseball is sick," a guy said, "from the minors to that bush league fence in Los Angeles. Chances are this will be the first year in history that every club in the American League shows a loss in attendance. But there's nothing wrong with the playing rules. It seems to me they are just about perfect, with a system of checks and balances that makes the game what it is.

"For example, when a genius like Fred Haney here uses a pinch-hitter, he has to sacrifice something—defensive strength, maybe, or some quality he was looking for when he spelled out the starting line-up. That's the way it's supposed to be."

"Right," another said. "Maybe there'll come at time later in the game when he needs one of those guys but can't have him because he's already used him. He's got to take that chance."

"Exactly. Allow the manager to bring a man back into the game and the sacrifice is gone. The calculated risk is gone. Then what good are Haney's brains? If there's no risk involved, you have a game where anybody can make the decisions."

Mr. Haney dimpled prettily.

"The only genius in this game," he said, "was the guy who set the bases ninety feet apart."

The same topic came up a little later in the Giants' dugout. Bill Rigney wasn't altogether clear on details of the proposal.

"This would apply to any player in any position?" he asked. "Pitchers, too?"

"Yes."

"You could bring a man back at his original position, or would he have to play somewhere else?"

"Bring him back anywhere you like."

"In other words," Rigney said, "I could hit for my pitcher, use Antonelli to pitch against three lefthanded batters, then come back with my starting pitcher?"

"Yep."

Bill was silent, thoughtful. In his mind's eye, he saw himself maneuvering twenty-five pawns in a game, switching from righthanders to lefthanders, substituting power for defensive skill, then swiftly reforming his defenses—making Casey Stengel's platoons as obsolete as Heinie Groh's bottle bat. Visitors tiptoed away leaving him to his reverie. It was a shaking experience.

—August 7, 1958

Reunion

IT WAS BARELY noon, and already the crowds outside Yankee Stadium were almost as dense as those in the dugouts, where the lions of the past commingled with the lambs of the present. Here were the Red Sox of 1946, the only pennant winners Boston has cheered in forty years, mixing with the heroes who have held New York to a lead of sixteen and a half games in this year's tingling race. Across the field the tyrants of 1958 sat cheek by jowl with the world champions of 1947, and the pin-striped flannels made them kin.

This was "Oldtimers" Day in the Bronx, the annual reunion of yesterday's stars with the apprentice demigods of today. It was a rare sort of occasion, when an infielder batting .202 could sit on the same bench as a man who had hit .400 three years out of four.

It was a rare sort of crowd, too, with scarcely an unoccupied seat discernible on the lofty slopes of the great playground. Obviously, the spell of the past exerts a mighty pull, even in a season devoid of championship competition, even in a town that one major league has forsaken.

The fans poured in and the kids came clamoring down toward the grandstand rail, begging for autographs. In the aisle alongside the Yankees' dugout, it took three cops to keep them from spilling onto the cluttered field. One couldn't help thinking of the clubs that have quit New York—because, they said, baseball interest was dying here.

"On you," a guy told Allie Reynolds, "that suit looks good."

Side by side in the Yankees' bench sat Rogers Hornsby, Bill Terry and George Sisler, .400 hitters in their day, with the incomparable Dizzy Dean. Hornsby was talking quietly to the Yankees' first baseman, Bill Skowron:

"—and when you hit with your weight on your front foot, you don't get no power. You're striding ahead of your swing, Bill. Do anything you want with that front foot, but when you come back here to swing, your weight shifts to your back foot. And when you're ready to hit, have your arms away from your body. . . ."

Skowron nodded, listening with the respect a .424 hitter commands from a guy batting .291.

Bucky Harris was prowling the dugout, seeking out and greeting the guys who made him manager of the world champions a decade ago—Bill Bevens, Spud Chandler, Joe Page, Vic Raschi, Spec Shea, Aaron Robinson, Bobby Brown, Bill Johnson, George McQuinn, Snuffy Stirnweiss, Charley Keller, Johnny Lindell.

There was added weight on some of them, but they wore the uniform with an air. On all of them, it looked good.

The regular game was to be preceded by a two-inning exhibition between the Red Sox and Yankees of 1946–'47. "You playing in that one?" Enos Slaughter was asked, for it was he whose wild dash from first base beat Boston in the 1946 World Series.

"Hell, no," Slaughter said. "I'm just a kid."

"How you hitting now?" Bill Terry asked him. "Are you getting the pitch up here?" He lifted a hand to armpit level.

"They don't call that a strike any more," Slaughter said, grinning.

"When I was managing the Giants," Terry said, "there was one pitcher this guy couldn't hit."

"Jumbo Brown," Slaughter said.

"Brownie," Bill agreed. "He'd start pitching him up here and make each one a little higher, and this guy would pop it straight up in the air."

"And every time I came up to pinch-hit," Slaughter said, "you'd bring in Brown."

"By the way," a fellow asked Terry, "is Brooklyn still in the league?"

One by one, Mel Allen called the guests out to the mound and there were roaring cheers for each. One of the last was Joe DiMaggio. The ground seemed to tremble.

With Al Schacht clowning as umpire-in-chief and both sides changing pitchers after virtually every time at bat, they ambled through two untidy innings. The Bostons scored three runs, if you could call them that, and the Yankees went hitless.

DiMaggio was in center field. Seeing him there recalled a remark overheard during a World Series after Joe had loped across the meadow to intercept a screaming drive with almost contemptuous ease.

"I've been watching the guy for years," a man said then, "and I've never seen him have a hard chance."

In the second inning, Wally Moses hit a droopy little fly that looked as though it had to drop safely behind second base. Not running at all, Joe floated in and the ball settled into his glove. It was so easy.

—August 10, 1958

Stengel for Senator

WHEN CASEY STENGEL appeared before the Senate subcommittee on anti-trust and monopoly, the papers made a good, game try at summarizing the Yankee manager's testimony—a task comparable with transcribing the Dead Sea Scrolls on the head of a pin. Now the transcript of the hearing has become available, and voters may read and discover for themselves just what their representatives have to contend with down in Washington.

The lawgivers cannot complain, however, that they didn't have fair warning. Fairly early in the transcript, the following colloquy is recorded:

Sen. Estes Kefauver: "Mr. Stengel, I am not sure that I made my question clear."

Mr. Stengel: "Yes, sir. Well, that's all right. I am not sure I am going to answer yours perfectly, either."

As usual, Mr. Stengel erred on the side of modesty. If the answers which follow aren't perfect, then of what does perfection consist?

Sen. William Langer: "This is the Anti-Monopoly Committee that is sitting here."

Mr. Stengel: "Yes, sir."

Sen. Langer: "I want to know whether you intend to keep on monopolizing the world's championship in New York City."

Mr. Stengel: "Well, I will tell you. I got a little concerned yesterday in the first three innings [of the All-Star game] when I saw the three players I had gotten rid of and I said when I lost nine what am I going to do and when I had a couple of my players I thought so great of that did not do so good up to the sixth inning I was more confused but I finally had to go and call on a

Casey Stengel

young man in Baltimore that we don't own and the Yankees don't own him, and he is doing pretty good, and I would actually have to tell you that I think we are more of the Greta Garbo type now from success.

"We are being hated I mean, from the ownership and all, we are hated. Every sport that gets too great or one individual—but if we made 27 cents and it pays to have a winner at home why would not you have a good winner in your own park if you were an owner?

"That is the result of baseball. An owner gets most of the money at home and it is up to him and his staff to do better or they ought to be discharged."

Sen. Langer: "That is all, Mr. Chairman, thank you."

Sen. Joseph C. O'Mahoney: "Did I understand you to say that in your own personal activity—"

Mr. Stengel: "Yes."

Sen. O'Mahoney: "—as manager you always give a player who is to be traded—"

Mr. Stengel: "Yes, sir."

Sen. O'Mahoney: "—advance notice?"

Mr. Stengel: "I warn him that—I hold a meeting. We have an instructional school, regardless of my English, we have got an instructional school."

Sen. O'Mahoney: "Your English is perfect and I can understand what you say, and I think you can understand what I mean."

Mr. Stengel: "Yes, sir. You have got some very wonderful points in. I would say in an instructional school we try you out for three weeks and we clock you, just like I mean how good are you going to be in the service before you go out of the service we have got you listed. We know if you are handicapped in the service and we have got instructors who teach you. They don't have to listen to me if they don't like me.

"I have a man like Crosetti, who never has been to a banquet, he never would. He does a big job like Art Fletcher, he teaches that boy and teaches his family he will be there, I have a man for first base, second base, short, that is why the Yankees are ahead. We have advanced so much we can take a man over to where he can be a big league player and if he does not we advance him to where he can play opposition to us.

"I am getting concerned about opposition. I am discharging too many good ones."

Mr. Stengel (asked to sketch his background and state his views on pending legislation): "I have been up and down the ladder. I know there are some things in baseball, 35 to 50 years ago, that are better now than they were in those days. In those days, my goodness, you could not transfer a ball club in the minor leagues, Class D, Class C ball, Class A ball.

"How could you transfer a ball club when you did not have a highway? How could you transfer a ball club when the railroads then would take you to a town you got off and then you had to wait and sit up five hours to go to another ball club?

"How could you run baseball then without night ball? You had to have night ball to improve the proceeds, to pay larger salaries and I went to work, the first year I received $135 a month. I thought that was amazing. I had to put away enough money to go to dental college. I found out it was better than dentistry, I stayed in baseball.

"Any other questions you would like to ask me?"

—August 13, 1958

Story of Braves' Fall

MILWAUKEE—At 3:15 p.m., Central Standard Time, a character in a brown suit who may or may not have been sampling the stuff that made Milwaukee famous, escaped from the stands in County Stadium and sprinted across the right field turf before the sorrowing, lackluster gaze of 46,367 witnesses.

Coattails flying, he slid grandly into second base, arose and struck up a conversation with Gil McDougald while a posse converged on him from three sections—two cops in official blue, three ushers in red jackets and two groundskeepers in pale blue coveralls.

As pursuit drew near the stranger fled, weaving, circling, reversing his field. A cop lunged for him and both went sprawling. Scrambling up, the fugitive headed for center field. By the time he was collared, he had made better progress around the diamond than all the Braves did all this long and summery afternoon.

He had also furnished the last opportunity of 1958 for a Milwaukee baseball fan to cheer. Twenty-two minutes later, as the downcast crowd trudged toward the exits, four pallbearers named Lou Perini, Fred Haney, John Quinn and Joe Cairnes emerged from the Braves' dugout and walked across the field toward the tunnel leading to the visiting team's clubhouse.

The money and brains of the Braves were on their way to congratulate the Yankees for accepting the championship which Milwaukee declined.

Achieving their third straight victory, 6 to 2, on a four-run spree in the eighth inning, the despots of the American League reclaimed their hereditary title and baronial estates from the upstarts who despoiled them last year and who should have done it again.

Until Casey Stengel's forces got up off their knees after three defeats in four games, only the Pittsburgh Pirates of 1925 had come back to win a seven-game World Series after trailing, three games to one.

New York won because Milwaukee wouldn't. The Braves had their second title wrapped up as far back as last Sunday night, but they tried to carry the bundle by the string. By mechanical bungling and sinful squandering of opportunities, they betrayed the admirable Lew Burdette today as they had betrayed the blameless Warren Spahn yesterday.

They didn't deserve a championship, though Spahn and Burdette did, richly. So did Bob Turley, who shut Milwaukee out last Monday, pitched to one batter and saved yesterday's victory, then hurried to Don Larsen's relief this afternoon and allowed only one home run and one single in six and two-thirds innings.

Technically, the teams were on even terms for this seventh match, for each had won three times and the starting pitchers were the ones who had started the seventh game last year, Burdette and Larsen. Actually, though, the Yankees had momentum going for them after two straight victories, and the wasteful Braves had invited disaster by their prodigality.

"They had plenty of chances to finish the job yesterday," men were saying, "and they let the Yankees off the hook. How many opportunities can a team waste in a short series?"

The answer was soon to come: "At least two more." In the first inning, the Braves filled the bases with one out, filled them again with two out, and collected one run.

In the third they knocked Larsen out with two singles, filled the bases against Turley with two out, and got nothing.

In between these crimes, Frank Torre committed two foul misdemeanors at first base and the Yankees gained a lead of 2 to 1 without a base hit.

At this point it seemed possible, if not likely, that Burdette would become the first pitcher in World Series annals to lose a no-hit game. The no-hitter vanished when McDougald doubled in the third inning, but the specter of defeat didn't.

Lew Burdette is a large, perhaps insanitary, West Virginia hillbilly with a dry wit and a moist delivery, who pitches with his arm and head and heart and tongue. Employing all the weapons which nature, a combative temperament and thirty-two years of living have given him, he beat the Yankees three times in last year's Series, beat them once in this struggle, and held them off for seven innings today, virtually unaided.

He got a mite of help in the sixth when Del Crandall hit a home run, but that only tied the score. Burdette must have been sick with weariness by that time, and sick of the sight of his teammates, too.

Still, he got the first two Yankee batters in the eighth. Then Yogi Berra doubled and Elston Howard singled home the winning run. After Andy Carey followed with an infield hit, Bill Skowron smashed a three-run homer, and the deed was done.

When the last Brave was retired, Berra plunged out from behind the plate and climbed Turley's burly torso in an excess of jubilation. Burdette wasn't there to watch. He had retired quietly after the eighth inning, without a handclap in his honor.

—October 10, 1958

Age Forty-Three

ENOS BRADSHER SLAUGHTER heard the news with a black scowl. "No comment," he said. He packed his duffle, picked up his pay check and his plane ticket, and stalked out of Yankee Stadium, bleakly silent. He was leaving the Yankees, already eliminated from their pennant race, to join the Braves, who still had a chance in theirs. Another ball player might have considered it a great break of luck. Slaughter was not deceived.

Moving to Milwaukee, he would be eligible to help the Braves win the pennant but he would not be eligible to play in the World Series or share in the Series swag. He is 43 years old. Win or lose this year, the Braves will start a new season next April with new hopes and some new players. What can Slaughter expect from employers who owe him no favors, from a club that has never had his allegiance? He knows. On April 27 he will be 44.

This is an unusual fellow, a professional and a tough one. He eats tobacco and he spits and he wants pitchers dead. Yet back in 1954 when the Cardinals traded him to New York, he cried like a girl. There was a picture of him packing his gear and snuffling into a handkerchief and it got into papers all over the country.

That was a chance for some magazine to get a real good story—"Why I Cried," by Enos Slaughter. Nobody got it. Maybe Slaughter wouldn't have been able to tell it to any ghost-writer. He is not one of the most articulate guys in the game.

If he were able, he might have told then what it means to a guy to feel that he belongs. In Slaughter's day in St. Louis, the Cardinals had a spirit of togetherness that may have been unique in professional sport. There was a special pride in being a Cardinal. They knew they were the best, and when somebody else won the pennant they wrote that off as a mistake and knew it would be different next year, and often enough it was.

The old Giants under McGraw had a pride like this, and surely the Yankees did in many years, and probably the Dodgers when they were in Brooklyn. With the Cardinals, though, it was a tight family feeling that went right on down through the minor leagues.

"In those days," Eddie Dyer used to say when he was still manager in St. Louis, "you knew that if you needed help there was a broad-tailed kid named Slaughter hitting .382 in Columbus, Ohio." (In conversation Eddie always mentioned the state like that, "Columbus, Ohio" or "Columbus, Ga.," because he'd managed Cardinal farms in both places.)

Well, there was that broad-tailed kid named Slaughter who came up to the Cardinals from Columbus, Ohio, and stayed for 16 years and felt he belonged. He played with Stan Musial and Marty Marion and Terry Moore and the rest of them, and the chances are he couldn't conceive of playing anywhere else. So then he got traded to the Yankees.

"What are you going to do with him," Casey Stengel was asked the day he got Slaughter. Casey was solid in the outfield in those days.

"All I know is, I got another player," Casey said. "I could use him talking to boys' clubs."

He didn't mean that exactly. Chances are Casey had never heard Slaughter make a speech. Possibly nobody has. What Casey meant was, here was a guy who was all ball player, a guy who hustled all the time, a guy so dedicated to the game that his mere presence on a club had to be good for morale.

Casey never changed his views about this. Even this year, when Slaughter didn't hit very often, it was Slaughter whom Casey sent up to the plate when the winning runs were on the bases. It must have been a hard wrench when Casey let the guy go.

Stengel wasn't alone in his admiration for the guy. Last year when Pete Reiser was managing the Dodgers' farm in Green Bay, Wis., some of his players asked him about a story they'd seen in the papers, where some major leaguer had said that a man who ran back and forth between his position and the bench every inning was "overhustling" and wasting his energy foolishly.

"All I can say," Pete told the kids, "is that there's a rightfielder in the American League who always beats the first baseman back to the bench, and he's forty-two years old and still playing ball in the big leagues. His name is Enos Slaughter."

If there's one more thing to say about Slaughter, Joe Garagiola said it. Joe played with the guy and now Joe is a radio fellow. The Yankees were taking batting practice before a World Series game with the Braves in Milwaukee. Slaughter was in the cage. There was a lot of stuff in the newspapers about space travel.

"There," Joe said, "is the guy who'll be the first man to play ball on the moon."

Any bets?

—September 12, 1959

Dearborn Massacre

CHICAGO—The settlers fought to the last man, but Fort Dearborn lies in smoking ruins tonight, every defender dead and scalped. Everybody but Mrs. O'Leary's cow got into the act today when a howling pack of savages from the West, cutting, shooting and burning, breached Comiskey Park's tall green stockade and laid waste to the championship dream which American League baseball fans here had clutched to their bosoms through forty barren years.

Not since the fire of '71 had inhabitants of this trading post seen such a disaster until the marauding Dodgers from Los Angeles sprang upon Early Wynn and Dick Donovan in the fourth inning and clubbed them for six runs which demolished the White Sox in the sixth and decisive game of the World Series, 9 to 3.

By the start of the eighth inning, women and children were fleeing for the exits but there was no escape. Charley Dressen, savage sub-chief of the merciless crew, was waiting in ambush to pick them off as they fled, having been excused from the Dodgers' dugout by the umpires.

It was the sort of thing ordinarily forbidden on Chicago's South Side except in the stockyards themselves. Strong men blanched, anti-vivisectionists swooned, and Lord, how the money rolled in.

In 1906, first time Chicago was the scene of this annual rounders tournament, 100,199 customers paid $106,550 to see the White Sox beat the Cubs in six games. The six matches that encompassed California's first world championship this year drew $2,626,973.44 at the box office from 420,784 clients. Not until 1919 did total receipts from a World Series match the haul that the players alone took from this one, and the entertainment of 40 years ago wasn't worth the price.

This one probably was, for it offered some splendid individual performances and a truly remarkable group achievement by the winners, who came clamoring up from seventh place to consummate California's first championship only 316 games after big league ball crossed the Rockies.

The new champions are a curious mixture of age and youth, seasoned survivors of the Dodgers' days in Brooklyn and rookies known only by vague rumor a few months ago.

Most heroic figure of them all when it ended was perhaps the rawest of them all, 24-year-old Larry Sherry, who was pitching, and losing, in St. Paul as recently as July.

He is a Los Angeles native son whose professional background is practically diaphanous. Just a couple of years ago he was capable of walking 15 batters while pitching a three-inning no-hitter (three innings were all his manager could stomach). Yet on four occasions when trouble beset Los Angeles in this struggle, he rushed to succor more famous colleagues.

Sherry was the winner today, though his team was far ahead when he arrived. Chances are the Dodgers would have stayed ahead no matter who went in to relieve Johnny Podres, for the moment of his arrival was strictly the moment of truth, graphically illustrating the basic difference between the contending teams.

It was the fourth inning. In the first half, the Dodgers batted around and made six runs. In the lower half the Sox batted around and scored three times.

Nothing could have been more revealingly characteristic of the two teams. The American League champions are a squad of many small skills, dexterous, swift, spirited and puny. The Dodgers have muscle.

They whacked three home runs today, one by Chuck Essegian who thus became the only pinch-batter ever to knock two out of the yard in one World Series. Chicago got one home run, from its one fully accredited purple pitcher-eater, Ted Kluszewski.

It was also characteristic of this series that Essegian got his chance almost accidentally, by a mere flicker of Walter Alston's intellect. Chicago's left-handed Billy Pierce had strained a muscle during the preceding inning but Al Lopez let him walk to the mound in the ninth, anticipating that the Los Angeles manager would replace Duke Snider, the lead-off hitter, with a right-handed batter. As soon as Alston sent Essegian up for Snider, the Chicago thinker called in Ray Moore, a right-hander, for Pierce. Alston beckoned Essegian back to the bench, then changed his mind and let him hit, but hard.

That was the day's only occasion for mental calisthenics by the flanneled Merlins on the bench. Carried this far by Alston's clairvoyant gifts, the Dodgers finished it on pure gristle.

An instant after the final putout, a great, bright rainbow arched across the sky, ostentatiously corny. It flamed on the dark and dismal horizon of the east, but the light that painted its coarsely garish hues came from the west.

Ah, Hollywood.

—October 9, 1959

1960s

Advice to a Rookie

ST. PETERSBURG, FLA.—When the baseball exhibition schedule opened here Saturday Mr. Charles Dillon Stengel, who manages the Yankees when Mr. Lawrence Peter Berra is busy behind the plate, suggested that Yogi lay aside his mask and mitt and armor and try out as a rookie third baseman. Humoring his old colleague, Mr. Berra complied. He played the position in a style described by Tommy Holmes, the author, as "revolutionary."

Over the weekend, furrows in the scholarly brow made it evident that Yogi had weighty matters on his mind. Today he was sunning himself outside the dugout when his thoughtful gaze fell on Mr. J. J. Dykes, manager of the visiting Detroit Tigers. Mr. Dykes is a fatherly man, generous with advice, who played the infield 22 years before his intellect outgrew his muscles. Mr. Berra hastened over.

"If I play third base," he asked, "will I last 22 years?" Mr. Dykes laid a paternal paw on his shoulder.

"Get a chest protector," he said, "a little short one, like a bib, that you can wear under your shirt. If you're going to play third, Yogi, remember this one rule: 'They can hit it over my head, okay. They can hit it past me, okay. But through me, never.' "

Absently, Yogi's fingers caressed his bosom. As the line drive flies, the distance between the plate and the third baseman's sternum is no greater than from here to eternity.

"It don't bother you hittin'?" he asked.

"Naw," Mr. Dykes said. "Wear it underneath, where nobody can see it. Get a pliable one. That means it bends easy."

Nodding pensively, Mr. Berra turned away. "Another thing," Mr. Dykes called after him, "when those big guys come up in a bunt situation, take your time about crowding in on 'em and never mind what Casey tells you, because sometimes they don't bunt."

Wearing the look of an Eagle Scout who has done his daily good turn, Mr. Dykes returned to the business at hand. He said he was going to show the Yankees a big young pitcher named Bob Bruce who could throw with some vehemence, though he might be nervous.

"You mean you haven't been saving Lary for the Yanks?" The Tigers' Frank Lary and Don Mossi beat the Yankees as a hobby. Lary, whose lifetime record against New York is 21 and 6, beat 'em five times last year. Mossi beat 'em six.

"I told Casey," Mr. Dykes said, "he wasn't going to see Lary or Mossi once before the season opens. I won't even bring 'em along for the bus ride. The Yankees might catch one of 'em cold and get the idea they can beat him."

Opening last season as a Pittsburgh coach, Mr. Dykes responded to an emergency call to replace Bill Norman after the Tigers lost 15 of their first 17 games.

"I was flying out from Pittsburgh," he said, "and every club in the league had had a shot at Detroit except Casey. The Yankees were coming in for a double-header. I thought, 'Oh-oh, maybe this plane better drop me right here,' but that day Lary and Mossi pitched and we won both games. That was May 3."

The Tigers went on to finish fourth. Harvey Kuenn won the batting championship; Al Kaline was runner-up; Lary, Mossi and Jim Bunning won 17 games each and Paul Foytack won 14.

"I think it was John Carmichael in Chicago," Dykes said, "asked me, 'How is it you got the batting champion, the second hitter and all those winning pitchers, and still you lose? Is it the manager?'

"Fact is, we had nothing in the batting order once you got past the four top guys. I think we left 1,161 runs on bases, lost 27 games by one run. Probably 600, 700 men left on bases normal. Our bullpen—well, four pitchers won 65 games and the other six won 11 altogether. This year—"

He launched into the hymn that every manager has sung every spring since some prehistoric Berra took his first cut with the shinbone of a dinosaur—Detroit's pitchers will be better, the batters stronger, the outfielders fleeter, the infielders niftier.

"How's your first baseman?" he was asked.

"Bilko? Fine, he can move around there all right. Be kind. Write something nice about him."

That's easy to do. Stephen Thomas Bilko has been coming up to play first base for one club or another since the dawn of history. He has hit as high as .360 in the top minors and as low as .220 in the majors. There are 235 sweet-natured pounds of him. He needs to feel wanted.

When he was with Cincinnati he shared an apartment with three other players. Steve did the cooking. He is a wonderful cook. His roommates appreciated him and sent him a Mother's Day card, but the Reds sent him to Los Angeles, who sent him to Spokane.

"Anyhow," somebody said to Dykes, "your club doesn't figure to lose 15 of the first 17 again."

"If we do," the manager said, "move over."

—March 15, 1960

Man Who Found Aaron

FORT MYERS, FLA.—The way it figures out, Hank Aaron must have been 17 when Dewey Griggs saw him. Hank's birthday is down in the records as Feb. 5, 1934, and the book shows he was with Eau Claire, Wis., in the Northern League in 1952. Dewey Griggs caught up with him before he got into organized baseball, which couldn't have been later than 1951.

Dewey Griggs is a stocky, grave little man who dresses like a claim adjuster and talks like a long-playing record. When he was a scout for the Braves he found guys like Wes Covington and Johnny Logan, not to mention Aaron. Now he works for the Phillies and he's down here scouting the other big league clubs, just in case they should turn loose a live one.

The Braves were warming up for a game and Charley Dressen was saying pooh, he wasn't worried about who would play second base, just so long as Del Crandall's back was all right. Everybody asks about second base, where Charley has several candidates who might get by, but the Braves would be stone cold dead in the marketplace if Crandall couldn't catch for them, and he has had a pinched nerve or something in his back that sent him up to the Mayos.

He seems to be all right now, though, and Mr. Dressen seems content with the odds in the Las Vegas future books, where the Braves are the favorites to win in the National League. Being an old horse player with a proper respect for bookmakers, Charley reckons that if Crandall's condition were serious Las Vegas would know about it.

So the manager chattered along, cheerful as a cricket, while off in the stands a piece Dewey Griggs talked about Aaron. "It was in Buffalo," he said, "where Aaron was playing shortstop for the Indianapolis Clowns against the Kansas City Monarchs. I had two days to make up my mind on him because Sid Pollock, who owned the Clowns, was going to sell him and there were a lot of other guys looking at him.

"Well, they were playing a double-header and here was Hank just kind of loafing over to pick up ground balls and giving it the big, easy toss to first base, throwing them out by a short step. When he ran he ran lazy-like on his heels, and in that first game I never saw him go over into the hole for a ground ball.

"At the plate, though—well, they threw one high right up here on him, and he powered it over the wall and out of sight. He reached out for another one low and outside and pulled it over the wall, across the street and on to the roof of a building.

"To make a long story short, he got seven for nine in that double-header, but between games I went to Pollock and told him I wanted to talk to Aaron before the second game.

"I told the kid, 'Hank, you haven't showed me anything. I don't know if you can run. I haven't seen you field, I don't even know if you can throw. You're not putting out.'

"He said to me, 'I kin run and throw all right. My daddy told me never exert yourse'f if it ain't necessary.'

"So in that second game he got up on his toes and he went over in the hole to field ground balls and he threw bullets to first base. He wanted to show me he could run so he dropped a bunt down and beat that out. I don't think I've ever seen him bunt once since he got to Milwaukee, but he can bunt as well as anybody if he wants to.

"As I say, he went seven for nine in that double-header, hitting a couple out of sight.

"After the game I grabbed Pollock on the field and I said, 'I'll give you five thousand right now.' Pollock said to me, 'Turn around, just turn around and look up there behind you.'

" 'Those are three guys from the Giants,' he told me, 'and they're going to be coming down here talking.' I said, 'All right, ten thousand.' 'It's a deal,' he said, and we closed it right there on the field. Then I phoned Milwaukee.

" 'You like him?' they asked me. 'Look,' I said, 'I don't know anything about baseball, but, if I had ten thousand dollars I'd pay it just for his hitting, even if he couldn't do anything else.' So we got him, and I don't think anybody is going to get another Aaron right away."

There was a brief, respectful silence.

"Funny thing, though," Dewey said, "there was a shortstop playing for the Kansas City Monarchs that day and I bet I could have got him for nothing. I think he made four errors. Probably you've heard of him since. A shortstop named Ernie Banks."

—March 27, 1960

His Last Bow?

PITTSBURGH—When Hal Smith hit the ball Jim Coates turned to watch its flight over left field, and as it vanished beyond the ivied wall of brick the pitcher flung his glove high, as though renouncing forever the loathsome tools of his trade. Before the runners had circled the bases, C. D. Stengel was out of the dugout, his knee-sprung gait taking him rapidly toward the forlorn young man on the mound.

Five times earlier this sultry, sunny, hazy, implausible day, the greatest man in baseball had shaped up front and center, asking questions, making decisions, issuing orders, while the Yankees and Pirates threshed and clawed through the sudden-death seventh struggle for the championship of their species.

Now Casey spoke briefly to Coates, who turned and shuffled to the dugout on dragging feet, his head low. The manager waited until Ralph Terry arrived from the bullpen, then walked warily back to his seat.

It may have been his last exit from the stage he has occupied through most of his 70 years. Maybe it wasn't, and next year they may have to write pieces captioned, "The return of Casey Stengel." But if this was his final bow, then it was made in circumstances more gaudily theatrical than the wildest mummery this old trouper could have dreamed up for himself.

Perhaps there have been other World Series games as extravagantly melodramatic as this, which the Yankees seemed to have won with a come-from-behind rush in the middle innings; which flipped over to dizzy abruptness when Smith's home run with two on base topped off a five-run burst for Pittsburgh in the eighth; which slipped out of Pirate paws when the Yankees tied the score with two runs in the ninth, then blew up with the shattering crash of Bill Mazeroski's bat against Terry's last pitch.

The home run went where Smith's had gone, giving Pittsburgh the game, 10 to 9, and the set, 4 to 3. Terry watched the ball disappear, brandished his glove hand high overhead, shook himself like a wet spaniel, and started fighting through the mobs that came boiling from the stands to use Mazeroski like a trampoline.

Maybe there've been other finishes like this, but this is Pittsburgh's first world championship in 35 years. As this is written, the pitching mound heaves and squirms with kids whose parents may not have been born when the Pirates last won a pennant. From somewhere under the stands comes burst after burst of cheering for every blessed little Buccaneer down to Joe Christopher, a pinch-runner from the Virgin Islands. Over and over, screeching trebles sing a tinny horror entitled, "The Bucs Are Going All the Way." On the field a meaty introvert in a brown suit poses for snapshots with a spade over one shoulder and, on the other, the Forbes Field home plate which he dug up as cops looked on.

In his own good time, Casey Stengel will reveal whether he means to manage again or retire with his matchless seasons. His Yankee teams won seven world championships and it was obvious from the outset that he wanted this eighth title so much he could taste it.

He sent his non-alcoholic, denicotinized, clean-living, right-thinking, brave, pure and reverent right-hander, Bob Turley, out to pitch against the equally unblemished Latter Day Saint, Vernon Law, but the lofty moral tone of the duel didn't stay his hand. When Rocky Nelson hit a two-run homer in the first inning and Smoky Burgess led off the second with a single, out came Turley like a loose tooth, and when Pittsburgh added a third and fourth run off Bill Stafford, that young man vanished also.

For five innings, Bobby Shantz stopped the Pirates cold with one single while the Yankees got hunk with Law and the accomplice who had helped him win two games, Roy Face. Bill Skowron got a home run against Law and a six-inning rumpus brought in Face, in time for a three-run shot that Yogi Berra smashed high and far to the right-field gallery.

The four runs scored in the sixth put the Yankees ahead 5 to 4, and there was lovely poetic justice in this. If this was Casey's last game, how sweet that it should be a gift from Yogi, the only Yankee who was a Yankee when Casey arrived in New York, the only one who has shared his triumph and disaster since 1949.

Somebody up there hates sentiment. Somebody up there waited until the Yankees padded their lead by two more runs, then slipped a pebble in front of a double-play grounder hit by Bill Virdon. The double play would have averted trouble in the eighth inning, but the ball leaped and struck at Tony Kubek like an angry cobra, sending him to hospital with a smashed larynx. Moments later, Shantz was out of there and Hal Smith was capping that five-run binge.

With the score 9 to 7 against them, fortune turned a false smile on the Yankees. Singles by Bobby Richardson, Dale Long and Mickey Mantle got one run home, put men on first and third with one out. Berra grounded out to Nelson, who stepped on first base for what he may have believed the final putout, then gazed incuriously at Mantle, sprawled face down a few feet from the bag. Mickey wriggled like a snake back to safety as Nelson made a belated stab and the tying run scampered home.

Casey's old heart sang. A swan song? A brief song, and how. Mazeroski was first up for Pittsburgh.

—October 14, 1960

Exit, Talking

MANY YEARS AGO, the late Ring Lardner gave his friend, Charles Dillon Stengel, a bit of advice on press relations.

"Casey," he said, "just keep talking. When a newspaper man comes around, don't try to feed him some particular story. Chances are it'd be nothing he could use. Just keep talking and he'll get his story."

If Lardner had lived, he might have been shaken to observe how faithfully his advice was followed. No doubt his conscience would have been clear, but there would have been times when throbbing temples and a numbed sensation about the ears forced him to wonder whether his well-meant counsel had really been necessary.

Appropriately, it was Casey who did the important talking yesterday when the press assembled to hear the answer to the question everybody had been asking through the World Series and the late weeks of the season preceding it.

"I was told," said the great manager of the Yankees, "that my services would not be desired any longer."

This was the leave-taking of the most successful manager that ever lived. Thus ended an era in baseball. So closed a glorious chapter in the life of New York.

Sometimes the effects of listening to Casey are a good deal like those the scientists expect spacemen to experience. One has the sensation of being whirled through emptiness, weightless and practically disembodied, untouched by gravity, sealed away from reality. When he chooses, however, he can speak with a directness that erases misunderstanding as a wet thumb wipes chalk from a blackboard.

"I was told my services would not be desired any longer," leaves no room for doubt as to whose decision it was. There was a halfhearted effort to imply that Casey sought leisure to spend with his wife, but he brushed that aside and laid the responsibility where it belongs, with Dan Topping and Del Webb.

Their reluctance to assume the responsibility was understandable, if not enormously admirable. It required no clairvoyance to foresee that their action would be unpopular. They had the evidence of a petition urging Casey to stay, signed by 35 New York newspaper men at the Series in Pittsburgh.

So they groped for sugar to coat the pill, suggesting plaintively that there ought to be an age limit in baseball—which would serve no purpose except to ease their own embarrassment—calling on the baseball writers to waive their rules and elect Casey to the Hall of Fame without delay, making a point of the profit-sharing arrangement that will give Casey $160,000 in severance pay.

None of this altered or concealed the essential fact that Topping and Webb, wisely or unwisely, with or without good reason, fairly or not, fired the man who has done more for them and their club than any other human and probably has done as much for the game as anybody else this side of Babe Ruth.

It is indicative of the man's stature that the big question raised by the announcement was not "who's the new manager?" but rather, "what'll you do now, Casey?" It will be no stunning surprise if Ralph Houk is introduced as the new manager tomorrow, but there was the liveliest interest in Casey's answer:

"Well, I'm glad you asked me that question because that's what everybody seems to want to know and I expect my wife will ask me when I get home. . . . I've always been able to get along in baseball. . . . I've been very successful and I've met some wonderful friends in baseball, men from the cafes and men from the homes and men from the churches. . . . I don't know, I never been able to make any plans. . . . If you're wanted, they always seem able to get you on the telephone."

If that wasn't opening the door for baseball offers, then a lot of listeners guessed wrong.

Casey Stengel is seventy years old. The age of employees is a factor which the heads of any competitive business are forced to consider. It is a factor for the employee to consider, too, for as Red Blaik said when he resigned at West Point: "It is unthinkable to overstay a career."

A man can be overtaken by age unawares. He can doze past his bus stop. It is doubtful, though, that the most keenly clinical observer could detect signs of failing in Casey Stengel this summer and fall. It is doubtful that a club ever was handled more skillfully than the Yankees in their rush to the pennant and their seven World Series games. Right down to the last inning of the last game in Pittsburgh, he had the winning combination, and but for a little pebble on the infield he would be the first manager of a world champion ever fired.

The feeling here is that he had earned the right to call his own play. Nudging him out was sheer effrontery.

—October 19, 1960

The Hot Seat

THE SCENE is the directors' room high in the tower of the Wrigley Building in Chicago. It is simply but richly furnished, with a diamond-shaped council table of polished sapodilla, flannel upholstery on the chairs, bearskin scatter-rugs and walls painted a restful spearmint green. On a window many floors above the river is a painted X marking the spot where Lou Boudreau, Charley Grimm, Bob Scheffing and predecessors as manager of the Cubs jumped, fell or were pushed.

At the head of the table sits Phil K. Wrigley, president of the Cubs, flanked by six or eight vice presidents. The next eight chairs are occupied by coaches. At the foot of the table stands a squat metal contraption with electric wires affixed. The seat, obviously hot, is unoccupied.

(Central casting has promised to furnish players for all parts by the time this drama goes into rehearsal. At present, the only performers who have accepted roles as coaches are Rip Collins, Elvin Tappe, Vedie Himsl and Harry Craft.)

As the curtain rises, all are chewing rhythmically. The president raps briskly with a gavel.

Wrigley: The meeting will come to order. Doublemint, anyone? Mr. Collins, you're new here. That isn't, uh—that couldn't be a Topps wrapper in your pocket, surely? Good heavens! Beechnut cut plug! Ah, Mr. Holland (addressing a vice president), perhaps you'd have a little chat with Mr. Collins after the meeting? Thank you.

Wrigley (resuming after a stern silence): Now, gentlemen, you've probably guessed why I asked you here today. Possibly some of you have learned through the newspapers that we are seeking a man to occupy that empty chair down there, the right man, the best possible man.

Mr. Boudreau was the last occupant but unfortunately he is no longer with us. Mr. Grimm was here before him—for the third time, I think it was, or maybe the sixth. Not an easy man to keep track of, Mr. Grimm, an itinerant banjo player. Then there was Mr. Scheffing and, let's see . . . yes, Mr. Phil Cavaretta. Fine men all of them but none, in my judgment, the right man.

As you probably know, gentlemen, our past policy has been for the vice presidents, general managers and myself to hire a man to occupy that seat with the title of manager. He would then select four or five pinochle cronies as coaches and then I would fire him if somebody in our little family here hadn't already cut the ground from under him.

This year we're going at it differently. You coaches down there are going to choose the manager, but we're not going to call him by that title. Smacks of feudalism, in my opinion. We'll call him head coach, perhaps, or chairman of the board. First, however, a chicle break. Do try a stick, Mr. Collins. Refreshing, isn't it?

(All chew silently until the president wields the gavel again.)

Wrigley: Delicious. Amazing how the flavor lasts. Now perhaps some of you gentlemen feel that we're going about this business in an unusual fashion, even an unorthodox fashion. I should explain that this organization has always been receptive to new ideas.

Years ago when my father was in charge here, there was a sports writer on one of the papers named William Veeck, Sr., whose articles were sharply critical of the operation. I daresay no other man in baseball would have defied tradition as William Wrigley did. Instead of writing to the editor demanding that Veeck be fired, he called the young man in and said: "You know so much about how a ball club should be run, why don't you try?" "I will," Veeck said, and he got winners, too.

I had a similar experience with another newspaperman, a chap named Jim Gallagher. He did quite well after I hired him as general manager, but I was adding vice presidents at the time and it became so crowded around here that Mr. Gallagher found himself elbowed all the way to Philadelphia.

Now then, gentlemen, are we ready? There are pencils and pads in front of all you coaches. You understand what we want. I'd like each of you to write down the name of one man, the right man, the best man. Then fold your ballots and pass them up here, if you please.

A pregnant silence falls, in which can be heard faint sounds—heavy breathing, teeth gnawing on pencils, the scratch of labored writing. Eight slips are passed to the president, who takes them to a window where they can be read, this being the only directors' room in baseball without artificial lighting.

Wrigley (muttering as he reads): Let's see, now . . . the right man . . . Collins, one vote . . . Tappe, one vote . . . Himsl, one vote . . . Craft, one—"

(The curtain falls heavily.)

—December 26, 1960

Cubs, Fraught with Thought

MR. PHIL K. WRIGLEY, a thinking man who believes that nine heads are better than one, has renewed his lease on the towering intellect of Charley Grimm, a Chicago landmark as familiar to tourists as the Lindbergh Beacon on the Palmolive Building, and has taken title to the brain of Verlon Walker, younger brother of the former Brooklyn base-runner, Rube Walker.

This gives him seven craniums, so round, so firm, so fully packed, to think the Cubs out of the slums of the National League next summer, but Mr. Wrigley will not expect them to accomplish this unaided. Before the players check into Mr. Wrigley's hotel in Mesa, Ariz., for spring training, at least one more cerebellum will be added, and the gray matter of Richie Ashburn, the club's player representative, will be drafted for part-time service as "ex officio member of the management team."

The Cubs are going to soar to sixth place this year if their owner has to dragoon every cerebrum and medulla oblongata, every nerve, lobe ventricle and peduncle in baseball to turn the trick.

He is sick and tired of hiring managers like Lou Boudreau and seeing his team finish seventh, one game out of last place and 35 games out of first. He is also sick of firing managers. To a thinking man, the escape hatch in this dilemma is obvious: Don't have a manager at all.

There is an erroneous impression around that the Cubs are the only team in baseball planning to operate without a manager in 1961. Actually, there are two others—the Chicago farms in San Antonio, Tex., and Wenatchee, Wash.

When the Chicago brainbund has been fully staffed, its members will take turns thinking for the Cubs as "rotating head coaches," leaving at least two intellects free to serve San Antonio and Wenatchee as "roving coaches." Never has such a smothering mass of intelligence been directed to the business of hitting a ball with a stick.

Already under contract, and presumably striking off mental sparks like thunderbolts, are the Messrs. Grimm and Walker, Harry Craft, Vedie Himsl, Elvin Tappe, Rip Collins and Goldie Holt.

Grimm, a vice president of the Cubs lately retired from radio broadcasting, is an old head, having served three hitches as a lonely genius in Wrigley Field. During his three terms as manager, he had to brood alone. Craft, Himsl, and Tappe helped Boudreau ponder last summer. Collins and Holt are newcomers in the noodle department. Walker has been sharpening his mind in the Cubs' minor league organization since 1948. It will be taken for granted, at least by those who can recall the stately progress of Brother Rube from the plate to first base, that Walker's first assignment will be as instructor in running and sliding.

Roving coaches are expected to put in about a month each in San Antonio and Wenatchee but up to now there has been no decision regarding the tenure of the revolving Merlins of Lake Michigan. Splitting the season into eight short terms has at least one obvious advantage. Knowing that he has only 19¼ games to go instead of 154, the head thinker needn't try to pace himself to spare his wits, but can shoot the works with all his keenest analyses, most incisive judgments and cleverest stratagems.

Naturally, it will be imperative to arrive at a clear understanding regarding the order of rotation. Managers have been known to send batters up out of turn and lose track of the pitching rotation. Forgetting whose turn it was to bring off the daily miracle could be disastrous.

Suppose, for example, the Cubs had their eight-man brain trust deployed on the bench and the coaching lines and also had a couple of runners on the bases—an unlikely prospect, to be sure, but this is a hypothetical situation. Confusion on the board of strategy could result in the following signal on a single pitch:

"Hit, take, bunt, hit-and-run, steal, suicide squeeze, Kansas City squeeze, and get out of that uniform and under the shower."

Frankly, there is a growing suspicion in baseball circles that Mr. Wrigley has popped his chicle. This is uncharitable, however. When you recall some of the managers he has had over the years, it is small wonder that he should seek a new approach. Some of the creeps chewed tobacco.

P. K. is a sound and successful business man, an analytical thinker who has a printed motto in his office that could serve as a text for the mightiest minds in baseball.

"Anyone," it reads, "who remains calm in the midst of all this confusion, simply does not understand the situation."

—January 13, 1961

The Cheerful Haggler

THEY GENERALLY LAUGH when Bill Veeck gets up to make a speech, and his public dicker with Roy Sievers the other day was typical. The White Sox outfielder, in Chicago for a sporting goods convention, had been haggling with the boss over his 1961 contract. He was in the audience when Veeck addressed the convention. Things were never like this, said the White Sox president, when he was running the threadbare Browns, and employees like Sievers would leap like salmon at a $200 raise.

"Right now," he told the conventioneers, "I'd give Roy an extra $2,000 if I could get him to sign today."

"I'll take it," Sievers hollered, and that was that.

Contract time serves Veeck well in his campaign to keep fans talking baseball. He was addressing a New York gathering about this time of year when his Indians were world champions. Steve Gromek, the Cleveland pitcher, was in the audience, and Bill interrupted himself to toss an aside his way.

"Steven, there isn't that much money," he said gently, and resumed his topic.

At that time the salary hassle between George Weiss and a Yankee star, probably Mickey Mantle, was in the papers. Both were present and Veeck never could pass up a chance to needle New York's thinking man. He spoke with soaring eloquence of Mantle's great skills, paused, and addressed the outfielder directly, "Mickey, you're worth every penny of it."

Contract matters get a lot of newspaper space at this time of year because there isn't much else going on in sports, unless you regard throwing eggs at round-ball players as a sport. At that, it's more fun than watching them play.

It must have shaken Roger Maris, the American League's "most valuable" player, when the mail brought a contract calling for the same wage he got last year. "Mere routine," said Roy Hamey, serving his first turn as the Yankee's resident Scrooge, but Maris was moved to mention it in Rochester, where he was attending a dinner.

Because of his lively hitting in the first half of the season, the inevitable question came up about somebody breaking Babe Ruth's record of 60 home runs. Maris, who hit 39 in his first season as a Yankee, hastily disclaimed any designs on the mark. It is a rare year, he pointed out, when somebody hits 50.

After 33 years, Ruth's record is new by comparison with, say, Hugh Duffy's 1894 batting average of .438, yet the chances are it has inspired more rich, crunchy prose than any other individual accomplishment in sports. That's only partly because it was a remarkable performance. Mostly it's because of the performer's personality.

When Ted Williams was at his peak, Joe McCarthy was asked whether he thought Williams would have broken Ruth's record if he'd been a Yankee playing 77 games in the Stadium, whose right field fence is 80 feet closer to the plate than Fenway Park's.

"Lou Gehrig didn't," McCarthy said simply.

That's really the measuring stick, the number of musclemen who have played through the era of the lively ball, whip-handle bat and big swing without matching the Babe's total. Never a year passes without the papers noting that somebody is running ahead of Ruth's pace, and now and then a Mantle or Ralph Kiner or Willie Mays or Hack Wilson or Ernie Banks or

Johnny Mize keeps going long enough to preserve the illusion that he might score bingo.

Actually, the only men who ever had a good shot at it were Hank Greenberg and Jimmy Foxx. With one frequently forgotten exception, Foxx came closest, though his 58 in 1932 was matched by Greenberg six years later. Jimmy's 1932 performance would have topped Ruth a few years earlier, for that season he hit about four drives against a new screen fencing off the right field pavilion in St. Louis.

The forgotten exception, by the way, the guy who came closest to Ruth's mark, was Babe Ruth with 59 in 1921.

Now they're suggesting that the American League's expanded schedule of 162 games may improve somebody's chances of breaking 60. It's unlikely the eight extra games will make any difference. Hugh Duffy had to swing at a discolored blob of dough and was charged with a time at bat for a sacrifice fly, but nobody is crowding his .438. Baseball's reverence for records is stupid, anyway. Some year somebody will hit 61 home runs but if he hit 120 he still couldn't dim the Babe's memory.

Incidentally, inasmuch as Jimmy Foxx was mentioned a moment back, if Maris is aggrieved about that contract he could have an instructive chat with old Double-X regarding the rewards of virtue. Jimmy was the League's "most valuable" in 1932 and 1933, with 58 homers and 169 runs-batted-in one year, 48 and 163 the next.

So for 1934, Connie Mack gave him a handsome wage cut.

—January 25, 1961

Spit

THE RULE IS No. 6.02 and it declares: "The pitcher shall not be allowed to—(1) apply a foreign substance of any kind to the ball; (2) expectorate either on the ball or his glove; (3) rub the ball on his glove, person or clothing; (4) deface the ball in any manner; (5) deliver what is called the 'shine' ball, 'spit' ball, 'mud' ball, or 'emery' ball. The pitcher, of course, is allowed to rub the ball between his bare hands.

"Penalty—For violation of any part of this rule the umpire shall at once order the pitcher from the game, and in addition he shall be automatically suspended for a period of 10 days, on notice from the President of the League."

It seems clear enough, yet the chances are there is more misinformation current on this subject than on any other topic in sports.

The matter of the drooling delivery is in the news once more, and this time for a change the discussion does not concern Selva Lewis Burdette Jr., the Milwaukee hero whose relative humidity has been a controversial issue for years and years. Recently the unsanitary but elusive spitter won a powerful ally when Joe Cronin, president of the American League, no less, implied that he saw nothing sinful in saliva. Mike Higgins, manager of the Red Sox, concurs, and so does the baseball commissioner unofficially. For years Ford Frick has been saying, "Bring back the spitter," in informal conversations, but if he ever urged the rule makers to action nothing was done about it.

It was 1920 when the spitball was declared verboten, with the proviso that big league pitchers already accustomed to slobbering on the sphere would not be required to break this untidy habit. Last of the licensed droolers was Burleigh Grimes, who ran dry with Bloomington in the Three-Eye League in 1935.

Myths can grow tall in four decades. Fans today who never saw a kosher spitter thrown will tell you that the damp delivery was banned because it is difficult to control and consequently a menace to life and limb, or because it is unsportsmanlike, or because it might offend fastidious customers, or because there is something intrinsically dishonest, not to say immoral, about moistening the hide of a dead horse.

In a baseball novel by an author born in 1922, a pitcher wiped his sweaty brow with his fingertips and threw a juicy curve. Though he had never employed this sordid tactic before, he controlled the pitch perfectly, breaking it over for a third strike. The catcher, the third baseman, the leftfielder, the batter and all his comrades on the bench and even people watching on television—everybody, in fact, except the umpire—instantly recognized the loathsome thing with grief and shock. The miscreant's father, an old sandlot lefthander himself, wept.

That was a few years ago. Today if a pitcher sneaked in a soggy one, his crime could go undetected except in the radio-television booth, where the eagles of electronics can identify curves, sliders, sinkers, screwballs, knucklers, forkballs and palmballs at 300 yards.

Well, sir, the fact is that in 1920 the baseball people and the fans were power-happy. Babe Ruth had shattered all records by hitting 29 home runs in 1919 and would belt 54 in 1920. In spite of ugly rumors soon to be confirmed by the disclosure that the 1919 World Series had been crooked, customers were tearing their pants getting up gold to see the Babe swing.

Club owners of that time were not like today's sportsmen. They liked money. To encourage the long hitters and stimulate business they hopped up the ball and forbade doctoring the hide—packing the seams with mud, buffing up a shiny spot, roughening the cover with emery paper, lubricating it with spittle or using any other artificial aid to make a pitch misbehave.

That is the real and only reason why these useful devices are prohibited. The spitter never was more lethal than the fastball, nor less godly. Thrown by a man who has mastered the delivery, it is not more difficult to control. Slobberers like Spittin' Bill Doak, Clarence Mitchell, Red Faber and Frank Shellenback weren't notorious for braining batters, and if Burleigh Grimes occasionally tucked one under a guy's chin or stuck it in his ear, this was due more to the venom in his soul than the slippery elm in his mouth.

With a two-day stubble on his jowls, eyes blazing with hate and yellow fangs bared, old Burleigh wasn't exactly a pretty sight as he drooled or pretended to drool into his cupped paws, but he was a sight to remember.

The spitter was not only a serviceable tool in the pitcher's trade, but apparently it was one he could use without great physical hardship. Craftsmen like Grimes, Doak, Mitchell and Faber enjoyed exceptionally long careers and seemed immune to arm ailments.

It is the exception today when a starting pitcher lasts nine innings. He needs every weapon he can command, yet everybody picks on him and they even have rules against playful forms of retaliation like parting a hitter's hair with a high hard one.

It's high time the poor slob got a break. These days he can't even depend on his catcher having a raised eyelet on his mitt and carving up the ball for him now and then. Sure as anything, some interfering ape of an umpire would ring in a new ball on the very next pitch.

—June 8, 1961

The Long Ball

MONTICELLO, N.Y.—Dan Devine, of Missouri, had diagrammed "student-body left" and "student-body right," the sweep plays that beat Navy last winter, and the student body attending the football-basketball coaching clinic at Kutsher's Country Club retired to the Ibo Lele Room to build character. In the group was a big guy who had tried out with the Philadelphia Athletics after finishing Notre Dame in the early '30s.

"I was a catcher," he said, "and Mickey Cochrane was working with me. He said, 'You can hit and you can throw, but let's see if you can catch.' So we were working behind the plate when Connie Mack came along and stood watching us for a while.

"'Mr. Mack' Mickey said, 'look at this kid. Don't you think he's got his left foot in the wrong place?'

"'He's got both feet in the wrong place,' Connie said. 'They should be in Williamsport.' And two days later they were. I still tell my boy what a hitter I was, though. A little while back Jake Kline, the Notre Dame baseball coach, visited us.

"'Is it true?' my boy asked him, 'could Dad really hit the long ball?'

"'I guess he could son,' Jack said, 'It was that little round one that gave him trouble.'"

The long ball hitter is a director of athletics now in a high school where, from time to time, he has coached all sports. He also teaches a course in health—"for athletes who can't handle biology."

"There was a question in an exam," he said, "reading: 'What is meant by acute fatigue?' I saw one of my stars having trouble with it. He spelled out 'what' and 'is,' but the next word, 'meant,' was tough. I know you don't syllabilize 'meant' but I covered the last three letters with my finger and he read, 'me,' and I took my finger away and he read, 'ant.' 'Me ant,' he said, 'that's wrong, it should be my ant.'

"'The word is 'meant,' I told him. 'Now, what is meant by—.' I put my finger over 'acute' and he read 'a' and then 'cute.' 'Oh,' he said, 'what is meant by a cute fat guy? Hey that's you, a cute fat guy!'

"I was correcting papers at home the other night and there was a two-part question: '(a) What is a compound fracture? (b) Give an example.' One of my scholars had the first part right but for the second he wrote, '715 times 12.' I told my wife, 'I thought I'd seen everything, but this beats me.' She looked at the paper a while and then broke up. 'He gave an example,' she said, 'an example in multiplication.'

"We had a really good basketball player who began to get letters from colleges around the country. I'm not sure he could read 'em but he enjoyed getting mail. One from Kansas enclosed a card you could fill out if you wanted to visit the campus. 'That's the school for me,' he said, 'I've got this weekend off from work. I'll go out there then.'

"'Wait a minute,' I told him, 'the card won't have time to get there before this weekend. Do you have any idea where Kansas is?'

"'It's over thataway,' he said.

"I'm no Michelangelo, but I sketched an outline of the United States and put in the Great Lakes and the Mississippi. 'What does that look like?' I asked. 'A cow,' he said. He worked in a butcher shop. I said, 'This is a map of the United States. Now show me where we are.'

"He made a dot with the pencil. 'That would be Savannah, Ga.' I told him. 'Here's where we are, and this little dot out here is Kansas. How far would you say it is from here to there?'

"He squinted a second or two. 'About six and a half inches,' he said. I took a ruler and measured, and it was six and a half inches exactly. No wonder he could shoot baskets.

"On my baseball team, I had nobody who could pitch. There was this kid, said he was a shortstop, so I started him on the mound. By the time he got two outs, the score was nine to nothing. I walked out to him.

" 'That's enough,' I said, 'We'll try somebody else.'

" 'Lemme pitch to one more hitter,' he said. 'I struck this guy out last time.'

"I looked at the batter and it was so. 'You struck him out,' I said, 'but that was this inning. Get out of here.' "

—June 28, 1961

Battling Bob

ROBERT MOSES, A Rhodes scholar who was the first American on the Oxford debating team, can still heave the 56-pound rebuttal, fling the javelin-sharp riposte and lay about with the bruising rejoinder. In the news sections of Sunday's papers there appeared brief excerpts of his remarks at the groundbreaking ceremonies for the new ballpark on Flushing Meadow.

The sports page, it seems to me, can afford space for fuller publication, partly because of the richness of the prose, partly in fairness to the one public official who strove to keep the Dodgers and Giants in New York and, failing that, aided the successful battle for a playpen for a new National League team.

"Well," he said after turning his spadeful of earth, "here we are at last. When the Emperor Titus opened the Colosseum in 80 A.D., he could have felt no happier. We shall never know whether in the bistros and narrow alleys of ancient Rome the aficionados who owned pieces of gladiators or of circus wild beasts muttered against Trajan for his dumb and artless arena.

"No doubt there were contemporary sportswriters, relaxing between bouts in the nearby holes in the walls where the vino flowed, who had the gift of tongues and talked and wrote about legendary heroes with sly, salty humor, happy metaphors, and, of course, scrupulous fairness. Perhaps among them there were a few unhappy souls who viewed their gladiatorial world through jaundiced eyes, talked out of the corners of their mouths and dipped their pens in vitriol. It was always thus.

"I have lived through many denunciations of what proved in the end to be eminently successful enterprises, but none more outrageous than those aimed at this stadium by some who, in their hearts if not in their typewriters, knew better. It is all part of the great American game of editing.

"The Colosseum at Rome seated 50,000 and, unlike the edifice of the Emperor Shea, had no provision for expansion or for a future cover. That's where we have it all over the old Romans. If the future proves we need more room and a plastic dome, we have the flexibility to provide them.

"Hold your bile, you laureates of sports. We bureaucrats, smarting under attacks, sometimes get good and mad at you. And then we reflect that out of the 'terl,' sweat and tears of the ring, the cursing and prayers of the arena, the hyperbole of track, field, tank, ice and water, the rancid smells of gymnasiums and dressing rooms, the Rabelaisian gossip of taverns, trains and planes, have come many of our most honest, earthy and genuine American authors.

"Sportswriters are not, like the French Academy, the final arbiters of our American tongue, but sporting lingo at its best is an influential source of changing colloquial English. If it is embellished now and then by a classic allusion or a hint that the bozo has mitted Shakespeare and come away with a whiff of the classics, the fans will take it along with the good sweaty, peppermint smell of Omego Oil.

"This, my fine friends, is an event in literature as well as sport. The folklore of baseball will climb like ivy over this stadium, encrust it with tradition, mellow it with the lurid colors of fiction, invest it with the visions of boyhood and the dreams of age, challenge the giants of Homer, Rabelais, Bret Harte, Mark Twain and Daudet, and put Paul Bunyan to shame.

"When I think back over the dilemma of Walter O'Malley, torn between his love of Ebbets Field and the desire to be on the side of Los Angeles, I am weak with the perspiration of dramatic suspense. . . . More influences were brought to bear to hold the Dodgers in Brooklyn than to keep the French in Algiers. . . .

"Walter O'Malley's rendering of 'Tosti's Goodbye' made the first cornetist of Sousa's band look like a National Guard bugler. . . . How could we compete with an entire arroyo in California? The question, my friends, is rhetorical and calls for no answer. It is all, as the French say, of a great sadness. . . .

"Joy has returned to our favored Flushing Meadow, the sun shines, bands play, children shout and a great Macedonian cry rises from the crowd as another Casey, Casey Stengel, armed with fractured English, comes to bat. . . ."

—October 31, 1961

Lonesome Charley

IT WAS THE last day of an eastern team's final series in Kansas City, during the late and lamentable American League baseball season. The road secretary of the visiting club, needing tickets for a ball player's relatives or somebody, telephoned the girl in the Athletics' office who handled such matters for him in the past.

"Thanks," he said, when she told him the tickets would be left at the gate, "I'll see you next year."

"Next year?" The lady said. "Not me, you won't."

"Did you see that item in the papers recently," one guy asked another at the World Series, "about the Kansas City scouting staff, six or seven of 'em quitting in a body? Well, today the final blow fell. Finley learned that the clubhouse boy was going to the Yankees."

If true, it was a heavy blow, indeed, but not the last. That didn't fall until the other day when Bill Bergesch, assistant general manager, quit the Athletics to become farm administrator for the New York Mets.

The little world of Charles O. Finley keeps shrinking. First thing he knows he'll have to start speaking to the boys from the "Kansas City Star," lest the solitude drives him mad.

It was 11 months ago when Charles Finley, demon insurance peddler, bought the Athletics from the heirs of Arnold Johnson. Along with franchise, player contracts and used sweat socks, he got title to the massed brains of Parke Carroll, general manager; Joe Gordon, manager; George Selkirk, supervisor of player personnel; and Henry J. Peters, head of a minor league chain extending from Sanford, Fla., to Honolulu.

None of them could tell a double indemnity clause from a 20-year endowment but among them they must have represented several centuries of baseball experience.

Deftly snatching the swivel chair out from under Carroll, the new owner installed Frank Lane in his place and Lane hired Bergesch as chief assistant. Finley beamed upon the shining morning faces of his staff. This was the matchless body of men, he announced, who would lead the Athletics onward and upward from last place to heights undreamed of in Kansas City's philosophy.

The flourish of trumpets died. The next sound heard was the slam of a door closing behind Joe Gordon. Hank Bauer, a blameless outfielder who had never done anything to deserve such a fate, was the new presiding genius in the dugout.

Quiet fell and so did the team, both uneasily. For a time the president and chairman of the board kept himself occupied second-guessing the manager, blackguarding the Kansas City press and threatening to punish the fans by taking his dreary team elsewhere. In a few months he knew all there was to know about running a farm system.

"Just leave your files with Bergesch on your way out," he told Hank Peters.

"Oh-oh," said George Selkirk, who may have lost some of his speed since his days as a Yankee outfielder but whose sense of smell remains acute. "That's my cue." Pausing only long enough to pick up his laundry, George walked out.

By process of elimination, this brought Lane into focus as a target. The first time Frank turned his back he sustained a direct hit between the shoulder blades. With the exception of Gordon, none of these men was replaced. Instead, Finley brought in his man Friday, first name Pat, as general manager. Like his employer, Friday has a rich background in the insurance business.

It is not true that at the end of Charles Finley's first baseball season there was nobody left in the Kansas City Office who knew first base from third, though if Bill Bergesch happened to be out to lunch there might have been hell to pay getting the infield fly rule defined.

Now 38, Bergesch started as an apprentice executive in the Cardinals' chain in Albany, Ga., about 15 years ago, worked up to Omaha and after the coming of Castro he handled the transfer of Havana's International League franchise to Jersey City. Since the Kansas City purges, he has had nothing to occupy him except George Selkirk's work as personnel director, Hank Peters's work as farm director and his own work as assistant general manager. This left him a minimum of time to point out second base for the president and general manager.

Possibly the work load he was carrying impressed George Weiss, the Mets' president, who has never asked a subordinate to work longer than the 26-hour day that George himself observes. Or maybe it was simply that when Weiss was running the Yankees and needed help he always turned to Kansas City, and can't break the habit now.

Anyhow, Bergesch is in New York. Kansas City has Finley and Friday. That's two days of fasting and abstinence.

—November 7, 1961

Slug-Nutty

SCHOLARS VERSED IN the art of swatting a round ball with a round stick have commanded a good deal of space lately explaining, too late to help a pitcher named Tracy Stallard, why Roger Maris was able to hit 61 home runs in

1961. Maris himself, who may or may not qualify as an authority, credits scientific refinements in bat design. Ted Williams says American League pitching, which used to be bonded stuff, was cut by addition of a soupçon of bushers, just as a honkytonk cuts the whisky with water.

This guy says it's all on account of the lively ball and somebody else insists that lively ballplayers are the answer. Hardly anybody remembers that a schedule of 162 games gave hitters more chances to punish curves than Babe Ruth had in 1927, and more than Maris had in 1960, for that matter.

Some day, no doubt, a big league season will comprise 200 games and some meaty characters with pointed ears will hit 70 home runs, and then we'll hear about the lively ball, the lively bat, the lively batter and the moribund pitcher all over again.

The notion here is that there is a degree of validity in each of these explanations, but that it is over-simplifying to offer just one factor as the whole answer. Chances are all were contributing factors, and all were part of the most important influence of all—the change that has come about in the offensive strategy of the game.

As Maris says, the bat he and most other players use today is a bulbous wand, comparatively light, with a long, slender handle and all the wood in the head end. It doesn't produce anywhere near so many handle hits as the old, thick-barreled models—witness the striking decrease in .300 and .350 hitters in the last 30 years—but when a well-timed swing connects with a pitch up where the wood is, the ball leaves the neighborhood.

Williams offers a perfectly sound mathematical proposition. When the American League opened wide, ardent arms to cuddle Los Angeles and the Twin Cities, it became necessary to staff ten teams instead of eight. This meant a thinning out of talent in all departments and especially in pitching, for a club needs more men at that position than at any other.

Counting 11 pitchers to a team, Williams points out that in 1961 the American League employed 22 pitchers who would have been crowded off the big time in 1960. Even before expansion, there were inferior pitchers making big league salaries because the supply never did meet the demand. In 1961 the number of unqualified pitchers had to be increased by 25 per cent, making life at least that much sweeter for the hitters.

As to the lively ball and lively ball players, that is an argument nobody can resolve. The manufacturers insist that the ball hasn't been changed and oldtimers jeer at the suggestion that there are better hitters today than Hornsby and Cobb and Ruth and Sisler and Heilmann and Speaker, none of whom ever hit 61 home runs in a year.

There can be no denying, however, that the nature of the game and the batters' approach to it have undergone changes. Teams still employ the hit-and-run, the bunt, the steal and the squeeze, but rarely by comparison with the old days.

Just as a football team like the Philadelphia Eagles fills the air with passes, reckoning that one out of three will produce a first down, so the batters parade to the plate and swing for the fences. More often than not they strike out or pop up or beat a little nubber along the ground, and they compile no such averages as a batter would, and used to do, protecting the plate.

If they catch one, though, it goes. And it is an article of faith among knowledgeable blondes that the girl who thinks mink will be well advised to bestow her favors on the longball hitter. The 1962 contract of Roger Maris, a .270 hitter, will do nothing to destroy this belief.

This was not, of course, a change that came about suddenly in one year. It has been the trend ever since the rise of Babe Ruth, and the long-ball cult has known many prophets from Hack Wilson to Mickey Mantle. Maris got 61 home runs where the Greenbergs and Foxxes and Mizes failed because he is a pull hitter who had his best season in a year when all other factors were in his favor.

This is no knock on the guy who swings for distance. The home run may be too highly esteemed as a weapon, but the crowds drawn by Maris and Mantle in an otherwise drab season are evidence of its sucker appeal.

Back in 1946 when Eddie Dyer over-shifted the Cardinals' defense against Williams in the World Series, Babe Ruth remarked that teams had tried the same tactic against him years before.

"Especially one season," he said. "I could of hit .500 that year pushing the ball to left."

The obvious question was asked. Why hadn't he?

"That ain't what I was getting the dough for," he said simply. "That ain't why they came out to see Baby swing."

—January 11, 1962

"Negro Outspoken"

ON THE DAY the news was released that Jackie Robinson and Bob Feller had made the Baseball Hall of Fame, a copy of "Newsweek" arrived containing an interview with the former Brooklyn second baseman. It quotes Robinson thus:

"I'm positive I won't be accepted this year. Maybe someday, but regardless of what my achievements were, many writers are going to disregard this because of Jackie Robinson, Negro outspoken."

By a similar happy coincidence, the election returns came out almost simultaneously with another magazine piece in which Feller criticizes the voting procedure, complaining that it militates against players of recent vintage, especially pitchers.

There ought to be the text of a lecture of some sort here. Something about good will among men and not hollering copper until you've been wronged. Under the rules, no ballplayer gets into the Cooperstown Mahal until five years or more after retirement. Feller and Robinson last played in 1956, so both were chosen the very first time they were eligible.

To them, congratulations on honors fairly earned. To the Baseball Writers' Association of America, a salute in lieu of the apologies that are not likely to be forthcoming from any other source.

With 160 members of the association voting, a player had to be mentioned on 75 per cent of the ballots (120) to make the grade. Feller got 150 votes, Robinson 124. The discrepancy is not necessarily due to Robinson's penchant for remarks like those quoted in "Newsweek." Though both had exceptional ability, Feller was a greater standout at his position than Robinson at his.

Feller was unquestionably the most gifted pitcher of his era. Barring crippling injury, his feet were set on the road to Cooperstown almost from the day Cy Slapnicka detoured him from a plow furrow at Van Meter, Iowa.

So was Robinson destined for fame from the moment Branch Rickey signed him to a Montreal contract in 1945, but for a different reason. If he could present acceptable credentials on the field, he must inevitably be elected on historical grounds, as the first Negro to win recognition in organized baseball.

His credentials were more than acceptable. There have been men with higher lifetime batting averages than Robinson's .311 who are not in the Hall of Fame, men who hit more home runs than he, men who stole more bases, men who were his match on defense and men who were equally earnest competitors.

However, Robinson combined many qualities in high degree—as hitter, fielder, base-runner and competitor—and he was one of the most exciting performers of his time. To call him the single most exciting is to ignore the fact that his day overlapped with those of Willie Mays, Joe DiMaggio, Ted Williams and Stan Musial.

At the beginning, Robinson asked to be judged only as a ballplayer without regard to pigmentation. This is the least any man can ask and the least any man is owed in common human decency, though of course it was never either possible or desirable to ignore the historical and social significance of Robinson's presence in the game.

After his first season or two, though, it was almost invariably Robinson himself who brought up the question of color when the question did arise. When he was involved in controversy, and that was frequently, he was the first to impute bias to the other party or parties to the dispute.

He was a superior ballplayer who made a mighty contribution to baseball and America and human rights. This above all is the reason he belongs in the Hall of Fame and the reason he is there.

To put it in simpler words, it was primarily because of his color that he was voted in by men whom he was still accusing of bias while the ballots were being counted.

Once there was a high school athlete who, called before a crowd to accept an award, blurted: "I don't appreciate this honor, but I deserve it from the bottom of my heart."

Even while baseball was honoring Robinson, he was telling an interviewer: "One thing I am sure of. If I had been white with the things I did—and I know I had leadership ability—they would never have allowed me to get out of baseball."

"They" were the New York Giants who, on Dec. 13, 1956, bought his contract in good faith from the Dodgers for $35,000 and Dick Littlefield, a pitcher. "They" were prepared to pay him what was fair to keep him in baseball.

On Jan. 5, 1957, in a magazine article sold in advance, he announced that he was quitting baseball of his own free will.

—January 25, 1962

New, New Look

ST. PETERSBURG, FLA.—Once it was called Crystal Lake Park, and the spikes that gouged its clipped turf were worn by Babe Ruth, Lou Gehrig, Bob Meusel. Then it was rechristened Miller Huggins Field and the idlers who clustered in the unroofed stands each March morning watched Joe DiMaggio, Bill Dickey, Tommy Henrich and Mickey Mantle. It is still Huggins Field, but only the name is unchanged.

In right field is a brand new clubhouse. In the clubhouse is a brand new team. Opening off the carpeted main room is a combination office-boudoir with oddly familiar names on the lockers: Hornsby, Lavagetto, Hemus, Kress, Ruffing, and one that is a household word in California banking circles—Stengel.

The flannel playsuits have orange and blue trim with "New York" in block letters across the bosom. Stretched above Fourth St., where for years and years the city fathers hung a sign saluting the Yankees, a new banner reads: "Welcome New York Mets."

It was the first day of exercise in the club's first training season, and looking on with George Weiss, the president, was a new owner, Mrs. Charles Shipman Payson.

"So this is the National League," an onlooker said. "I'll bet there isn't a razor in the camp."

"Elementary, Wilson," his companion said. "I can see Hornsby hasn't shaved today and those players never have."

Rogers Hornsby was standing close behind the batting cage, though not necessarily close enough for his lifetime average of .358 to rub off on the downy cheeked lads taking turns at the plate. Most of them were young catchers or pitchers, and for each he had a quiet word of advice.

"All right, Jimmy, just relax. Be comfortable up there."

"Fitz, you're looking down. The ball's going to come from the pitcher, keep your eye on him and pick up the ball when he shows it."

"Wait for the ball to get to you, Ed. You're hitting off your front foot too much."

"Now this pitcher isn't throwing as hard as the last one, so you have to adjust your timing. Wait for the ball, and then whip your wrist through."

To a visitor he said: "We're just trying to help 'em learn the strike zone. Between the shoulders and knees, and over the plate. If the pitch is anywhere between the middle of the plate and the inside corner, we want 'em to pull the ball. From the middle to the outside, punch it to the opposite field. Righthanders or left, you can't pull an outside pitch successfully."

On the first pitch to each batter, the catcher moved out front of the plate to field a bunt.

"We're trying to teach 'em to bunt for a sacrifice," Hornsby said. "How many games have you seen where the pitcher came up with a man on base and the manager had to pinch-hit for him because the pitcher couldn't move the runner over? If the pitcher can lay down a bunt, the manager could keep him in the game.

"Bunting for the sacrifice is the easiest thing a man can do with a bat, if he's willing to give up his turn at bat. That's what sacrifice means, giving up your turn to move a runner over. Half of 'em can't bunt correctly because they're moving, trying to beat it out for a hit. Or you'll see 'em holding the bat at an angle, trying to foul off a couple for strikes so they'll get that one chance to swing and maybe hit a home run. They don't fool me, or any professional."

"All right," he told one kid, "but be out front."

"Farther than that?" the kid asked.

"Yes."

"We want 'em to do three things," the coach went on, "stand still, have the bat out in front at least six inches, and have the bat level. Anybody can learn to bunt if he'll do that. There's no excuse for any pitcher not learning.

"In our day we'd bunt in the first inning if it would help get a run. Now everybody swings for the home run and the pitchers can't protect a one-run lead so you play for the big inning. From the seventh inning on, though, you might play for one run."

It was not what you'd call an advanced course, but this is a kindergarten. Such old pros as the Mets pried out of their benevolent lodge brothers have until next Monday to report.

"Now that you've seen your team, tell us where the Mets will finish," a joker urged Mr. Stengel.

"That's what a radio fella wants to ask me," the banker said. "Wants me to make a five-minute tape. He said, 'I'll just ask you—' and I said, 'No you won't. I'll do the talking.' "

He will, too. Things have changed around Huggins Field, but not all that drastically.

—February 20, 1962

Ave Atque Vale

THERE IS THIS guy in New York who has been a sports fan all his life and a Yankee fan in particular. On Monday he was watching the play-off for the Masters golf championship on television and a friend asked casually, "You going to the baseball opener tomorrow?"

"Tomorrow?" the guy said. "It's Friday."

This is what the Mets accomplished, without so much as showing their bright morning faces in the city that is now their home. They showed those faces for the first time yesterday, and tens of thousands whooped a welcome as they made their way up Broadway from Bowling Green to City Hall.

There wasn't a ball game in town, and yet Thursday, April 12, 1952, is a date to be remembered in the metropolitan world of sports, for at the same hour when the citizenry was showering its new baseball team with ticker tape, a slightly smaller but even more devout group was heaping encomiums on Rufus Stanley Woodward, the Herald Tribune's retiring sports editor.

In Toots Shor's it was hail and farewell. Up Broadway it was hallelujah. And if the weather co-operates today, it will be a source of genuine astonishment if the grand opening in the Polo Grounds doesn't draw substantially larger crowds than they had in Yankee Stadium Tuesday for the triumphal return of the champions of the world.

Five years ago the National League shattered all existing records for knotheaded stupidity by abdicating its position in New York, the capital city where the Giants of John McGraw had reigned for so many years as the kings of baseball, the city in which the Dodgers grew from a hambone comedy act to a national institution.

Now the excitement attending the league's return—even with a club of the most dubious promise—emphasizes anew what a sorry mistake was made. If an observer can judge by the remarks he hears, the reopening of the Polo Grounds is a more meaningful event than the westward movement of big league ball to California and Texas.

At least, it seems to have more meaning throughout the league. Guys who were in Cincinnati Monday for the Reds' pennant-raising ceremonies report that they heard more talk about the Mets out there than about the homecoming of the National League champions.

The question asked most frequently in the Florida training camp this spring was, "How do you think the Mets will do?" And whenever National League players got into the discussion, it was clear that for them the prospect of playing in New York meant exactly what Broadway means to an actor. After four years on the road, they're going to make the big apple.

Several years ago a couple of tourists taking leave of the Braves in Bradenton, Fla., encountered Red Schoendienst, a friend of Toots Shor. "We'll be seeing Fat Stuff in a day or so," one of them said. "Any messages for him?"

"Yes," Schoendienst said, "tell him to buy a National League club so we can get to New York once in a while."

The other day in Cincinnati Don Demeter, now with the Phillies, mentioned his eagerness to see the Polo Grounds. This seemed odd, for one thinks of Demeter as a Dodger of rather long standing, but the fact is he didn't make the team until it had quit Brooklyn. He said he had never laid eyes on the park, and added that this was true of many of the Phillies' young men, all of whom were looking forward to playing there.

"So are our guys," said Jim Brosnan, the Cincinnati pitcher. "They can't wait to hit in that park."

"What about you?" he was asked. "Won't it bother you to pitch with the outfield wall just behind your shoulder?"

"It would," Brosnan said. "If I had to pitch to hitters."

Here, obviously, is a realist who recognizes the significance of the return to New York, but does not deceive himself about the quality of the team, as now constituted, that represents the big town in the National League.

Brosnan has demonstrated before his gift for recognizing facts. When the World Series moved from Yankee Stadium to Cincinnati last fall, a guy who hadn't seen Crosley Field in years remarked that he'd forgotten what a snug little playground it was.

"That's right," Brosnan said, "a pitcher can't afford to make mistakes here."

"As a matter of fact," he added, "it's a small town. You can't afford *any* mistakes."

—April 13, 1962

Maysville

STANDING AT HOME plate just before the game, Ralph Kiner called the Giants from the dugout one by one. He reeled off 24 names to perfunctory applause and indifferent boos. "And," he concluded, with a tiny pause for emphasis, "Willie Mays!" "Yyyea! Yea! Yea!" Halfway up the bleachers in left center field a youngish man with a blue baseball cap stood tiptoe, arms uplifted, both hands waving. "Yyyyea!" he shouted, drawing it out long and hoarse. "Yea! Yea! Yea! —," maybe 20 times all together. His face was alight.

Mays was a block and a half away with his back turned. In the clamor around him, he couldn't have picked out any single voice at the range of 10 feet. Yet somehow that guy in the bleachers achieved actual communion with the distant figure in gray. The guy turned and bounded up the steps, springing with happiness.

Except for a lower corner where the view is shut off by a green wall to give the batters a background, the bleachers were filled. For seven wonderful summers this was Willie's kingdom, his realm, his loyal domain. Now after four years of exile he was home.

Willie McCovey, the Giants' second batter, hit a towering home run, and drew indulgent laughter from the bleachers. There was no derision in the laughter. The attitude seemed to be, "These are the Mets. What can you expect?"

There was stir and a straining forward. Cramped knees prodded the backs of fans on the slat ahead. "C'mon Willie!" No announcer had to identify the Giants' third hitter, a faraway figure with a wide stance, bat cocked. Mays hit a hard liner straight to Felix Mantilla at third base. Orlando

Cepeda grounded out—for some reason, he was booed on every appearance—and here came Willie jogging out to center field.

There were smiles all around but Willie took up his position too far from the seats for any shouted exchanges. Several times he looked back over his shoulder, a little like a monarch surveying his court but probably just checking the flags for wind direction.

A rhythmic clapping began as Elio Chacon led off for the Mets. At first it was a little difficult deciding exactly how loyalties were divided here in the bleachers, but gradually it became clear. These were Willie's fans first, the Mets' fans second, and baseball fans all the time. Where Willie wasn't directly involved, they rooted for the home team, but as the game went on good plays on either side were applauded noisily.

High above the Polo Grounds a jet left a curling trail of gold against the sunset sky. "Ain't that pretty?" a woman said, "and they takin' pictures of this park." She was an avid fan who called every pitch and noted every play on her scorebook. She was strictly a Mets rooter.

With Chacon on third base and two out in the first, Frank Thomas took a third strike. Somewhere up back an argument was going, "Ya, he had a hitting streak 14 days, what's he done since?"

"Ayruh! Ayruh!," the woman with the scorecard cried when José Pagan booted a grounder by Harry Chiti in the second. Then Joe Christopher walked. Before he could move toward first base, she had called it. "Too low. 'At's ball four, 'at's ball four."

"'At ain't nothin'," the woman said, disgusted when Jim Hickman popped up. She told her escort, "I could send you up there and do that." From up back came the argumentative voice. "Billie Pierce, for cryin' out loud? He's won seven straight games."

In the third, McCovey hit another home run and Mays grounded out. This time when the Giants took the field the cheers were for McCovey, who tipped his cap. Charley Neal tripled to left center for the Mets. A morose man spoke for the first time to the stranger beside him. "Shoulda had a home run. Too slow."

"That's Charley Neal," the other protested, "he can run."

"Bushers," the man said. "Believe it or not. Hodges hit one to the same spot and got a home run inside the park."

Still the Mets didn't score. "Makes me sick they can't bring 'em in," the woman said. "Trip and break a leg awready," a man suggested while Tom Haller was chasing a pop foul in the fourth, but the Giant catcher made the putout and the Mets remained scoreless.

Now it was Mays coming up for the third time amid cheers, whistles, and a few surprising boos. "Imagine if the Mets got ahold of him," a voice said. Then everybody was on his feet and upstretched fingers were pointing, tracing the flight of a ball to the grandstand in right. Screams, fists brandished high, a guy in the aisle yelling, "Say hey, baby! Say hey, baby!"

A toothless old guy rocked and cackled. "I can go home now! I can go home now! 'At's what I wanted to see!"

He started out. "Whatsa idea you're goin'!" somebody shouted. "Ya mean ya ain't a fan?"

—June 3, 1962

Moment of Truth

San Francisco—For this they played 339 ball games from April into October, 171 by the Giants, 168 by the Yankees, who win their pennants before the season ends. It was 2:25 p.m., Pacific Daylight Time, and for the first time all day those scandalous Candlestick Park winds moderated from gales to a mere menace. It was the least the gods could do. Willie Mays was up, and the rounders championship of creation trembled in the balance.

All day long, those winds had jeered at batters. Howling in from dead center field, they snatched every ball hit into the air, tossed it about, pushed it twisting back toward the plate. In the fifth inning, Bill Skowron and Clete Boyer had rifled low shots to left for singles, and after a walk filled the bases with none out, Skowron had scored on a double play.

That was all, and now came Willie with two out in the ninth, Matty Alou on first base, Yankees in front, 1–0, and one putout to go for New York's 20th world title. For five and two-thirds innings, Ralph Terry had pitched a perfect game, turning back 17 batters in order while in the San Francisco bullpen the only perfect pitcher of World Series history, Don Larsen, sat watching this brazen infringement of his copyright.

In the sixth inning, Jack Sanford had singled with two out. In the seventh, Willie McCovey had tripled with two down. Alou's perfect drag bunt in the ninth was the third Giant hit.

On the mound, Terry went into a bellyache crouch to take the sign from Elston Howard. His gloved left hand rested on his knee, nude right fist hiding the ball behind his hip. Mays waited with knees bent, bat cocked high.

Ball one, low and inside. Ball two, across the letters, as Willie fell away. Mays was a mile late with his swing on the third pitch. The ball rode a trolley into right field and Alou got going. It was an automatic double, but Roger Maris was in front of the ball, fielded it swiftly and threw to Bobby Richardson, who had hustled out into short right.

Richardson pivoted, and saw he could take it easy with his relay to the plate, for Alou had ground to a halt after rounding third. The ball reached Howard on one big, easy hop. Had Richardson been forced to hurry, he might have thrown wild, but as the play was made, Whitey Lockman, the coach, was dead right not sending Alou in to extinction.

In the stands, the vigilantes rode again, bawling for Lockman's blood. Then suddenly, all was still as in a cathedral. Under the prayerful eyes of 43,948, the monstrous McCovey shuffled to the plate. Away back in the dark ages when this World Series was not quite two games old, Willie had smashed a pitch by Terry across the county line as Sanford shut the Yankees out, 2–0.

It was 2:29 p.m. McCovey swung on the first pitch. "There it goes!" The ball arched toward the cyclone fence in right, curving as it flew, and the stubborn wind pushed hard, forcing it foul. "I don't know why they don't walk—" a fan began.

The sentence hasn't ended yet, but the World Series has. McCovey hit the second pitch on a line into Richardson's glove.

For an instant there was neither sound nor movement. Then Terry brandished a fist aloft. He did a half-dozen unrehearsed dance steps toward first base. He snatched his cap off, flung it away, and disappeared beneath a swirling wave of gray flannel.

Whether he was carried to the clubhouse, dragged, or allowed to make it on his own, it was impossible to see. It doesn't matter, anyhow, for henceforth he will travel by sports car, the only natural method of locomotion for the outstanding player in a World Series. Thrice a starter and twice a winner in this seven-game, 13-day war of attrition, the lean gentleman from Big Cabin, Okla., was a galloping winner of the prize given annually by "Sport Magazine."

Thus endeth, and not a moment too soon, the first transcontinental World Series, the golden hour of San Francisco's dream. A departing native summed it up: "Seven games, and the last one is 1 to 0. How could you get a better match?"

He was about right. In spite of a tardy start and four rain-outs, it was a good and entertaining struggle all the way, tied three times in victories—which is perfect for the course—with superior pitching giving luster to every game.

Best of the pitchers were Terry and Sanford. The Giants' 24-game winner shut all the Yankees out in his first start, shut out eight of them in his second, and the only run they could get on seven hits in his third was scored on a double play.

Once Tom Tresh beat Sanford, and won for Terry, with his bat. Yesterday he performed the same service with his glove, bringing off a brilliant racing catch, back-handed, on Willie Mays, just ahead of McCovey's triple.

Tom was the first player out of the clubhouse after the final game. He was already two days late for classes at Central Michigan University. They're teaching him physical education—him.

—October 17, 1962

The High Cost of Baseball Success

THE LETTER IS so obviously sincere it must be presented as fully and as faithfully as possible. After a preamble it begins:

"Last year when Bill McKechnie was inducted into the Baseball Hall of Fame, he opined that the trouble with baseball was the inadequate salaries paid those who disport in the minor leagues. This remark did not seek to set the owners on fire with enthusiasm to grant pay increases.

"As the mother of a young pitcher about to embark on his second season as a professional baseball player, I feel there is some validity in his remarks. Our son's contract was of the Class B level, and his take-home pay was about $75 a week for four months.

"From this sum he had to pay for his room, board, laundry and entertainment, keep himself in sweat shirts, spikes, gloves, etc., pay his own hospitalization and assume any obligation for medical or dental expenses not incurred as the direct result of his antics on the diamond. This is not a princely salary, and hardly adequate for saving sufficient money to see him through the off-season with its haphazard employment opportunities.

"I am sorry to say employers are not overwhelmed with joy at the prospect of hiring a 20-year-old minor leaguer who can work only during the winter months. Summer is the time for hiring this type of help.

"I wish someone would explode the myth of the rich baseball player, leading his gay, jaded life a la Bo Belinsky. The men who own baseball and its serfs should interest themselves in the off-season employment of their hired hands. This dreadful uncertainty about a decent annual income costs baseball much talent.

"If love flies in the door, baseball must of necessity fly out the window. These kids are sitting ducks for a sympathetic young female, since they are lonely, away from home, bored by their enforced daily idleness, and starved for company.

"They are viewed with alarm, I am sure, by the parents of nice girls, and rightly so. What do these people know of the background and morals of these boys? The way some of our major leaguers are written up as playboys and lady-killers would frighten any parent interested in the welfare of his daughter.

"But enough of my complaint. Perhaps you do not agree with me that these boys deserve some off-season help from their owners, and I use word 'owner' in its literal sense.

"I may be a mother anguished and overwhelmed by her son's uncertain future. I suppose that, could we go back a year to two to the day we signed him away, we would still do the same thing. He wants to play ball and we cannot deny him his chance.

"However, a little thought from the owners would certainly make the job more appealing and less nerve-wracking. Baseball is said to need talent. How much talent is lost because baseball players cannot afford to play baseball?

"Am I right in my estimate of this situation? It is only through the press that any reform can be effected. The bubble of the affluent baseball player should be pricked."

When this country was young, it must have been difficult for a mother in Pennsylvania to understand why her son had to quit the security of the home farm and push west into the wilderness. Yet without those adventuresome kids we would not have the United States.

Professional baseball is a poor career except for the kid who reaches the major leagues. So is professional golf for the guy who finishes 35th in the tournament; so is race riding for the boy who gets one $25 mount a week; so is writing for the author whose novel sells 412 copies.

Success comes seldom in any field without some sacrifice. The boy with a steady job in the corner delicatessen gets a pay check every week, but he may pay too much for his security. There are some who cannot keep pace with their companions because they hear a different drummer.

"Let him step to the music which he hears," Mr. Thoreau advised all parents, "however measured or far away."

—February 15, 1963

The Field Was Moist, the Eyes Were Dry

WHEN THE New York Giants played their first game in the old Polo Grounds in 1891, they beat the Pirates, 7 to 5. The big man in New York that year was Amos Rusie, of Mooresville, Ind., whose fast ball caused it to be said for the first time, "You can't hit 'em if you can't see 'em."

Rusie won 33 games that year and lost 20 as the Giants finished third.

Green grew the legends then at the base of Coogan's Bluff. From the days of Buck Ewing to the time of Willie Mays, there never was another shrine like the Polo Grounds, never a team like the swaggering Giants of John McGraw.

Then, after 66 years, the Pirates beat the Giants, 9 to 1. It was Sept. 29, 1957, the day the New York Giants ceased to be. As the game ended, a kid popped from the stands, cut second base loose from its moorings and fled with it, lateralling the bag to a pal as two members of the grounds crew closed in on him.

It was, Tommy Holmes wrote that day, the last hurrah at the Polo Grounds. Tommy didn't know, nor did anybody else then, about the New Breed.

When they shouted the first of those last hurrahs, they meant it. There were 11,606 customers and before the players could break for the club house in center field, the crowds were all around them.

Clawing with fingernails and pen knives, the fans dug up home plate and the pitcher's rubber. They tore away the green canvas screen behind the plate, made off with the padding on the dugout benches, dismantled the little lean-to in the right field bullpen.

They even pried loose the plaque on the Eddie Grant Memorial in center field, but cops recovered that. Massed in deep center at the foot of the clubhouse steps, the crowds sang "Auld Lang Syne," shouted for favorite players and yelled abuse of Horace Stoneham, who was taking the Giants to San Francisco.

It wasn't a great team they mourned that day, for the Giants of 1957 were a sixth-place club. They grieved for their memories, and the loss of something that had been a part of New York through all their lives.

Since then, two baseball seasons have been played to completion in the Polo Grounds. With the end of each, a farewell scene was played, but the stuff of drama wasn't there. These were merely moving days, and the first turned out to be less than that.

When the Mets finished their first season a year ago, it was thought they were forever done with the grimy old slum beside the Harlem. Having wound up with a 2–1 victory over the Cubs, Casey Stengel stood at the plate and gabbed into a microphone with Lindsey Nelson, Bob Murphy and Ralph Kiner.

Fans lingering in the stands couldn't hear his words, but they applauded when he was done and he responded, first with a deep bow, then with a jig that took him as far as the mound, then with a bounding scamper clear out to the clubhouse steps.

It was a comic leave-taking, tinged with no sweet sorrow.

So yesterday they warmed over the old routine once more. The new playground on Long Island which the Mets expected to occupy this season isn't ready yet; the promise is that it will be completed for next spring's opening game.

Again the team took temporary quarters at 155th St. and Eighth Ave., kicking up some excitement now and then, playing to a total of 1,080,104 as they trudged through their second summer in tenth place.

On the last day, the team and the customers and the script were tired. The weather was dismal. The paid attendance was 1,752. Jim Hickman got a home run but the Mets were never in the ball game as the Phillies made it easy, 5 to 1.

Once more Nelson, Murphy and Kiner held Stengel at the microphone. They played to an audience of cops, groundskeepers and news photographers, who brought Edna Stengel out to pose with her husband. Once more Casey made his way to the clubhouse, just walking this time, trailed by a covey of cameramen.

From the public address system issued the canned strains of "Auld Lang Syne." The playing field was moist, but eyes were dry.

—September 19, 1963

New Manager

MIAMI—Lee MacPhail said that when Baltimore decided to replace Billy Hitchcock as manager, Hank Bauer automatically became the leading candidate. But the Orioles were determined to take their time. "If there'd been somebody who would have given us a big lift at the box office," the general manager said, "we'd have been interested. Frankly, we considered Yogi Berra until the Yankees let us know he positively wasn't available."

"We open our home season against Yogi," Bauer said. "At the winter meetings in Los Angeles I told him, 'I'll tell you who you're going to pitch against us. Ford, Bouton and Downing.'

" 'How the hell did you know that?' Yogi said. He told me, 'I know who you're gonna pitch against us. Barber, Pappas and Roberts.' I said, 'You could be right!'

"Yogi," Hank said, "has the toughest job in baseball. If he finishes second he's a bum. If we finish second, I'll demand a 10-year contract."

Bauer was sitting in the clubhouse with a towel over his nakedness and a sandwich in his fist. The talk rambled from Oshkosh, Wis., to Sugar Loaf Hill on Okinawa to Washington where Hank was leading off for the Yankees with Willie Grieve the umpire. . . . "First pitch of the game is this high. 'Strike,' he says, and I turned around. 'Don't get mad, Hank,' Willie said, 'I'm not warmed up yet.' "

Sooner or later a name had to come up and it did—Charles Dillon Stengel, Bauer's boss for 11 seasons in Yankee Stadium.

"I disagreed with him," Hank said, "but looking back I know he prolonged my career a few years. But that platooning! I was mad all the time. Once I hit two home runs and a double for him, and in the top of the eighth he pinch-hit for me! Know who he sent up?"

Bauer nodded across the small room to where the coaches were dressing. Gene Woodling grinned back evilly.

"If I'd had a bat when Woodie walked up there," Hank said, "I'da broken both his legs. Another time against Detroit it's the first inning, nobody out, we already got two runs in and the bases filled. I'm hitting sixth and I start to the plate. Wheeet!"

Hank whistled and swung a beckoning arm. "Come back here. He pinch-hit for me, and I haven't been up yet."

"The things he'd do," Hank said. "One time in Washington Gil McDougald was up with the bases filled. Wheeet! He sends up Johnny Mize. Now Mize had never hit a home run in the Washington ball park in his life.

"Remember that runway back of the dugout where we used to cop a smoke? I'm sitting back there with Gil and I can see the red coming up on his neck. About the second pitch to Mize and whack, there it goes out of the park.

" 'What you gonna tell him now?' I said: 'Nothin',' McDougald said.

"Casey could keep you burned to a cinder. One year we've won the pennant and I hear him down the bench talking about me—'but he just can't hit the righthander.' After a while I walked down to him.

" 'What's the idea telling those writers I can't hit righthanders? Sal Maglie's starting the World Series tomorrow and you know damn well I'm going to be leading off.'

"Know what he said? Nothing. Just gave me that big circus wink."

"For years," Hank said, "I couldn't understand why he kept me leading off. Finally I asked him why. 'I'm no base on balls hitter,' I told him.

" 'Well, I'll tell you,' he said, 'you might open the game for me with a home run.' 'Yeah,' I said. I think I did that six times one year. 'You can score from first on a double,' he said. 'Yeah,' I said. 'Going down to second you'll break up the double play.' 'Sure,' I said.

" 'You might break it open for me with an extra base hit,' he said. 'A double or a triple and I don't have to sacrifice. If I can open with one run in the first inning, it changes the whole aspect of the game.'

" 'I can see that,' I said. 'That's why you're leading off,' he said. 'Oh,' I said."

—March 3, 1964

Yogi and Casey

FORT LAUDERDALE, FLA.—The first time Roger Maris went to bat he was booed just as though this were an ordinary ball game, but it wasn't. You could tell that on arrival in the pressbox where houris in sarongs and gloriously inadequate halters swayed down the aisle serving rare viands and pale yellow daiquiris to authors from Nashville and Newark, Washington and Rochester, and other exotic points.

This was the confrontation, eyeball to eyeball, like Khrushchev and Mao, Goldwater and Rockefeller, Macy and Gimbel. The Mets were playing the Yankees and it was teacher against pupil, the first summit meeting of those mighty baseball intellects, Charles Dillon Stengel and Lawrence Peter Berra.

Trailed by authors from Nashville and Newark, Washington and Rochester, Mr. Stengel moved across the field, encountered Mr. Berra a little short of the Yankee dugout and bowed from the waist, removing his cap with a sweeping gesture.

"You see I got a Beatle haircut," the great man said. Authors from Nashville and Newark, Washington and Rochester scribbled frantically to preserve the words for history alongside "What hath God wrought?" "Lafayette we are here" and "I'll pay you next week."

"I hear you're ketchin' batting practice," Mr. Stengel said. Mr. Berra confirmed the rumor modestly.

"When you worked for me," the master told the pupil, "you said I was killin' you if I wanted you to ketch batting practice."

"But you had me ketchin' doubleheaders too," Yogi said.

"Yeah, I was killin' you," Casey said. "You don't look so dead to me. You look pretty rich. And before they had highways you always got sick two days before Orlando."

"I went there every year," Mr. Berra said.

"You did not. Now it's two hours on these highways or quicker if you fly but when it was 5½ hours St. Pete to Orlando you always got sick. You and about four others. That Mantle, he always had something happen to him, too."

"Whitey's the one," Yogi said. "Seventeen years in the American League and Ford hasn't seen Florida yet."

"Tell him he's a coach now and he's gotta make the trips," the master said. "He'll be a good coach for you."

"You can ketch batting practice one-handed," Mr. Stengel said, "and you know which pitchers are throwin' hard."

"That's right," Yogi said.

Yogi Berra with Mickey Mantle in 1956

"And you can tell something about the hitters, your own men. You can find out what some guys can't hit."

Yogi nodded, grinning. "You can see a lot behind that cage, too, but the best place—"

"—is out in center field," Casey said, and again Mr. Berra nodded agreement. "You can see what they're doin' and they don't know you're watchin' 'em. They say, 'I can't swing natural when he's standin' behind me,' but if you're out there in center they don't know you're watchin'."

"They think you're just out there talkin' to somebody," Mr. Berra said. "Hey, Rich and Kubek want to say hello."

Yankees who had played for Mr. Stengel had halted their warmup pitch-catch and edged in, grinning at the sparkling repartee.

"Good to see you, boys," Casey told them. "I hope you all do splendid and I know you will."

The umpires appeared, the players deployed, the thinkers took their seats in the dugouts, the battle was joined.

Ralph Terry shut out the Mets for five innings on four hits. Carl Willey shut out the Yankees for six innings on four hits. Pete Mikkelsen and Hal Reniff each pitched a scoreless inning for the Yankees. In the seventh Larry Bearnarth picked up where Willey left off.

Suddenly Larry Napp, umpiring behind the plate, whirled and leveled an imperious forefinger at the Yankee dugout. Whitey Ford and Jimmy Gleason, coaches, who had been commenting audibly on Napp's judgment, were through for the day, costing Mr. Berra one-half of his brain trust.

The manager protested with spirit. While Yogi and the umpire jawed, nose to nose, Mr. Stengel stuck his neck up out of the visitors' dugout and blew a kiss.

In the eighth Frank Thomas singled home a run against the Yankees' Tom Metcalf. Bearnarth protected the shutout through the last two innings and the Mets had their fourth victory in four starts against American League teams.

"Every day a crisis," Mr. Stengel said.

—March 25, 1964

Pepper Martin

FT. LAUDERDALE, FLA.—Johnny Keane, a Cardinal from his first day in baseball until he managed the world champions 32 years later, was reminiscing about last year's struggle for the National League pennant when Joe Reichler, of The Associated Press, came into the Yankees' dugout.

"Sorry to bring bad news," Joe said, "but Pepper Martin is dead."

Keane's gray, lined face was stricken. It is unlikely he and Pepper ever were intimate, for when John Leonard Martin was the biggest name in the game John Keane was 19, going on 20, and had just completed his second season as a bush league infielder. In a baseball sense, the towns where Keane had played—Globe, Ariz., Waynesboro in the Blue Ridge League, and Springfield, Mo.—were a million light years from Sportsman's Park.

But as a kid in St. Louis Johnny had been a card-carrying member of the original Knothole Gang, sitting in left field and screeching, "We want a homerrr!" whenever Rogers Hornsby and Chick Hafey or Jim Bottomley went to bat. Then in Globe and Waynesboro and Springfield he was a member of the family. And for any kid in the Cardinal chain in those days, the beau ideal, the model, the hero larger than life, had to be Pepper Martin, the Wild Horse of the Osage.

"Oh my," John said at Reichler's news. "Oh, my. I saw Pepper just—well, maybe it was at the World Series. He was in St. Louis and he looked fine. What a sweet guy, and what a ball club that was! Do we have them as tough as that today? These were guys who just hated to play in clean suits."

Perhaps that was a curious way of expressing it, but the words brought memories back in a flood—a hundred memories of the cutting, slashing desperadoes who were the Cardinals of 1931, and most vivid in all the image of a rawboned, ungainly country boy who couldn't play one inning without looking like something drug out of a potato field.

They could send Pepper Martin out of the clubhouse all scrubbed and combed and laundered and pressed, though there never was a tailor who could cut flannels to look natty on those preposterous shoulders. Then he'd go busting down to second base with one of those headlong, belly-whopping slides and up he'd come out of the dusty whirlwind that was his native habitat with his sweat-soaked, haberdashery blacked with loam, a glistening film of grime on the homely face with its great, beaked prow.

Pepper Martin wasn't the greatest hitter of all time, or the greatest fielder or thrower or base runner, but he did everything well and no more fiery competitor ever lived in any sport.

In the highly colored judgment of one who was a young sports writer at the time covering the Cardinals and all wrapped up in the team's fortunes, Pepper was, for at least one ten-day span in his life, the most exciting ballplayer of human history. That was in the 1931 World Series when he was a living flame laying waste to what may have been Connie Mack's greatest team.

This was the team of Lefty Grove, George Earnshaw and Rube Walberg, Al Simmons, Jimmy Foxx, Mickey Cochrane and the rest, overpowering favorites to win their third straight world championship. Almost literally, Pepper broke them between his soiled and reddened hands.

He didn't hit everything Grove and Earnshaw threw and he didn't steal Cochrane's underwear. It only seemed that way. By the time the series was three games old, newcomers arriving in the park were asking first of all, "Which one is Martin?"

In enemy Philadelphia, the hotel lobby was a maelstrom with Pepper its center. "Pepper, how do you account for the way you're going?" "I dunno. I'm just takin' my natural swing and the ball is hittin' the fat part of the bat." "Mr. Martin, where did you learn to run the way you do?"

"Well, sir, I grew up in Oklahoma, and once you start runnin' out there there ain't nothin' to stop you."

In Philadelphia's Broad Street Station Judge Kenesaw Mountain Landis, the commissioner who never was unaware of an audience, bellowed above the crowd: "Young man, I'd like to change places with you right now."

Quoth Pepper, never unaware of salary discrepancies: "Well, Judge, $75,000 against $7,500—I'll swap you."

After the World Series Pepper toured in vaudeville for more money than he had collected in baseball—people would fill theaters just to see and hear a ballplayer in those days of innocence. Then he loaded his shotgun and his midget racing car and other necessities of life into the pickup truck which was his idea of a wealthy young sportsman's equipage, and took off for Oklahoma.

He never changed. He played the big cities and he managed in the top minors but in all his travels he never found anything more beautiful in his eyes than a tractor. There was passionate honesty in him, and an almost ministerial sincerity, yet on a team of indefatigable merry-Andrews he had a hand in every prank.

He was one of those who, disguised in white coveralls and carrying paint buckets, marched into a dinner in a Philadelphia hotel and began redecorating the room, somewhat to the consternation of the speaker. He was maestro of the Mississippi Mudcats, a jug-and-washboard band in the Cardinal clubhouse. When the team was tossed out of a Boston hotel for shooting pigeons from the windows, Pepper was there.

He did not clown on the field, though. An umpire in the minors found that out when Pepper, then a manager, dissented from a decision.

"Pepper," the league president asked later, "when you had your hands on that man's throat, what could you have been thinking!"

"I was thinking I'd choke him to death," Pepper said earnestly.

—February 7, 1965

Houston's Blister

HOUSTON, TEX.—A double platoon of space cadets from du Pont, who built the biggest blister in Texas, huddled like frightened quail in a box eight stories above left field in Houston Friday night and tried to look like baseball fans. From overhead, a great wedding band of diamonds flooded the playing field with light. Above the 4,596 panels of translucent plastic, the night sky made a background of black velvet for fly balls.

"I suppose," a sympathetic visitor said, "that when you manufacture something like this you have to service it for a long time."

"Forever," a du Ponter said, staring straight ahead.

"Oh, well," the visitor said, "I'm sure it will be all right. As a last resort, day games could be moved outside to old Colt Stadium."

"That may be the solution," the man said quietly, "but we're not making suggestions right now. These people are, er, emotional."

It was an understatement of rare beauty. "These people" had spent four years and close to $32 million creating a playpen proof against rain and snow, heat and cold, wind and darkness and fog and predatory mosquitoes. And now the horrid truth was out: they couldn't play big league baseball in sunlight here.

Already word had come that an "optical physicist" was flying out from du Pont, though when he got there he would not find the problem at its most acute. In a dress rehearsal last Thursday, the Astros had discovered that fielders could not follow the flight of a white ball with sunlight glaring through the skylight. However, the scientist would arrive for afternoon games Saturday and Sunday under overcast skies, with a minimum of glare.

There was talk of experimenting with colored baseballs, of painting the skylight black or covering it with tarpaulin, which would mean playing afternoon games under lights.

"How could they spend all that money," some fans are asking, "without discovering this flaw?"

Well, it happens all the time. Hotels have been built without elevators, without a kitchen. A great oil plant was opened in Texas without provision for removing salt from the crude oil. A fortune had to be spent to replace lines and machinery ruined by salt.

Engineers and architects and scientists and planners took every precaution here that their slide rules and light meters and wind tunnels and computers advised but it didn't occur to them to have an outfielder try to shag fungoes on a bright day.

They'll find a solution, though. "Roy Hofheinz," Paul Richards said of the Astrodome's astroprophet, "meets disaster at 11:59."

Meanwhile, one worm in the apple shouldn't obscure the fact that something truly revolutionary has been accomplished. This is the greatest change in baseball since Candy Cummings invented the curve. From the business side, it is impossible to over-estimate the importance of the Dome.

For the first time, weather ceases to be a factor in scheduling, in selling tickets. Rain, wet grounds, wind, fog, cold, heat and darkness no longer exist.

There are no rainchecks on the Astros' tickets. Regardless of conditions outside, the game will be played as scheduled and the fans will watch in perfect comfort, relaxed on upholstered theater seats in a climate tailored to their taste.

All this is equally applicable to football and other sports. Today championship fights are run indoors because a postponement would mess up the closed-circuit commitments in theaters across the country. A promoter could sell 60,000 seats for a fight here without fear of a rainout.

They have licked every problem except good weather.

Because turf doesn't prosper in the diffused sunlight, Hofheinz is talking about putting in plastic grass. In the light of this experience, he would be well advised to run extensive tests first with batted balls; it could be that grounders would skid on that stuff instead of bouncing.

Be the difficulties small or big, it must be remembered that this, after all, is Texas. On Friday a large cowboy ambled into the shimmering jewelry shop in Houston's Shamrock-Hilton and perched on a stool at a glass counter. His ten-gallon hat was snow white, its brim exquisitely curled. Across the yoke of his hand-stitched shirt a double row of rhinestones glittered.

The high heels of his boots were solid silver. Filigreed caps of polished silver covered the toes. An obsequious attendant unlocked a showcase and drew out a ring with a stone the size of a walnut.

A witness walked away, his faith restored. Nothing fazes the men of this master race.

—April 12, 1965

Big Poison

PAUL WANER HAD been one of baseball's finest hitters for a dozen years before a chance remark dropped in the dugout disclosed that he couldn't read the advertisements on the outfield walls. He never had been able to read them from the bench and he hadn't given it a thought, for in his philosophy fences were targets, not literature.

Naturally, steps were taken immediately. With his weak eyes, Paul was batting only about .350. It stood to reason that with corrected vision he'd never be put out. So the Pirates had him fitted with glasses and he gave them a try.

He hated them. For the first time in his life, that thing the pitchers were throwing turned out to be a little thing, a spinning, sharply defined missile no bigger than a baseball. He had always seen it as a fuzzy blob the size of a grapefruit.

Near-sighted millions read about the experiment and chuckled in sympathetic appreciation of his disgust. We in the myopia set see the world as a rather pleasant blur where vaguely outlined objects any distance away appear larger than life, like a street lamp in fog.

The point is, Waner had been whacking that indistinct melon in exact dead center ever since he left the town team in Harrah, Oklahoma.

When Paul Waner died, the obituaries cited the statistical proof of his greatness as a ball player, mentioned his election to the Hall of Fame in 1952, and, of course, referred to the nicknames he and his kid brother Lloyd bore in the game—Big Poison and Little Poison.

Both were small men physically but Paul, with a batting average of .333 for twenty big league seasons, was somewhat more poisonous to pitchers than Lloyd, who hit .316 for eighteen years. Actually, though, Paul's nickname was neither a tribute from the pitchers' fraternity, nor a reference to his preference in beverages, appropriate though it would have been in either case.

"Poison" is Brooklynese for "person." A fan in Ebbets Field was supposed to have complained, "Every time you look up those Waner boys are on base. It's always the little poison on thoid and the big poison on foist."

Maybe the quote is apocryphal but the facts support it. Between them, the brothers made 5,611 hits, about four times as many as a whole team gets in a season. Since Eve threw the first curve to Adam, only eight men have made more than three thousand hits. Paul's 3,152 put him ahead of some pretty fair batsmen named Rogers Hornsby, Ted Williams, Lou Gehrig and Babe Ruth.

By rights the records should credit Paul with 3,153 hits or else there should be a separate page in the book for him alone. It would read: "Most Hits Rejected by Batter Lifetime—1, P. Waner, Boston NL, June 17, 1942."

When the second game of a doubleheader started that day, Waner had 2,999 hits. He had opened the season with 2,955 and had struggled through fifty-two games toward the shining goal of 3,000. In twenty-five games he'd been shut out, but now one more hit would do it.

With Tommy Holmes a baserunner on first, the hit-and-run was on. Holmes broke for second on the pitch and as Eddie Joost, the Cincinnati shortstop, started over to cover the bag. Paul hit toward the spot Joost had vacated. Joost slammed on the brakes, spun back and got his glove on the ball but couldn't hold it.

In the press box the official scorer lifted a forefinger to indicate a single, which it was. A roar saluted the three-thousandth hit. Beans Reardon, the umpire, retrieved the ball and trotted to first base with the souvenir.

Waner was standing on the bag shaking his head emphatically and shouting, "No, no, no!" at the press box. Reluctantly the scorer reversed his decision. Two days later Paul got number three thousand off Rip Sewell, of Pittsburgh, and this was a clean single to center.

Because his hitting overshadowed everything else, Waner's defensive skill is rarely mentioned, but he was a superior outfielder, one of the swiftest runners in the National League with a wonderful arm. One season he threw out thirty-one baserunners to lead the league.

"He had to be a very graceful player," Casey Stengel has said, "because he could slide without breaking the bottle on his hip."

Casey was Waner's manager with the Braves and he knew it was a myth that he enjoyed his nips between games. Most of the tales told of him around the ball parks tell how he might show up somewhat bleary after a night of relaxation, strike out three times, then triple the winning runs home on his fourth trip.

The late Bill Cissell, an American League infielder, spent some time with the Waners and their friends in Sarasota one winter. They had a field baited for doves, but not every shot fired there came out of a 12-gauge. In fact, Bill reported—and he was an excellent jug man himself—sometimes the safest place in the county was out in the field with the birds.

—August 1965

Eyeball to Eyeball

ST. LOUIS—The match was on, the real thing, the eyeball-to-eyeball bit in the seventh game of the World Series. The confrontation they had talked about before they had set Bob Gibson against Denny McLain, but nothing much came of that. Now it was Gibson against the lefthanded motorcyclist, Mickey Lolich. Each had won twice in the series but they had never opposed each other. Now they were head to head.

Gone was the foul weather when foul deeds had been done. While Gibson was in there against them the Tigers had scored one run in 18 innings but then he had sat huddled in the dugout and watched while they scored 18 runs in two games. This, though, was spotless Indian summer and customers stood coatless in sunshine as Mary Eileen O'Reilly Schoendienst, wife of the Cardinals' manager, sang the National Anthem in a sweet soprano.

"Lovely," said a music critic. "She's having a better series than Red."

Away back last Sunday Gibson had stomped Detroit for the second time and given the Schoendienst forces a lead of three victories to one but the Cardinals had frittered that away. Thursday the teams went in even, and even they stayed as the innings hurried past.

Lolich, working with two days' rest, and Gibson with three, matched one-hitters for four innings. For the baleful despot of the National League it was a perfect game until Mickey Stanley slapped a grounder toward left field with one out in the fourth. Dal Maxvill raced to his right and cut it off but couldn't get set to wheel and throw, and Stanley had an infield single.

Stanley was Detroit's only baserunner for six and two-thirds innings. St. Louis had only three up to the sixth. It was beautiful, and suddenly it was dreadful.

Warning cracks showed an inning before the crash, and they showed at the top. Lou Brock, who makes the impossible look easy, led off the home sixth with a single. Every soul in the park waited to see him go down for his eighth steal of the series. Contemptuous of Lolich's lefthanded motion toward first, he strolled off to a lead of at least 15 feet, taunting the pitcher to pick him off. Lolich threw to first and Brock broke for second. The same audacious tactic had worked against Lolich in the second game but this time Norm Cash's relay retired Brock at second.

Even for a baserunner of Brock's spectacular gifts, this was arrogance beyond the call of common sense, impossible to justify with nobody out in a scoreless World Series game. It was the first crack. The second came after Julian Javier lined out and Flood singled. The only player on either team good enough to bat .300 this season got himself picked off, too.

Flood wasn't trying to draw a throw. He just got caught leaning the wrong way when Lolich trapped him. Spectators stared at one another, speechless. It could have been a big inning, a winning inning for the Cardinals. Two of the best ball players in the world had run the opportunity over a cliff.

Gibson got the first two Tiger batters in the seventh, then Cash singled and so did Willie Horton. And then it happened.

Jim Northrup raised a long fly to center. Flood broke in, tried to slam on the brakes, and skidded like a hog on ice. Arms flailing, he struggled for a foothold in the soft turf that was the goal line when the football Cardinals played in the rain here last Sunday.

There are no better center fielders than Flood, who catches 100 flies like this in 100 chances. The 101st went far over his head for a two-run triple. Bill Freehan drove in a third run, getting a double when his low drive eluded Brock's one-handed stab, and three Detroit singles made it 4–0 in the ninth.

Now it was the last of the ninth with the Tigers three putouts away from the championship of the world. Flood went out, Orlando Cepeda went out. Mike Shannon hit a home run and the score read 4–1. Lolich, whose almost cherubic expression of tranquil concentration had not shown a flicker of change all afternoon, watched Shannon circle the bases and then pitched once to Tim McCarver.

The Cardinal catcher lifted a high foul toward first base. Freehan waited under it, facing the seats, and Lolich seemed to tiptoe up behind him. Freehan caught the ball. A split-second later Lolich sprang on him from the rear, riding him piggyback.

The pitcher was screaming, his mouth was wide open, face contorted. He had his legs wrapped around the catcher's middle, one fist brandished aloft. Tigers descended on the pair of them. Hands beat on Lolich, yanked off his cap, scrubbed at his haircut, pawed his features. Somebody's big glove, with a hand in it, smacked him full in the face as the gray-flanneled throng swirled away like chips in a freshet.

—October 11, 1968

Sick Sport

BASEBALL IS SICK and even the men who own the game know that, but they don't know why. They fire their commissioner, they lower the pitcher's mound, they worry about the length of the first baseman's sideburns, and they appoint a committee to devise a plan for "bold and imaginative restructuring" of their business. By none of these measures do they approach the root of the trouble.

The real trouble is that they still think like Joe Engel. Joe Engel was a capable and colorful operator in the minor leagues who once traded a ballplayer for a turkey.

Like Joe, the men who own baseball believe that barnyard fowl and outfielders are created equal. This is the mentality that rules the game, and that is why baseball is sick.

If anybody doubts this, he is referred to the statement issued this week by the owners' committee that has been haggling with the players about the loot from television. The statement said in effect that labor was not entitled to share in the fruits of labor. It said that labor was entitled to nothing. Nevertheless, it added, labor was going to get something because the owners were generous to a fault.

Baseball can show the world how to succeed in alienating the help without really trying. A year ago the player representatives of 20 teams went to Mexico City hoping to get labor negotiations off the ground during the winter meetings there. Their bosses brushed them off without a nod, and the players went home as sore as a sick thumb.

Now, after another year of glacial progress, the labor relations committee representing the owners announces what the powers intend to do about whacking up the increasing spoils from television.

In 1969 National Broadcasting Co. will pay $16.5 million for the World Series, All-Star Game, and game of the week, plus an amount not yet determined for the leagues' divisional playoffs. This is an increase of more than $4.2 million. The owners say they'll hike contributions to the players' pension fund by a million, raising the annual payment to $5.1 million.

It was their first proposal on this thorny issue, yet it was presented as a fait accompli before the players had a chance to consider it. Moreover, in a crude rebuff to Marvin Miller, director of the Players Association, the committee coolly advised him that it was bypassing his office and sending copies of the offer to all players.

Pointing out that it would require half the million-dollar increase to cover the players on the four expansion teams scheduled to start in 1969, Miller called the offer totally inadequate. Steve Hamilton of the Yankees called it "almost an insult."

The manner of its presentation would infuriate a turnip.

And on top of everything else, the committee went out of its way to insist that "when the players claim, as they do, the right to share in national television and radio revenue, they are claiming a property right they do not now have, nor ever had."

The sad fact—sad for baseball—is that the chumps believe this. Call them Young Turks or Old Romans, feudal blindness seems to come with the franchise. They think they own not only the business but also the players, who have no rights at all but only the rare privilege of working for Big Daddy.

It is, of course, easily provable that the players do have a vested right to a share of TV swag, but that isn't the point here. The point is that this attitude of the owners is typical of the lemming mentality that is guiding baseball to disaster.

Also typical was the recent adoption of the "Lonborg Rule," providing that if a player is injured away from the ball park—as Boston's Jim Lonborg was injured on a ski slope—he can be placed on a "temporarily inactive list," without pay. The idea that a club can retain ownership of a man without supporting him does not please the players.

The owners don't quite understand this, though they wouldn't expect to keep a bird dog without feeding him. They don't quite understand a fellow like Rep. Frank Thompson, Jr., of New Jersey, chairman of a House

Labor Subcommittee investigating the firing of two American League umpires, when he says the inquiry may be extended to include the labor problems of professional athletes generally.

They think a fellow like that must be some kind of Bolshevik.

—December 20, 1968

The Most Ridiculous

"IT HAS ALL been very interesting," a man said before the game, "but what can they do for an encore?"

"They'll think of something," said another, a true believer. He had been watching the Mets ever since they introduced the pratfall to baseball back in 1962. He had faith.

They thought of something. They thought of the most ridiculous, the most preposterous, the most widely improbable absurdities that ever encumbered a World Series match. And now that the foolishness is ended the New York Mets, those golden-hearted clowns of all creation, stand assured forevermore of their place in baseball mythology.

It happened in Shea Stadium yesterday. Shea Stadium was the name of a playpen that used to stand on Flushing Meadow. Two-legged termites took it down piece by piece immediately after the Mets chopped up the Baltimore Orioles for the fourth successive time and won the championship of this dizzily whirling globe, four games to one.

This is how the fates, laughing fit to split, arranged for the Orioles to snatch a 5–3 defeat from the jaws of a 3–0 victory:

In the sixth inning, Cleon Jones led off for New York against Dave McNally, who had allowed three hits up to that point. Jerry Koosman had allowed only five hits, but three of them had come in the third inning in this order: Pop single by Mark Belanger, two-run homer by McNally, of all people, and a drive struck angrily by Frank Robinson that went screaming clear over skeleton bleachers built for this series beyond the fence in left-center.

It was high time the Mets do something if they were to avoid a return to Baltimore for a sixth and possibly a seventh game. But what? "Let's dig up the old Shinola play," somebody up there suggested.

The Shinola play was introduced to World Series competition in 1957 in Milwaukee. Nippy Jones of the Braves howled that a pitch by the Yankees' Tommy Byrne had struck him on the foot but Augie Donatelli, the umpire, wouldn't believe him until he was shown a smudge of shoe polish on the ball. Thanks to his neat grooming, Jones was awarded first base, he scored the winning run, and Milwaukee won the championship.

Lou Dimuro was Thursday's plate umpire. A skeptic like Donatelli, he had coldly rejected Frank Robinson's claim that a pitch by Koosman in the top of the sixth had struck him. Even when Robinson stalked off the field and held up the game five minutes while he applied ice to his bruised thigh, Dimuro stood his ground, embarrassed but obstinate.

So now in the same inning, the umpire was understandably cool to Jones's claim that he'd been nicked on the toe by a McNally pitch. "Shut up and bat," Dimuro was saying, when here came the Mets' manager, Gil Hodges, carrying the ball which had skidded into the Mets' dugout. It bore the telltale smear.

Waved to first base, Jones cantered home ahead of Donn Clendenon when that tall citizen busted his third home run of the series. Now it was a 3–2 ball game. What could the Mets think of next?

You wouldn't believe this. They thought of Al Weis. Al Weis has played baseball in the major leagues for seven years and in that space he had hit six home runs. So he led off the seventh inning with his seventh. It gave this .215 hitter an average of .500 for the World Series; it gave the Mets a 3–3 tie. Now what?

Having started it all with his elegantly polished booties, Cleon Jones was elected to signal the closing flourish. Leading off in the eighth, he slugged a double against the wall in center. Then with one out, up stepped Ron Swoboda, the archetypal Met. He looks like L'il Abner; he forgets things; he gets lost; he swings a bat with a wild, impassioned dedication.

Eddie Watt was pitching now. With first base open, prudence advised against giving the muscular Swoboda a pitch he could hit. Watt's first delivery was low and outside. His second was higher and not so wide. Swoboda placed it neatly just inside the left field line for two bases.

In came the winning run, and nothing else mattered. Swoboda scored the fifth run when the Orioles, beaten and aware of it, butchered a play. In the ninth, Koosman held them off at the pass. The last play of 1969 was a fly to Jones. He caught the ball and dropped to his knees in thanksgiving, but Koosman didn't see that. With the crack of the bat, Jerry Grote had rushed out from behind the plate and flung himself on the pitcher's bosom. When it ended, Koosman was wearing his catcher like prayer beads.

—October 17, 1969

1970s

Curt's 13th Amendment

CURT FLOOD WAS 19 years old and had made one hit in the major leagues (a home run) when his telephone rang on Dec. 5 of 1957. The call was from the Cincinnati Reds, advising him that he had been traded to the St. Louis Cardinals.

"I knew ball players got traded like horses," he said years later, "but I can't tell you how I felt when it happened to me. I was only 19, but I made up my mind then it wouldn't ever happen again."

It happened again last October. The Cardinals traded Flood to Philadelphia. "Maybe I won't go," Curt said. Baseball men laughed. Curt makes something like $90,000 a year playing center field, and less than that painting portraits in his studio in Clayton, Mo. "Unless he's better than Rembrandt," one baseball man said, "he'll play."

It was a beautiful comment, superlatively typical of the executive mind, a pluperfect example of baseball's reaction to unrest down in the slave cabins. "You mean," baseball demands incredulously, "that at these prices they want human rights, too?"

Curtis Charles Flood is a man of character and self-respect. Being black, he is more sensitive than most white players about the institution of slavery as it exists in professional baseball. After the trade he went abroad, and when he returned his mind was made up. He confided his decision to the 24 club representatives in the Major League Players Association at their convention in San Juan, Puerto Rico.

He told them it was high time somebody in baseball made a stand for human freedom. He said he was determined to make the stand and he asked their support. The players questioned him closely to make sure this was not merely a ploy to squeeze money out of the Phillies. Then, convinced, they voted unanimously to back him up.

Realizing that if Flood lost his case through poor handling they would all be losers, the players arranged—through their executive director, Marvin Miller—to retain Arthur J. Goldberg, former Secretary of Labor, former Justice of the Supreme Court, former United States ambassador to the United Nations, and the country's most distinguished authority on labor-management relations.

Baseball's so-called reserve clause, which binds the player to his employer through his professional life, had been under fire before. Never has it been attacked by a team like this.

The system is in deep trouble, and yesterday's action by the baseball commissioner, Bowie Kuhn, did nothing to help it out. Because the news was out that Flood was going to take baseball to court, Kuhn released to the press the following correspondence:

"Dear Mr. Kuhn," Flood wrote on Dec. 24, 1969, "after 12 years in the major leagues I do not feel that I am a piece of property to be bought and sold irrespective of my wishes. I believe that any system that produces that result violates my basic rights as a citizen and is inconsistent with the laws of the United States and of the several states.

"It is my desire to play baseball in 1970, and I am capable of playing. I have received a contract offer from the Philadelphia club, but I believe that I have the right to consider offers from other clubs before making any decisions. I, therefore, request that you make known to all the major league clubs my feelings in this matter, and advise them of my availability for the 1970 season."

Kuhn replied:

"Dear Curt: This will acknowledge your letter of Dec. 24, 1969, which I found on returning to my office yesterday.

"I certainly agree with you that you, as a human being, are not a piece of property to be bought and sold. That is fundamental in our society and I think obvious. However, I cannot see its application to the situation at hand.

"You have entered into a current playing contract with the St. Louis club which has the same assignment provisions as those in your annual major league contracts since 1956. Your present playing contract has been assigned in accordance with its provisions by the St. Louis club to the Philadelphia club. The provisions of the playing contract have been negotiated over the years between the clubs and the players, most recently when the present basic agreement was negotiated two years ago between the clubs and the Players Association.

"If you have any specific objections to the propriety of the assignment I would appreciate your specifying the objections. Under the circumstances, and pending any further information from you, I do not see what action I can take, and cannot comply with your request contained in the second paragraph of your letter.

"I am pleased to see your statement that you desire to play baseball in 1970. I take it this puts to rest any thought, as reported earlier in the press, that you were considering retirement."

Thus the commissioner restates baseball's labor policy: "Run along, sonny, you bother me."

—January 1, 1970

Sparky

ST. PETERSBURG, FLA.—"When you come into baseball," Sparky Anderson said, "I don't care what organization, they give you a manual telling you how to play. If you read it, you're in trouble."

Sparky Anderson, of the Cincinnati Reds, has been a manager in the major leagues ever since Oct. 9, but he says he's no smarter now than he was when he managed St. Pete in the Florida State League.

"You can't read a book and learn about baseball," he said. "You have to see it with your eyes. See that Number 3 out there?" He gestured toward George Kissell, the Cardinals' third base coach. "He says you should be able to walk into a park with the scoreboard blacked out and know which team is ahead from the way they're playing.

"That Kissell, you take the 24 managers in the major leagues, including me, and put 'em on one side, with Kissell on the other side and he'll eat 'em up on fundamental baseball. I roomed with him three years in the St. Louis organization.

"So Doubleday wrote the book saying hit behind the runner and send him from first to third, but do you want John Bench to go to the other field? The other day we had a man on first and John sliced a couple fouls trying to hit to right. I knew what he was doing. Finally he popped one up to right, and when he came in I said, 'How would you hit best, swinging like John Bench or trying to punch it to the opposite field?'

"He said, 'I'll hit best swinging.' I said, 'Well, then why handicap yourself? When you hurt yourself, you hurt us.' I want him and Lee May and Tony Perez to be swinging. Then if he happens to hit to right it will be well hit. Bobby Tolan, now, and Pete Rose batting lefthanded, they have to wait for a pitch they can pull until two strikes. After that they hit it where it's pitched.

"You can't play by the book. Runners on first and second, would you bunt 'em over against—" he named a pitcher with a big, soft earned-run-average. "No, you play for the big inning. But against Larry Dierker you'll bunt 'em over because you're never going to get more than two runs off him.

"You have to see it with your eyes. You look around the field, from first base all around. Maybe you're playing a hitter to pull but you want your fielders spaced evenly, all over to right the same distance or all over to left except against Matty Alou. With him you shade him to left and left-center and he can pull the ball so you have to play him in right, but you give him all of right-center."

During one 24-hour span last fall, Sparky Anderson was employed by three big league clubs. A coach with San Diego, he accepted a coaching job with his old friend Lefty Phillips, manager of the California Angeles, on Oct. 8. The next day Bob Howsam of Cincinnati asked permission of Dick Walsh, the Angels' general manager, to talk business with Anderson.

"My head was whirling," Sparky said. "I was in Dick Walsh's office when Howsam called, but I didn't have any idea of what it was about. Dick hung up and closed the door and said, 'they're probably going to make you an offer.' I said, 'cut it out, don't do that to me.' I knew Dave Bristol was out, but I thought they'd go for a name, not somebody like me.

"Sure, I wanted to manage in the majors. I tell my coaches, if anybody asks if you want to manage in the majors, tell 'em yes, because if you don't you're no baseball man.

"The writers say to me, 'You're under pressure. You have to win.' I say, 'Hell, you're under pressure if you can't write.' "

"About your team," a visitor said. "I notice you have the batting champions of three leagues."

"Yes," Anderson said. "Bravo from the Coast League and Carbo from the American Association and—" he groped. "Pete Rose," the visitor said and Anderson laughed at himself.

"I only remember minor leaguers," he said. "All right, now I'm managing in the majors but does that make me smarter than I was in the minors? Do you think any of my coaches couldn't manage in the majors? 'Up here,' I hear guys saying, and I wonder where are we, heaven or someplace? I wouldn't be ashamed to go back and manage in the minors. It's still the same game.

"They ask me, 'Have you changed?' I don't think so. I hope not. I know some guys manage in the majors two or three years and they fall in love with themselves. They see you and they don't know who you are. They stick out a hand like this. 'How are the wife and kids?' they say. Look, you tell me if I change. Come around five years from now if I'm still here and see if I ask how are the wife and kids."

—March 17, 1970

One Vote for Morganna

CINCINNATI—The game was one putout old and Tom Seaver had missed the strike zone with a pitch to Carl Yastrzemski when Morganna the Wild One (44–23–37) vaulted out of the grandstand in short left field. A private cop named Thomas Burton caught her like a pop foul and they went to the mat with his arms wrapped around 37.

As they struggled to their feet, a clutch of Cincinnati's Finest swooped. Morganna was blindsided by one of the fuzz who wound the long arms of the law around 44, found a firm handhold, and did not let go.

Kicking and squirming under callused male hands, the helpless bit of fluff was hustled to an exit, yet another victim of police brutality. All the sweet thing wanted was to kiss Seaver's catcher, John Bench, through his mask. Yet they treated her like a common felon.

There will be repercussions, for this is one case where the Administration cannot plead ignorance. Sitting right there watching with a mouthful of teeth was Richard Milhous Nixon himself, and he did not lift a finger. Neither did Pat nor Julie nor David nor Rep. Robert Taft, Jr., nor Bowie Kuhn nor president Joe Cronin of the American League nor president Chub Feeney of the National League nor Chub's predecessor Warren Giles nor the hundred or so Secret Service men and six umpires who witnessed the sorry affair.

For the benefit of readers on Mars, it should be explained that Morganna Roberts is a stripper who has been undressing in a joint across the Ohio River in Newport, Ky. She is a shy, timorous creature whose distaste for publicity drives her into baseball parks where she has smooched Pete Rose of the Reds, Clete Boyer of the Braves, Wes Parker of the Dodgers, Billy Cowan of the Angels, Frank Howard of the Senators, and a roundball player named Bob Verga.

Ads in the local papers had promised that she would be in Riverfront Stadium last night to ornament the 41st All-Star Game and—if the vernacular may be forgiven—she did indeed shape up. She wore a tousled black wig and dark glasses, with her interesting contours encased in a green sweatshirt and brown bell-bottoms.

Her trouble, and that of most of the batters on the field, was over-eagerness. Through the early innings the batters twitched and lunged and swung and missed, especially when Seaver or Jim Merritt or Jim Palmer or Sam McDowell was pitching.

Like them, Morganna simply couldn't wait. She should have held her fire until, say, the eighth inning when punishing heat and smothering boredom had put the crowd of 51,838 into a somnolent stupor. At that point the show needed her desperately and she would have been cheered to the sultry skies. Instead, she chose to make her pitch soon after the arrival of the Presidential party when security forces were still on the alert for infiltrating Democrats.

Due in part to the misfeasance of Cincinnati deities, the first eight innings were tedious and tidy. "Tricky Dick loves the big red machine," read one of the bedsheet banners that festooned the new playpen in celebration of Cincinnati's 10-game lead in the National League West. But over the normal nine-inning distance, the only contributions from Tony Perez, Pete Rose, and John Bench, all cogs in the machine, were seven strikeouts.

It was enough to make Nixon burn his card of honorary membership in the Baseball Writers Association of America, but he contented himself by explaining the game to the baseball commissioner and shaking hands. In the fifth inning when there were no unshaken paws left within reach, Ed Roush, who made the Hall of Fame as a Cincinnati outfielder, was brought to the royal box to have his knuckles clutched. In the ninth the President risked a hernia hanging over the rail to press the flesh of Al Barlick, the plate umpire.

At this point the Americans led, 4–1, and could taste their first victory in eight years. Bud Harrelson, the littlest Met, had singled and scored the Nationals' only run. In the ninth the Giants' Dick Dietz smashed a home run, Harrelson singled again, and by the time the side was out the score was tied.

Not until the 12th inning did Rose score the Nationals' winning run. The job required three suffocating hours and 19 sweltering minutes. Few husbands would be surprised to hear that Mrs. Nixon mentioned the time of game later when she inspected the seat of her pretty red plaid frock.

Yastrzemski made four hits, scored a run, drove in another, and was chosen most valuable player in a pressbox poll.

Morganna got one vote and Mr. Nixon none, even though he wore his arm out throwing a first ball to Bill Freehan for the American League, a first ball to Bench for the National League, and three balls for deserving Republicans in the second deck of stands.

Considering how much grimacing effort he put into his performance, this must have been his most galling defeat since the California gubernatorial election of 1962. He is expected to call a news conference when the soreness leaves his shoulder and turn in his baseball writer's card. He will, informed sources report, tell the writers:

"You won't have Nixon to kick around anymore."

—July 16, 1970

A Matter of Timing

BOWIE KUHN'S RECENT announcement that the Cubs were not going to win a pennant in 1971 must have come as a blow to the players, the fans on Chicago's North Side, and Philip Wrigley, the owner.

It is painful to think what the disappointment must be doing to the morale of a sincere and sensitive competitor like Ron Santo, or how it must dampen the spirits of Ernie Banks, who for 18 consecutive springs has shown up in training camp with a song on his lips, buoyed by faith that this was the year when he would play in a World Series.

Phil Wrigley must be asking himself why he should bother opening the park.

It's enough to make Leo Durocher take a full-time job as counselor in that Wisconsin boys' camp.

Unlike professional oddsmakers such as Jimmie the Greek Snyder and Denny McLain, Kuhn did not write off the Cubs' chances merely on the basis of his own independent judgment. He had the assistance and advice of Carl Lindemann, sports director of NBC.

They kicked the idea around from the time of the All-Star Game last July. Then Bowie broke the news: The fourth game of the 1971 World Series, tentatively scheduled for Wednesday, Oct. 13, would be played at night.

It goes without saying that with six months for study the thinkers considered all aspects of the proposition. It must have occurred to somebody that in 1971 the National League champions would be the home team in the fourth game, that the Cubs are members of the National League and that there are no lights for night games in the Cubs' park.

Since the announcement included no conditional clauses, it follows that Kuhn and Lindemann had ruled out the Cubs as candidates for the National League championship.

However, it would be underestimating the ingenuity of the planners to suggest that they couldn't find a way around the difficulty if the Cubs should win. They could move the fourth game to some lighted playground like White Sox Park or Milwaukee County Stadium or, if protocol demanded a National League park, to Cincinnati or St. Louis.

Failing that, they could present the game in Wrigley Field in total darkness. Television cameras are perfectly capable of photographing the action by infrared light, and since this light is not visible to the human eye it would not offend Phil Wrigley.

It is possible that neither of these arrangements would delight the Bleacher Bums and other supporters of the Cubs who have contributed $40 or $50 million at the gate in the quarter-century since they were last rewarded with a championship. Still, the freeloaders would get to see the game on TV, and that's all that counts.

There is no secret about the origin of the idea of playing the World Series at night. The network people, Kuhn said, were "intrigued" by the higher ratings the All-Star Game got after it was changed from afternoon to evening. According to surveys, 25,390,000 sets were tuned in for the 1970 All-Star Game under the lights in Cincinnati compared with 15,960,000 for the daytime game in Washington the summer before.

When the network people are "intrigued," Commissioner Kuhn is submissive. He has made it clear that he believes baseball is healthy when the largest possible number of viewers are watching it free on television. He has let TV dictate starting times for the pennant playoffs and now he will permit the space cadets to put the sport's showcase attraction into direct competition with go-go dancers, Johnny Cash and "Oh! Calcutta!"

If the fourth World Series game is scheduled for Los Angeles or San Diego or San Francisco, the home fans will be told they must show up before 5 p.m. and sit through their dinner hour so effete snobs in the East can enjoy the game in prime time.

It is a pity the commissioner isn't a boxing fan. If he were, he could remember a time when the networks had three evening fight shows a week. The insatiable medium sucked boxing dry, then cast it out to die of overexposure.

—January 27, 1971

Mr. Cub

"THERE'S TWO-THREE guys ought to be ruled out of baseball," Garry Schumacher of the Giants has said, "because they make the game look too easy. And the biggest offender of them all is Ernie Banks."

"They voted Joe Cronin the greatest living shortstop," said Cliff Keane of Boston during the All-Star festivities of 1969 in Washington, which celebrated a centennial of professional baseball. "He couldn't wear Ernie Banks's spikes."

"I wish colleges didn't always feel they had to save their honorary degrees for fat cats who give them a lot of money," a member of the Roosevelt University administration in Chicago confided one day. "I want Roosevelt to confer a doctorate on Ernie Banks."

"I call it Picasso's fiasco, a rising heap of rusting iron," said Alderman John Hoellen when Pablo Picasso presented his five-story metal sculpture to the city of Chicago in 1967. Hoellen introduced a resolution in city council rejecting the gift and proposing for its place in front of the civic center a five-story statue of Ernie Banks as "a living symbol of a vibrant city."

These are a few of the people who have had their say about Ernie Banks since Sept. 8, 1953, when the Chicago Cubs bought him from the Kansas City Monarchs of the Negro American league. Now Ernie Banks has his. With Jim Enright as collaborator, Ernie tells his own story under the title, *Mr. Cub.*

Nobody who has felt the sunny warmth of Ernie Banks, either in personal contact or by reflection through the sports pages, will be surprised to learn that his book has little in common with other recent products of the sweaty literati, such as Jim Bouton's *Ball Four* and Curt Flood's *The Way It Is.*

Bouton's opus made the best-seller lists on the strength of the intimacies he reveals about some former teammates and the sneers he directs toward others. Flood says he detested Solly Hemus, one of his managers. If Banks ever met anybody he didn't like, the secret is still locked inside him.

His choice of a collaborator is evidence of his tolerance, for although Jim Enright is a jovial soul and an amiable pressbox companion who has covered the Cubs longer than Ernie has played with them, he has a black past as a basketball referee. It was only a few years ago that Enright, a spherical man, went square after breathing through a whistle practically all his adult life.

In his years with the Cubs, Banks played under Phil Cavaretta, Stan Hack, Bob Scheffing, Charley Grimm, Lou Boudreau and Leo Durocher. He not only has warm words for all of them; he also esteems Phil Wrigley as the most considerate of employers and Jim Gallagher and John Holland as general managers, and even speaks well of the college of coaches that presided during the five seasons when the Cubs had no manager at all.

"It has been my good fortune," Ernie recalls, "to have exceptional rapport with all my managers, but Bob Scheffing paid me the most flattering compliment I've ever received." In an interview, Scheffing said:

"During my first 26 years in baseball, Joe DiMaggio is the only player I'd ever consider rating ahead of Ernie Banks after the year Ernie

A young Ernie Banks

had for me in 1959. He batted fourth behind three hitters who didn't come even close to averaging .260 and still he batted in 143 runs. He also hit 45 homers and I figure that his bat was directly responsible for 27 of our 74 victories that season. Afield he was the equal of any shortstop I've seen."

Ernie, of course, was on the team whose collapse in 1969 prompted Durocher to say he "could have dressed nine broads up as ball players and they would have beaten the Cubs." "That's Leo all the way," Ernie tells us. "A bark now, a good laugh a little later . . . Leo can build a player's morale like no one else."

The author, it must be remembered, is a man who says of his high school football coach: "I've never known a man who coached with more dedication than Coach Hollie. He made us practice until dark, and if you made a mistake he rapped you across the rump with a board he always carried."

Though it has much to enjoy and admire, *Mr. Cub* is not recommended as reading for fans of the Giants, Mets, Expos or any other National League club outside of Chicago. It makes you root for the Cubs so Ernie Banks can play in a World Series.

—May 25, 1971

Slugging Manager

EVER SINCE Billy Martin was a street kid in Oakland, getting into fights under his square name of Alfred Manuel Pesano, he has been characterized by what Joseph Conrad called "an open, generous, frank, barbarous recklessness."

He was a rookie riding the Yankees' bench in 1952 when the Marines called up Jerry Coleman, the best second baseman in the American League, for service in Korea. This gave Martin a chance to play regularly but he did not exclaim, "Oh, goodie!" Finding his name eighth in the batting order, he sought out Casey Stengel. "What is this, a joke?" he demanded. "I suppose tomorrow I'll be hitting behind the groundskeeper."

"Where do you think you should be hitting?" the manager asked. "Third?"

"Where else?" the young man said.

Still a museum piece among heedless World Series plays is one Martin employed to insure the Yankees' defeat in the fourth game of their 1953 struggle with the Brooklyn Dodgers. With the Dodgers leading, 7–3, Gene Woodling and Martin singled in the ninth inning and Gil McDougald walked, filling the bases. There was promise of a big Yankee rally, but Clem Labine relieved Billy Loes, struck out Phil Rizzuto and got the second out on a fly by Johnny Mize. Mickey Mantle singled to left, scoring Woodling with the Yankees' fourth run, and Martin gambled that he could get home from second base with a meaningless fifth. Running with great resolution, not to mention open, generous, frank and barbarous recklessness, he ran the Yankees plumb out of the ball game.

Those were Martin's salad days, when he was green in judgment. In fairness, it should be added that he was the star of the series, which the Yankees won in six games. He batted .500 and his 12 hits equaled the World Series record that Pepper Martin had set 22 years earlier in seven games.

On May 16, 1957, when Martin attained to the wisdom of 29 years, he celebrated the birthday in the Copacabana, a popular waterhole in New York, in company with Hank Bauer, Yogi Berra, Whitey Ford and their wives. Toasts were drunk, words spoken, a stranger awoke the next day with a lump on his jaw, and Martin wound up in Kansas City.

"I never dared to be a radical when young," Robert Frost has told us, "for fear it would make me conservative when old." It didn't work that way as Billy Martin matured. As a coach with the Minnesota Twins, he punched Howard Fox, the traveling secretary.

When he succeeded to the dignity of manager, he slugged his star pitcher, Dave Boswell, stiff as a straw hat, in a brawl outside a saloon. He complained publicly about the work of the club's personnel director, a relative of the boss, and when the Twins finished first in the American League West, under Martin's direction, Calvin Griffith, the owner, handed Martin his head as a token of his esteem.

This is Martin's second season as licensed wonder worker for the Detroit Tigers. Since training camp opened he has been promising that his team would win in the American League East.

Arriving in New York last week with his club in first place, he said that if it hadn't been for the players' strike last spring the Tigers would be out of sight.

The Tigers lost three of their four games in Yankee Stadium. They went home, lost twice to Cleveland, and dropped out of first place.

So Martin tried a novel experiment. Before Sunday's doubleheader with the Indians, he put the names of his eight regulars in a hat, shook well, and had Al Kaline select the batting order in a blind draw. Norm Cash, the club's leading power hitter, led off, and Ed Brinkman, hitting .205, batted clean-up. Detroit won, 3–2. For the second game, Martin revised the batting order according to his best judgment. For the sixth time in eight games, Detroit lost.

John E. Fetzer, owner of the Tigers, has not yet fired Martin and hired Martin's hat, but if he should, Martin will know where he got the idea.

—August 16, 1972

Unconquerable

IN THE SCENE that doesn't fade, the Brooklyn Dodgers are tied with the Phillies in the bottom of the 12th inning. It is 6 p.m. on an October Sunday, but the gloom in Philadelphia's Shibe Park is only partly due to oncoming evening. The Dodgers, champions-elect in August, have frittered away a lead of 13½ games, and there is bitterness in the dusk of this last day of the 1951 baseball season. Two days ago, the New York Giants drew even with Brooklyn in the pennant race. Two hours ago, the numbers went up on the scoreboard: New York 3, Boston 2. The pennant belongs to the Giants unless the Dodgers can snatch it back.

With two out and the bases full of Phillies, Eddie Waitkus smashes a low, malevolent drive toward center field. The ball is a blur passing second base, difficult to follow in the half-light, impossible to catch. Jackie Robinson catches it. He flings himself headlong at right angles to the flight of the ball, for an instant his body is suspended in midair, then somehow the outstretched glove intercepts the ball inches off the ground.

He falls heavily, the crash drives an elbow into his side, he collapses. But the Phillies are out, the score is still tied.

Now it is the 14th inning. It is too dark to play baseball, but the rules forbid turning on lights for a game begun at 2 o'clock. Pee Wee Reese pops up. So does Duke Snider. Robin Roberts throws a ball and a strike to Robinson. Jackie hits the next pitch upstairs in left field for the run that sets up baseball's most memorable playoff.

That was the day that popped into mind when word came yesterday that Jack Roosevelt Robinson had died at 53. Of all the pictures he left upon memory, the one that will always flash back first shows him stretched at full length in the insubstantial twilight, the unconquerable doing the impossible.

The word for Jackie Robinson is "unconquerable." In *The Boys of Summer,* Roger Kahn sums it up: "In two seasons, 1962 and 1965, Maury Wills stole more bases than Robinson did in all of a 10-year career. Ted Williams' lifetime batting average, .344, is two points higher than Robinson's best for any season. Robinson never hit 20 home runs in a year, never batted in 125 runs. Stan Musial consistently scored more often. Having said those things, one has not said much because troops of people who were there believe that in his prime Jackie Robinson was a better ball player than any of the others."

Another picture comes back. Robinson has taken a lead off first base and he crouches, facing the pitcher, feet fairly wide apart, knees bent, hands held well out from his sides to help him balance, teetering on the balls of his feet. Would he be running? His average was 20 stolen bases a year and Bugs Baer wrote that "John McGraw demanded more than that from the baseball writers."

Yet he was the only base-runner of his time who could bring a game to a stop just by getting on base. When he walked to first, all other action ceased. For Robinson, television introduced the split screen so the viewer at home as well as the fan in the park could watch both the runner on first and the pitcher standing irresolute, wishing he didn't have to throw.

Jackie Robinson established the black man's right to play second base. He fought for the black man's right to a place in the white community, and he never lost sight of that goal. After he left baseball, almost everything he did was directed toward that goal. He was involved in foundation of the Freedom National Banks. He tried to get an insurance company started with black capital and when he died he was head of a construction company building housing for blacks. Years ago a friend, talking of the needs of blacks, said "good schooling comes first."

"No," Jackie said, "housing is the first thing. Unless he's got a home he wants to come back to, it doesn't matter what kind of school he goes to."

There was anger in him and when he was a young man he tended to raise his falsetto voice. "But my demands were modest enough," he said, and he spoke the truth. The very last demand he made publicly was delivered in the mildest of terms during the World Series just concluded. There was a ceremony in Cincinnati saluting him for his work in drug addiction and in his response he mentioned a wish that he could look down to third base and see a black manager on the coaching line.

Seeing him in Cincinnati recalled the Dylan Thomas line that Roger Kahn borrowed for a title: "I see the boys of summer in their ruin." At 53 Jackie was sick of body, white of hair. He had survived one heart attack, he had diabetes and high blood-pressure, and he was going blind as a result of retinal bleeding in spite of efforts to cauterize the ruptured blood vessels with laser beams. With him were his wife Rachel, their son, David, and daughter, Sharon. Everybody was remembering Jack Jr., an addict who beat the heroin habit and died at 24 in an auto accident.

"I've lost the sight in one eye," Jackie had told Kahn a day or so earlier, "but they think they can save the other. I've got nothing to complain about."

—October 25, 1972

One of a Kind

GRANTLAND RICE, the prince of sportswriters, used to do a weekly radio interview with some sporting figure. Frequently, in the interest of spontaneity, he would type out questions and answers in advance. One night his guest was Babe Ruth.

"Well, you know, Granny," the Babe read in response to a question, "Duke Ellington said the Battle of Waterloo was won on the playing fields of Elkton."

"Babe," Granny said after the show, "Duke Ellington for the Duke of Wellington I can understand. But how did you ever read Eton as Elkton? That's in Maryland, isn't it?"

"I married my first wife there," Babe said, "and I always hated the gawdam place." He was cheerily unruffled. In the uncomplicated world of George Herman Ruth, errors were part of the game.

Babe Ruth died 25 years ago but his ample ghost has been with us all summer and he seems to grow more insistently alive every time Henry Aaron hits a baseball over a fence. What, people under 50 keep asking, what was this creature of myth and legend like in real life? If he were around today, how would he react when Aaron at last broke his hallowed record of 714 home runs? The first question may be impossible to answer fully; the second is easy.

"Well, what d'you know!" he would have said when the record got away. "Baby loses another! Come on, have another beer."

To paraphrase Abraham Lincoln's remark about another deity, Ruth must have admired records because he created so many of them. Yet he was sublimely aware that he transcended records and his place in the American scene was no mere matter of statistics. It wasn't just that he hit more home runs than anybody else, he hit them better, higher, farther, with more theatrical timing and a more flamboyant flourish. Nobody could strike out like Babe Ruth. Nobody circled the bases with the same pigeon-toed, mincing majesty.

"He was one of a kind," says Waite Hoyt, a Yankee pitcher in the years of Ruthian splendor. "If he had never played ball, if you had never heard of him and passed him on Broadway, you'd turn around and look."

Looking, you would have seen a barrel swaddled in a wrap-around camel-hair topcoat with a flat camel-hair cap on the round head. Thus arrayed he was instantly recognizable not only on Broadway in New York but also on the Ginza in Tokyo. "Baby Roos! Baby Roos!" cried excited crowds, following through the streets when he visited Japan with an all-star team in the early 1930s.

The camel-hair coat and cap are part of my last memory of the man. It must have been in the spring training season of 1948 when the Babe and everybody else knew he was dying of throat cancer. "This is the last time around," he had told Frank Stevens that winter when the head of the H. M. Stevens catering firm visited him in French Hospital on West 30th Street, "but before I go I'm gonna get out of here and have some fun."

He did get out, but touring the Florida training camps surrounded by a gaggle of admen, hustlers and promoters, he didn't look like a man having fun. It was a hot day when he arrived in St. Petersburg but the camel-hair collar was turned up about the wounded throat. By this time, Al Lang Stadium had replaced old Waterfront Park where he had drawn crowds when the Yankees trained in St. Pete.

"What do you remember best about this place?" asked Francis Stann of "The Washington Star."

Babe gestured toward the West Coast Inn, an old frame building a city block beyond the right-field fence. "The day I hit the adjectival ball against that adjectival hotel." The voice was a hoarse stage whisper; the adjective was one often printed these days, but not here.

"Wow!" Francis Stann said. "Pretty good belt."

"But don't forget," Babe said, "the adjectival park was a block back this way then."

Ruth was not noted for a good memory. In fact, the inability to remember names is part of his legend. Yet he needed no record books to remind him of his own special feats. There was, for example, the time he visited Philadelphia as a "coach" with the Brooklyn Dodgers. (His coachly duties consisted of hitting home runs in batting practice.) This was in the late 1930s when National League games in Philadelphia were played in Shibe Park, the American League grounds where Babe had performed. I asked him what memories stirred on his return.

"The time I hit one into Opal Street," he said.

Now, a baseball hit over Shibe Park's right field fence landed in 20th Street. Opal is the next street east, just a wide alley one block long. There may not be 500 Philadelphians who know it by name, but Babe Ruth knew it.

Another time, during a chat in Hollywood, where he was an actor in the film *Pride of the Yankees,* one of us mentioned Rube Walberg, a good left-handed pitcher with the Philadelphia Athletics through the Ruth era. To some left-handed batters there is no dirtier word than the name of a good left-handed pitcher, but the Babe spoke fondly:

"Rube Walberg! What a pigeon! I hit 23 home runs off him." Or whatever the figure was. It isn't in the record book but it was in Ruth's memory.

Obviously it is not true that he couldn't even remember the names of his teammates. It was only that the names he remembered were not always those bestowed at the baptismal font. To him Urban Shocker, a Yankee pitcher, was Rubber Belly. Pat Collins, the catcher, was Horse Nose. All redcaps at railroad stations were Stinkweed, and everybody else was Kid. One day Jim Cahn, covering the Yankees for "The New York Sun," watched two players board a train with a porter toting the luggage.

"There go Rubber Belly, Horse Nose and Stinkweed," Jim said.

Don Heffner joined the Yankees in 1934, Ruth's last year with the team. Playing second base through spring training, Heffner was stationed directly in the line of vision of Ruth, the right fielder. Breaking camp, the Yankees stopped in Jacksonville on a night when the Baltimore Orioles of the International League were also in town. A young reporter on "The Baltimore Sun" seized the opportunity to interview Ruth.

"How is Heffner looking?" he asked, because the second baseman had been a star with the Orioles in 1933.

"Who the hell is Heffner?" the Babe demanded. The reporter should, of course, have asked about the kid at second.

Jacksonville was the first stop that year on the barnstorming trip that would last two or three weeks and take the team to Yankee Stadium by a meandering route through the American bush. There, as everywhere, Ruth moved among crowds. Whether the Yankees played in Memphis or New Orleans or Selma, Ala., the park was almost always filled, the hotel overrun if the team used a hotel, the railroad depot thronged. In a town of 5,000, perhaps 7,500 would see the game. Mostly the players lived in Pullmans and somehow word always went ahead when the Yankees' train was coming through. At every stop at any hour of the night there would be a cluster of men on the platform, maybe the stationmaster and telegrapher, a section gang and the baggage agent watching the dark sleeping cars for the glimpse of a Yankee, possibly even the Babe.

It was said in those days, probably truly, that receipts from the preseason exhibitions more than paid Ruth's salary for the year, even when he was getting $80,000, which was substantially more than any other player earned, or any manager or baseball executive. It was more than President Herbert Hoover received, but if this was ever pointed out to Ruth he almost surely did not reply, as the story goes: "I had a better year than he did." He would have been correct, but the Babe was not that well informed on national affairs.

Crowds were to Ruth as water to a fish. Probably the only time on record when he sought to avert a mob scene was the day of his second marriage. The ceremony was scheduled for 6 a.m. on the theory that people wouldn't be abroad then, but when he arrived at St. Gregory's in West 90th Street, the church was filled and hundreds were waiting outside.

A reception followed in Babe's apartment on Riverside Drive, where the 18th Amendment did not apply. It was opening day of the baseball season but the weather intervened on behalf of the happy couple. The party went on and on, with entertainment by Peter de Rose, composer-pianist, and May Singhi Breen, who played the ukulele and sang.

Rain abated in time for a game the next day. For the first time, Claire Ruth watched from a box near the Yankees' dugout, as she still does on ceremonial occasions. Naturally, the bridegroom hit a home run. Rounding the bases, he halted at second and swept off his cap in a courtly bow to his bride. This was typical of him. There are a hundred stories illustrating his sense of theater—how he opened Yankee Stadium (The House That Ruth Built) with a home run against the Red Sox, how at the age of 40 he closed out his career as a player by hitting three mighty shots out of spacious Forbes Field in Pittsburgh, stories about the times he promised to hit a home run for some kid in a hospital and made good, and of course the one about calling his shot in a World Series.

That either did or did not happen in Chicago's Wrigley Field on Oct. 1, 1932. I was there but I have never been dead sure of what I saw.

The Yankees had won the first two games and the score of the third was 4–4 when Ruth went to bat in the fifth inning with the bases empty and Charley Root pitching for the Cubs. Ruth had staked the Yankees to a three-run lead in the first inning by hitting Root for a home run with two on base. Now Root threw a strike. Ruth stepped back and lifted a finger. "One." A second strike, a second upraised finger. "Two." Then Ruth made some sort of sign with his bat. Some said, and their version has become gospel, that he aimed it like a rifle at the bleachers in right center field. That's where he hit the next pitch. That made the score 5–4. Lou Gehrig followed with a home run and the Yankees won, 7–5, ending the series the next day.

All the Yankees, and Ruth in particular, had been riding the Cubs unmercifully through every game, deriding them as cheapskates because in cutting up their World Series money the Chicago players had voted only one-fourth of a share to Mark Koenig, the former New York shortstop who had joined them in August and batted .353 in the last month of the pennant race. With all the dialogue and pantomime that went on, there was no telling what Ruth was saying to Root. When the papers reported that he had called his shot, he did not deny it.

He almost never quibbled about anything that was written. During the 1934 World Series between the Cardinals and Detroit Tigers, "The St. Louis Post-Dispatch" assigned its Washington correspondent, Paul Y. Anderson, to write features. His seat in the auxiliary press box was next to Ruth, a member of the sweaty literati whose observations on the games would be converted into suitably wooden prose by a syndicate ghost-writer. Babe was companionable as usual.

"You see the series here in '28?" he asked.

"No," Anderson said, "was it a good one?"

"That was when I hit three outta here in the last game."

"Gee," Anderson said, "a good day for you, eh?"

"Yeah," Babe said, "I had a good day. But don't forget, the fans had a hell of a day, too."

Paul Anderson was at ease with men as dissimilar as Huey Long, John L. Lewis and Franklin D. Roosevelt but he had never encountered anyone quite like this child of nature. He devoted his story to the bumptious bundle of vanity seated beside him. To his discomfort, a press-box neighbor asked Ruth the next day whether he had read the story. Ruth said sure, though he probably hadn't. "What did you think of it?" the other persisted while Anderson squirmed.

"Hell," Babe said, "the newspaper guys always been great to me."

A person familiar with Ruth only through photographs and records could hardly be blamed for assuming that he was a blubbery freak whose ability to hit balls across county lines was all that kept him in the big leagues. The truth is that he was the complete ballplayer, certainly one of the greatest and maybe the one best of all time.

As a left-handed pitcher with the Boston Red Sox, he won 18 games in his rookie season, 23 the next year and 24 the next before Ed Barrow assigned him to the outfield to keep him in the batting order every day. His record of pitching 29⅔ consecutive scoreless innings in World Series stood 43 years before Whitey Ford broke it.

He was an accomplished outfielder with astonishing range for his bulk, a powerful arm and keen baseball sense. It was said that he never made a mental error like throwing to the wrong base.

He recognized his role as public entertainer and understood it. In the 1946 World Series the Cardinals made a radical shift in their defense against Ted Williams, packing the right side of the field and leaving the left virtually unprotected. "They did that to me in the American League one year," Ruth told the columnist, Frank Graham. "I coulda hit .600 that year slicing singles to left."

"Why didn't you?" Frank asked.

"That wasn't what the fans came out to see."

Thirteen years after Ruth's death, when another rightfielder for the Yankees, Roger Maris, was threatening the season record of 60 home runs that Babe had set 34 years earlier, I made a small sentimental pilgrimage in Baltimore where the Yankees happened to be playing. The first stop was the row house where the Babe was born. A gracious woman showed visitors through the small rooms. Next came a drink in the neighborhood saloon Babe's father ran when Babe was a boy. Nobody ever came in who remembered the Ruth family, the bartender said. The tour ended at St. Mary's Industrial School, which the wrecker's big iron ball was knocking down.

St. Mary's was Babe's home through most of his boyhood because his parents weren't interested in rearing him. He left the home on Feb. 27, 1914, three weeks after his 19th birthday, to pitch for the Baltimore Orioles of the International League. Jack Dunn, the owner, paid him $600 and sold him late that summer to the Red Sox for $2,900. He was 6-foot-2 and an athlete, thick-chested but not fat. "A big, lummockin' sort of fella," said a waiter in Toots Shor's who had worked in a restaurant near the Red Sox park where young Ruth got sweet on one of the waitresses.

When his hard-pressed employers sold him to the Yankees, he was still a trim young ballplayer who had hit 29 of the Boston club's 32 home runs that season of 1919. He hit an unthinkable 54 in his first New York summer, 59 in his second, and became a god. His waistline grew with his fame, until the legs that nobody had considered spindly began to look like matchsticks and his feet seemed grotesquely small.

He changed the rules, the equipment and the strategy of baseball. Reasoning that if one Babe Ruth could fill a park, 16 would fill all the parks, the owners instructed the manufacturers to produce a livelier ball that would make every man a home-run king. As a further aid to batters, trick pitching deliveries like the spitball, the emery ball, the shine ball and the mud ball were forbidden.

The home run, an occasional phenomenon when a team hit a total of 20 in a season, came to be regarded as the ultimate offensive weapon. Shortstops inclined to swoon at the sight of blood had their bats made with all the wood up in the big end, gripped the slender handle at the very hilt and swung from the heels.

None of these devices produced another Ruth, of course, because Ruth was one of a kind. He recognized this as the simple truth and conducted himself accordingly. Even before they were married and Claire began to accompany him on the road, he always occupied the drawing room on the team's Pullman; he seldom shared his revels after dark with other players, although one year he did take a fancy to a worshipful rookie named Jimmy Reese and made him a companion until management intervened; if friends were not on hand with transportation, he usually took a taxi by himself to hotel or ball park or railroad station. Unlike other players, Ruth was never seen in the hotel dining room or sitting in the lobby waiting for some passerby to discard a newspaper.

St. Louis was one town where he was always met. When the team left St. Louis, his friends would deliver him to the station along with a laundry basket full of barbecued ribs and tubs of home brew. Then anybody—player, coach or press—was welcome in the drawing room to munch ribs, swill the yeasty beer and laugh at the Babe's favorite record on the Babe's portable phonograph. He would play Moran & Mack's talking record, "Two Black Crows," a hundred times and howl at the hundredth repetition: "How come the black horses ate more'n the white horses?" "Search me, 'cept we had more black horses than white horses."

Roistering was a way of life, yet Ruth was no boozer. Three drinks of hard liquor left him fuzzy. He could consume great quantities of beer, was a prodigious eater and his prowess with women was legendary. Sleep was something he got when other appetites were sated. He arose when he chose and almost invariably was the last to arrive in the clubhouse, where Doc Woods, the Yankees' trainer, always had bicarbonate of soda ready. Before changing clothes, the Babe would measure out a mound of bicarb smaller than the Pyramid of Cheops, mix and gulp it down.

"Then," Jim Cahn says, "he would belch. And all the loose water in the showers would fall down."

The man was a boy, simple, artless, genuine and unabashed. This explains his rapport with children, whom he met as intellectual equals. Probably his natural liking for people communicated itself to the public to help make him an idol.

He was buried on a sweltering day in August, 1948. In the pallbearers' pew, Waite Hoyt sat beside Joe Dugan, the third baseman. "I'd give a hundred dollars for a cold beer," Dugan whispered. "So would the Babe," Hoyt said.

In packed St. Patrick's Cathedral, Francis Cardinal Spellman celebrated requiem mass and out in Fifth Avenue thousands and thousands waited to say good-bye to the waif from Baltimore whose parents didn't want him.

"Some 20 years ago," says Tommy Holmes, the great baseball writer, "I stopped talking about the Babe for the simple reason that I realized that those who had never seen him didn't believe me."

—1973

Little Things in a Great Big Game

FORT LAUDERDALE, FLA.—Behind the batting cage, Ron Swoboda said to Ralph Houk: "Keeping the ball low is the most important thing for an outfielder?" They call Swoboda "Rocky," short for "Rock Head," and it is a bum rap. There isn't a more sincere or more thoughtful player in baseball, or one who strives more conscientiously to improve himself. He is getting ready for his ninth season in the majors and he must have been familiar with the cutoff play as an undergraduate at Maryland. Yet he is not ashamed to be asking questions still, taking refresher courses, reminding himself that when he fields a hit with a runner in scoring position he must aim his throw at the chest of the cutoff man, who will have stationed himself on a line between the outfielder and the plate. If there is a play at home, the cutoff man lets the throw go through; otherwise, he catches it to prevent the hitter from taking second base.

"You mean for the cutoff?" Houk said. "Yes, because as soon as the hitter sees the ball high, he'll take off for second. As a base-runner, you know that when you round first it's hard to tell exactly where the throw is going if it's low."

"And the first-base coach has the same angle," Ron said. "The only man who could help the hitter is the third-base coach, and he's too far away."

"That's right," said the manager of the Yankees. "Say the tying run is on second with two out. You know they're going to send that runner in and the outfielder is determined to cut him down. So he hurries his throw, puts too much on it, and it comes in high. The tying run scores and the winning run goes to second."

"We use the third baseman as the cutoff man," Swoboda said.

"Yes. They say taking the third baseman off the bag lets a runner make the wide turn at third, but how often do you see that? Before that runner comes into third, the coach is either sending him or holding him. On some teams the third baseman is the cutoff man on hits to left or center, and the first baseman on hits to right. But with first base unprotected, the hitter takes a lead of 30 feet toward second.

"Where we look bad, there's a good right-hand hitter up and we're playing him deep, but he crosses us and hits to right. Now the third baseman can't get over from where he is to make the cutoff. Then it's up to the catcher to decide whether he's going to have a play at the plate. If not, he goes out and takes the throw short."

Swoboda nodded thoughtfully and walked away. Around a corner of the grandstand, Jim Hegan was pitching balls into the dirt for Jerry Moses, the catcher the Yankees got from Cleveland.

"He wants to block a wild pitch and keep the ball in front of him," the coach explained. "If his body is turned at an angle or if the mitt is, the ball can glance away and let runners advance. We don't want him to catch the wild pitch, just block it. He wants to be square on his knees with the mitt square between the knees and the meathand behind the mitt.

"Little things. You'd be surprised how many catchers don't know them. Like I ask them, on the double play that goes to the plate and then first base, what foot steps on the plate? The left foot does, and as you throw your stride takes you toward first so the man sliding home doesn't hit you. If the throw is off here to your left, then you have to shift and your chance for the double play is gone anyway.

"Or I ask them, where are your feet when you block the plate? You want to be up on the left front corner. That way, the runner has to slide away to your left and there's no way he can score except to touch the plate with his hand. You don't chase him, you chase the plate. You have the ball down here on the corner because this is where he's got to come.

"Or when you chase a bunt or a topped ball out in front of the plate, how do you throw to first? Do you turn right and throw underhand, or do you pivot left? There are two ways to do anything and usually the most comfortable is the best. If you come out and pivot left, your arm will be in position to throw, and the overhand throw is easiest to handle. The throw from down here tends to veer off.

"Usually the catcher has more time than he thinks, time enough to pivot left. Same when the runner is stealing second. If the pitcher doesn't let him get too big a jump, the catcher usually has plenty of time unless it's an exceptionally fast man. Most of these little things, the fans don't even think about."

—March 14, 1973

Wait, Fellows, Where's the Fire?

It is reported that some of the men who own baseball are beginning to look kindly upon the idea of interleague play in midsummer and may even vote to experiment with the innovation next year. If this seems like rash and headlong haste uncharacteristic of the rounders' hierarchy, well, it is. Only a little more than half a century has passed since William L. Veeck Sr. first proposed interlocking schedules at a National League meeting in 1922. The American League had outdrawn the Nationals that season, 4.8 million to 3.9 million, and Veeck, president of the fifth-place Cubs, thought it might help their gate if the Nationals could occasionally present new faces like that fellow Cobb over in Detroit, or the fastball pitcher Johnson, or Ken Williams of the Browns, who had beaten out Ruth for the home-run championship.

Some years later when the Nationals got around to mentioning the scheme at a joint meeting, the Americans weren't interested. They had the Yankees, the biggest draw in baseball, and were not disposed to waste their sweetness on the desert air of Boston's Braves Field and Philadelphia's Baker Bowl. More recently the American League came to favor the plan and the Nationals, outdrawing the other tong by four or five million, cocked a snoot.

Now the word is that the Nationals' attitude is thawing. Although they beat the American League at the gate last season by more than 4 million customers, their own attendance dropped 1,795,000 below 1971's and the 12 clubs now in the league drew about 1,000 fewer customers per day than eight clubs a dozen years earlier.

Something, the boys feel, has to be done, but they're still not going to abandon themselves to any visionary schemes. At most they'll dip a toe into the water, letting each club schedule half a dozen games with nearby teams in the other league. Thus the Mets might play two games with the Yankees, two with the Orioles and two with the Red Sox; Oakland might meet the Giants, Dodgers and Padres.

This might increase crowds fractionally, but it's like putting a Band-Aid on a leper.

Time and again it has been argued here that baseball could stimulate business and substantially reduce expenses by reassigning the 24 teams into three eight-club leagues organized on geographic lines.

On the basis of Sunday morning's standings, this is how the pennant races would look:

ATLANTIC LEAGUE

	W.	L.	Pct.	G.B.
Detroit	23	20	.535	—
Mets	20	19	.513	1
Yankees	22	21	.512	1
Baltimore	18	19	.486	2
Pittsburgh	17	19	.472	2½
Boston	17	20	.459	3
Montreal	17	20	.459	3
Philadelphia	17	24	.415	5

CENTRAL LEAGUE

White Sox	24	14	.632	—
Cubs	26	17	.605	½
Cincinnati	25	18	.581	1½
Minnesota	21	19	.525	4
Milwaukee	19	22	.463	6½
Cleveland	19	23	.452	7
Atlanta	17	25	.405	9
St. Louis	15	24	.388	9½

PACIFIC LEAGUE

	W.	L.	Pct.	G.B.
San Francisco	29	19	.604	—
Houston	27	19	.587	1
Los Angeles	26	19	.578	1½
California	22	18	.550	3
Kansas City	24	20	.545	3
Oakland	23	21	.523	4
San Diego	16	29	.356	11½
Texas	12	27	.308	12½

Out of the four divisions now in existence, only the American League East has a closer race than these, and the tight fit in that division is the result of beautifully balanced mediocrity. Until recently, nobody in this ghetto could beat one side of anybody else. That isn't a race, it's a slough.

It has been demonstrated many times that the most profitable item baseball has to sell is neighborhood rivalry. Even in seasons when neither team could get arrested, Brooklyn–New York matches always drew the biggest crowds to Ebbets Field and the Polo Grounds. This has continued to be true since the Giants and Dodgers moved West. It would be true of the Mets and Yankees, White Sox and Cubs, Oakland and San Francisco, Los Angeles and Anaheim.

Interlocking schedules among the three leagues are perfectly feasible, and the ratio of interleague to intraleague games could be adjusted as experience dictated. Just for openers, a team could play 14-game home-and-home series in its league and four-game series in the other two, for a total of 162. Playing most of its games around home, a team would save on travel expenses, reduce line charges for television and have comparatively few telecasts from California starting at 11 p.m. Eastern time.

The World Series would create no difficulties the Commissioner couldn't handle with the help of his advisers at National Broadcasting Company. If it were provided that the team with the best winning percentage over the season drew a bye while the other two played off for a place in the World Series, this would keep interest alive even after a pennant was decided. However, if anybody boggled at the thought of a pennant winner being left out, the World Series could be a round-robin. The plan makes so much sense it will never get off the ground.

—May 28, 1973

About Dusters and Dust-ups

THE MOST INTERESTING thing about the brawls that have enlivened baseball's first month is the identity of the combatants. The Giants have gone to battle at least twice and so have the Cardinals, and in recent years these have been among the most docile clubs in the game, making trouble for nobody. Back in the days when the Giants' home base was New York and John McGraw was their leader, the manager punched more people in a social evening at the Lambs Club than the San Francisco team does in a season. And for the last half-dozen years the Cardinals have performed with a decorum that would bring a blush of shame to the St. Louis Gas House Gang of 40 years ago. There has been raffish deportment on the part of other habitually quiescent groups, too, like the Angels, Padres and Indians, but in one respect the combatants have been faithful to tradition: nobody has thrown a punch that would break the Mother Superior's glasses.

Most of the donnybrooks have been set off by that staple of the pitcher's repertory, the beanball, or duster, or brushback pitch. Pitchers and batters may drink together in their spare time, but during business hours they are tribal enemies in perpetual conflict.

The batter has the most difficult assignment in sports—to gauge the changing flight of a round ball traveling 85 miles an hour and hit it with a round stick. To hit it hard he takes a toehold, leans into the pitch and swings from Boro Hall. In the pitcher's eyes, these are acts of war demanding retaliation. He could remonstrate, reminding his adversary that his control is imperfect and a fast ball high and inside could seriously inconvenience a batter who was not prepared to duck. He finds, however, that a hard ball whistling under the batter's chin gets the message across effectively. The Mets' Tom Seaver delivered the message yesterday to Dave Winfield of the Padres.

"It's a battle for the strike zone," Jon Matlack of the Mets told Joe Durso of "The Times" the other day. Early Wynn, a pitcher whose built-in glower could draw blood at 60 feet 6 inches, phrased it a little differently.

"That space between the white line," Early said, "that's my office. That's where I conduct my business. Anybody crowds me there has got to get a broken leg."

Hardly anybody ever enjoyed getting a baseball stuck in his ear, but it does seem that today's players are touchier about it than their elders were. When Uncle Wilbert Robinson, manager of the old Brooklyn Dodgers, said some big young pitcher was "fast and pleasingly wild," he meant it as a high compliment. Before he went to the big dugout in the sky, Frank Frisch used to speak with grudging respect about a pitcher who answered this description—a dark menace from Mississippi named Guy Bush.

When you walked up against Bush, Frank said, you went up knowing you were going to hit the dirt not once but twice. Against a good hitter, Bush liked to deliver the message with his first pitch and underline it with his second. After that he would throw strikes. Frisch, a .316 hitter over 19 years, accepted this as a compliment, knowing that Bush didn't give such attention to .220 hitters.

Then, as now, tempers sometimes wore thin and fisticuffs ensued. Then, as now, the ballplayer who could break a soda cracker with a punch was an exception.

When Bill Dickey was catching for the Yankees, he broke the jaw of Carl Reynolds, a Washington outfielder, with a single shot. And when Billy Martin was managing Minnesota, he flattened his star pitcher in front of a saloon. However, most fights on the field are like a hair-pull in a sorority house.

One of the few baseball battles that wouldn't have been hooted out of Madison Square Garden matched two teams that are now extinct, the Washington Senators and Philadelphia Athletics. Memory suggests that it started when Washington's Buddy Myer slid hard into the Athletics' third baseman, Bill Werber. In an instant both dugouts were empty and gladiators were taking their best shots.

Frank Hayes, the Philadelphia catcher, was moving around on his toes like Sugar Ray Robinson. Still wearing his catcher's mitt, he would stiff-arm an opponent with his left, pop him with his right and move on to the next subject. Huge Cal Hubbard, who had played in the line for the Green Bay Packers, was one of the umpires and he surged through the melee knocking heads together.

Strangest sight of all was Bob Johnson, the noble Cherokee who played left field for the A's. He probably could have whipped any two players on the field, yet he stood a little removed from the fray, looking on with a dreamy smile.

Suddenly a late arrival came lurching across the diamond with an ungainly lope. It was Big Joe Krakauskas, a left-handed pitcher. Fist cocked, he charged up behind Skeeter Newsome, the Athletics' little shortstop, but just as he was about to bushwhack him, a hand caught his shoulder and spun him, a fist dropped him. Krakauskas said later that he thought it must be Hubbard who hit him. He scrambled up and fled for the bench without looking back.

"You weren't mad at anybody," a man said to Johnson afterward, "and yet you really crammed that Krakauskas. What made you hit him like that?"

"Because I never could hit the crumbum when he was pitching," Bob said.

—May 10, 1976

Of Accidie and Longevity

JACK ORR, WHO used to be a newspaperman himself, saw a recent piece here about an insurance company's discovery that third basemen lived longer than shortstops and first basemen longer than managers. On occasion in the dear dead past, one thing or another might drive Jack to drink, but this piece drove him to his typewriter. He wrote: "Speaking of death, which seems to be a preoccupation of mine along with I. W. Harper, Liv Ullman and don't-bring-the-infield-in-now-dummy, I find myself reading the obituary page first, before turning to the team standings. Wasn't there an Englishman—Waugh, perhaps—who said he read the obits in 'The London

Times' in bed and if his name wasn't there, got up and shaved? [Don't know about Waugh, but our sportswriting friend Caswell Adams used to say it and then one morning his name was there.—Ed. note]

"You didn't mention catchers in your mortality rundown, but wouldn't you think they're particularly vulnerable? Offhand, I think of Mickey Cochrane [58], Jimmy Wilson [47], Bill DeLancey [45], Pinky Hargrave [46], Brucie Ogrodowski [44], Willard Hershberger [28]—but maybe he shouldn't count since he did a Dutch—Aaron Robinson [51], Shanty Hogan [61], Mike Tresh [52] and Johnny Grabowski [46].

"Well, maybe Connie Mack, Branch Rickey and Wally Schang, still going at 87 as far as I know, bring up the mean.

"Not long ago I renewed a correspondence with a college buddy [San Diego State, 1936], one Leon Kucher. Forty years ago he was the most talented essayist, newspaper editor and wit we had. He is still in southern California and he is some kind of executive in the shoe business. I asked him what the hell happened.

" 'Well,' he wrote back, 'for years I thought it was thyroid deficiency. If you take thyroid extract for reducing, your heart pounds, your pulse goes up, you become overactive. So I don't have enough of it, so I goofed. As Thurber said, "it is better to have loafed and lost than never to have loafed at all.' "

" 'Later I found a name for what ailed me. The name is "accidie,' " and Aldous Huxley wrote of it. He says it's a demon recognized in the Middle Ages, "a fiend of deadly subtlety who was not afraid to walk by day."

" 'Inaccurate psychologists of evil are wont to speak of accidie as though it were plain sloth,' Huxley wrote, 'but sloth is only one of the numerous manifestations of the subtle and complicated vice of accidie.' "

"Quoting Chaucer, he goes on to say, 'it paralyzes human will. It forsloweth and forsluggeth a man whenever he attempts to act. From accidie comes dread to begin to work any good deeds, and finally wanhope, or despair. On its way to ultimate wanhope, accidie produces a whole crop of minor sins, such as idleness, tardiness.'

" 'Boy,' said Kucher, 'now there's a classy excuse. It beats the hell out of a lousy thyroid.'

"I told him it was better than my answer: blaming the booze for the twilight of my career of mediocrity [as Frank Sullivan, the pitcher, once said]. For years I went around quoting my Scotch father's toast: 'It killed me father, it killed his father, and here's revenge!'

"If I ever got fired, I blamed that. I leaned on the story about John McNulty, fired from "The Daily News" for drinking, who went up to the city editor the next day and said, 'Sire, I understand there's a vacancy on your staff because a man was indiscreet about alcohol. I happen to be a Methodist from Des Moines and I neither smoke nor drink.' The city editor, bless him, rehired John.

"I also told him about a wise old advertising director I met when I was doing publicity at NBC. He used to direct his salesmen to have three or four martinis at business lunches. 'I'd rather have them think you're drunk than stupid,' he would say.

"Then I told Kuch what we had to be thankful for: longevity.

"'Look at it this way, Kuch. We've already outlasted [if not outdistanced] Rabby Burns [37], de Maupassant [43], Heywood Broun [50], St. Thomas Aquinas [47], Lou Gehrig [38], Mad Anthony Wayne [49], Humphrey Bogart [57], the real Thomas Wolfe [38], Joseph Goebbels [48], Vanzetti [39], Chic Sale [50], Christy Mathewson [45], Balzac [49], all the Lardners save Ring Jr., [48, 48, 25, 24], Nathaniel West [37], Eddie Sinclair [50], Alan Seeger [28], both Kennedys [46, 40], Spike Jones [55], Kurt Weill [49], Saki [46], Lenny Bruce [40], Amerigo Vespucci [56], John Fletcher [45], Wally Cox [48], Caruso [48], Lenin [53], Hart Crane [33], Harvey Swados [52], Warren Pack [49], Stephen Vincent Benet [45], the Babe [52], John Garfield [39]—and what a way he went, in the sack with a chick in an apartment in Gramercy Square and they say it took a week for the funeral people to get the smile off his face—Jack London [40], Dylan [39], Don Marquis [49], Jackie Robinson [42], Chekhov [44], James Agee [44], Snuffy Stirnweiss [39], Michael Dunn [39], O. Henry [48] and Jesus Christ Himself [37?].'"

—September 5, 1976

Feast of Reason and Flow of Soul

WHEN THE GAME ends, the two managers and the players who performed key roles are herded into a room below decks for inquisition by the flower of American letters. Questions from the assembled press are repeated into a microphone by Bob Fishel of the American League office and are piped with the replies into the press box for the benefit of those still working up there. A fan attending the session would marvel at the searching, incisive, trenchant quality of the questions, and at the wit that illumines the answers like a lambent flame. The truth, these are not impromptu. Questions and answers are composed in advance with blank spaces for the names, which are filled in as the game progresses. Before the final playoff between the Yankees and Kansas City Royals last night, "The New York Times" obtained a copy of the script prepared for the post-game interview, which follows:

FISHEL: Gentlemen (Whitey Herzog–Billy Martin.)

LOSING MANAGER: First of all I want to congratulate (Billy-Whitey.) He knows I'll be rooting for him in the World Series. Second of all, I wanta say I'm proud of my club. They're a great bunch of guys and they come to play or they wouldn't of brought us this far. They got nothing to be ashamed of. That ball of (Name) in the sixth, if it had of dropped in we got their pitcher out of there and it's a whole new ball game, but those are the breaks. It's part of the game.

Q. Did you consider pinch-hitting for (Name) in the eighth?

A. No, because he's the guy that's been doing the job for me all year. Maybe he hasn't hit for too big of an average but he's a guy that comes to play. He knows how to protect that plate and I wasn't going away from him after he brought us this far.

Q. What did you learn about the (Yankees-Royals) in this series?

A. What our scouts told us before. They're a good ball club that put their pants on one leg at a time.

Q. What were you thinking when it was two out in the ninth? Were you discouraged?

A. No, because the ball game's never over till the last man is out.

FISHEL: Thanks (Billy-Whitey.) Now (Whitey-Billy.)

Q. Was this the biggest win for your club this year?

WINNING MANAGER: You better believe it. Biggest of my career. But I wasn't surprised. This club has been doing that all year.

Q. How do you feel about playing the Big Mean Machine, and what strategy are you planning against Cincinnati?

A. First of all, we look forward to playing 'em because that's the name of the game. They're the champions, and if you want to be the best you got to beat the champions. Second of all, as far as strategy, we're gonna play this Series the way we've played in our own league all year—one game at a time.

Q. Who's your opening pitcher?

A. Haven't decided yet. I'll talk to (Name), and we'll decide who we think can do the best job for us. The pitchers understand that we've brought 'em this far and we'll be deciding what we think is best for the whole club.

Q. How close were you to changing pitchers in the sixth tonight? Was (Name) getting tired?

A. He said he felt all right. I only went out there to remind him he had that fast man on first base and not to let him take too big of a lead. I wasn't thinking about taking him out because he's the guy that's been doing the job for me all year and I'm not going away from him now. If he was a little tired, well, if he don't get out of that inning, he's gonna have all winter to rest, because there's no tomorrow.

Q. Do you feel you have momentum going for you now, coming off this game into the World Series?

A. Hopefully, yes. You got to respect the Cincinnati club, they're the champions, but they had a five-day layoff last week and now they've just been sitting around since Tuesday. Hot hitters can cool off in that time, and you saw for yourself tonight what we can do when we put it all together.

Q. Did you tell (Name) last night that he would be starting the deciding game tonight?

A. I didn't have to. He's a smart kid and he read it in the paper.

FISHEL: Thanks, (Billy-Whitey). Here's (Name), who got the key hit.

Q. Tell us a little about what you were looking for when you were up there. Were you trying to hit to right?

A. I was just up there swinging. I haven't been swinging the bat all that good lately and I must've changed my stance five or six times before I got to feeling comfortable up there tonight. I'm just sorry it took me so long.

Q. How did their pitcher compare with the last time you hit against him? Was he as sharp tonight?

A. He had good stuff but he was getting his breaking stuff up tonight. I hit a fastball across the letters.

Q. How do you feel about playing the Big Mean Machine?

A. It's kind of like a dream. I've been reading about those guys for years, Bench and Morgan and those guys. They're great ballplayers but they still put their pants on one leg at a time.

—October 15, 1976

The Moving Finger Writes, Etc.

IT HAD TO happen this way. It had been predestined since Nov. 29, 1976, when Reginald Martinez Jackson sat down on a gilded chair in New York's Americana Hotel and wrote his name on a Yankee contract. That day he became an instant millionaire, the big honcho on the best team money could buy, the richest, least inhibited, most glamorous exhibit in Billy Martin's pin-striped zoo. That day the plot was written for last right—the bizarre scenario Reggie Jackson played out by hitting three home runs, clubbing the Los Angeles Dodgers into submission and carrying his supporting players with him to the baseball championship of North America. His was the most lurid performance in 74 World Series, for although Babe Ruth hit three more home runs in a game in 1926 and again in 1928, not even that demigod smashed three in a row.

Reggie's first broke a tie and put the Yankees in front, 4–3. His second fattened the advantage to 7–3. His third completed arrangements for a final score of 8–4, wrapping up the championship in six games.

Yet that was merely the final act of an implausible one-man show. Jackson had made a home run last Saturday in Los Angeles and another on his last time at bat in that earthly paradise on Sunday. On his first appearance at the plate last night he walked, getting no official time at bat, so in his last four official turns he hit four home runs.

In his last nine times at bat, this Hamlet in double-knits scored seven runs, made six hits and five home runs and batted in six runs for a batting average of .667 compiled by day and by night on two seacoasts 3,000 miles and three time zones apart. Shakespeare wouldn't attempt a curtain scene like that if he was plastered.

This was a drama that consumed seven months, for ever since the Yankees went to training camp last March, Jackson had lived in the eye of the hurricane. All summer long as the spike-shod capitalists bickered and quarreled, contending with their manager, defying their owner, Reggie was the most controversial, the most articulate, the most flamboyant.

Part philosopher, part preacher and part outfielder, he carried this rancorous company with his bat in the season's last 50 games, leading them to the East championship in the American League and into the World Series. He knocked in the winning run in the 12-inning first game, drove in a run and scored two in the third, furnished the winning margin in the fourth and delivered the final run in the fifth.

Thus the stage was set when he went to the plate in last night's second inning with the Dodgers leading 2–0. Sedately, he led off with a walk. Serenely, he circled the bases on a home run by Chris Chambliss. The score was tied.

Los Angeles had moved out front, 3–2, when the man reappeared in the fourth inning with Thurman Munson on base. He hit the first pitch on a line into the seats beyond right field. Circling the bases for the second time, he went into his home-run glide—head high, chest out. The Yankees led, 4–3. In the dugout, Yankees fell upon him. Billy Martin, the manager, who tried to slug him last June, patted his cheek lovingly. The dugout phone rang and Reggie accepted the call graciously.

His first home run knocked the Dodgers' starting pitcher, Burt Hooton, out of the game. His second disposed of Elias Sosa, Hooton's successor. Before Sosa's first pitch in the fifth inning, Reggie had strolled the length of the dugout to pluck a bat from the rack, even though three men would precede him to the plate. He was confident he would get his turn. When he did, there was a runner on base again, and again he hit the first pitch. Again it reached the seats in right.

When the last jubilant playmate had been peeled off his neck, Reggie took a seat near the first-base end of the bench. The crowd was still bawling for him and comrades urged him to take a curtain call but he replied with a gesture that said, "Aw, fellows, cut it out!" He did unbend enough to hold up two fingers for photographers in a V-for-victory sign.

Jackson was the leadoff batter in the eighth. By that time, Martin would have replaced him in an ordinary game, sending Paul Blair to right field to help protect the Yankees' lead. But did they ever bench Edwin Booth in the last act?

For the third time, Reggie hit the first pitch but this one didn't take the shortest distance between two points. Straight out from the plate the ball streaked, not toward the neighborly stands in right but on a soaring arc toward the unoccupied bleachers in dead center, where the seats are blacked out to give batters a background. Up the white speck climbed, dwindling, diminishing, until it settled at last halfway up those empty stands, probably 450 feet away.

This time he could not disappoint his public. He stepped out of the dugout and faced the multitude, two fists and one cap uplifted. Not only the customers applauded.

"I must admit," said Steve Garvey, the Dodgers' first baseman, "when Reggie Jackson hit his third home run and I was sure nobody was listening, I applauded into my glove."

—October 19, 1977

Joe McCarthy

WHEN TOMMY HENRICH was a rookie with the Yankees, Joe McCarthy told him: "They're making a sucker out of you with that outside curve. I want you to lay off it." A week or 10 days later, McCarthy said: "Tommy, I told you to lay off that pitch. Now, either you lay off it, or you'll learn to hit it in Newark."

"When he put it that way," Henrich said later, "you listened."

The sports world in general had its attention fixed on New Orleans and Super Bowl XII when Joseph Vincent McCarthy stepped quietly off this mortal coil. He was 90 and, by all accounts, still the same square-jawed intelligent Irishman who, as a manager in both major leagues, was able to bring out the best in such disparate individuals as Hack Wilson, Rogers Hornsby, Babe Ruth, Lou Gehrig, Joe DiMaggio and Ted Williams. "Williams was no problem," McCarthy told Don Honig last year when

Honig interviewed him for "The Man in the Dugout," wherein 15 present or former managers have their say. "He was in the ball game every day. He played. He hustled. Followed orders. Of course I only gave him one order—hit. No insubordination there. He hit."

Drunks can argue till they're sober about who was the greatest of all managers—John McGraw, who had 10 pennant winners; Casey Stengel, who had 10 with five in a row; Connie Mack, who built eight championship clubs on his way to sainthood; or men with special credentials, like Billy Southworth, Bill McKechnie, Miller Huggins, Al Lopez, Fred Hutchinson. For old Yankees like Henrich, Phil Rizzuto or DiMaggio it is no contest. There never was another like Joe McCarthy, who steered them to seven championships in eight years.

Yankee-haters called him a push-button manager, implying that the batboy could have won with those players, but it has been shown that not even managers as brilliant as Charlie Finley or George Steinbrenner can win with bad ball players. Remembering the richness of his Yankee talent, it is easy to forget McCarthy's first job in the majors. In 1926 he took over the Chicago Cubs, a last-place club the coroner had pronounced dead and partly decomposed. In Joe's four years in Wrigley Field, the Cubs finished fourth, fourth, third and first.

The Athletics creamed the Cubs in the World Series, putting on a 10-run inning in the fourth game when Chicago was leading, 7–0. McCarthy got fired. A year later he was back in Philadelphia, a spectator at the World Series this time, when the Yankees came after him. There had been feelers from other clubs, so Joe called Kenesaw M. Landis to ask the commissioner's advice.

"I want you to get the best job in baseball," Judge Landis said. "I can't," Joe said.

"Why not?"

"Because you have it."

"Then get the next best," the Judge said, and Joe did.

One Yankee who was happy to see him in New York was Earle Combs, the center fielder, who had not forgotten his own experience in Louisville, where McCarthy was manager when Combs joined the Colonels as a scared country schoolteacher. In his first game for Louisville, Combs dropped the first ball hit to him. McCarthy said nothing. Combs misplayed a single into extra bases. McCarthy was silent. In the eighth inning with the score tied and two runners on base, the hitter drove a single to center. The ball hopped between Combs's knees and rolled to the fence.

In the clubhouse, McCarthy strolled over to the rookie's locker. "Forget it," he said. "I told you today you were my center fielder. You still are." Then Joe laughed. "Listen," he said, "if I can stand it, I guess you can."

Joe McCarthy

The year before McCarthy took over, the Yankees ran third. "I will stand for you finishing second this year," said Col. Jacob Ruppert, the owner, "because you are new in this league. But I warn you, McCarddy, I don't like to finish second."

Joe looked him in the eye. "Colonel," he said, "neither do I."

The Yankees did finish second. Then they finished first, again and again. After one World Series, Joe went to call on the Colonel, who was sick in bed. "Colonel," he said, "you're the champion again."

"Fine, fine, McCarddy," Ruppert said. "Do it again next year."

McCarthy's favorite story about the Yankees concerned a game with the Red Sox. Johnny Broaca, a student-athlete from Yale, was the New York pitcher. He had a 1–0 lead in the top of the ninth with two out, the tying run on first base, and Joe Cronin coming up. On deck behind Cronin was Jimmy Foxx.

"Broaca starts pitching to Cronin," Joe told Honig, "and he's not coming close to the plate. I couldn't believe it—he's walking Cronin to get to Foxx. I yelled out to Bill Dickey, 'What the hell's going on?' Bill just shrugged. There wasn't anything he could do about it. And Broaca was pitching such a good game I couldn't take him out.

"So Foxx comes up and now the tying run is on second. And Jimmy laid into one. He hit it into deep center field, as far as any ball I ever saw hit in Yankee Stadium that wasn't a home run. DiMaggio went out there and caught it. It didn't miss by much from going into the bleachers in dead center. But Joe got it and the game was over.

"In the clubhouse I went over to shake hands with Broaca. 'Johnny,' I said, 'that was quite a game. But will you tell me why you didn't pitch to Cronin?'

"'I was afraid of Cronin,' he said, 'but I knew I could get Foxx.'

"'You did, eh?' I said. I looked around. DiMaggio still hadn't come in with the ball."

—January 22, 1978

Crime and Punishment

RAY KROC has been on television lately doing commercials for McDonald's hamburgers. Lucky he's working. He's got to scuffle up $100,000 one way or another for Bowie Kuhn, and at 76 it isn't easy to get a new job.

In his 10 years as baseball's ayatollah, Bowie Kuhn has exhibited the bold crusading spirit of the "Waxahachie Light," a Texas newspaper that once employed that elder statesman of baseball, Paul Richards. The "Light's" inflexible editorial policy opposed the boll weevil and favored an early spring. Going even further, Bowie stoutly supports baseball in Washington and takes an uncompromising stand against autographing the bare bottoms of lady fans. Nor does he stop there. The other day he fined Kroc, owner of the San Diego Padres, $100,000 for admiring Graig Nettles and Joe Morgan out loud.

This reflects a view of justice that is unorthodox if not unique. Obviously, Bowie's object all sublime is not to let the punishment fit the crime but rather to make the penalty fit the criminal's bankroll. Can it be that Princeton, the ayatollah's alma mater, does not teach that all men are equal in the eyes of the law?

Founder of the world's largest fast-food chain, Kroc is reputed to be worth $500 million. Nevertheless, the harshness of Kuhn's action so offended him that this lifelong fan quit the game he loves and put his stepson-in-law in charge of the Padres.

"The fun in it is all gone for me," he said. "Baseball isn't baseball anymore. Baseball has brought me nothing but aggravation."

Kroc is a feisty cuss who can be altogether charming one minute and as arrogant as $500 million the next. In his five years in baseball he has committed his share of errors, sometimes after having one too many Dublrich Chocolate Malteds Too Thick for a Straw. However, one thing must be said for him that cannot be said for Bowie Kuhn: He made major league baseball important in a disaster area.

In their first five years, the Padres' top attendance was 644,272. The franchise was a flat failure and it was about to be sold to Washington when Kroc galloped to the rescue in a curtain scene worthy of "East Lynne." Pumping his millions and his enthusiasm into the club, he built a healthy enterprise that has tripled its business.

Kuhn regularly takes bows for baseball's prosperity. If he has chased the savior of San Diego baseball out of the game, he deserves full credit for that, too.

Since he lowered the boom on Kroc, baseball people have been asking what Kuhn would have done if Calvin Griffith had said he'd like to have Nettles and Morgan on the Twins, or if Charlie Finley had uttered those subversive words in Oakland. Calvin doesn't have $100,000 to spare, if we may believe what he tells his players. Finley has been the ayatollah's severest critic and most rebellious subject. More than one of Kuhn's mandates concerning Charlie have smacked of reprisal.

Kroc's public view of the ayatollah has been less than idolatrous, too. He has said there were too damn many lawyers in baseball, and the last time Bowie got a pay raise, Kroc cast the only opposing vote in the National League. It is said that all power corrupts, and absolute power corrupts absolutely. Baseball invests the commissioner with extraordinary powers, trusting that he will use them impartially.

Naturally, the gravity of Kroc's crime dictates the severity of his penalty. He did not attempt to buy political favors or ask employees to commit perjury; he is not a banker who played put-and-take with depositors' savings; he never went to jail for income tax evasion; he never even sniffed cocaine in Studio 54. This is Kroc's version of what happened:

He was talking to a newspaperman—he says he cannot remember which of the half-dozen who phoned him that day, but probably it was Norman Clark of the Associated Press. Kroc said he was prepared to spend up to $10 million to improve the Padres and the interviewer asked if he would be interested in potential free agents like Nettles, Morgan and Al Oliver. Kroc said yes.

That may be the biggest three-letter word in the English language. Helen of Troy said it, and started a war that lasted 10 years. Kroc said it, and it cost him $100,000 for the baseball sin of "tampering" with somebody else's players. Figures even smaller than $100,000 have been known to irritate Kroc. When the Padres were training in Yuma, Ariz., he made a visit of inspection to a McDonald's franchise incognito and was annoyed when the counterman recognized him. "I don't understand it," he told Buzzie Bavasi, who ran the Padres for him then. "I just walked in and ordered a hamburger like anybody."

"In Yuma, Ariz., Ray," Buzzie told him, "a guy pulls up behind a chauffeur in a white Rolls Royce and orders a hamburger every day." Hearing the colloquy, Jack Murphy quoted it in the "San Diego Union" and a wire service picked it up.

On opening day of the season in Cincinnati, Kroc came to breakfast in a grouchy mood. Murphy asked what was wrong.

"I just turned on the television in my room," Kroc said, "and there was my picture. A girl told about me pulling up to McDonald's in a $90,000 Rolls Royce and being recognized."

"Isn't that about right?" Murphy asked.

"Dammit!" Kroc said. "I never paid more than $40,000 for a car in my life!"

Since then, the Rolls of his model has gone to $90,000.

"What damfool would pay $90,000 for a car?" he demanded of the Rolls representative.

The man looked him in the eye. "The same damfool that paid $40,000 for one," he said.

—August 27, 1979

A Call from Jimmy

IN BOSTON SOMEBODY said Carl Yastrzemski had made his first hit when John F. Kennedy was President and might not make his 3,000th until Teddy was. However, after a delay that was beginning to make everyone's teeth hurt, Yaz did the deed in time to be congratulated by President Carter. "Give me a number," a member of the White House staff had said several days ago to Bill Crowley, the Red Sox vice president for public relations, "and we'll call within 20 minutes after the game ends." "I can't keep the Boston press waiting 20 minutes," Crawley had said. "They're more important to me than you are."

When Cap Anson reached 3,000 hits in 1897, there was no congratulatory phone call from President McKinley, who was preoccupied getting a protective tariff through Congress. When Ty Cobb made it in 1921, news accounts of the game mentioned his achievement in the 12th or 14th paragraph. When Sam Rice retired in 1934 with 2,987 hits, it didn't occur to him that maybe he should stick around for 13 more.

In those days, Media was where the Medes and Persians came from.

Many years ago a wise man wrote that baseball was the game of professional athletes and amateur statisticians. Today it sometimes seems that statistics are bigger than the game or the players, in the eyes of the "media," at least.

Carl Yastrzemski has been playing professional ball for 21 years. He has made hits in All-Star games, in pennant playoffs and in World Series, yet not one of them commanded such attention or stirred such emotions as his ground single to right field off the Yankees' Jim Beattie Wednesday night in the eighth inning of a game the Red Sox had already won.

If it weren't for press and television and radio, nobody would be willing to pay $10,000 for Yaz's footprints in plaster. If the 3,000th hit had not become a "media event" it wouldn't have cost Yaz $600 a day to keep 26 visiting relatives in Boston to see history made, and his kids wouldn't be overdue in school in Florida.

When Anson made his 3,000th hit, nobody realized that the number would attain significance. Nobody knew Anson was founding a club so exclusive that 82 years later it would have only 15 members. When Cobb reached that plateau, he was en route to 4,191 hits and he hardly noticed the milestone as he passed. The first time in memory that there was any special commotion over somebody joining the 3,000 Club was in 1958 when Stan Musial made it, and there were special circumstances then.

The Cardinals were on the road when Stan hit No. 2,999 and Fred Hutchinson, the manager, announced he would hold Musial out of their last game in Chicago so he could get the big one at home. This was understandable. Given his choice, Musial would prefer that the event take place before a friendly crowd, and the prospect of seeing it happen would attract additional customers in St. Louis, as it did for the last week in Fenway Park.

It was only mid-May, though, and nobody knew the Cardinals were destined to finish in a tie for fifth place. With his team in the pennant race, a victory in May would count as much as a victory in September. In the circumstances, it was felt that Hutch had no right to sheathe his principal offensive weapon.

Defying his critics, Hutchinson did leave Musial out of the starting batting order, but in the sixth inning he saw a chance to win and called on Stan. Musial ripped a double for No. 3,000, rousing spectators to silence.

To say that there was a time when the 3,000th hit didn't alter the course of the stars in their flight is not to disparage the hitter's achievement. Babe Ruth's 60th home run in 1927 caused no wild excitement, either; he was only breaking his own record of 59 and there was no reason to doubt that he would hit 61 in another year. But Babe never made 3,000 hits and neither did Lou Gehrig or Rogers Hornsby or Joe DiMaggio or Ted Williams.

"I haven't had the greatest ability in the world," Yaz said. "I'm not a big, strong guy. I've made nine million adjustments, nine million changes. I've worked hard over the wintertime. I've paid the price. And God gave me a tremendous incentive and body to excel and that desire inside of me."

That's what it takes—the willingness to pay the price—and keep paying it year in and year out, summer and winter. Along with the willingness, there must be the opportunity, for nobody has made his 3,000th hit earlier than his 16th season, and only a tiny minority can stay in the majors that long.

This is Yaz's 19th season with Boston. His 40-year-old Achilles tendons punish him day and night. When he made No. 3,000 he was wearing a spiked shoe on his left foot and a sneaker on his right. He is ready for carpet slippers but instead he runs all winter and now he means to get Nautilus exercising equipment because, "If it can help Freddie Lynn get 37 homers, I'm going to pump it."

—September 14, 1979

1980s

McGraw: 'Then I Hit Him'

BILL MADLOCK, a spirited Pittsburgh infielder known to admirers as "Mad Dog," has been fined $5,000 and suspended 15 days for feloniously wiping an umpire's nose with his glove. Billy Martin, the peace-loving manager of the Oakland A's, wants an umpire suspended because, Martin says, the umpire game him a villainous and unprovoked shove. In both cases, the dispute was over a strike called on a checked swing, one of the most ticklish decisions an umpire has to make.

Madlock says that any contact between his glove and Gerry Crawford's profile was unpremeditated, accidental and purely coincidental, not to say benign. Dale Ford says he did not punch, push, poke, prod or nudge Martin. The way of aggressors is hard.

"Then I hit him," John McGraw, manager of the New York Giants, wrote to John K. Tener, president of the National League, in his report on a postgame colloquy with Bill Byron, the Singing Umpire.

Now, there is a statement that should be preserved in the Hall of Fame. It is.

The McGraw-Byron confrontation took place at the end of a game in Cincinnati on June 8, 1917. As related by Frank Graham of "The New York Sun," one of four reporters traveling with the Giants, players on both teams had quarreled with the umpire almost constantly, and as they left the field Tom Clark, the Reds' catcher, was still snarling at Byron. At the entrance to the runway to the clubhouses, McGraw caught up with them.

"I don't know what you just said, Tom," he told Clark, "but whatever it was, it goes double for me."

"You talk big," Byron said, wheeling on McGraw. "I guess you didn't use to be so tough. They say you were run out of Baltimore."

McGraw was fiercely proud of his achievement as star third baseman for the legendary Orioles of the National League, with whom his batting average had ranged from .321 to .391.

"What did you say?" he demanded.

"They say you were run out of Baltimore," Byron said.

"They say! They say I was run out of Baltimore! Would you say it?"

"Yes," Byron said. "I'd say it."

McGraw hit him a short right hand that split Byron's upper lip. As the umpire staggered back, McGraw was on him again, but Matty Schwab, the Reds' groundskeeper, flung both arms around McGraw. Bill Rariden, the Giants' catcher, cracked Schwab alongside the head. As players of both teams plunged in, cops wrestled through the tangle, pulled McGraw and Byron out and led them to their dressing rooms.

In his room in the Hotel Havlin, McGraw talked freely. Byron had delivered the insult deadly. McGraw would have hit anybody who told that black lie, and the fact that Byron was an umpire had nothing to do with the case. President Tener would understand that this was a personal matter not connected with any ball game or decision. It had not happened on the playing field but in the mouth of the runway. McGraw's written report to the league president summarized the verbal exchange with Byron.

"Then I hit him," it concluded. "I maintain I had reason to resent his insulting statement."

The Giants were in Pittsburgh five days later when "The Sun" wired Frank Graham that Tener had slapped a $500 fine on McGraw and suspended him for 16 days. Graham was out when the wire arrived and it was opened by his roommate, Sid Mercer of "The Globe," in keeping with an agreement between them. Mercer brought the news to McGraw, who blew a gasket.

He denounced Tener and all his umpires. He accused the league president of bias against the Giants, adding that he had been railroaded into office by the Philadelphia club and had run the league from there.

"Do you want to be quoted?" Mercer asked.

"Every word!" McGraw said. "Tell the other newspapermen. I want this in every paper in New York."

Sid wrote a story and showed it to McGraw, thinking he might take them back when he saw how the words looked on paper. But McGraw merely glanced at the copy. "That looks all right," he said. "Have you told the others?"

"I'll tell them now," Sid said. He ran down Graham, Sam Crane of "The Evening Journal" and Jimmy Sinnott of "The Evening Mail."

Wire services picked up the story, and when Pittsburgh reporters ran at McGraw the next day he told them: "I've nothing more to say. It's all in that story."

With an open date between the Pittsburgh series and an engagement in Boston, the Giants played an exhibition in Wellsville, N.Y., where McGraw had played 27 years earlier for $60 a month. When the team went on to Boston, though, McGraw wasn't along; he had received an urgent call to New York.

Next day the four reporters had a shock. Called before the National League board of directors, McGraw had submitted a signed statement denying that he had made the remarks attributed to him. Queried by their offices, the reporters stuck to their story and their papers backed them up.

Privately, Graham, Crane and Sinnott told their editors that they had got the facts second-hand, but nobody doubted Mercer's integrity and competence and, anyway, McGraw had expressed the same sentiments to the other reporters later.

Before the second game in Boston, McGraw faced two of the reporters in the visitors' clubhouse. He said that when he got to New York, Cornelius J. Sullivan, the Giants' attorney, had the statement already prepared and that Sullivan and Harry Hempstead, the owner, kept at him until he signed it.

"I made them make one change in it, though," he said. "It said you fellows had written scurrilous stories. I made them strike out 'scurrilous.' "

"You still called us liars," a reporter said.

"Well," McGraw said, "the hell with it."

By now the Baseball Writers Association of America was in the act. It clamored for an investigation, and Tener appointed John Conway Toole, counsel for the league, to take testimony. The hearing left nobody in doubt as to who had lied. Tener fined McGraw another $1,000.

"It cost Mac $500 for fighting and $1,000 for talking about it," a baseball writer said.

Mercer stopped talking to McGraw. Nowhere do the available records show what was done about the 16-day suspension.

—June 15, 1980

Loathsome Ploy: d.h.

"The outlook wasn't brilliant for the Mudville ten that day;
The score stood four to two with but one inning more to play . . ."

CHANCES ARE Ernest L. Thayer, who created the mighty Casey, and DeWolf Hopper, whose recitations immortalized him, have got beyond the stage of whirling in their graves. The game they knew as baseball, the nine-man game, is played only in the National League and Japan's Central League today, and it came perilously close to eradication from the National League the other day. By the narrowest of margins, the league voted against adopting the loathsome designated hitter rule in slavish imitation of the American League.

As Bill Lee, the thinking man's pitcher, pointed out several years ago, the designated hitter serves one useful purpose. It relieves the manager of all responsibility except to post the lineup card on the dugout wall and make sure everybody gets to the airport on time.

Once there was a theory that devising strategy, dictating and altering tactics, matching wits with the licensed genius across the way were part of the manager's job and that his degree of success in these areas accounted for his ranking in his profession. In the 10-man game, most decisions are made for the manager automatically. If he wants to phone his bookmaker in the third inning, there is seldom anything else demanding his attention.

The only excuse anybody gives for adopting the d.h. rule is that baseball is in a rut and cries aloud for some change, any change. The fact is, baseball has had longer to test and polish its rules than any other team game in this country, and this process of evolution has produced a code that seldom demands change because it is beautiful in its fairness and balance. If you don't know a rule governing a certain situation, give it some thought; when you have arrived at a decision that is fair to both sides, you will have the rule as it is written.

Tested, altered and adjusted over a century, the rules for nine-man baseball became a triumph of checks and balances. There are moves the manager can make in the interest of offense, but he must pay for them. When to remove the pitcher used to be, and in the National League still is, one of the major decisions up to a manager. Suppose the pitcher allowed a run in the first inning and none since. It is now the eighth inning, it is his turn to bat, and the team is still trailing, 1–0. The pitcher is strong enough to work at least a couple more innings but he can't win without a run and he isn't likely to contribute much to the offense.

If you take him out for a pinch-batter, you lose his services and must rely on the bullpen, and that's the way it should be. This charming balance is a major factor in the attraction of the game.

With the corruption called designated hitter, the balance is destroyed, the challenge to the manager eliminated. He pinch hits for the pitcher every time around, and it costs him nothing. National League managers have to think; American Leaguers don't, and maybe that helps explain the result of the annual All-Star Game.

A designated hitter has added a few points to the team batting average and presumably added a few runs to the season's score. The men who own baseball have long had the notion that more hitting and scoring produces more business, but there is no proof of that. The d.h. rule is in its eighth year now, and as yet nobody has been overheard saying, "Let's go out and watch the designated hitter."

By the winter of 1972 the governing intellects in the American League were in a panic. For more than a decade A.L. attendance had run substantially behind business in the National League. One year the N.L. had drawn 17,324,857, a tidy 5,456,297 more than the American.

"So what can we do about it?" the Americans asked one another.

"My cook says the public wants more hitting and scoring," one replied.

"Well," said another, "suppose we pinch-hit for the pitcher every time up but let the pitcher stay in the game. Think that might add some pizzazz?"

"Can't hurt to try," said still another. "Sure, it changes the whole game but who cares? Alexander Cartwright is dead."

So it came about, and the changes were immediately reflected at the box office. That is, the American League and its 10-man game continued to run behind the National League every year, millions behind, until 1977, when it added franchises in Seattle and Toronto, expanding to 14 clubs while the Nationals remained at 12.

Then A.L. figures inched up, edging past the other league for the first time in many years. In the American League press guide, the 1979 attendance of 22,371,979 is marked with two asterisks, denoting "major league and professional sports league records." Broken down on a team-by-team basis, the American League average was 1,597,999 and the Nationals? 1,764,468. And still those chumps almost went for the d.h.

—August 18, 1980

Leave Him to the Angels

A YOUNG WOMAN asked, "What was Casey Stengel like?" I thought she was pulling my leg until I realized that she was nine years old when Casey, retiring as manager of the New York Mets, dropped out of public view. "Casey Stengel," I said, "was—well, just a minute." I dug out my copy of Casey's testimony before the Senate Subcommittee on Antitrust and Monopoly on July 9, 1958. It seems to me that those of us who covered Casey in his time owe it to history to reintroduce him to readers in this fashion at least once a decade.

Senator Estes Kefauver: Mr. Stengel, you are the manager of the New York Yankees. Will you give us very briefly your background and your views about this legislation?

Stengel: Well, I started in professional ball in 1910. I have been in professional ball, I would say, for 48 years. I have been employed by numerous ball clubs in the majors and in the minor leagues.

I entered in the minor leagues with Kansas City. I played as low as Class D ball, which was at Shelbyville, Kentucky, and also Class C ball and Class A ball, and I have advanced in baseball as a ballplayer.

I had many years that I was not so successful as a ballplayer, as it is a game of skill. And then I was no doubt discharged by baseball in which I had to go back to the minor leagues as a manager, and after being in the minor leagues as a manager, I became a major league manager in several cities and was discharged, we call it discharged because there is no question I had to leave.

And I returned to the minor leagues at Milwaukee, Kansas City and Oakland, Calif., and then returned to the major leagues. In the last 10 years, naturally, with the New York Yankees, the New York Yankees have had tremendous success and while I am not a ballplayer who does the work I have no doubt worked for a ball club that is very capable in the office.

I have been up and down the ladder. I know there are some things in baseball 35 to 50 years ago that are better now than they were in those days. In those days, my goodness, you could not transfer a ball club in the minor leagues, Class D, Class C ball, Class A ball.

How could you transfer a ball club when you did not have a highway? How could you transfer a ball club when the railroads then would take you to a town you got off and then you had to wait and sit up five hours to go to another ball club?

How could you run baseball then without night ball? You had to have night ball to improve the proceeds, to pay larger salaries, and I went to work, the first year I received $135 a month. I thought that was amazing. I had to put away enough money to go to dental college. I found out it was not better in dentistry. I stayed in baseball.

Any other questions you would like to ask me?

Kefauver: Mr. Stengel, are you prepared to answer particularly why baseball wants this bill passed?

Stengel: Well, I would have to say at the present time, I think that baseball has advanced in this respect for the player help. That is an amazing statement for me to make, because you can retire with an annuity at 50 and what organization in America allows you to retire at 50 and receive money?

Now the second thing about baseball that I think is very interesting to the public or to all of us is that it is the owner's fault if he does not improve his club, along with the officials in the ball club and the players.

Now what causes that?

If I am going to go on the road and we are a traveling ball club and you know the cost of transportation now—we travel sometimes with three Pullman coaches, the New York Yankees, and I'm just a salaried man and do not own stock in the New York Yankees, I found out that in traveling with the New York Yankees on the road and all, that it is the best, and we have broken records in Washington this year, we have broken them in every city but New York and we have lost two clubs that have gone out of the city of New York.

Of course, we have had some bad weather. I would say that they are mad at us in Chicago, we fill the parks. They have come out to see good material. I will say they are mad at us in Kansas City, but we broke their attendance records.

Now on the road we only get possibly 27 cents. I am not positive of these figures, as I am not an official. If you go back 15 years or if I owned stock in the club, I would give them to you.

Kefauver: Mr. Stengel, I am not sure that I made my question clear.

Stengel: Yes, sir. Well, that is all right. I am not sure I'm going to answer yours perfectly, either.

Senator Joseph C. O'Mahoney: How many minor leagues were there in baseball when you began?

Stengel: Well, there were not so many at that time because of this fact: anybody to go into baseball at that time with the educational schools that we had were small, while you were probably thoroughly educated at school, you had to be—we had only small cities that you could put a team in and they would go defunct.

Why, I remember the first year I was at Kankakee, Illinois, and a bank offered me $550 if I would let them have a little notice. I left there and took a uniform because they owed me two weeks pay. But I either had to quit but

I did not have enough money to go to dental college so I had to go with the manager down to Kentucky.

What happened there was if you got by July, that was the big date. You did not play night ball and you did not play Sundays in half of the cities because of a Sunday observance, so in those days when things were tough, and all of it was, I mean to say, why they just closed up July 4 and there you were sitting there in the depot. You could go to work some place else, but that was it.

So I got out of Kankakee, Illinois, and I just go there for the visit now.

Senator John A. Carroll: The question Senator Kefauver asked you was what, in your honest opinion, with your 48 years of experience, is the need for this legislation in view of the fact that baseball has not been subject to antitrust laws.

Stengel: No.

Carroll: I had a conference with one of the attorneys representing not only baseball but all of the sports, and I listened to your explanation to Senator Kefauver. It seemed to me it had some clarity. I asked the attorney this question: What was the need for this legislation? I wonder if you would accept his definition. He said they didn't want to be subjected to the *ipse dixit* of the Federal Government because they would throw a lot of damage suits on the *ad damnum* clause. He said, in the first place, the Toolson case was *sui generis*, it was *de minimus non curat lex.*

Stengel: Well, you are going to get me there for about two hours.

Kefauver: Thank you, very much, Mr. Stengel. We appreciate your presence here.

Mr. Mickey Mantle, will you come around?

Mr. Mantle, do you have any observations with reference to the applicability of the antitrust laws to baseball?

Mantle: My views are just about the same as Casey's.

—January 18, 1981

Index

A NOTE ON THE AUTHOR

Walter W. (Red) Smith was born September 25, 1905, in Green Bay, Wisconsin. After graduating from the University of Notre Dame in 1927, he went to work as a reporter for the *Milwaukee Sentinel.* There and at the *St. Louis Lone Star* and the *Philadelphia Record,* he became in rapid succession a copyreader, rewrite and assignments man, and sportswriter. In 1945 he was named a sports columnist for the *New York Herald Tribune.* Soon after the *Tribune*'s demise, he moved to the *New York Times* where he was the primary sports columnist until his death in January 1982. His many awards over the years included an honorary L.L.D. degree from his alma mater, Notre Dame; the George Polk Award for outstanding reporting; and in 1975, long overdue, the Pulitzer Prize.